Psychology Revivals

Psychological Mindedness

Psychological Mindedness: A Contemporary Understanding was first published in 1997. At the time, psychodynamically-oriented clinicians had long emphasized the relevance of psychological mindedness to effective therapy. But what does the term mean? That had been a difficult question to answer. There had been a variety of definitions and measures not only of psychological mindedness but of related constructs such as alexithymia, private self-consciousness, self-focused attention, social perspective taking, and personal intelligence.

Over the previous decade, McCallum and Piper had developed their own definition and measure of psychological mindedness, and examined the extent to which it predicted patient response to psychodynamic psychotherapy. This book is both a collection of both their own efforts and those of their fellow researchers in this broad field. It attempted to increase mental health practitioners' understanding of psychological mindedness and its importance to patient assessment and treatment at the time. It also provides practical methods for assessing psychological mindedness and addresses its relevance to interpersonal contexts outside the mental health field.

This book was intended to facilitate clinicians' efforts to select the most appropriate patients for their particular approaches to therapy, which would in turn reduce client dropout rates and maximize therapeutic processes and outcomes.

Psychological Mindedness

A Contemporary Understanding

Edited by

Mary McCallum and William E. Piper

Routledge
Taylor & Francis Group
LONDON AND NEW YORK

First published in 1997
by Lawrence Erlbaum Associates, Inc.

This edition first published in 2025 by Routledge
4 Park Square, Milton Park, Abingdon, Oxon, OX14 4RN

and by Routledge
605 Third Avenue, New York, NY 10158

Routledge is an imprint of the Taylor & Francis Group, an informa business

Publisher's Note

The publisher has gone to great lengths to ensure the quality of this reprint but points out that some imperfections in the original copies may be apparent.

Disclaimer

The publisher has made every effort to trace copyright holders and welcomes correspondence from those they have been unable to contact.

A Library of Congress record exists under ISBN: 0805817220

ISBN: 978-1-041-08501-0 (hbk)
ISBN: 978-1-003-64567-2 (ebk)
ISBN: 978-1-041-08668-0 (pbk)

Book DOI 10.4324/9781003645672

Psychological Mindedness

A Contemporary Understanding

Edited by
Mary McCallum
University of Alberta

William E. Piper
University of Alberta

LAWRENCE ERLBAUM ASSOCIATES, PUBLISHERS
1997 Mahwah, New Jersey London

Lawrence Erlbaum Associates, Inc., Publishers
10 Industrial Avenue
Mahwah, New Jersey 07430

Library of Congress Cataloging-in-Publication-Data

Psychological mindedness: a contemporary understanding / edited by Mary McCallum & William E. Piper.
p. cm.
Includes bibliographical references and index.
ISBN 0-8058-1722-0 (alk. paper).
1. Psychological mindedness. 2. Psychodynamic psychotherapy.
I. McCallum, Mary, Ph.D. II. Piper, William E., Ph.D.
RC489.P74P77 1997
616.89'14—DC21

97-2440
CIP

Books published by Lawrence Erlbaum Associates are printed on acid-free paper, and their bindings are chosen for strength and durability.

Printed in the United States of America
10 9 8 7 6 5 4 3 2 1

To my mother, Mary, for instilling in me the courage to try. To my father, Jimmy, for the perseverance to continue. To my husband, Don, for always welcoming me over the finish line.

—*M.M.*

To my family, colleagues and patients, who over the years have contributed to my appreciation and understanding of the world of psychological events.

—*W.E.P.*

CONTENTS

PART III: INTEGRATION AND IMPLICATIONS

PREFACE

BACKGROUND

Psychological mindedness is a term commonly used in dynamically oriented clinical settings to describe patients, trainees, and staff. It is usually regarded as a positive (desirable) attribute. Sometimes, its absence is used to explain lack of progress. It is different from intelligence, although an intelligent person is often thought to possess high psychological mindedness. Like other familiar terms in clinical settings, for example, ego strength, its use often lacks precision and contributes to conceptual ambiguity. Over time, as a result of our experience with the concept, we became more curious about its meaning and usefulness. Consequently, we decided to explore it more formally by incorporating it into our clinical research.

In 1977, the second author (William Piper) included psychological mindedness among a set of 15 variables therapists used to rate psychotherapy patients after conducting initial interviews. The set was used to predict process and outcome in a clinical trial comparing four forms of time-limited psychotherapy (Piper, Debbane, Bienvenu, & Garant, 1984). Psychological mindedness emerged as a significant predictor of the degree to which patients disclosed and worked in short-term individual therapy (Piper, de Carufel, & Szkrumelak, 1985), and therapy outcome in short-term group therapy (de Carufel & Piper, 1988). These results were regarded as promising, primarily because only a global, relatively undifferentiated definition of psychological mindedness had guided the ratings. We wondered what a more refined measure might provide in the way of prediction.

In 1981, the first author (Mary McCallum) began developing that more refined measure of psychological mindedness as part of her doctoral dissertation (McCallum, 1989). The measure was influenced by her experience using a process analysis system that identifies therapist interpretations. That system, the Therapist Intervention Rating System (Piper, Debbane, Bienvenu, & de Carufel, 1987) defined interpretations as therapist interventions that identified one or more components of an intrapsychic conflict, for example, wish, anxiety, defense. When using the system to rate the individual therapy sessions from the aforementioned comparative study (Piper et al., 1984), differences were noticed among patients' response to interpretations. Some patients stumbled, seemingly perplexed, whereas others ran with them, often formulating elegant interpretations of their own and others' dynamics. These latter patients seemed to be receptive to the therapists' hypotheses that current difficulties were linked to unconscious conflicts between wishes, fears, and defenses. It was as if they entered therapy "speaking the same language" as the therapist. We postulated that these were highly psychologically minded patients. We proceeded to develop scoring criteria reflective of these patients' ability to identify dynamic (intrapsychic) components and to relate them to difficulties.

The test stimulus was a simulated patient-therapist interaction that we scripted and videotaped. The use of the videotape reflected our goal of assessing psychological mindedness in a manner more congruent with preferences of the current era. We also wanted to protect our assessment of psychological mindedness from the possible confounds of education and intelligence. Specifically, we did not want to bias the performance of those individuals, especially those with limited formal education, who were often astute about others' dynamics but apprehensive about forms or "tests." The videotape and a manual for applying the scoring criteria became the Psychological Mindedness Assessment Procedure (PMAP; McCallum & Piper, 1987).

Beginning in the mid-1980's, we have explored the usefulness of our measure for predicting patients' response to psychodynamic psychotherapy. We used the PMAP with four populations, three of which were psychiatric. In preparation for these studies, we repeatedly reviewed the clinical and research literature concerning psychological mindedness, and noticed several trends.

Clinicians aligned with the psychodynamic theoretical orientation emphasized the relevance of psychological mindedness to working within all forms of psychodynamically oriented therapy. The term *psychological mindedness* has been used interchangeably with other concepts, for example, *insight*, *introspection*, *intraception*, *self-awareness*, *self-reflection*, and the *capacity for self-observation*. There have also been different ways of conceptualizing psychological mindedness. It has been viewed as a motive, an ability, an expectancy, an attributional style, a preference, and an interest. In addition, there have been different approaches to the measurement of psychological mindedness, for example, self-report questionnaires, appraisals based on clinical interviews, and appraisals derived by combining scores from variables conceptually related to psychological mindedness. This diversity in terminology, conceptualization, and measurement resulted in a confusing conceptual literature and a limited empirical literature.

Another factor that may have added to the confusion was revealed by the results of our computerized literature searches for articles pertaining to psychological mindedness. These searches invariably yielded articles about related concepts from other areas of study. These other concepts included *alexithymia*, *private self-consciousness*, *self-focused attention*, and *personal intelligence*. Their applications included but were not restricted to the area of psychotherapy. Initially, we discarded these other articles without much consideration. We suspect that other psychotherapy investigators and investigators from other areas of psychology may have also discarded articles that overlapped somewhat with their area of research. That would explain our eventual observation that each area's inquiries seemed to proceed along separate lines with each investigator being unaware of the discoveries of the others. As such, it appeared that theoreticians, clinicians, and researchers had not benefited from the contributions of each other's work.

In order to try to connect these separate yet related lines of investigation, we decided to edit a book on psychological mindedness and related concepts. We invited contributions from authors whom we regarded as being among the leading North American researchers in this area. We provided each author with an outline consisting of seven topics, requesting that they be addressed in each chapter. The common topics covered information about each concept's (a) origin, including its theoretical background and evolution, (b) conceptual definition, (c) operational definition, (d) psychometric properties, and (e) research findings. We also asked each author to provide a (f) summary, and some suggestion for (g) future directions. The authors' compliance with our request is evident in the content of their chapters, which cover very well the common topics.

PURPOSE OF THE VOLUME

The primary purpose of this volume is to increase mental health practitioners' understanding of the concept of psychological mindedness and its importance to their everyday work in assessing and treating patients. The volume also provides practical methods for assessing psychological mindedness. Consequently, we hope it will facilitate clinicians' methods of selection of the most appropriate patients for their particular approaches to therapy. By choosing the most appropriate patients, clinicians may minimize dropout rates and optimize the process and outcome of therapy.

A secondary purpose of this volume is to address the relevance of psychological mindedness to interpersonal contexts outside of the mental health field. We attempt to fulfill this second purpose by assembling, in Part II, chapters about concepts related to psychological mindedness developed by professionals in other areas of study. As Part II depicts, these related concepts have emphasized various aspects of psychological mindedness, for example, the interpersonal, motivational, developmental, creative, cognitive, and emotional. We hope that an exploration of the relationships among the related concepts will enhance the understanding and knowledge base of professionals in diverse areas.

READERSHIP

This volume is primarily addressed to mental health practitioners who provide services to psychiatric patients, including the staff of public and private clinics, and private practitioners. They are typically from the disciplines of psychiatry, psychology, social work, occupational therapy, and nursing. We believe the volume is relevant to both students (trainees) and experienced clinicians. The book may be of particular interest to practitioners who utilize a psychodynamic theoretical orientation. However, practitioners who utilize other theoretical orientations may find the book useful in considering the relevance of the concept of psychological mindedness and related concepts to their clinical procedures and as a model for developing operational definitions of concepts central to their approach to psychotherapy. Clinicians whose practice is more eclectic routinely match particular technical approaches with suitable patients. For these clinicians, this volume can facilitate matching decisions. For example, they may offer an interpretive technical approach to their highly psychologically minded patients and offer a more supportive technical approach to their minimally psychologically minded patients. Because of the attention paid to the research grounding of the assessment of psychological mindedness, we believe the volume is also relevant to researchers and evaluators of mental health delivery systems.

This volume is also relevant for professionals from other areas of psychology, for example, educational, industrial–organizational, developmental, and social. While specific chapters may be more or less relevant to each school of psychology, the variety of approaches reviewed here should provide an interesting comparison across the schools of thought. We hope you enjoy it and find it useful!

CHAPTER CONTENT

The present book is the result of collaboration. It is composed of three major parts. Part I presents various ways of conceptualizing and measuring psychological mindedness. Chapter 1, co-authored by Conte and Ratto, reviews questionnaire measures of psychological mindedness. In chapter 2, we summarize alternative methods of assessing psychological mindedness by using information from the clinical interview and by combining other variables—an indirect method of assessing psychological mindedness. Chapter 2 also presents a description of our measure of psychological mindedness, which uses a standardized video stimulus. Part I concludes with Hatcher and Hatcher's work on the assessment of the psychological mindedness of children. By surveying the various measures of psychological mindedness in Part I, readers can become familar with methods of assessing psychological mindedness. They can select those meeting their specific needs.

Findings concerning related concepts from other fields of investigation compose the second part of the volume. Five related concepts are reviewed. In chapter 4 Taylor and Taylor begin the section with a review of thc concept and measurement of *alexithymia*. Fenigstein presents the area of *personal and private self-consciousness* in chapter 5. Chapter 6 provides Park and Park with an opportunity to discuss *personal intelligence*. In chapter 7 Dollinger traces his many years of investigating the concept of "reading between the lines." Menna and Cohen review, in chapter 8, the work of themselves and others in the area of *social perspective taking* among children. It is our goal that Part II of the book provides readers with the opportunity to benefit from the discoveries in other areas of investigation with which they may not be acquainted.

Part III consists of two integrative chapters. Chapter 9 coauthored by Farber and Golden, presents a semifictional account of a developing psychotherapist as the authors discuss the *psychological mindedness* of the psychotherapist. In chapter 10, we attempt to integrate and discuss the previous chapters. We organize this integration around a number of common themes emerging throughout the volume. These include: (a) development, (b) dimensions, (c) basic characteristics, (d) focus, (e) advantages and disadvantages, (f) current state of knowledge, and (g) future research directions associated with psychological mindedness and related concepts. In addition to reviewing the various authors' work, we compare and contrast the various measures of psychological mindedness and related concepts.

ACKNOWLEDGMENTS

We wish to extend our appreciation to all of the authors who contributed chapters to this volume. Their cooperation in following our content outline and responding to our editorial feedback created an informative and productive collegial process.

The program of clinical research presented in chapter 2 began in the mid-1970's and continues to the present. The successful development and implementation of the PMAP reflects the collaboration of many people. We wish to express our thanks and appreciation to them. First, we are indebted to Ms. Jocelyne Lauziere and Mr. Carl Aboud for graciously agreeing to skillfully portray the patient–therapist dyad on the videotape.

Over the years, many research assistants were involved in the daily routine of our clinical research. Their consistently careful contribution has resulted in the nearly seamless continuity of the research. We especially want to acknowledge the contribution of the research coordinators, Hillary Morin, Bonnie Stephanson, Suzanne B. Korpela, Colleen S. Poon, and Carol E. Wilson. We wish to express a special appreciation to our clinical research assessors, Drs. Anthony Joyce and Scott Duncan.

We extend our sincerest gratitude to the clinical staff of the Psychiatric Walk-In Clinic who served as the intake assessors and primary referral base for patients in the three clinical studies. We also appreciate the participation of the projects' therapists who represent the staffs of the Walk-In Clinic, the Day Treatment, and the Evening Treatment programs.

The cooperation of the service chiefs, Drs. Hassan F. A. Azim, John S. Rosie, and John G. O'Kelly was also essential for the successful implementation of the studies. We additionally wish to acknowledge the support for our clinical research expressed by the past and present chairmen of the Department of Psychiatry, University of Alberta, Drs. William G. Dewhurst and Roger C. Bland. Our gratitude is also extended to Claire Leighton-Morris for her meticulous preparation of the final and uniform manuscript. Finally, we sincerely and respectfully acknowledge the contribution of the patients in the clinical trials and the subjects of the initial study for their trust and patience with the research procedures.

This program of research was supported by the following provincial and national granting agencies: Medical Research Council of Canada; the National Health, Research, and Development Program, Health and Welfare Canada; the Canadian Psychiatric Research Foundation; the Alberta Mental Health Research Fund; and the Special Services and Research Committee of the University of Alberta Hospitals.

—Mary McCallum
—William E. Piper

REFERENCES

de Carufel, F. L., & Piper, W. E. (1988). Group psychotherapy or individual psychotherapy. Patient characteristics as predictive factors. *International Journal of Group Psychotherapy, 38,* 169–188.

McCallum, M. (1989). *A controlled study of effectiveness and patient suitability for short-term group psychotherapy.* Unpublished doctoral dissertation, McGill University, Montreal, Quebec, Canada.

McCallum, M. & Piper, W. E. (1987). *The psychological mindedness assessment procedure.* Unpublished manual and videotape.

Piper, W. E., de Carufel, F. L., & Szkrumelak, N. (1985). Patient predictors of process and outcome in short-term individual psychotherapy. *Journal of Nervous and Mental Disease, 173,* 726–733.

Piper, W. E., Debbane, E. G., Bienvenu, J. P., & de Carufel, F. L. (1987). A system for differentiating therapist interpretations and other interventions. *Bulletin of the Menninger Clinic, 51,* 532–550.

Piper, W. E., Debbane, E. G., Bienvenu, J. P., & Garant, J. (1984). A comparative study of four forms of psychotherapy. *Journal of Consulting and Clinical Psychology, 52,* 268–279.

Chapter 1

Self-Report Measures of Psychological Mindedness

Hope R. Conte
Rosemarie Ratto
Albert Einstein College of Medicine of Yeshiva University

There is consensus among clinicians working within the area of dynamically oriented psychotherapy on the importance and relevance of the concept of psychological mindedness. Because of the widespread belief that psychological mindedness is a prerequisite for success in this form of treatment, clinicians routinely make specific recommendations on the basis of an individual's perceived capacity to be psychologically minded. In fact, it is often stated that the prospects of a psychologically minded patient benefitting from treatment are greatly enhanced regardless of other factors that might appear to mitigate against improvement. Many theorists and clinicians also contend that effective therapy requires psychological mindedness on the part of both patient and therapist (Coltart, 1988; Farber, 1985).

This complex concept appears to be intuitively understood by clinicians. Nevertheless, as it is used in the literature, its definition is far from precise. For example, with Appelbaum's (1973) definition, the emphasis was on the individual: "A person's ability to see relationships among thoughts, feelings, and actions, with the goal of learning the meanings and causes of his experiences and behavior" (p. 36). Consistent with Appelbaum's definition, but less specific, McCallum and Piper (1990b) stressed an understanding of intrapsychic dynamics. They defined psychological mindedness "as the ability to identify dynamic (intrapsychic) components and to relate them to a person's difficulties" (p. 412).

Farber (1985) specifically introduced the notion of "others," and saw psychological mindedness as a trait rather than an ability, calling it ". . . the disposition to reflect upon the meaning and motivation of behavior, thoughts, and feelings of oneself and others" (p. 170). Wolitsky and Reuben (1974) chose to keep the notions of interest and ability separate and thus considered psychological mindedness as a tendency to "view behavior as expressing and communicating information about the needs, wishes, purposes, intentions, conflicts, defensive strategies, etc. of the person in question, oneself or another" (p. 26).

In contrast, Hall (1992) characterizeed the concept as reflecting both an inclination or disposition, and an ability, and defined it as "reflectivity about psychological processes, relationships, and meanings, and is displayed by an individual to the extent that he or she displays both interest in and ability for such reflectivity across both affective and intellectual dimensions" (pp. 139–140).

Much theoretical attention was, therefore, devoted to this concept. Empirical data concerning psychological mindedness (PM) has been more limited. Wolitzky and Reuben (1974) developed a measure of the concept based on assessment of a person's response to Thematic Apperception Test (TAT) stories. Dollinger, Greening, and Tylenda (1985) have used a task based on word associations. Ryan and Cicchetti (1985) constructed a rating scale on which PM is rated from high (internal orientation) to low (external orientation) on the basis of interview data. McCallum and Piper (1990b) developed the Psychological Mindedness Assessment Procedure (PMAP), which uses a standardized video and interview format to assess PM.

Considering the importance of this concept, only a few self-report scales were developed to measure psychological mindedness. These include the Private Self-Consciousness Scale (Fenigstein, Scheier, & Buss, 1975) used by Farber (1989), the Insight Test, developed by Tolor and Reznikoff (1960), the Py scale of the California Psychological Inventory (CPI; Gough, 1957, 1975) and the Psychological Mindedness Scale (Conte et al., 1990). The latter three test instruments are described in detail in this chapter, and Fenigstein et al.'s (1975) is discussed in chapter 5.

THE INSIGHT TEST

Tolor and Reznikoff created the Insight Test because the literature at that time contained few empirical investigations of insight, even though the concept occupied a major position in theories of psychotherapy. Their premise was based on the idea that insight can be measured by determining the degree to which an individual accurately interprets a number of hypothetical situations representing the operation of various defense mechanisms. It was their belief that this approach, linking insight to defensive reactions, created a more dynamic, motivation-oriented context as opposed to what they considered to be only a poorly understood domain of traits.

These authors considered insight as the ability to realistically perceive the environment and the ability to comprehend the causative factors determining the attitudes and behaviors of others, both of which are presumed to underlie an understanding of one's own motivation. This definition assumes that insight involves an understanding of one's own attitudes and behaviors as well as those of others. Such a capacity is broadly related to what others have called self-awareness, reflectiveness, and introspectiveness.

Development of the Technique

A number of hypothetical situations were constructed that depicted the use of common defense mechanisms. For each situation, four explanatory statements were created, and then rank ordered independently by the authors and three other judges who were unaware of the purpose of the study, according to the degree of insight shown. Those situations agreed on by four of the five judges were retained. The scale was then administered to a sample of nurses and college students who were asked to choose, for each situation, the explanatory statements indicative of the most and least amount of insight.

Analyses of these data led to the form of the test selected for further study. It included 27 different, brief hypothetical situations, 2 representing each of 13 different defense mechanisms and one in which a number of defenses were combined. The following defenses, varied systematically so that no defense ever occurred twice in succession, were included: denial, displacement, identification, introjection, isolation, compensation, projection, rationalization, reaction formation, regression, repression, sublimation, and undoing. The test is scored by summing the number of times the subject's choice of most and least insightful explanations correspond with the choices for each situation determined by the judges. Thus, insight as operationally defined by Tolor and Reznikoff is: The ability to chose, in 27 different hypothetical situations depicting the operation of various defense mechanisms, the two explanatory statements indicative of the defenses presumably representing the most and the least insightful interpretations of the situations depicted.

The following is an example of a hypothetical situation and its explanatory statements:

A man who intensely dislikes a fellow worker goes out of his way to speak well of him.

1. The man really doesn't dislike his coworker.
2. The man believes he will make a better impression on others by speaking well of him.
3. The man is overdoing his praises in order to cover up for his real feelings of dislike.
4. The man doesn't want to hurt anyone's feelings.

This situation exemplifies the defense mechanism of reaction formation. The third response represents the most insightful and the first item the least insightful choice.

Reliability

The only reliability data presented by Tolor and Reznikoff (1960) was a test–retest coefficient of .86 obtained on a sample of 27 introductory psychology students after a 1-week interval. No measure of internal consistency was given. Abramowitz and Abramowitz (1974) did, however, report an alpha coefficient of .60 for a 12-situation distillation of the Insight Test used to assess pre- to posttherapy changes after insight-oriented group therapy. This coefficient was described as "considerably higher than that found for the longer but less cohesive parent inventory" (p. 612), yet the reliability of that inventory was not mentioned.

Validity

The validity of the 27-situation Insight Test was studied by comparing test scores obtained by 68 adult hospitalized and clinic patients with independent insight ratings made on each of these patients by 28 psychiatrists and psychologists. They rated the patients at the time they were administered the Insight Test on a 5-point scale ranging from 1 *significantly below average for most patients* to 5 *significantly above average for most patients*. The patients were then divided into high, low, and middle groups on the basis of these ratings. Analyses indicated that Insight Test scores differed significantly for patients in the two extreme groups, indicating that judges' ratings of insight are significantly related to Insight Test scores and that the test possesses a measure of discriminant validity.

However, sensitivity and specificity determinations obtained with a variety of cutoff scores were not adequate for use in making individual predictions. In addition, no meaningful relationships were found between test scores and diagnoses, age, or gender. There was some indication that test scores and intelligence were related.

Tolor and Reznikoff (1960) found additional evidence of discriminant validity for their test in a study comparing 56 psychiatric patients, 115 untrained nurses, and 106 trained psychiatric nurses. Patients' mean scores were significantly lower than those of both groups of nurses, and a significant difference was found between trained and untrained nurses. This latter finding was regarded as indicative that training of this type can play an important ancillary role in increasing level of insight.

A separate study by Tolor (1961) provided evidence of concurrent validity for the Insight Test. In a survey of 67 psychiatric aides, he investigated the relationship between insight and intraception, defined by Edwards (1953) as the need to "analyze one's motives and feelings, to observe others, to understand how others feel about problems, to put one's self in another's place, to judge people by why they do things rather than by what they do, to analyze the behavior of others, to analyze the motives of others, to predict how others will act" (p. 11). As predicted, a low, significant, positive relationship was found between the two constructs.

There were only two studies that used test scores on the Insight Test as a predictor of outcome in psychotherapy. Abramowitz and Abramowitz (1974) randomly assigned a sample of 26 college students to one of four therapy groups, two described as insight-oriented and two not insight-oriented, meeting twice weekly for 5 weeks, all led by a single psychologist. The previously mentioned modified 12-situation Insight Test was used to assess pre- to posttherapy changes in insight. An ANOVA with post hoc mean comparison showed a trend ($p < .15$) toward increased insight among the members of the analytically oriented groups, but not for the noninsight groups. In addition, those patients having greater pretherapy insight made greater strides in the insight-oriented therapy. Their counterparts in the noninsight groups fared no better than did less insightful members.

The results of this study offer evidence that psychological mindedness, at least as measured by the modified Insight Test, relates to positive outcome for insight-oriented groups. However, as the authors pointed out, the generalizability and persuasiveness of these data are limited due to the small, homogeneous, relatively healthy sample, the brevity of the treatment, and the use of only a single therapist who, coincidentally, was the senior investigator with an admittedly proinsight orientation.

A more recent study (Piper, Azim, McCallum, & Joyce, 1990) used Insight Test scores as one measure of psychotherapy outcome in an investigation of the relationship of the effects of time-limited, short-term individual dynamic psychotherapy and the quality of patients' object relations. Thirty-eight patients, representing a variety of clinical diagnoses, served as their own controls by completing both the waiting list control condition and the therapy condition. A comparison of residual change scores on the Insight Test during the control condition with residual change during the treatment period showed significantly greater improvement for the treatment period ($p < .05$). However, no significant improvement was found on the Insight Test for the between group comparison, that is, the immediate treatment versus control condition. These findings thus provide partial support for Tolor and Resnikoff s (1960) assertion that exposure to psychological concepts can play an important role in increasing insight and, taken together with the findings of Abramowitz and Abramowitz (1974), provide some evidence for the predictive validity of the Insight Test.

Studies Relating Insight to Other Personal Characteristics

In examining the relationship between level of insight and adjustment in a sample of 24 patients from a schizophrenic population, Roback and Abramowitz (1979) found somewhat paradoxical results. High scorers on the

Insight Test were not significantly different from low scoring patients on any of 22 measures of adjustment, yet a disproportionate number were in the predicted direction. Staff rated higher insight-scoring patients better adjusted on 9 out of the 12 behavioral adjustment measures. However, these same patients rated themselves as less well-adjusted on all 10 of the self-report measures of well-being. For a number of reasons, including small sample size, these results are tentative. But the notion that insight may intensify subjective distress while concomitantly helping behavioral adjustment is an intriguing one and consistent with Appelbaum's (1976) comment on the dangerous edge of insight and Farber's (1989) conclusion that the "benefits of psychological-mindedness are inextricably linked to its costs: greater awareness of dysphoric emotions and greater awareness of untenable possibilities" (p. 216).

Schulberg (1962) administered the Insight Test to 218 college students to test Adorno, Frenkel-Brunswik, Levinson, and Sandford's (1950) hypothesis that nonauthoritarians are more insightful and perceptive than are authoritarians. Even after the effect of insight's relationship to intelligence was partialed out, insight's association with nonauthoritarianism as measured by the F scale (Christie, Havel, & Seidenberg, 1958) was significant.

Tolor and Reznikoff (1967) found mixed results in their test of hypotheses regarding personality characteristics and insight. First, they hypothesized that subjects who sensitize, characterized by alertness and approaching behaviors, tend to be more insightful than those who repress, defined by avoidance and denial. Second, using Rotter's (1966) theory of internal versus external control, Tolor and Reznikoff hypothesized that those individuals who believed rewards follow one's own behavior (internal control) would be more insightful than those who believed that rewards are contingent on forces independent of their own actions (external control). Data from 79 college students again showed insight and intelligence to be highly related. Partial correlations, controlling for the effect of intelligence, between Insight Test scores and scores on the Repression–Sensitization (R–S) scale (Byrne, 1961) and Rotter's (1966) Internal–External (I–E) Scale confirmed the hypothesis that those individuals who possessed internal control were more insightful. However, no relationship was found between insight and repression–sensitization.

Finally, a series of studies utilized the Insight Test as a means of investigating the relationship between insight and competence among students in the mental health field (Goldney & McFarlane, 1986; Goldney & Pilowsky, 1976; Lenarz & Vestre, 1964; McFarlane, Goldney, & Kalucy, 1989). Lenarz and Vestre's results showed that Insight Test scores of a group of 54 nurses were significantly higher after a 12-week course in psychiatric nursing than were scores for a comparable group who did not take the course. Similar results occurred in the other three studies dealing with medical students. In all cases, Insight Test scores increased significantly as a result of training programs. In addition, final Insight scores were significantly correlated with criterion measures such as test scores and supervisors' ratings.

Summary

The grounding of the Insight Test in a psychodynamic theoretical perspective is one of its greatest assets and gives it both clinical and training relevance. It has been used over the past 30 years to link the concept of insight to such important variables as psychopathology and adjustment, outcome of psychotherapy, personality traits, and training issues. Although the research is sparse—only 11 articles found since its conception in 1960—a variety of populations were studied. These include psychiatric in- and outpatients, but most of the investigations were with relatively healthy college and medical students and nurses. This limited sampling may provide at least a partial explanation for two key findings: First, a considerable amount of the variance on the Insight Test is accounted for by intellectual factors; and second, it shows no consistent relation to diagnostic categories.

Although evidence for the test's discriminant, predictive, concurrent, and convergent validity was provided, there is a paucity of data on reliability. Tolor and Reznikoff (1960) reported only a test–retest coefficient of .86 on a small number of students who took the test after just a 1-week interval, which is hardly long enough to dilute the influence of responses on the first testing. The only measure of internal consistency, reported by Abramowitz and Abramowitz (1974) for a modified 12-situation version of the Insight Test, is a relatively low coefficient alpha of .60.

A major criticism that can be leveled at the Insight Test revolves around the definition of psychological mindedness. This concept is generally thought to presume an understanding of one's own motivation, feelings, and behavior as well as those of others. Tolor and Reznikoff's (1960) assumption (that the ability to appreciate others' motivations and to see below the surface of a clinical situation presupposes a similar self-understanding) is questionable (Dollinger et al., 1985; Markova & Berrios, 1992). This test approaches the measurement of psychological mindedness as a skill somewhat independent of the respondent's insight into himself or herself. Future investigations could, perhaps, address the following issues: (a) whether self-insight and insight into others are positively correlated, (b) the relationship between insight and the use of various defense mechanisms, and (c) whether (as one might hypothesize) various diagnostic groups demonstrate any consistent differences in overall insight.

THE PSYCHOLOGICAL MINDEDNESS SCALE OF THE CPI

The Psychological Mindedness scale (Py) is one of 18 subscales of the CPI developed by Gough (1957, 1975) to create a measure of descriptive concepts relevant to an individual's personal and social context. The CPI was an attempt to create a measure of interpersonal behavior different from those available at the time, which were primarily used in special settings such as psychiatric clinics or for a particular problem such as vocational choice. Consequently, the goals of the inventory (Gough, 1987) were to "assess the kind of everyday variables that ordinary people use in their daily lives to understand, classify, and predict their own behavior and that of others the CPI seeks to appraise folk concepts—concepts that arise from and are linked to ineluctable processes of interpersonal life, and that are found everywhere that humans congregate into groups and establish societal functions" (p. 1).

The 18 subscales of the self-report CPI are divided into four conceptual classes, not on the usual basis of psychometric factors or clusters, but rather for the purpose of facilitating clinical interpretation of the profile generated by the scales. Class I scales measure Poise, Ascendancy, Self-Assurance, and Interpersonal Adequacy; Class II assesses Socialization, Responsibility, Interpersonal Values, and Character; Class III has scales for Achievement Potential and Intellectual Efficiency; and Class IV, which contains the Psychological Mindedness scale (Py) along with scales for Flexibility and Femininity, is called, somewhat ambiguously, Intellectual and Interest Modes.

Development of the Scales

In the late 1940s and early 1950s, Gough assembled a pool of 300 experimental items. He then used the external–criterion method (Megargee, 1972) to construct a preliminary inventory. The 300 items were given to 25 "outstanding" young psychologists, whose responses (true–false) were compared with those of a large sample of subjects in other fields and training programs. Items that discriminated between these groups were next administered to approximately 50 graduate psychology students, whose responses were then correlated with instructors' ratings of competence and "potential." Items that correlated with this second criterion were retained (Gough, 1968). Thus, item selection was guided solely by the empirically determined relationship between test item and the two criterion measures.

The 22-item Py scale consists of 6 items that are keyed true and 16 keyed false. Gough (1957) originally defined the psychologically minded individual as one who "is interested in, and responsive to, the inner needs, motives, and experiences of others" (p. 11). He or she is "observant, spontaneous talka tive, resourceful, and changeable verbally fluent and socially ascendant r ebellious towards rules, restrictions and constraints" (p. 11). In contrast, low scorers on the Py scale are "apathetic, peaceable cau - tious slow and deliberate " (p. 11). A more recent definition (Gough, 1987) described the high scorer as "more interested in why people do what they do than in what they do; good judge of how people feel and what they think about things" (p. 7). The emphasis in both definitions is on the "other." Neither the definitions themselves nor the descriptions of high scoring individuals suggest that psychological mindedness involves introspection or self-understanding.

Some items have a degree of face validity. For example, "I like to keep things neat and tidy and in good order" (F) implies that psychological mindedness involves a tolerance of ambiguity. Others, like "I have a tendency to give up easily when I meet with difficult problems" (F) suggest a person who is resourceful enough to concentrate on a problem. Many items, however, such as "We ought to pay our elected officials better than we do" (T), "I do not have a great fear of snakes" (T), and "I would like to write a technical book" (T) do not appear to even describe an individual who is interested in and responsive to others, much less one who has any degree of self-understanding.

Reliability

The original manual reports test–retest correlations over a 1-year period for 125 female high school students as .49 and for 102 males as .48. The test–retest correlation for 200 male prisoners tested 4 weeks apart was .53. (Gough, 1957, 1975). Stability of the Py scale over 1 year as reported by Hase and Goldberg (1967) for 234 men and women was in the same approximate range, .48. They also report internal consistency, calculated by KR–20 for 179 freshman women, as .44.

In 1987, Gough reported a KR–20 coefficient for 400 college students as .62 on a longer Py form. Stability, as assessed by parallel forms completed by 85 male and 38 female high school students 1 week apart, was reported as .50 and .46, respectively. Test–retest over a 1-year period was .58 and .63 for 102 males and 128 females, respectively.

Validity

Evidence for the validity of the original scale was demonstrated when a rank ordering of the mean Py scores for 14 male and 7 female samples, ranging from psychology graduate students to prison inmates, corresponded "fairly well" to the continuum one might theoretically expect. Additional data was presented by Gough (1957, 1964b, 1975) to demonstrate that Py measures psychological mindedness. First, the Py scores of a sample of 70 medical student applicants and a group of 152 adult males correlated .44 and .40, respectively, with the Psychologist scale of the Strong Vocational Interest Blank. Second, the mean correlation between Py scores and course grade was .24 for samples representing 5,103 introductory psychology students. This coefficient, significant due to the large number of subjects, still only accounts for 6% of the variance.

The construct validity of the Py scale was investigated by other researchers as well. Findings were mixed. For example, Hase and Goldberg (1967) reported that the correlation between college students' peer ratings of psychological mindedness and Py scale scores was an unexpected –.12. In contrast, McCallum and Piper (1990b) reported a significant correlation of .42 between the Py scale and their measure of psychological mindedness, the PMAP, on data obtained from normal adults. Somewhat more difficult to interpret is Burkhart, Gynther, and Christian's (1978) finding that in a sample of 60 college students, high scorers on the Py scale also endorsed items characterized as "very subtle" and "somewhat subtle" on the MMPI.

To date, only one study assessed the predictive validity of the Py scale (Yalom, Houts, Zimerberg, & Rand, 1967). In this investigation of five outpatient groups led by 10 therapists using a "dynamic interactional" style, pretreatment scores on Py failed to correlate with interviewer ratings of improvement in three areas of psychosocial adjustment and with self-rated improvement in two of these three. The only significant correlation was with self-reported improvement in interpersonal relationships.

Studies Relating Py to Other Personal Characteristics

In their study of the relationships between alexithymia and a number of measures of personality and psychopathology, Bagby, Taylor, and Ryan (1986) found Py to be negatively correlated with scores on the Toronto Alexithymia Scale (TAS) for 81 college students, suggesting that individuals who are characterized by poorly differentiated and poorly verbalized affect are not psychologically minded. Py scores were also negatively related to scores on the Beck Depression Inventory, but positively related to a scale designed to measure the tendency to engage in and enjoy effortful cognitive endeavors.

Evidence for the construct validity of the Py scale obtained in another study of college students (Dollinger, Reader, Marnett, & Tylenda, 1983) is less consistent. This study examined the relations among three indirect measures of psychological thinking (e.g., describing another person in psychological terms), the Py scale, and the Intraception scale (a measure of social intelligence) of the Adjective Check List (ACL). No meaningful relations were found between Py scores and the indirect measures, whereas Py scores did relate significantly, in a positive manner, to scores on the Intraception scale. The authors believed this relationship exists primarily because both tests appear to elicit socially desirable responses. They concluded that psychological mindedness is not a unitary characteristic of a person.

Other studies, all conducted with students, report findings consistent with the way in which Gough claimed high scorers on the Py scale tend to be seen. Vingoe (1973), for example, found significant positive relationships between Py scores and peer ratings of how well a specified person is felt to be known (socially ascendent). Hoffnung (1975) reported that among male Orthodox Jewish students differing in the extent of their orthodoxy, those students scoring highest on the Py scale were also from the least dogmatic and orthodox group. This finding is consistent with Schulberg's (1962) results showing a significant relationship between high scorers on the Insight Test and nonauthoritarianism.

Studies on the relationship between psychological mindedness and drug use describe high Py scorers as less likely to be substance abusers. For example, in a study comparing 122 recovering alcoholics to a group of 61 adult controls, those alcoholics with at least 4 years of sobriety scored higher on the Py scale than did those with either shorter periods of sobriety or the control group (Kurtines, Ball, & Wood, 1978). Similarly, marijuana nonusers scored higher than occasional users, regular users, or heavy users, in that order (McGuire & Megargee, 1974). These findings, although consistent with Gough's description of high Py scorers being resourceful, are not in line with his notion that low scorers tend to be cautious, overly conforming, and conventional.

A number of research studies showed individuals involved in health care provision scored significantly higher on the Py scale than did comparison groups of various kinds (Dyer, Monson, & Van Drimmelen, 1972; Hersch, Kulik, & Scheibe, 1969; King, McGowen, Doonan, & Schweibert, 1980).

Finally, and not unexpectedly considering the way in which the scale was constructed, scores on the Py scale correlated significantly and positively with academic achievement (Gough, 1964a; Gough & Lanning, 1986; Hogan & Weiss, 1974; Holland, 1959; Maxwell, 1960; Murray & Walsh, 1976; Repapi, Gough, Lanning, & Stefanis, 1983; Snider, 1966).

Summary

The Py scale is without doubt the most widely used questionnaire measure of psychological mindedness. It is the only such scale with enough empirical research to allow the user to evaluate the probable utility of his or her predictions of behavior patterns in such everyday situations as academic achievement, interpersonal effectiveness, and professional performance. The scale has normative data based on over 6,000 men and 7,000 women, but is most applicable to students and young adults, both because of the larger size of these samples and because the content of the items appears more relevant to younger, academically oriented groups. The advantage of these extensive norms is, however, somewhat tempered by the scale's quite modest reliabilities.

A definite weakness of the scale, as it is for all the scales of the CPI, is that the manual does not provide a detailed description of Gough's scale construction procedures. The reader would like to know, for example, how and why the original 300 items were selected and what constituted the "longer" form used in the 1987 reliability studies.

Gough never adopted a formal theoretical position. The items of the Py scale were selected almost entirely on the basis of their ability to distinguish groups believed a priori to be highly different in terms of psychological mindedness. Those that also correlated significantly with ratings of "competence" of psychology students were then retained and the scale named Psychological Mindedness. As Walsh (1972) in his review of the CPI pointed out, the criterion approach to scale construction has enough problems of its own in the sense that it often results in scales without basic psychological meaning. The use of extreme groups for item selection can only serve to lessen the scale's psychological significance.

Thus, from the derivation of the scale, an inspection of item content, and the validity data presented (which rely heavily on academic achievement and proficiency), we agree with Megargee (1972) that the Py scale does reflect attitudes and behaviors associated with psychologists, but psychologists more as scientists than as clinicians. Furthermore, neither the definitions given nor the content of the items themselves imply that psychological mindedness involves self-understanding or insight into one's own thoughts, feelings, or behavior. Consequently, as Hall (1992) commented, the preference for the use of the Py scale can be criticized on the grounds that there is no clear reason, outside of precedence, to prefer it.

THE PSYCHOLOGICAL MINDEDNESS (PM) SCALE

There were a large number of quantitative investigations of pretreatment variables that might predict who will benefit most from psychotherapy. Luborsky, Crits-Christoph, Mintz, and Auerbach (1988) provided the most recent review of factors influencing the outcome of psychotherapy and research support for them. As these authors noted, such pretreatment variables as amount of motivation for treatment, positive attitudes toward self and therapist, and a relatively high level of intelligence tend to be associated with positive outcome. However, although psychological mindedness was seen as a criterion for motivation for psychotherapy (Rosenbaum & Horowitz, 1983; Sifneos, 1972) and was previously associated with therapeutic outcome (Appelbaum, 1973; Piper, deCarufel, & Szkrumelak, 1985; Sifneos, 1981), it is one pretreatment variable that was not systematically studied in its own right.

The Psychological Mindedness (PM) Scale (Conte et al., 1990) is a new measure of psychological mindedness designed to measure a patient's suitability for dynamically oriented psychotherapy and to determine the extent to which it can predict other variables related to psychotherapy outcome. The PM Scale is not theoretically based, as it does not attempt to operationalize psychoanalytic variables. It does, however, have a theoretical frame of reference in that it attempts to measure characteristics such as a willingness to commit oneself to the therapeutic alliance and a basic agreement with those values and norms associated with good prognosis in dynamic psychotherapy.

Development of the Technique

The PM Scale represents a shortened version of a 65-item scale originally used by Lotterman[1] in a pilot study (Lotterman, 1979). As used by Lotterman, it consisted of 45 self-report items and 20 items that were part of a multiple-choice test to be completed after reading two clinical vignettes. The present PM Scale contains only the 45 self-report items, some of which were revised or reworded. They represent multiple facets of this complex concept, involving an ability to be introspective about one's own feelings, thoughts, and behavior as well as an interest in understanding why others feel, think, and behave as they do.

Items are in a self-report format, scored on a 4-point scale ranging from 1 (*strongly disagree*) to 4 (*strongly agree*). Content validity was determined by asking five experienced clinicians to judge whether the items adequately covered a representative sample of the concept of PM as they understood it clinically and as it is described in the literature. They agreed that it did. They further agreed that if endorsed, 24 of the items loaded positively for PM whereas 21 loaded negatively. These latter items are reverse scored. A total PM score is obtained by summing the scores for all items.

Reliability

Conte et al. (1990) reported good internal consistency of the PM Scale (coefficient alpha = .86) based on the data of 69 psychiatric outpatients. The coefficient alpha was recomputed on the data of an additional 250 outpatients and again showed good internal consistency for this population (.87). Test–retest reliability over a 2-week period for a sample of 22 normal adults was .92, indicating good stability as well (Conte, Ratto, Clutz, & Karasu, 1993).

Validity

A study of 44 psychiatric outpatients (Conte et al., 1990) seen in primarily individual psychodynamically oriented psychotherapy provided preliminary evidence for the predictive validity of the PM Scale. Their pretherapy total PM scores were found to be significantly correlated ($r = .39$; $p < .01$) with the number of psychotherapy sessions attended ($M = 19.70$, $SD = 24.36$), with an increase in global functioning as judged by an independent rater ($r = .33$; $p < .05$), and with a decrease in psychosocial symptoms and problems as rated by clinicians ($r = -.37$; $p < .05$). There was no significant relationship between pretherapy PM scores and initial functioning, symptomatology, or years of education, suggesting that regardless of educational level or initial severity of psychological problems, the higher an individual's PM, the greater the likelihood of his or her becoming engaged in therapy and benefitting from it.

---

[1]Copyright © 1993 by Andrew C. Lotterman.

The 20 items selected to be the best predictors of outcome served as the basis for an operational definition of PM. That is, one is considered to be psychologically minded if one has access to one's feelings, is willing to talk about one's intrapsychic and interpersonal problems, has the capacity and motivation for behavioral change, and is interested in what motivates other people's behavior.

A subsequent study (Conte et al., 1993) attempted to replicate, on a larger sample of psychiatric outpatients at the same clinic, the PM Scale's ability to predict measures of outcome in terms of clinicians' and an independent rater's ratings and in terms of length of time spent in psychotherapy. One hundred sixteen patients who completed the PM Scale at admission were discharged over a 4-year period and attended at least four sessions of psychotherapy (M = 22.61; SD = 30.16). As found in the original study (Conte, et al. 1990), PM scores were basically uncorrelated with initial global functioning and level of psychosocial symptoms and problems at admission. A significant relationship was found between PM scores and level of education ($r = .17$; $p < .10$). Also as in the original study, a high level of PM at intake was significantly and positively correlated with number of therapy sessions attended ($r = .25$; $p < .01$). However, the findings with respect to the predictive validity of the PM Scale in terms of an independent rater's and clinicians' ratings of level of functioning and symptoms and problems did not replicate.

These results are consistent with those of McCallum and Piper (1990b) who found that PM was predictive of remaining in short-term group therapy, but failed to find significant direct relationships between PM and a large battery of outcome indices. They are inconsistent, however, with the finding that for patients in a group-oriented day treatment program, PM was significantly related to favorable outcome (Piper, Joyce, Azim, & Rosie, 1994; Piper, Joyce, Rosie, & Azim, 1994). Nevertheless, none of these findings are inconsistent with Meltzoff and Kornreich's (1970) belief that in a complex, multidetermined enterprise such as psychotherapy, the relation of any single patient variable to outcome is apt to account for only a small portion of the total variance.

An additional measure, not used in the Conte et al. (1990) study, was the Self-Report Symptoms and Problems Questionnaire (SRPQ). This instrument was constructed for a previous survey of recently discharged patients (Conte, Plutchik, Buckley, Spence, & Karasu, 1989) and was mailed to all of the 116 discharged patients, 42 of whom returned scorable forms. The SRPQ consists of 24 frequently encountered symptoms or problems such as panic, depression, shyness, irritability, sleep problems, lack of enjoyment of life, problems in getting along with people, and problems with alcohol and drugs. Patients were asked to indicate whether they experienced at discharge more or fewer problems than they had on admission to treatment, or whether there was no change. A total score represents the patient's rating of improvement. The lower the score, the greater the perceived improvement. Item 25, representing the patient's subjective global rating of improvement in therapy, asked on a 4-point scale how much they believed they were helped at the clinic. The last item, 26, asked for ratings, again on a 4-point scale, of how satisfied the patients were with their therapists.

Although PM was unrelated to measures of patient outcome from the therapists' and independent rater's points of view in this study, for the 42 patients who returned their SRPQ survey, PM scores were significantly correlated with their assessment of the extent of their psychosocial symptoms subsequent to termination of treatment (items 1–24; $r = -.32$; $p < .05$). In addition, these self-ratings of symptomatology subsequent to discharge were significantly correlated with patients' global ratings of improvement in therapy (Item 25 of the SRPQ; $r = -.31$; $p < .05$). There was also some evidence that these global ratings of improvement were related to ratings of satisfaction with therapists (Item 26; $r = -.27$; $p < .10$). What this suggests is that for high psychologically minded individuals, self-ratings may be more sensitive to change in dynamically oriented psychotherapy than are ratings made from other vantage points. Nevertheless, these findings need replication on a larger sample.

Bagby, Taylor, and Parker's (1994) investigation of the psychometric properties of their scale for alexithymia (TAS–20) provides evidence for construct (discriminant) validity of the PM Scale. The alexithymic state was characterized (Moore & Fine, 1990) by "poorly differentiated and poorly verbalized affects that do not serve the signal function adequately (do not communicate effectively)" (p. 11). One would predict, therefore, that a measure of this concept would correlate negatively with PM scores, which is what these investigators found. Negative correlations were obtained between the PM Scale and the TAS–20, (r –.68; $p < .01$), as well as between PM and each of the TAS–20's three factors, defined as (a) difficulty identifying feelings, (b) difficulty describing feelings, and (c) externally oriented thinking (rs = –.44; –.51, and –.54, respectively; $p < .01$). These findings suggest that the PM Scale is measuring the converse of the concept of alexithymia.

Studies Relating PM to Other Personal Characteristics

Two recent studies by Conte and her colleagues (Conte, Buckley, Picard, & Karasu, 1995) investigated the construct validity of the PM Scale by assessing whether psychiatric outpatients' scores on the scale would be related in theoretically expected ways to their scores on a personality test and to their scores on measures of ego functioning. Also explored was the ability of the PM Scale to differentiate, between two groups of psychiatric outpatients who differed significantly in numbers of years of education.

Study 1 was conducted on a sample of 46 medical students attending a special personnel clinic within a large psychiatric outpatient department affiliated with their medical school. Patients were diagnosed primarily as affective, anxiety, and adjustment disorders. At the time of their admission to the clinic they were administered the Personality Profile Index (PPI; Plutchik & Conte, 1989).

The PPI consists of 89 items in a self-report format. Although it is theoretically based, the actual items chosen for the test have their origins in the empirically derived circular ordering of trait terms reported by Conte and Plutchik (1981). Eight dimensions of personality are rated: acceptance, submission, passivity, depression, rejection, aggression, assertion, and sociability. The PPI also provides a conflict measure and a meassure of social desirability. Good internal consistency and evidence for discriminant validity were demonstrated (Conte, Plutchik, Picard, & Karasu, 1991; Conte, Plutchik, Picard, Karasu, Galanter, & Jacoby, 1991; Plutchik, & Conte, 1989).

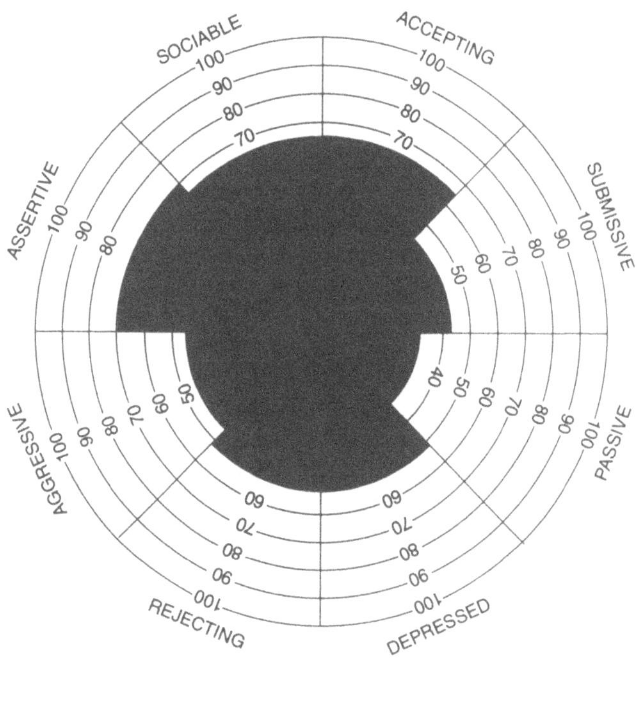

FIG. 1.1. Personality profile of psychiatric outpatients scoring in the top one-third of the distribution of scores on the PM scale. ($N = 15$). Adapted from Conte et al. (1995) with permission.

Results showed that high PM scores were significantly associated with high assertiveness ($r = .57; p < .001$), sociability ($r = .40; p < .01$), low passivity ($r = -.59$; $p < .001$), and depression and conflict ($rs = -.34$ and $-.30$, respectively; $p < .05$). Those students with high scores on PM also tended not to be submissive ($r = -.27$; $p < .10$) and could be considered above average in their tendency to be accepting rather than rejecting of others ($rs = .24$ and $-.24$, respectively; $p < .10$).

Another way of looking at these data is presented in Fig. 1.1, which graphically shows the personality profile, expressed in percentiles, of those students who scored in the top one third of the distribution of total PM scores ($N = 15$). Although conflict is not represented on this circular diagram, their average scores put them in the 52nd percentile, or normal, range.

These characteristics are those one might theoretically expect from individuals who are psychologically minded and who, presumably, will do well and benefit from psychodynamically oriented psychotherapy.

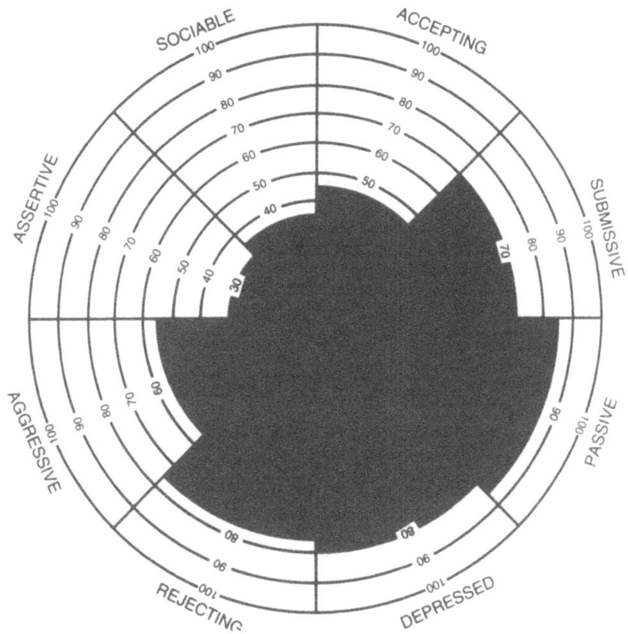

FIG. 1.2. Personality profile of psychiatric outpatients scoring in the bottom one-third of the distribution of scores on the PM scale. ($N = 15$). Adapted from Conte et al. (1995) with permission.

That is, individuals who are interested in the meaning of their own behavior and that of others and who derive insight from discussions about their problems, would tend to be sociable, assertive, and accepting of others. Being low on rejection, they would also be open to new ideas and, not being exceptionally passive or depressed, they would have a capacity for change.

Figure 1.2 presents the contrasting personality profile of those patients who scored in the bottom one third of the distribution of PM scores. Most notable are high passivity, depression, submission, and rejection, whereas those traits characteristic of the patients with high PM (assertion, sociability, and acceptance) are below average. The mean conflict score of the low scorers, which falls at the 77th percentile, is also well out of the normal range. This profile represents a group one would not expect to be insightful nor be open to, motivated for, or have the capacity for change.

The average PM score of these high and low scoring medical student patients was significantly different, as were their average scores on all dimensions of the PPI except aggression. These data may be seen in Table 1.1.

Study 2 (Conte et al., 1995) reported the results of another investigation conducted at the same outpatient clinic, but with a sample of 192 regular clinic patients. This sample was similarly diagnosed with affective, adjustment, or anxiety disorders, but also had patients diagnosed with schizophrenic and psychoactive substance use disorders.

Results of this study also provided evidence for construct validity of the PM Scale. Total PM scores were correlated with scores on the Self-Evaluation Questionnaire (Conte et al., 1995), which contains four scales whose items were based on Bellack's Ego Function Assessment (Bellak, 1984) and a fifth scale, Ego Strength, based on a subscale of Grygier's (1970) Dynamic Personality Inventory.

These five scales, (a) Stimulus Barrier, (b) Autonomous Functioning, (c) Synthetic-Integrative Functioning, (d) Mastery–Competence, and (e) Ego Strength, consist of 10 items each in a self-report format rated on a 4-point scale ranging from 0 (*never*) to 3 (*often*). The higher an individual's score on any scale, the better is that individual's functioning in that area. The internal

TABLE 1.1

Comparison of Personality Profile Index Scores of Patient-Scoring High and Low on the Psychological Mindedness (PM) Scale

	High Scorers (N = 15)		Low Scorers (N = 15)		
	M	*SD*	*M*	*SD*	*t*
PM scores	154.33	8.44	125.93	5.77	10.39****
Passive	31.1	30.17	83.93	27.94	4.81****
Assertive	70.20	15.92	31.27	27.54	4.58****
Sociable	64.53	24.09	37.47	26.63	2.65***
Depressed	54.67	26.04	80.07	26.93	2.53***
Submissive	42.27	32.12	69.87	28.15	
Rejecting	53.13	29.12	74.00	24.19	2.06**
Accepting	63.60	22.74	47.27	29.56	1.64*
Aggressive	44.67	22.48	56.13	25.28	1.27
Conflict	52.33	29.16	77.13	20.20	

*$p < .010$. **$p < .05$. ***$p < .01$. ****$p < .001$.

TABLE 1.2
Relations Between Psychological Mindedness and Ego Functions (N = 192)

Variables	Correlation
Ego Strength	.58**
Mastery–Competence	.53**
Synthetic–Integrative functioning	.49**
Autonomous functioning	.29*
Stimulus barrier	.19

*$p < .01$. **$p < .001$.

consistency (coefficient alpha) of the five scales ranged from .73 to .86, with a mean of .82.

Table 1.2 presents the relations between PM scores and each of the five scales. The highest correlation is with Ego Strength, which presumably reflects an individual's ability to function well in any of the ego areas. Next, in descending order of magnitude, is PM's relation to Mastery Competence (actual performance in relation to capacity to interact with and master the environment), Synthetic–Integrative Functioning (capacity to reconcile or integrate discrepant or potentially contradictory attitudes, values, affects, and behavior), Autonomous Functioning (degree of freedom from impairment of primary autonomy–e.g., attention, concentration–and of secondary autonomy–e.g., learned complex skills), and Stimulus Barrier (sensitivity to external stimuli impinging upon various sensory modalities and effectiveness of coping mechanisms in relation to the degree of stimulation).

Implied in the high positive correlation between PM and Ego Strength, which can be considered an umbrella concept, is that an individual who has a strong ego is one who is willing to explore potentially dangerous psychological events. He or she is, for example, willing to face embarrassment or potential shame as a consequence of disclosing personal information or to face the possibility of uncovering unacceptable impulses within him or herself.

The significantly positive correlations between PM and the next three ego functions (Mastery–Competence, Synthetic–Integrative Functioning, and Autonomous Functioning) are also what one would expect theoretically. A person high on psychological mindedness, who is open to new ideas and has the capacity for change, would also be effective in coping with the environment and to have a subjective sense of competence. Similarly, someone who is insightful and has access to his or her feelings would be expected to function relatively autonomously and have the potential to reconcile the ambiguities and incongruities of daily life.

These correlations suggest that PM and these three ego functions are all part of a multifaceted concept that deals with adaptive functioning and that psychological mindedness may be an additional aspect of ego functioning. This idea was suggested before (Appelbaum, 1972; Conte et al., 1995). Perhaps, then, PM has no direct relation to outcome and is, in fact, a moderator variable between predictors and outcome. If this notion is credible, perhaps an individual's PM facilitates remaining in therapy and enables that individual to become emotionally attuned to intrapsychic or interpersonal functioning that might not necessarily be detected by others. This could at least partially explain why patients' initial PM scores were significantly related to a decrease in self-report ratings of symptoms and problems at discharge in the outcome replication study, whereas ratings made by others were not.

The one ego function essentially unrelated to psychological mindedness was Stimulus Barrier. A possible explanation lies in the fact that this ego function reflects an individual's sensitivity to, or registration of, sensory stimulation. Of the four ego functions, it is the least concerned with cognition which, presumably, is a primary characteristic of psychological mindedness.

Previous studies (Conte et al., 1990; McCallum & Piper, 1990a, 1990b) did not find a significant correlation between education and PM in relatively homogeneous populations. However, it was hypothesized that the medical student patients of Study 1, with a mean of 16.98 (SD = 1.15) years of education, which was significantly greater than that of the regular clinic patients of Study 2, (M = 12.10; SD = 2.24 year; $p < .0001$) would also be more psychologically minded. This hypothesis was confirmed. The medical students' average PM score was significantly higher than that of the regular clinic patients, thus providing a measure of discriminant validity. A likely explanation for this finding is the former group's greater exposure to abstract, analytical thinking, greater psychological sophistication, and presumably greater openness to new ideas, although education is only one among a number of variables that might distinguish the two populations.

Factor Structure of the PM Scale

As one aspect of an earlier mentioned study (Conte et al., 1993), the factor structure of the PM Scale was investigated using the principal components method with orthogonal (Varimax) rotation. The scales of 250 psychiatric outpatients, 105 males and 145 females, served as the database. The option of inserting 1.0 for each communality (diagonal) cell of the correlation matrix, followed by the extraction of all factors that had eigenvalues greater than or equal to 1.0 was used (Rummel, 1970). This procedure resulted in the rotation of 14 factors accounting for 63% of the variance. However, no factor after the fifth had more than two items whose factor loadings were .40 or greater. The first five factors acounted for 38% of the variance. Table 1.3 presents the five factors that were identified, the number of items loading .40 or greater on each, and one item with the highest factor loading on each of the five factors.

Twenty-nine of the 45 items of the PM Scale were accounted for by this factor structure, with item-total correlations ranging from .06 to .52 with a

TABLE 1.3

Factor Structure of the Psychological Mindedness Scale (N = 250)

Factor	Number of Items	Factor Loading
I. Avoidance of insight and reluctance to discuss one's problems "I frequently don't want to delve too deeply into what I'm feeling."	12	.66
II. Openness to new ideas and capacity for "At work, if someone suggested a different way of doing a job that might be better, I'd give it a try."	5	.65
III. Access to one's feelings "Often, even though I know I'm having an emotion, I don't know what it is."	5	.73
IV. Insight through discussing one's problems with others "Talking about your worries to another person helps you to understand your problems better."	3	.82
V. Interest in the meaning and motivation of one's own behavior and that of others "I often find myself thinking about what made me act in a certain way."	4	.75

mean of .35, indicating that they all contribute to the overall concept of psychological mindedness without being redundant. It would be premature, however, to revise or shorten the scale on the basis of these data alone, as the remaining 16 items had item-total correlations that ranged from .01 to .44, with a mean of .20. Additional data are needed to determine if this factor structure and the items contributing to it remain stable.

The factors identified in this analysis add additional facets, such as willingness to discuss one's problems with others, openness to new ideas, and a capacity for change, to the concept of psychological mindedness as previously defined by other investigators. Nevertheless, they are compatible with previous conceptual definitions. That is, they reflect Appelbaum's (1973) notion of PM as a process of insight that allows an individual to see that thoughts, feelings, and actions are interrelated, and also Farber's (1985) view of PM as interest in the motivation and meaning of one's own and others' behavior, thoughts, and feelings. It is also compatible with Hall's (1992) more recent conceptual model, which defined psychological mindedness in terms of an interest in, and ability to, develop understanding of psychological processes. On the basis of the present study, we propose the following definition of psychological mindedness: PM is an attribute of an individual that presupposes a degree of access to one's feelings that leads, through discussion of one's problems with others, to an ability to acquire insight into the meaning and motivation of one's own and others' thoughts, feelings, and behavior, and to a capacity for change.

Summary

Unlike the Insight Test (Tolor & Reznikoff, 1960) and the Py Scale (Gough, 1957, 1975, 1987), the PM Scale (Conte et al., 1990) is a relatively new test instrument for the measurement of psychological mindedness. More data are, therefore, necessary before a conclusive assessment of its clinical and research value can be made.

A definite strength, however, is that the rationale guiding item selection (i.e., that items represent characteristics associated with good prognosis in dynamic psychotherapy) ensured that, unlike the previous two tests, items specifically reflect an interest in, and a desire for understanding, one's own as well as others' feelings, thoughts, and behavior. Another strong point of the PM Scale is that it has good reliability, both in terms of internal consistency and stability.

The scale's ability to discriminate between groups that differ significantly on level of education was demonstrated; however, evidence for predictive validity is more problematic. Although preliminary data were indicative of the PM Scale's ability to predict outcome of therapy (Conte et al., 1990), only those results pertaining to remaining in therapy replicated. A study using a shortened version of the PM Scale based on its factor structure and including the SRPQ is planned.

There is good evidence for the construct validity of the PM Scale. Total scores were related as predicted (negatively) to scores on a test of alexithymia (Bagby et al., 1994). They also correlated in theoretically expected ways with scores on the PPI (Plutchik & Conte, 1989) and with scores on a number of measures of ego functioning (Conte et al., 1995).

The five-factor structure obtained for the PM Scale (Conte et al., 1993) was consistent with earlier findings in terms of the content of items most predictive of psychotherapy outcome (Conte et al., 1990). However, those findings need to be replicated to determine whether or not the factors remain stable and to ascertain the extent to which the items with high loadings on each factor remain stable.

A disadvantage of the PM Scale is that, with the exception of Bagby et al.'s (1994) study, it has, to date, only been administered to outpatient psychiatric populations. Enough outpatients were already tested to derive normative data for this group of subjects. Normative data is needed for nonclinical populations which could be used to test the stability of the factor structure that was obtained.

Because PM appears to be highly related to adaptive aspects of ego functioning, a question to be addressed in a future study might be the degree to which PM and various defense mechanisms are related, and the extent to which there is an increasingly positive relationship with those defenses considered to be the most adaptive.

CONCLUSION

The three self-report measures of psychological mindedness reviewed in this chapter each present a different aspect of the concept. The Insight Test (Tolor & Reznikoff, 1960) focuses on understanding causative factors of others' behaviors, with the assumption that this leads to an understanding of one's own behavior. The Py scale from the CPI (Gough, 1957) empirically defines the concept as describing a person who is a good judge of others' feelings and thoughts. Finally, the PM Scale (Conte et al., 1990) conceives of the concept as an ability to access one's own and other's feelings and utilize these for changing behavior.

Considering the complexity of the concept, researchers must have an understanding at the outset of what is meant by the term psychological mindedness as exemplified by the instrument that they are using. Thus, having an adequately defined and reliable measure is of primary importance.

Further research is needed to broaden our comprehension of this concept that has been in the empirical literature since before 1960. The possibilities that psychological mindedness functions as a moderator variable between predictors and outcome and that it may be related to such a multifaceted construct as ego functioning, are suggested in this chapter. More focused research exploring these and other important theoretical issues should help us develop a better understanding of the role of psychological mindedness in psychotherapeutic practice.

REFERENCES

Abramowitz, S. I., & Abramowitz, C. V. (1974). Psychological-mindedness and benefit from insight-oriented group therapy. *Archives of General Psychiatry, 30*, 610–615.

Adorno, W. T., Frenkel-Brunswik, E., Levinson, D. J., & Sandford, R. N. (1950). *The authoritarian personality*. New York: Harper & Row.

Appelbaum, A. (1972). A critical reexamination of the concept 'motivation for change' in psychoanalytic treatment. *International Journal of Psychoanalysis, 53*, 51–59.

Appelbaum, S. A. (1973). Psychological mindedness: Word, concept and essence. *International Journal of Psychoanalysis, 54*, 35–46.

Appelbaum, S. A. (1976). The dangerous edge of insight. *Psychotherapy: Theory, Research and Practice, 13*, 202–206.

Bagby, R. M., Taylor, G. J., & Parker, J. D. A. (1994). The twenty-item Toronto Alexithymia Scale-II. Convergent, discriminative, and concurrent validity. *Journal of Psychosomatic Research, 38*, 33–40.

Bagby, R. M., Taylor, G. J., & Ryan, D. (1986). Toronto Alexithymia Scale: Relationship with personality and psychopathology measures. *Psychotherapy and Psychosomatic Research, 45*, 207–215.

Bellack, L. (1984). The flexibility of EPA. In L. Bellack & L. A. Goldsmith (Eds.), *The broad scope of ego function assessment* (pp. 6–19). New York: Wiley.

Burkhart, B. R., Gynther, M. D., & Christian, W. L. (1978). Psychological mindedness, intelligence, and item subtlety endorsement patterns on the MMPI. *Journal of Clinical Psychology, 34*, 76–79.

Byrne, D. (1961). The Repression-sensitization scale: Rationale, reliability, and validity. *Journal of Personality, 29*, 334–349.

Christie, R., Havel, J., & Seidenberg, B. (1958). Is the F scale irreversible? *Journal of Abnormal and Social Psychology, 56*, 143–159.

Coltart, N. E. (1988). The asssessment of psychological mindedness in the diagnostic interview. *British Journal of Psychiatry, 153*, 819–820.

Conte, H. R., Buckley, P., Picard, S., & Karasu, T. B. (1995). Relations between psychological mindedness and personality traits and ego functioning: Validity studies. *Comprehensive Psychiatry, 36,* 11–17.

Conte, H. R., & Plutchik, R. (1981). A circumplex model for interpersonal personality traits. *Journal of Personality and Social Psychology, 40,* 701–711.

Conte, H. R., & Plutchik, R., Buckley, P., Spence, D. W., & Karasu, T. B. (1989). Outpatients view their psychiatric treatment. *Hospital and Community Psychiatry, 40,* 641–643.

Conte, H. R., Plutchik, R., Jung, B. B., Picard, S., Karasu, T. B., & Lotterman, A. (1990). Psychological mindedness as a predictor of psychotherapy outcome: A preliminary report. *Comprehensive Psychiatry, 31,* 426–431.

Conte, H. R., Plutchik, R., Picard, S., & Karasu, T. B. (1991). Can personality traits predict psychotherapy outcome? *Comprehensive Psychiatry, 32,* 66–72.

Conte, H. R., Plutchik, R., Picard, S., Karasu, T. B., Galanter, M., & Jacoby, J. (1991). Sex differences in personality traits and coping styles of hospitalized alcoholics. *Journal of Studies on Alcohol, 52,* 26–32.

Conte, H. R., Ratto, R., Clutz, K., & Karasu, T. B. (1993, June). *The Psychological Mindedness Scale: New findings.* Paper presented at the annual meeting of the Society for Psychotherapy Research, Pittsburgh, PA.

Dollinger, S. J., Greening, L., & Tylenda, B. (1985). Psychological mindedness as "reading between the lines." Vigilance, locus of control, and sagacious judgment. *Journal of Personality, 53,* 603–625.

Dollinger, S. J., Reader, M. J., Marnett, J. P., & Tylenda, B. (1983). Psychological-mindedness, psychological-construing, and the judgment of deception. *Journal of General Psychology, 108,* 183–191.

Dyer, E. D., Monson, M. A., & Van Drimmelen, J. B. (1972). Male registered nurses differences on the California Psychological Inventory. *Psychological Reports, 30,* 956.

Edwards, A. L. (1953). *Manual for the Edwards Personal Preference Schedule.* New York: Psychological Corporation.

Farber, B. A. (1985). The genesis, development and implications of psychological-mindedness in psychotherapists. *Psychotherapy: Theory, Research, and Practice, 22,* 170–177.

Farber, B. A. (1989). Psychological-mindedness: Can there be too much of a good thing? *Psychotherapy: Theory, Research and Practice, 26,* 210–217.

Fenigstein, A., Scheier, M. F., & Buss, A. H. (1975). Public and private self-consciousness: Assessment and theory. *Journal of Consulting and Clinical Psychology, 43,* 522–527.

Goldney, R. D., & McFarlane, A. C. (1986). Assessment in undergraduate psychiatric education. *Medical Education, 20,* 117–122.

Goldney, R. D., & Pilowsky, I. (1976). Assessment of insight change in medical students doing psychiatry. *Medical Education, 10,* 503–507.

Gough, H. G. (1957). Manual of the California Psychological Inventory. Palo Alto, CA: Consulting Psychologists Press.

Gough, H. G. (1975) *Manual of the California Psychological Inventory.* Palo Alto, CA: Consulting Psychologists Press.

Gough, H. G. (1964a). Academic achievement in high school as predicted from the California Psychological Inventory. *Journal of Educational Psychology, 55,* 174–180.

Gough, H. G. (1964b). Achievement in the first course in psychology as predicted from the California Psychological Inventory. *Journal of Psychology, 57,* 419–430.

Gough, H. G. (1968). An interpreter's syllabus for the California Psychological Inventory. In P. McReynolds (Ed.), *Advances in psychological assessment* (Vol. 1; pp. 55–79). Palo Alto, CA: Science & Behavior Books.

Gough, H. G. (1987). *Administrator's guide for the California Psychological Inventory.* Palo Alto, CA: Consulting Psychologist Press.

Gough, H. G., & Lanning, K. (1986). Predicting grades in college from the California Psychological Inventory. *Educational and Psychological Measurement, 46,* 205–213.

Grygier, T. (1970). Validity of the Dynamic Personality Inventory. *British Journal of Projective Psychology and Personality Study, 15,* 25–29.

Hall, J. A. (1992). Psychological-mindedness: A conceptual model. *American Journal of Psychotherapy, 46,* 131–140.

Hase, H. D., & Goldberg, L. R. (1967). Comparative validity of different strategies of constructing personality inventory scales. *Psychological Bulletin, 67,* 231–248.

Hersch, P. D., Kulik, J. A., & Scheibe, K. E. (1969). Personal characteristics of college volunteers in mental hospitals. *Journal of Consulting and Clinical Psychology, 33,* 30–34.

Hoffnung, R. A. (1975). Personality and dogmatism among selected groups of Orthodox Jews. *Psychological Reports, 37,* 1099–1106.

Hogan, R., & Weiss, D. S. (1974). Personality correlates of superior academic achievement. *Journal of Counseling Psychology, 21,* 144–149.

Holland, J. L. (1959). The prediction of college grades from the California Psychological Inventory and the Scholastic Aptitude Test. *The Journal of Educational Psychology, 50,* 135–142.

King, G. D., McGowen, R., Doonan, R., & Schweibert, D. (1980). The selection of paraprofessional telephone counselors using the California Psychological Inventory. *American Journal of Community Psychology, 8,* 495–501.

Kurtines, W. M., Ball, L. R., & Wood, G. H. (1978). Personality characteristics of long-term recovered alcoholics: A comparative analysis. *Journal of Consulting & Clinical Psychology, 46,* 971–977.

Lenarz, D. M., & Vestre, N. D. (1964). The effect of a course in psychiatric nursing on insight test scores of nursing students. *Journal of Psychiatric Nursing, 2,* 137–141.

Lotterman, A. C. (1979). *A questionnaire measure of psychological mindedness and the capacity to benefit from psychotherapy.* Unpublished manuscript.

Luborsky, L., Crits-Cristoph, P., Mintz, J., & Auerbach, A. (1988). *Who will benefit from psychotherapy: Predicting therapeutic outcomes.* New York: Basic Books.

Markova, I. S., & Berrios, G. E. (1992). The meaning of insight in clinical psychiatry. *British Journal of Psychiatry, 160,* 850–860.

Maxwell, M. J. (1960). An analysis of the California Psychological Inventory and the American Council on Education Psychological Test as predictors of success in different college curricula. *American Psychologist, 15,* 425.

McCallum, M., & Piper, W. E. (1990a). A controlled study of effectiveness and patient suitability for short-term group psychotherapy. *International Journal of Group Psychotherapy, 40,* 431–452.

McCallum, M., & Piper, W. E. (1990b). The Psychological Mindedness Assessment Procedure. *Psychological Assessment, 2,* 412–418.

McFarlane, R. D., Goldney, R. D., & Kalucy, R. S. (1989). A factor analytic study of clinical competence in undergraduate psychiatry. *Medical Education, 23,* 422–428.

McGuire, J. S., & Megargee, E. I. (1974). Personality correlates of marijuana use among youthful offenders. *Journal of Consulting and Clinical Psychology, 42,* 124–133.

Megargee, E. I. (1972). *The California Psychological Inventory Handbook.* San Francisco: Jossey-Bass.

Meltzoff, J., & Kornreich, M. (1970). *Research in psychotherapy.* New York: Atherton.

Moore, B., & Fine, B. D. (Eds.). (1990). *Psychoanalytic terms and concepts.* New Haven: Yale University Press.

Murray, R. E., & Walsh, R. P. (1976). Personality differences between levels of psychology majors. *Psychological Reports, 39,* 215–220.

Piper, W. E., Azim, H. F. A., McCallum, M., & Joyce, A. S. (1990). Patient suitability and outcome in short-term individual psychotherapy. *Journal of Consulting and Clinical Psychology, 58,* 475–481.

Piper, W. E., de Carufel, F. L., & Szkrumelak, N. (1985). Patient predictors of process and outcome in short-term individual psychotherapy. *Journal of Nervous and Mental Disease, 171,* 726–733.

Piper, W. E., Joyce, A. S., Azim, H. F. A., & Rosie, J. S. (1994). Patient characteristics and success in day treatment. *Journal of Nervous and Mental Disease, 182,* 381–386.

Piper, W. E., Joyce, A. S., Rosie, J. S., & Azim, H. F. A. (1994). Psychological mindedness, work, and outcome in day treatment. *International Journal of Group Psychotherapy, 44,* 291–311.

Plutchik, R., & Conte, H. R. (1989). Measuring emotions and their derivatives: Personality traits, ego defenses, and coping styles. In S. Wetzler & M. Katz (Eds.), *Contemporary approaches to psychological assessment* (pp. 239–269). New York: Brunner/Mazel.

Repapi, M., Gough, H. G., Lanning, K., & Stefanis, C. (1983). Predicting academic achievement of Greek secondary school students from family background and California Psychological Inventory Scores. *Contemporary Educational Psychology, 8*, 181–188.

Roback, H. B., & Abramowitz, S. I. (1979). Insight and hospital adjustment. *Canadian Journal of Psychiatry, 24*, 233–236.

Rosenbaum, R. L., & Horowitz, M. J. (1983). Motivation for psychotherapy: A factorial and conceptual analysis. *Psychotherapy: Theory, Research, Practice, 20*, 347–354.

Rotter, J. B. (1966). Generalized expectances for internal versus external control of reinforcement. *Psychological Monographs, 80* (1, Whole No. 609).

Rummel, R. J. (1970). *Applied factor analysis*. Evanston, IL: Northwestern University Press.

Ryan, E. R., & Cicchetti, D. V. (1985). Predicting quality of alliance in the initial psychotherapy interview. *Journal of Nervous and Mental Disease, 173*, 717–725.

Schulberg, H. C. (1962). Insight, authoritarianism, and tendency to agree. *Journal of Nervous and Mental Disease, 135*, 481–488.

Sifneos, P. E. (1972). *Short-term dynamic psychotherapy: Evaluation and technique*. New York: Plenum.

Sifneos, P. E. (1981). Short-term anxiety-provoking psychotherapy: Its history, technique, outcome and instruction. In S. H. Budman (Ed.), *Forms of brief therapy* (pp. 45–81). New York: Guilford.

Snider, J. G. (1966). Academic achievement and underachievement in a Canadian high school as predicted from the California Psychological Inventory. *Psychology in the Schools, 3*, 370–372.

Tolor, A. (1961). The relationship between insight and intraception. *Journal of Clinical Psychology, 17*, 188–189.

Tolor, A. , & Reznikoff, M. (1960). A new approach to insight: A preliminary report. *Journal of Nervous and Mental Disease, 130*, 286–296.

Vingoe, F. J. (1973). Comment on H. B. Gibson's report on the validity of the Eysenck Personality Inventory-extraversion, degree of acquaintanceship, and mean peer-ratings. *British Journal of Social and Clinical Psychology, 12*, 268–274.

Walsh, J. A. (1972). Review of the California Psychological Inventory. In O. K. Buros (Ed.), *The Seventh Mental Measurements* Yearbook. Highland Park, NJ: Gryphon Press.

Wolitzky, D. L., & Reuben, R. (1974). Psychological-mindedness. *Journal of Clinical Psychology, 30*, 26–30.

Yalom, I. D., Houts, P. S., Zimerberg, S. M., & Rand, K. H. (1967). Prediction of improvement in group therapy: An exploratory study. *Archives of General Psychiatry, 17*, 159–168.

Chapter 2

The Psychological Mindedness Assessment Procedure

Mary McCallum
William E. Piper
University of Alberta

Our interest in the concept of psychological mindedness evolved from our goal of developing valid selection criteria for psychoanalytically oriented group psychotherapy. The development of valid selection criteria involves determining the suitability of particular individuals for beneficial group treatment, that is, those who can be included and those who should be excluded. The relevance of identifying a suitable patient population is evident: If therapists accepted only those patients who are likely to benefit, they could minimize the wasted emotional and financial investments of therapists and patients. As Woods and Melnick (1979) wrote:

> As researchers, our challenge in identifying suitable patients was to: empirically identify...the group relevant behaviors requisite to achieving positive outcomes and then developing reliable and predictively valid pretherapy measures of these behaviors. (p. 162)

Theoretically, the achievement of positive outcomes in an analytic group depends on the patients' ability to contribute to the therapeutic objective. The objective of analytic groups is to help patients solve their presenting problems by achieving insight into how their difficulties are related to unresolved intrapsychic conflicts and by initiating a process of working through that will continue beyond the treatment sessions. The analytic group therapist uses an interpretive, here-and-now approach that focuses on unconscious conflicts. Specifically, the therapist endeavours to foster insight concerning how patients' presenting complaints are actually the manifestation of an underlying psychic conflict between unpermissable wishes, the anxiety or fear to which these wishes give rise, and the only partially effective defense mechanisms that are mobilized to cope with the anxiety and to maintain the repression of the wish. This insight is fostered by interpreting or hypothesizing a link between the patients' current patterns of behavior, feelings, and cognitions with these unconscious processes. In addition, the therapist hypothesizes a link between the patients' patterns of past relationships, current relationships, and their interactions within the group.

The relevant behaviors required for success in an analytic group involve an ability to work with interpretations. Working with interpretations requires that the patients have an "ability to see relationships among the thoughts, feelings, and actions, with the goal of learning the meanings and causes of his experiences and behavior" (Appelbaum, 1973, p.36). Although this definition identifies an ability requisite for working with interpretations, it was intended as a definition of psychological mindedness. Hence, we concluded that psychological mindedness represents a patient dimension conceptually related to relevant analytic group behavior. That conclusion was shared by several other authors in the psychotherapy literature. Psychological mindedness is believed to be important for working within all forms of psychoanalytically oriented therapy.

Consistent with the definitions by Silver (1983) and Appelbaum (1973), we define psychological mindedness as the ability to identify dynamic (intrapsychic) components and to relate them to a person's difficulties. The patient needs to be receptive to the hypothesis that current difficulties are linked to unconscious conflicts. Terming this receptivity "psychological" mindedness is consistent with literature wherein the concept was conceptualized by analytically oriented authors. However, the primary aim in operationalizing psychological mindedness according to analytic concepts was to identify patients best suited to analytically oriented therapies. The identification of patients best suited to other approaches to therapy will likely require pretherapy measures of variables that are precisely relevant to work within those orientations.

When we began to construct our measure of psychological mindedness, we were aware of three general approaches to assessing the variable: self-report questionnaires, appraisals based on clinical interviews, and appraisals derived by combining scores from variables conceptually related to psychological mindedness. In chapter 1 of this volume, Conte and Ratto reviewed self-report measures including their own questionnaire. Although the use of self-report questionnaires to measure psychological mindedness has not provided a consensus regarding its meaning, the approach has been relatively direct and has involved minimal inference on the part of the assessor. In comparison, the other two approaches have been considerably more indirect and inferential. As mentioned previously, the first involves the use of the clinical interview, and the second, the combination of variables from different measurement sources. We consider these in turn.

CLINICAL INTERVIEW

The clinical interview, which is a standard part of nearly all clinical assessment procedures, provides a wealth of information about the patient. This ranges from information about the patient's presenting problems to information about his or her early life experiences. It is a natural place to acquire an impression of the patient's psychological mindedness. Presumably, as the patient provides information about the nature of his or her problems and possible causes, there are many opportunities to assess the patient's psychological mindedness. Despite the accessibility and relevance of the material from clinical interviews, its use to assess psychological mindedness is characterized by certain problems.

The problems stem from the fact that the assessment of psychological mindedness is usually not the primary purpose of the clinical interview. Acquiring information about diagnosis, prognosis, etiology, and general suitability for treatment usually takes precedence. Because multiple variables are being addressed, time to assess psychological mindedness is generally not reserved, nor are questions specific to its assessment raised. The definition and criteria for the concept are typically general and brief. Therefore, the process of rating psychological mindedness tends to be highly inferential. Under such circumstances (i.e., the lack of specific and standard scoring criteria), reliability suffers. Even if acceptable reliability is attained, another problem may exist. There is a strong possibility that the rating of psychological mindedness is influenced by impressions of other variables such as verbal ability or likability, the so-called *halo effect*. Thus, the independence of the rating, as well as its reliability, may be problematic.

An example of using the clinical interview to derive a rating of psychological mindedness came from a comparative psychotherapy outcome study of four forms of psychotherapy we conducted in Montreal (Piper, Debbane, Bienvenu, & Garant, 1984). After conducting an unstructured, initial clinical interview, each therapist was requested to rate the patient on a set of 15 variables, including psychological mindedness. Brief definitions and anchor-point criteria were provided to assist the therapist in making a 7-point, Likert-type rating ranging from 1 (*poor*) to (*excellent*) for each variable. The variables were investigated as predictors of therapy process (*therapeutic alliance*) and therapy outcome (de Carufel & Piper, 1988; Piper, de Carufel, & Szkrumelak, 1985). Although some evidence for the predictive ability of this simple rating of psychological mindedness was found, questions regarding its reliability of measurement and independence from the other predictor variables remained. A better measure may have produced stronger results.

A second example of using a pretherapy clinical interview to rate psychological mindedness was described in a study by Rosenbaum and Horowitz (1983). Videotapes of 57 patients were rated on 36 items. Five items from their 23-item Motivation for Psychotherapy Scale loaded on a factor labeled Psychological Mindedness. The other items loaded on three other factors.. This is an example of a post hoc derivation of an interview measure of psychological mindedness. A third example where psychological mindedness was assessed with four other variables on the basis of interview and other data is described in a study by Ryan and Cicchetti (1985). In this study, as well as the other two examples, the same generic interview data was used to provide ratings for a number of different variables. In none of the examples was the interview designed for the specific assessment of psychological mindedness. There is nothing inherently wrong with using the interview method to assess psychological mindedness, as long as sufficient attention is devoted to its careful measurement. In capitalizing on the potential of the clinical interview to generate multiple ratings, the assessment of psychological mindedness may have been compromised in the examples we have considered.

COMBINATION OF VARIABLES

As indicated, another approach to the assessment of psychological mindedness involved the combination of variables to create a psychological mindedness score. The variables are viewed as components of psychological mindedness. They may or may not have been designed with the measurement of psychological mindedness as an objective. In either case, this approach to assessment is an indirect one.

An example of this approach is found in work arising from the Psychotherapy Research Project of the Menninger Foundation (Kernberg et al., 1972). The study involved an intensive long-term examination of patients treated with psychoanalysis or analytically oriented psychotherapy. Using a general definition of psychological mindedness provided by Wallerstein and Robbins (1956), Appelbaum (1977) relied on a combination of variables from an extensive battery of tests to generate a rating of psychological mindedness. The components, which included ideational richness, reflectiveness, and control over emotions and affects, were regarded as the intrapsychic components of psychological mindedness. However, the components might have represented separate variables. Correlations among the components and the exact method of combining the scores to arrive at the overall rating of psychological mindedness were not provided by the investigators.

A second example of combining scores to arrive at an estimate of psychological mindedness was suggested by Horowitz, Rosenberg, and Kalehzan (1992). They used two self-report scales of psychological distress. The first, the Inventory of Interpersonal Problems (Horowitz, Rosenberg, Baer, Ureño, & Villaseñor, 1988), focused on interpersonal distress, and the second, the SCL–90 (Derogatis, 1977), focused on symptomatic distress. The simple difference between the overall scores for the two scales, known as the I–S score, represents the salience of interpersonal over symptomatic distress. After examining the relationship of the I–S score to other variables such as success in brief therapy and the ability to describe other people clearly, they suggested that components of psychological mindedness may have been assessed. Although possible, the measurement approach was clearly an indirect one.

A third example, which is somewhat more direct, was provided by Wolitzky and Reuben (1974). In contrast to the first two examples, these investigators initially set out to develop a measure of psychological mindedness. They empirically derived their measure of psychological mindedness from a set of 10 possible components of the concept. Ratings of the presence or absence of the components in subjects' appraisals of Thematic Apperception Test (TAT) responses were used to select six as representative of psychological mindedness. Although most of the six components appeared to be related theoretically, differences among some of the components suggest that an element of indirectness also characterized this measure of psychological mindedness.

To a certain degree, the work of these investigators represents creative attempts to combine possible components of psychological mindedness. They also represent practical efforts to work further with existing data. One wonders, however, whether a more direct approach to the measurement of psychological mindedness would have been more productive in advancing knowledge about the concept.

Our approach differed from past attempts to operationalize the variable. First, by emphasizing analytic concepts, we attempted to distinguish the construct from other specific and nonspecific therapeutic factors rather than incorporating related concepts into the assessment of psychological mindedness. Second, by constructing the Psychological Mindedness Assessment Procedure (PMAP) to utilize objective, clearly defined behavioral referents, we attempted to enhance reliability. We also hoped to avoid assessing psychological mindedness in conjunction with other variables. Third, consistent with the current era's preference for video stimuli, the PMAP is a videotape measure. Utilizing a standardized video and interview format to assess psychological mindedness decreases threats to validity (e.g., halo effects, patient response bias, practice effects) associated with extensive selection procedures.

THE PSYCHOLOGICAL MINDEDNESS ASSESSMENT PROCEDURE

The PMAP is individually administered and requires approximately 15 minutes to determine the psychological mindedness score. The videotape presents two simulated patient–therapist interactions or scenarios. The scenarios are portrayed by actors according to scripts developed to reflect various components of therapeutic process. The scenarios begin with an actress–patient describing a recent event in her life to her male therapist. In the first scenario, the woman describes seeing from a distance, her former husband. In the second scenario, the same woman describes an argument she had with her new boyfriend. The descriptions include verbalizations reflecting dynamic components (i.e., conflictual wishes and fears, defensive maneuvers) and links between internal and external events (i.e., links between cognitions–affects and behavior). The patient's account constitutes the test stimulus for assessing psychological mindedness. After viewing this account, the tape is stopped and the person being assessed is asked for his or her general impressions of "What seems to be troubling this woman?" The first part is then replayed (in an attempt to eliminate possible confounding effects due to memory differences among respondents) and the person is allowed to elaborate on his or her initial answer.

The administrator needs to be familiar with psychodynamic concepts and the measure's scoring criteria (to follow). When developing the PMAP for use in the first or pilot study, two doctoral candidates in clinical psychology were trained to reliably score responses to the PMAP. In subsequent studies, research assistants with their bachelor degree in psychology were successfully trained to administer and score the PMAP. Training sessions took about 10 hours. They consisted of didactic presentations of psychodynamic theory and its relationship to the PMAP's scoring criteria as well as exercises that applied the criteria to responses to the PMAP.

The PMAP (Table 2.1) differentiates nine levels of psychological mindedness. The criteria for each level reflect basic assumptions of psychodynamic theory (McCallum & Piper, 1987). They also reflect the ability to identify dynamic (intrapsychic) components and to relate them to a person's difficulty. To obtain a high psychological mindedness score, a person must reflect several of the basic assumptions held by psychodynamic therapists concerning human pathology. The rationale for the hierarchy is that the higher levels incorporate criteria from the lower levels such that each level becomes more comprehensive and complex in its focus. Based on clinical experience, the criteria for the higher levels of the scale require more sophisticated and complex explanations than those for the lower levels. In addition, the hierarchy reflects a temporal sequence that is consistent with psychodynamic theory; for example, a conflict develops before the ego attempts to resolve it.

The criteria for Levels 1 through 3 are based on the assumption of *psychic determinism*, whereby all human functioning is assumed to result, at least in part, from an internal or psychic process. For example, the statement "her loneliness is making her feel depressed" meets Level 3 criteria by clearly attributing the depression to the internal state of loneliness. Level 4 criteria require an understanding of the unconscious. The criteria for Level 5, the

TABLE 2.1
The Nine Levels of Psychological Mindedness

Level 1:	The subject identifies a specific internal experience of the patient.
Level 2:	The subject recognizes the driving force of an internal experience of the patient.
Level 3:	The subject identifies a result of a drive such that a causal link is made between an internal event and its resultant expression.
Level 4:	The subject recognizes that the motivating force in the patient is largely out of her awareness or is unconscious.
Level 5:	The subject identifies conflictual components of the patient's experience.
Level 6:	Subject identifies a causal link where the conflict is presented as generating an expression.
Level 7:	Subject identifies a causal link where tension (fear, anxiety) is presented as motivating an expression.
Level 8:	Subject recognizes that the patient is engaging in a defensive maneuver.
Level 9:	Subject recognizes that despite the defensive maneuver, the patient remains disturbed in some way by the conflict.

midpoint of the scale, correspond to the recognition of ambivalence or conflict. A basic assumption underlying the psychodynamic understanding of pathology is that internal impulses (id) come into conflict with the frustrating or nongratifying aspects of external reality or their internalized representatives (superego), and the ego acts as mediator. An example of a response meriting a Level 5 rating is: "Well, she wants to be with her husband again, but at the same time she's still very angry with him."

The criteria for Levels 6 and 7 reflect the assumption that a conflict generates tension and motivates attempts at resolution. These attempts are, however, only partially successful. The conflictual impulses are permitted expression only in a distorted or diminished form after being filtered through self-protecting or defensive mechanisms. This latter assumption is reflected in the criteria for Levels 8 and 9. An example of a Level 9 rating is: "That's sour grapes to say she's 'really better off without him,' I think she really feels that she'd be a lot happier with him." In research studies, we used psychological mindedness as a matching variable before assigning patients to either the treatment or control conditions. Hence, the scale was dichotomized such that scores of 0–5 constituted low psychological mindedness and scores of 6–9 constituted high psychological mindedness. However, when investigating relationships among variables, the scale was utilized as a continuous variable. In order to provide the reader with a sense of how patients respond to the PMAP, transcripts of two responses follow. The first was rated as high and the second as low.

Example 1:

> Well she's troubled by anxiety; she had an anxiety attack in the store. I think that's 'cause she's angry that her marriage didn't work out. Well, angry, maybe more disappointed than angry. Okay, she's angry and disappointed, and still wants him back, and that's why she's having anxiety attacks; she doesn't know what she wants. Or she doesn't want to admit that she still wants him back. Yeah, she's angry 'cause she can't have what she wants. But she's in denial, she denies she wants him, wishing she had never met him, c'mon! If that were true, she wouldn't be so angry.

The patient identified the woman's internal experiences of disappointment and anger. The motivating force of those internal experiences was reflected in the statement: " s he had an anxiety attack in the store 'cause she's angry that her marriage didn't work out." The wish for the relationship with her husband is mentioned a couple of times. Reflecting an understanding of conflict, the patient identified the conflictual nature of her feelings: "Okay, she's angry and disappointed, and still wants him back. The patient proceeded to link the anxiety to those conflictual feelings ("and that's why she's having anxiety attacks"). Finally, the patient's understanding that the defensive maneuver that was activated to resolve the conflict was only partially successful is reflected in her statement: "But she's in denial, she denies she wants him, wishing she had never met him, c'mon! If that were true, she wouldn't be so angry." This response merited a Level 9 rating.

Example 2:

> Well she was in an abusive marriage and she wants to go back. It's terrible that she wants to go back. She must be really insecure. Men like that don't change. She should go on with her life. So what's troubling her is she's insecure.

In this second example, the patient identified an internal experience of the woman ("insecure") and her wish for the relationship with the husband ("she wants to go back"). Although she stated that the marriage was abusive, she did not link this with an internal experience of the woman. Therefore, her response did not meet the criterion of Level 5, the identification of ambivalent or conflictual feelings. Rather, the patient stated her opinion of what the woman should do, that is, "go on with her life." Example 2 merited a rating of Level 3.

In addition to psychological mindedness, the PMAP also assesses the degree to which a person understands psychodynamic interpretations. Following the assessment of psychological mindedness, an actor–therapist responds to the actress–patient by interpreting first the dynamic components of her conflict and then the transferential aspects, that is, her attempt to repeat with the therapist a past mode of interaction. Both types of interpretations are presented in three stages. At each subsequent stage, the degree of ambiguity and therefore, the degree of difficulty is less. The tape is stopped after each interpretation and the person being assessed is asked "Where is he getting that from?" or "What does he mean by that?" The therapist's responses constitute the test stimulus for assessing *interpretation comprehension*, defined as the ability to identify the referents of therapist interpretations. It has three subscores: the number of dynamics understood; the speed of recognizing dynamics, which reflects the ease with which the dynamics are understood; and the speed of recognizing transference, which reflects the ease with which the interpretation of transference phenomena is understood.

Psychometric Properties of the PMAP

The psychometric properties of the PMAP were investigated with four separate populations. The first population involved a nonclinical group of 30 adult volunteers (McCallum, 1989; McCallum & Piper, 1990a, 1996; Piper, McCallum, & Azim, 1992). The second involved using the PMAP in a controlled outcome study of short-term psychoanalytically oriented group psychotherapy for 154 patients suffering with loss (McCallum, 1989; McCallum & Piper, 1990a, 1990b, 1996; Pipe et. al., 1992). The third involved using the measure in a controlled trial of a day treatment program for 165 psychiatric patients suffering from serious long-term disorders, mainly affective and personality (Piper, Joyce, Azim, & Rosie, 1994; Piper, Joyce, Rosie, & Azim, 1994; Piper, Rosie, Azim, & Joyce, 1993; Piper, Rosie, Joyce, & Azim, 1996). The fourth involved using the PMAP with a psychiatric population engaged in a different partial hospitalization program. Specifically, the PMAP was used to predict the response of 190 patients suffering from serious long-term disorders, mainly affective and personality, who were admitted to an evening treatment program (McCallum, Piper, & O'Kelly, in press).

The three studies involving clinical populations took place in the Division of External Psychiatric Services at the University of Alberta Hospitals in Edmonton, Alberta, Canada. The 800-bed modern university hospital had a catchment area with a population of 1.5 million. The Division was composed of three clinical services, the Walk-in Clinic, the Day Treatment Program, and the Evening Treatment Program. The three services were well-integrated with the inpatient services of the Department of Psychiatry. In addition to providing various therapy programs, the Walk-in Clinic therapists performed the initial assessment and referral of patients to all three services.

These sections present the results of each study as they pertain to the PMAP, followed by a comparison of results from the four studies.

THE FIRST STUDY

The first study primarily addressed the rater reliability, test–retest reliability, and construct validity of the PMAP. It involved a nonclinical population. Because the study was reported in greater detail elsewhere (McCallum, 1989; McCallum & Piper, 1990a, 1996; Piper, McCallum, & Azim, 1992) for the purposes of this chapter only a brief summary of the study is presented.

Subjects

Thirty adult volunteers (19 women and 11 men) were recruited from the Montreal area to participate in a study on "the perception of psychotherapy." Their mean age was 36.3 years (range: 19–67). Sixty percent did not live with a partner. With respect to education, all of them had attended at least 1 year of postsecondary education.

Procedures and Design

Each subject was administered the PMAP and then asked to complete a few questionnaires. To determine rater reliability, all responses to the PMAP were audiotaped. A second rater, a doctoral candidate in clinical psychology, was trained to rate responses for the level of psychological mindedness they reflected. The responses of one half of the subjects were randomly chosen and rated by the second rater. To determine test–retest reliability, one half of the subjects were randomly chosen to be reassessed 1 month later.

Measures

To investigate convergent validity, two measures of psychological mindedness were administered: the Psychological Mindedness scale from the California Psychological Inventory (CPI, Gough, 1957) and the Insight Test (Tolor & Reznikoff, 1960). To investigate psychological mindedness's relationship with psychiatric symptomatology, subjects completed the Depression and anxiety subscales of the SCL–90 (Derogatis, 1977). To provide measures of relevant personality variables, subjects also completed the Cognitive Structure, Achievement, and Social Desirability scales of Jackson's (1974) Personality Research Form. The Quick Test (Ammons & Ammons, 1962), a measure of verbal intelligence, was also administered.

Results

Rater Reliability. For the 15 subjects whose responses were chosen randomly to be rated by a second rater, the rater reliability, calculated as an intraclass correlation coefficient [ICC(1, 1)], was .69.

Test–Retest Reliability. For those subjects who repeated the procedure, a Pearson correlation coefficient was calculated for the two scores. The results indicated that the test–retest reliability was $r(13) = .76, p < .001$ over the 1-month period.

Convergent Validity. Regarding the two other measures of psychological mindedness, the results indicated that the PMAP was significantly related to both the psychological mindedness scale of the CPI, $r(28) = .42, p < .05$, and the overall insight score of the Insight Test, $r(28) = .50, p < .01$.

Additional Aspects of Construct Validity. The results of chi square and correlational analyses revealed that psychological mindedness was not significantly related to age, gender, marital status, employment status, or level of education. In addition, psychological mindedness was not significantly related to the measures of personality, intelligence, or psychiatric symptomatology.

Implications of the First Study. Results of the first study supported the manner in which we had operationalized psychological mindedness. The PMAP was a reliable, easily administered measure whose construct validity was supported. We regarded it as a promising new instrument that might predict the response of a clinical population to psychodynamic psychotherapy.

THE SECOND STUDY

The second study, which involved a clinical population, gave particular emphasis to the exploration of the predictive validity of the PMAP. The measure's discriminant validity, rater and test–retest reliabilities were also explored. This study used the PMAP in a controlled outcome study of 16 short-term psychoanalytically oriented psychotherapy groups for patients suffering from loss. Because the study was reported in greater detail elsewhere (McCallum, 1989; McCallum & Piper, 1990a, 1990b, 1996; Piper et al., 1992) for the purposes of this chapter only a brief summary of the study is presented.

The objective of the short-term group program was to help patients solve their presenting problems by achieving insight into how their difficulties were related to unresolved intrapsychic conflicts and by initiating a process of working through that would continue beyond the treatment sessions. The groups utilized the single therapist model. Three therapists provided treatment in the study, two psychologists and one social worker. All were experienced with individual and group forms of time-limited, psychodynamic psychotherapy. The therapists used an interpretive, here-and-now approach that focused on unconscious conflicts.

Patients

The entire patient sample consisted of 154 adult outpatients who had presented to the Walk-in Clinic of the Division of External Psychiatric Services, University of Alberta Hospitals (Edmonton, Canada). The sample for outcome analyses consisted of 94 patients (68 women and 26 men). The following descriptive information is based on that sample. Their average age was 36.0 years (range: 18–57). Approximately two thirds (68%) of the patients did not live with a partner. The majority (85%) had at least a high school level of education. Of these, almost one third had attended or were attending a university and more than one third had attended or were attending a technical college. All patients had been assessed as experiencing a prolonged or delayed grief reaction following the loss of a person through death (29%), separation or divorce (12%), or both types of losses (59%). Depressive symptomatology, social isolation, and loneliness were common presenting features. In terms of the *Diagnostic and Statistical Manual of Mental Disorders* (3rd ed., [DSM–111] American Psychiatric Association (1980) most common Axis I diagnoses were affective disorder and adjustment disorder. One fifth also received an Axis II diagnosis, usually dependent personality disorder.

Investigations of different aspects of the PMAP's psychometric properties were based on different subsamples. Investigations of the PMAP's associations with outcome involved data from all 16 groups. Because the process analyses system was applied only to the first 12 groups, investigations of the PMAP's associations with process involved data from the first 12 groups. Investigations of the PMAP's rater and test-retest reliabilities and discriminant validity were based on the first eight therapy groups.

Procedures and Design

A Walk-in Clinic staff therapist conducted the initial clinical assessment. If suitable for the group, the therapist informed the patient, verbally and in writing, about the treatment and research procedures. After providing informed consent, the patients were assessed by two different members of the research team: the PM assessor and the independent assessor who administered the outcome battery. Both assessors were bachelor-level research assistants.

Patients were matched on level of psychological mindedness, gender, and age, and then randomly assigned to either the immediate treatment or the control condition. The control condition consisted of a 3-month waiting period after which patients proceeded into their therapy group. Length of therapy was also 3 months. The control condition represented, therefore, a delayed treatment condition. Each therapy group was composed of patients who were high on psychological mindedness and patients who were low on psychological mindedness. Therapists were blind to the patients' scores on the PMAP.

For patients in the control condition, the outcome battery was administered before and after the waiting period. The outcome battery was assessed to all patients before and after treatment to monitor change over treatment. To provide follow-up data, all patients completing the groups were invited back 6 months later to be reassessed with the outcome battery. All dropouts were asked to return for a second assessment interview and their reasons for premature termination explored.

Measures

Outcome Measures. A comprehensive battery of outcome measures were assessed before and after the delay period, the treatment period, and 6 months following the completion of treatment. The areas assessed included interpersonal functioning, psychiatric symptomatology, self-esteem, and personalized target objectives. The sources of evaluation included the patient, an independent assessor, and the therapist.

Process Measure. Therapy process was monitored for the first 12 therapy groups utilizing the Psychodynamic Work and Object Rating System (PWORS; Piper & McCallum, 1988). One feature of this process analysis system is its ability to reliably monitor the quality and quantity of psychodynamic work evidenced by group members. PWORS data were summarized to provide several ratios, for example, self-based work, or the proportion of a patient's work behavior relative to his or her total participation.

Results

Rater Reliability. Tape recordings of 15 patients' responses to the PMAP were randomly chosen and rated by a second rater. An intraclass correlation coefficient was calculated for the two raters. The results indicated that the rater reliability of the measure with this clinical population was ICC (1,1) = .96.

Test–Retest Reliability. To determine the test–retest reliability of the PMAP with this clinical population, Pearson correlation coefficients were calculated for control patients in the delayed treatment condition. The results indicated that the test–retest reliability for PM was r (27) = .59, $p <$ .001 over the 3-month delay period. Although significant, this coefficient is somewhat lower than that of the nonclinical population. Perhaps the patients, who had been waiting to enter therapy, were less motivated to do the task a second time. Or, they may have been indirectly expressing feelings about having had to wait for treatment. Alternatively, perhaps extending the period between test and retest from 1 month to 3 months resulted in differences among patients' memory capabilities playing a role in their performance. Specifically, perhaps some patients were better able to remember and be influenced by the (actor–) therapist's explanation of the woman that was presented during the interpretation comprehension part of the PMAP administration.

Convergent Validity. Following sessions 4, 8, and 12, the therapist was asked to provide ratings for a few patient variables, including psychological mindedness on a 7-point Likert-type scale that ranged from 1 (*poor*) to 7 (*excellent*). The relationship between the (mean) therapist rating of PM and the PMAP rating was determined for all patients who had completed therapy. The Pearson correlation coefficient was $r(40) = .30, p < .05$. This association offered clinical validation of the manner in which PM was operationalized. The coefficient also revealed that the two sources of assessment were not redundant.

Discriminant Validity. The discriminant validity of the measure was supported by finding that psychological mindedness scores were not highly associated with scores on the three interpretation comprehension variables provided by the PMAP. The Pearson correlation coefficients for the number of dynamics [$r(77) = .34, p < .01$], Speed of Dynamics [$r(77) = .25, p < .05$], and speed of transference [$r(77) = .20$] indicated that the PM score was not confounded by the method of assessment. Although the ability to generate a psychodynamic understanding of the woman's problems (PM) was somewhat related to comprehending the therapist's understanding of the woman's problems (number of dynamics and speed of dynamics), the former was probably more difficult.

Additional Aspects of Construct Validity. Additional analyses supported the construct validity of the PMAP. Level of psychological mindedness was again not found to be significantly associated with age, gender, marital status, employment status, level of education, or measures of psychiatric symptomatology and psychological distress. In addition, level of PM was not found to be significantly associated with the use of psychotropic medications.

Predictive Validity

Remaining. With respect to the measure's predictive validity, results of the second study revealed a strong association between level of psychological mindedness as assessed by the PMAP and remaining in therapy. A total of 33 of the 109 patients who actually started treatment dropped out prematurely. Although only 14% of the high PM patients dropped out, 53% of the low PM patients dropped out. A chi-square conducted on these percentages was significant: $X^2 (1, N = 109) = 17.58, p < .001$.

Process. The relationship between PM and work (as measured by the PWORS) was investigated by a Pearson product-moment correlation for 58 patients who had completed the first 12 therapy groups. The results revealed significant associations between psychological mindedness and high-level self-based work: $r(51) = .48$, $p < .001$, and between psychological mindedness and all self-based work in the groups: $r(51) = .43$, $p < .001$.

Outcome. Using a multivariate analysis (MANOVA), the relationship between PM and therapy outcome for all patients (in both the immediate treatment and waiting list control condition) was investigated. This analysis investigated whether high PM patients improved after 3 months whether or not they received treatment. The main effect for PM was nonsignificant. Thus, PM was not found to be a general prognostic predictor for loss patients.

However, it was still possible that PM was an important predictor variable for treated patients. The relationship between PM and therapy outcome for treated patients was investigated with a set of partial and Pearson product-moment correlations. The partial correlation statistic was used with 18 outcome variables that were measured both before and after therapy. The partial correlation statistic removed the effect of the pretherapy score on the correlation between PM and the posttherapy score. The Pearson correlation statistic was used with the two global rating measures that were assessed only after therapy. Those measures represented rated benefits and asked the patient and the therapist to rate the overall usefulness of therapy. None of the 20 correlations between PM and therapy outcome were statistically significant. The results failed to reveal significant direct relationships between psychological mindedness and the outcome variables.

Implications of the Second Study

The PMAP proved itself a reliable, valid, easily administered measure of psychological mindedness with a clinical population. It was found to be associated with remaining and working in the loss groups. It was not found to be associated with outcome. It was possible that the high number of low PM patients who dropped out of therapy prevented us from finding a significant relationship between PM and outcome. Overall, we were encouraged by the PMAP's performance. We decided to explore the utility of the PMAP with a different population and a different therapy format.

THE THIRD STUDY

The third study provided further information concerning the reliability and validity of the PMAP. As previously mentioned, this study involved using the PMAP in a controlled trial of a day treatment program for psychiatric patients suffering from serious long-term disorders, namely affective and personality disorders. Because the study was reported in greater detail elsewhere (Piper et al., 1993; Piper, Joyce, Azim, & Rosie, 1994; Piper, Joyce, Rosie, & Azim, 1994; Piper et al., 1996) for the purposes of this chapter only a brief summary of the study is presented.

The program is intensive, group-oriented, and time-limited. It is conducted weekdays for 18 weeks and consists of a large therapy group, a standard set of small therapy groups, and when indicated, family therapy and medication. The theoretical orientation of the program is psychodynamic with important influences from systems theory, therapeutic milieu concepts and biological psychiatry. The staff consists of a psychiatrist, a teacher, and a multidisciplinary team of eight therapists.

Patients

Investigation of different aspects of the PMAP's predictive validity was based on different subsamples: patients who began treatment (n = 165), patients who completed treatment (n = 99), and patients who completed the outcome study, that is, matched patients in the immediate treatment and control conditions (n = 120). For the outcome study, there were 80 women and 40 men whose mean age was 32.7 years (range: 14–57). Two thirds did not live with a partner. Most had high school education or less. About one third were employed full-time and nearly all had received previous psychiatric treatment. The most frequent Axis I lifetime and current diagnoses provided by the Diagnostic Interview Schedule were major depressive episode. Approximately two thirds also received an Axis II diagnosis, the most common being dependent, borderline, and atypical personality disorders. One half of the sample received life time diagnoses of both affective and personality disorders. All patients evidenced the presence of long-term psychiatric difficulties that disrupted familial, social, and work functioning.

Procedures and Design

Following the initial assessments, patients were matched in pairs according to Axis I diagnoses, age, and gender, and randomly assigned to immediate or delayed treatment. As with the second study, the control condition was a delayed treatment condition. Control patients were assigned to a wait list of 4 months which was the same duration as the treatment. Outcome variables were assessed before and after the treatment and the delay periods and at a follow-up interview conducted an average of 8 months posttreatment.

Measures

Outcome. The outcome variables covered areas of interpersonal functioning, psychiatric symptomatology, self-esteem, life-satisfaction, defensive functioning, and personalized target objectives. Sources of assessment included the patient and an independent assessor.

Process. Patient behavior in a small psychodynamic group meeting twice weekly for 12 weeks provided ratings of therapy process. After each session, each patient rated himself or herself and each of the other patients on how much they had worked during the session. These ratings generated three work variables: the patient's self-rating, the average of the other patients' ratings of the patient, and the patient's average rating of the other patients.

Results

Rater Reliability. The rater reliability of the PMAP for 15 randomly selected patients from this clinical population was ICC (1,1) = .88. This finding supported the results of the first two studies.

Test–Retest Reliability. The test–retest reliability was r(58) = .25 over a 4-month delay period. This correlation was considerably reduced compared to the first two studies. This finding may reflect the longer time period and the fact that the data were provided by waiting list patients may have been less motivated to perform the task a second time due to frustration over having to wait for treatment.

Discriminant Validity. Psychological mindedness scores were not highly associated with scores on the three other interpretation variables provided by the PMAP. As previously mentioned, those variables concern the patient's response to the therapist's interpretations of dynamics and transference. Hence, the PMAP's assessment of psychological mindedness was not confounded by the method of assessment.

Additional Aspects of Construct Validity. Other aspects of the PMAP's construct validity were again supported. In the day treatment study, level of psychological mindedness was not significantly associated with age, gender, marital status, employment status, or level of education. The use of psychotropic medication was not found to differ for patients obtaining high versus low psychological mindedness ratings. With respect to measures of psychiatric symptomatology and psychological distress, psychological mindedness was related to only one of the initial scores of the 21 outcome measures, a finding probably attributable to chance. Further, the prevalence of previous psychiatric treatment or hospitalization was not related to level of psychological mindedness. With respect to diagnoses, chi-square analyses revealed that psychological mindedness was not related to current Axis I or Axis II diagnoses. However, high psychologically minded patients were significantly more likely than low psychologically minded patients to warrant an Axis I lifetime diagnosis of major depression. Because major depression was only 1 of the 17 diagnoses investigated, that result may have been due to chance.

Predictive Validity

Remaining. We define a dropout as someone who starts therapy and then terminates prematurely. In the short-term group study, a strong negative association between level of psychological mindedness and dropping out was found. However, this result was not replicated in the day treatment study. Of the 165 patients who started the treatment phase of the study, 47 dropped out. A *t*-test revealed that for this patient population, psychological mindedness was not significantly related to attrition.

Process. In the short-term, group therapy study, psychological mindedness was positively and significantly associated with work as measured by a process analysis system. For this study, we investigated the relationship between psychological mindedness and the patient-generated work variables. Pearson product-moment correlations revealed significant associations between psychological mindedness and the patient's self-rating of work, $r\ (97) = .23, p < .05$, and between psychological mindedness and the other patients' rating of the patient, $r\ (97) = .30, p < .01$. The higher the psychological mindedness, the higher were the work ratings. Hence, results of the day treatment study supported the short-term, group therapy study concerning work.

Outcome. In the short-term group therapy study, psychological mindedness was not found to be significantly related to outcome. Because so many of the low psychologically minded patients had dropped out of

TABLE 2.2
Outcome Factors and Variables in DTP

Factor and Variables	Loading
I. *General Symptomatology and Target Objectives*	
Target objective severity, rated by assessor	.73
Depression	.70
Self-Esteem (low)	.70
Symptomatic distress (SCL–90)	.66
Maladaptive defensive style	.60
II. *Social Maladjustment* and Dissatisfaction	
Sexual interpersonal functioning	.69
Family interpersonal functioning	.64
Social (friendship) interpersonal functioning	.62
Life dissatisfaction	.58
III. *Pathological Dependency*	
Pathological attachment	.81
Emotional reliance	.73
IV. *Positive Interpersonal Functioning*	
Present interpersonal behavior	.86
Number of friends	.66

therapy, the ability to test the relationship between psychological mindedness and outcome was constrained. In the day treatment study, psychological mindedness was not significantly associated with attrition. Therefore, there was a better opportunity to test the relationship between psychological mindedness and outcome. These analyses used data from the 99 patients who completed treatment. The prescore–postscore data for each outcome variable were initially converted to residual gain scores. Residual gain scores represent postscores with the effect of the prescores removed. Next, the large set of outcome variables was reduced to a smaller set of factors using a principal components analysis. This technique helped eliminate redundancy and organized the variables under a few areas. The four factors that were derived and their factor loadings are presented in Table 2.2. We named them General Symptomatology and Target Objectives, Social Maladjustment and Dissatisfaction, Pathological Dependency, and Positive Interpersonal Functioning.

To investigate the relationship between psychological mindedness and outcome we calculated Pearson correlation coefficients for psychological mindedness and each of the posttreatment outcome factors. As indicated in Table 2.3, psychological mindedness was significantly related to each of the first three outcome factors. The more psychologically minded the patient, the better the outcome. The variance accounted for by psychological mindedness was 10% for the first outcome factor, 8% for the second, and 6% for the third. At the 8-month follow-up assessment, the relationships between psychological mindedness and the outcome factors were no longer significant.

Implications of the Third Study

The results of the day treatment study supported the manner in which the PMAP operationalized psychological mindedness. Many of the findings

TABLE 2.3
Correlations between Psychological Mindedness and Post-Treatment Outcome Factors in DTP

General Symptomatology and Target Objectives[a]	Social Maladjustment and Dissatisfaction[a]	Pathological Dependency[a]	Positive Interpersonal Functioning
−.32***	−.28**	−.25*	.02

[a] Low scores on outcome factors are desirable

*$p < .05$. **$p < .01$. ***$p < .001$.

were consistent with the previous two studies. The rater reliability was again found to be strong. Concerning its construct validity, psychological mindedness was again found to be independent of the method of assessment, several demographic characteristics, psychiatric symptomatology and psychological distress, medication use, and diagnosis. Concerning its predictive validity, psychological mindedness was again found to be significantly and directly related to working in group therapy. Some of the findings did not support the previous studies. The diminished test–retest reliability suggests that motivation may influence performance on the PMAP. The failure to find significant relationships between psychological mindedness and remaining in treatment suggests that the 4-month day program provided sufficient flexibility with respect to pace and variety of group modality for low psychologically minded patients to be assimilated. Perhaps the most important finding was that psychological mindedness was found to be related to outcome. The more psychologically minded the patient, the more he or she benefited from treatment. The usefulness of the PMAP was broadened to include a chronic psychiatric population. The PMAP's utility was generalizing across patient populations and therapy modalities.

THE FOURTH STUDY

The fourth study attempted to expand the usefulness of the PMAP by predicting patients' response to another form of therapy, the Evening Treatment Program (ETP). In addition to investigating the measure's reliability and construct validity, the same three aspects of the PMAP's predictive validity were investigated with the ETP patients: the relationships among psychological mindedness and remaining, working, and benefiting. Because the study was reported in greater detail elsewhere (McCallum et al., in press) for the purposes of this chapter only a brief summary of the study is presented.

The ETP is an intensive, dynamically oriented, group therapy program that is offered to patients who evidence a chronic, serious pattern of personal and interpersonal difficulties. Unlike Day Treatment (DTP) patients, ETP patients must be engaged in a meaningful daily activity such as work, school, or parenting. The program is offered 5 evenings per week, 4 hours per evening for 18 weeks. The theoretical orientation emphasizes psychodynamic principles with influences from systems, milieu, and social–learning theories as well as biological psychiatry. Implementing the program in a team approach are a psychiatrist, a psychologist, a social worker, an occupational therapist, two registered nurses and two psychiatric nurses. When the study was implemented, the staff had an average of 3.5 years of experience working in the ETP.

Patients

The entire research sample consisted of 190 patients who began the ETP during the 3 years of the project. Of those who began the program, 154 (81%) successfully completed it, 28 (15%) self-discharged, and 8 (4%) were asked to leave for failing to adhere to program policy.

For the sample of 154 completers, the average age was 33 years, 61% were female, over two thirds (68%) did not live with a partner, and the majority (92%) had at least completed high school. Decisionbase (Long, 1990), an interactive, computerized interview, provided initial diagnoses according to DSM–III and DSM–III–R criteria (American Psychiatric Association, 1980, 1987). According to this system, 99% of completers received an Axis I diagnosis, the most common being mood disorders and anxiety disorders. Approximately three quarters also received an Axis II diagnosis, the most common being avoidant, paranoid, dependent, and borderline personality disorder.

Procedures and Design

After obtaining informed consent and completing the initial assessments, patients immediately began the ETP. The outcome battery was assessed before and after treatment and at 4-month and 1-year follow-up interviews. The design involved a correlational study between pretherapy measures of patient characteristics, process measures obtained during the course of therapy, and outcome measures obtained before and three times after treatment. This chapter addresses results involving posttreatment outcome.

Measures

Outcome. The outcome battery assessed several areas of functioning: interpersonal and personality functioning, self-esteem, psychiatric symptomatology, personalized target objectives, and satisfaction with treatment. The sources of evaluation included the patient, the therapists, and the independent outcome assessor.

Process. The group chosen for an examination of process was a small psychodynamically oriented group. It was held once weekly for 7 weeks during the middle phase of the program and lasted 80 minutes. After each session, each patient rated the amount of work exhibited by him or her and by every other group member during that session. The therapists also provided a work rating for each patient. For each session, four work variables were derived: the patient's self-rating, the average of the other patients' ratings of the patient, the therapists' rating of the patient, and the patient's average rating of the other patients in his or her group.

Results

Rater Reliability. The PMAP's rater reliability was again supported with this population. Based on 30 randomly chosen cases, the ICC (2,1) in this study was .96 for the first scenario and .89 for the second, indicating strong interrater reliability.

Discriminant Validity. Psychological mindedness scores were again not found to be highly associated with the three other interpretation variables provided by the PMAP, thus supporting its discriminant validity.

Additional Aspects of Construct Validity. Other aspects of the PMAP's construct validity were again supported. In the evening treatment study, level of psychological mindedness was again not significantly associated with gender or level of education. However, in contrast to the previous studies, for this population psychological mindedness was significantly associated with age, marital status, and employment status. Specifically, younger, single patients scored higher than older or married patients. In addition, those working inside the home scored higher than those working outside the home.

The use of psychotropic medication was not found to differ for patients scoring high or low on the PMAP. With respect to measures of psychiatric symptomatology and psychological distress, none of the pretherapy measures were significantly associated with psychological mindedness. The prevalence of previous psychiatric treatment or hospitalization was not related to level of psychological mindedness. Finally, of the 20 F-tests conducted between psychological mindedness and lifelong diagnosis, only 1 was significant; those with a lifelong diagnosis of mood disorder scored significantly higher on the PMAP.

TABLE 2.4
Pearson Correlations Between Psychological Mindedness and Work in ETP

	Work			
	PP	OP	TP	PO
Psychological Mindedness	.20	.23*	.18	.10

Note. PP = Patient-rated, OP = Other-rated, TP = Therapist-rated, PO = Patient rating of others.

Predictive Validity

Remaining. Of the 190 patients who started the program, 36 dropped out. A *t*-test revealed that for this patient population, psychological mindedness was not significantly related to attrition.

Process. To investigate the relationship between psychological mindedness and work, Pearson correlation coefficients were calculated between the initial level of PM and each of the four indices of work: self-rated, other-rated, therapist-rated, and patient's rating of others. The results (Table 2.4) indicated significant direct relationships between PM and three of the indices of patient work. However, because of the number of variables being analyzed simultaneously, the probability of falsely obtaining significant findings was greater than .05. Therefore a Bonferroni adjustment was made to the individual p levels (.05 ÷ 4 = .012) to maintain an overall alpha level of .05. Only the correlation between psychological mindedness and the other patients' rating of work (OP) met this more stringent criterion. Hence, the more psychologically minded the patient, the more he or she worked in the psychodynamically oriented small group as rated by the other patients.

Outcome. Data for the outcome analyses were provided by 142 of the 154 completers whose data set was relatively complete. The 16 pre–post outcome variables were converted to residual gain scores and subjected to a principal components analysis (PCA). Rated benefit scores were not included in the PCA. The PCA yielded a five-factor solution. We named these factors Symptomatic Distress, Intrapersonal Malaise, Social–Sexual Dysfunction, Maladaptive Pattern of Relating, and Mature Defenses. Table 2.5 presents the five factors, the variance accounted for by each factor, and the measures associated with each factor.

To investigate the relationship between psychological mindedness and outcome, correlation coefficients were calculated between PM and the five pre–post outcome factors, and between PM and the two rated benefit scores. Again a Bonferroni adjustment was made such that the criterion for significance was $p < .01$ for the pre–post outcome factors and $p < .025$ for the rated

TABLE 2.5
ETP Outcome Factors, Percentages of Variance, and Loadings

Factor and Variables	% of Variance	Loading
I. *Symptomatic Distress*	36.7	
Interpersonal problems		.78
Immature/neurotic defenses		.76
Depression		.72
Anxiety		.59
SCL–90 symptomatology		.53
II. *Intrapersonal Malaise*	9.1	
Life (dis)satisfaction		.67
Global (current) dysfunction		.66
Targets severity, patient rated		.66
Targets severity, independently rated		.63
Self-esteem (low)		.60
III. *Social–Sexual Dysfunction*	8.0	
Sexual (dys)function		.72
Social (dys)function		.66
Number of friends (few)		.64
IV. *Maladaptive Pattern of Relating*	6.3	
Family (dys)function		.84
Interpersonal behavior		.53
V. *Mature Defenses*	6.3	
Mature defenses		.87

benefit scores. None of the seven correlations met the more stringent criterion of significance. Hence, patients tended to improve regardless of their level of psychological mindedness.

Additional Analyses. Unlike its application with the DTP, the PMAP was only partially successful in predicting patients' response to the ETP. One possible explanation was that patients' psychological mindedness increased as a function of their participation in the program, precluding finding a relationship between pretreatment PM and outcome. However, a correlated *t*-test conducted on the average PM score at pretreatment versus posttreatment was nonsignificant. The correlation coefficient was $r = .40$, $p < .001$, indicating the stability of the measure.

We next looked closer at the 16 measures of pre–post change of which the five pre–post outcome factors consisted. We investigated whether our failure to predict outcome using pre–post data was possibly due to the fact that patients had not improved over the course of treatment. We investigated the significance of pre–post change using multivariate and univariate statistics. We also calculated the magnitude of effect, or effect size, for all the pre–post variables according to a formula provided by Smith, Glass, and Miller (1980). The result of the MANOVA was significant [$F(16, 115) = 48.41$, $p < .000$], indicating significant pre–post change on outcome. The results of the univariate univariate analyses indicated that patients' scores improved significantly on each outcome variable. Finally, all effect sizes were positive in sign, indicating benefit and not deterioration. The average effect size for all 16 variables was 1.10, which is regarded as large in the psychotherapy literature.

We next investigated whether our failure to predict outcome was due to a restricted range in the outcome scores. When calculating the association between two variables, for example, PM and outcome, if the variability across patients is small for either or both variables, then the correlation will also be small.

To compare the variability in improvement across patients between the two studies, a series of *F*-tests was conducted between the outcome variance of the ETP and DTP for measures common to both studies. The results (Table 2.6) indicated that for 6 of the 11 measures common to both studies, the variance of outcome scores for the ETP was significantly smaller than that of the DTP. The ETP patients were more similar to each other in how much they improved than were the DTP patients. Stated another way, in the DTP study, some patients changed a lot and some changed very little, but in the ETP study, the amount of change among the patients was significantly less variable. Therefore, it is possible that the nonsignificant correlations between PM and the pre–post outcome factors, in the ETP, were partially due to the smaller variability in outcome in this study.

SUMMARY AND IMPLICATIONS OF THE FOUR STUDIES

Populations

The psychometric properties of the PMAP were investigated with four separate populations. The first population was a nonclinical group of 30 adult volunteers; the second was 154 patients suffering with loss referred to analytically oriented short-term groups for loss; the third was 165 psychiatric patients suffering from serious long-term disorders who participated in a controlled trial of a day treatment program; and the fourth population consisted of 190 patients who were admitted to an evening treatment program.

TABLE 2.6

Comparison of Variances for Outcome Variables Common to DTP and ETP

Common Variables	DTP Variance	ETP Variance	F
Social	2.59	1.93	1.34*
Family	2.53	1.99	1.27
Sexual	6.10	3.76	1.62**
Rosenberg self-esteem	0.36	0.25	18.60***
Target objectives			
patient-rated	.94	1.23	1.30
independently-rated	1.06	.55	1.93**
SCL-90 (GSI)	.48	.40	1.20
Life satisfaction	7.50	2.25	3.33**
Interpersonal behavior scale	623.50	554.13	1.12
Number of friends	2.82	1.14	2.47**
Satisfaction with friends	.49	.55	1.12

$^{*}p < .05$. $^{**}p < .01$. $^{***}p < .001$.

Reliability

In all four studies, the PMAP was found to have strong rater reliability. Its lowest reliability was found in the first study. Since then, and with three different clinical populations, its rater reliability has been consistently high. The strength of its rater reliability is particularly impressive given that the PMAP is easily and quickly administered. In addition, the rating procedure can be easily taught to raters who need not be particularly clinically sophisticated.

The test–retest reliability was strongest with the nonclinical population and the shortest retest period (1 month). Low patient motivation and memory differences may have influenced the poorer test–retest reliability when used with the clinical populations.

Convergent Validity

Scores on the PMAP were compared to three other measures of psychological mindedness. Results of the first and second studies revealed that the PMAP was significantly related to the Psychological Mindedness scale of the CPI, the overall insight score of the Insight Test, and therapist appraisals of psychological mindedness. However, the size of the correlations suggested that the PMAP was not redundant with these other measures.

Discriminant Validity

The discriminant validity of the measure was repeatedly supported by finding that psychological mindedness scores were not highly associated with scores on the three Interpretation Comprehension variables provided by the PMAP. Hence, the PM score was not confounded by the method of assessment.

Additional Aspects of Construct Validity

All four studies revealed that psychological mindedness was not significantly related to gender or level of education. In the first three studies, psychological mindedness was not significantly related to age, marital status, or employment status. However, in the fourth study patients who were younger, single, or worked inside the home scored higher on psychological mindedness than patients who were older, married, or worked outside the home.

Psychological mindedness was consistently not found to be significantly related to measures of personality, intelligence, psychiatric symptomatology, or psychological distress. Similarly, diagnosis, use of psychotropic medications, and the prevalence of previous psychiatric treatment or hospitalization were not related to level of psychological mindedness.

Predictive Validity

Attrition. In the study of short-term groups for loss patients, a strong relationship between psychological mindedness and attrition was found. Low PM patients were significantly more likely than high PM patients to drop out of this form of therapy. This relationship between PM and attrition was not found in the other two clinical studies. It is possible that the intense, accelerated pace of these dynamically oriented, short-term groups overwhelmed the low PM patients such that they felt they had to leave. That finding is consistent with the conception that patients who lack the ability required of therapy (low PM patients in the case of dynamically oriented therapy) are at high risk of dropping out. Budman, Demby, and Randall (1980) concluded that to remain and experience success in a short-term dynamically oriented therapy group, "a patient needs to be able to 'speak the same language' (as the other members)" (p. 15). In our short-term loss groups, "speaking the same language" can be taken to mean being psychologically minded. It is possible, therefore, that low PM patients may be better suited to a therapy group that utilizes a different theoretical orientation–for example, a more supportive or cognitive approach.

Conversely, for the two partial hospitalization programs studied, low PM patients were able to remain in treatment. This difference between the studies may be attributable to the salient differences between the types of treatment. The day and evening treatment programs are longer in duration, more intense, and offer a variety of groups within the program. Hence, low psychologically minded patients may be able to benefit enough from these other approaches to persist with the programs.

Process. In all three clinical studies, a direct and positive relationship between PM and work was found. Those who scored high on PM were suited to groups that utilized a psychodynamic approach to group therapy. It is possible, therefore, to identify the suitability of patients for a psychodynamic approach before therapy begins. Selection decisions can be based on such information. However, rather than excluding patients who score low on PM, therapists may wish to prepare them for psychodynamic work by requiring their attendance in a preadmission group where they can learn about the "language" and process of therapy. In the case of the day and evening treatment programs, the staff might also accomodate the low PM patients by initially emphasizing a more psychoeducational or supportive approach for all patients entering the program. For example, the first phase could emphasize rehabilitative, sociotherapy groups with the psychotherapeutic insight-oriented groups only being introduced at the next phase.

In the studies involving partial hospitalization programs, PM was most strongly related to Work as rated by the other patients (OP). As previously described, to score high on the PMAP, patients had to demonstrate an ability to identify intrapsychic components of another person (the actress on the videotape) and relate those components to the person's difficulties. When high PM patients entered the DTP or ETP, they probably continued to demonstrate that ability when conversing with the other group patients. The other patients may have felt understood by the high PM patients and appreciated their contribution to the group, thereby rating them as exhibiting higher levels of work.

Outcome. In the study of short-term groups for loss, psychological mindedness was not found to be significantly related to outcome. Because so many of the low PM patients dropped out, our ability to investigate this relationship in that study was constrained. Given that PM was not found to be significantly related to attrition in either of the partial hospitalization studies, those studies provided a better opportunity to test the relationship between PM and outcome.

In the study of the DTP psychological mindedness was significantly related to outcome. Conversely, in the study of the ETP, PM was not significantly related to outcome. Given the similarity between the two programs' goals and treatment approach, and the similarity between the two populations, this failure to cross-validate was perplexing. By analyzing the outcome variance between the two studies, we suggested that our failure to crossvalidate may have been partially due to the smaller outcome variance found for ETP patients compared to DTP patients. That difference in outcome variance may reflect differences among the two programs. For example, the ETP census (25) was quite a bit smaller than that of the DTP (43). It is possible, therefore, that in the ETP there was less chance of patients fading into the background. The staff and other patients may have more readily noticed and counteracted any such tendency. Consequently, a more inclusive milieu may have been created especially for the less suitable patients, that is, those with low psychological mindedness. Supporting this hypothesis was the smaller dropout rate for the ETP (19%) compared to the DTP (28.5%).

CONCLUSION

The PMAP approach to the measurement of psychological mindedness was fairly successful. Perhaps its greatest strength is that it is an efficient, easily administered, reliably scored, measure of psychological mindedness. It was found to be associated with measures to which it is conceptually related, such as other measures of psychological mindedness, and to be independent of possibly confounding variables, for example, intelligence and psychopathology. It was administered to three different clinical populations who seemed to enjoy the break from the usual battery of paper and pencil measures.

We attribute its success to the following factors. First, the PMAP was developed to assess the unique abilities required of work within analytically oriented therapy. Those abilities refer to understanding the relationships between intrapsychic conflicts and current difficulties. In this way, the concept could be distinguished from other specific and nonspecific factors. Clearly, the operationalization was theory driven. An objective was to predict success in analytically oriented group therapy. Therefore, a measure was devised that reflected the abilities required of work in analytic therapy and group therapy. Pretherapy behavior that approximated therapy behavior was assessed, that is, the subject was required to discuss the problems of another person (the actress–patient). That requirement is consistent with group therapy where patients are encouraged to listen and contribute to the therapeutic process of other patients.

The idea that the success of the PMAP may be attributable, in part, to the similarity between the pretherapy and therapy behavior, raises an important limitation of the measure. A significant characteristic of the PMAP is that it assesses the patient's psychological mindedness with respect to another person but not with respect to himself or herself. In part, the PMAP was developed this way in order to assess the person's ability to understand problems in a manner consistent with psychodynamic theory without the assessment being confounded by the person's own defensive processes. For the purpose of selecting patients for group therapy (and the reader should note that the PMAP has been used only with group forms of therapy), the PMAP's inability to assess the person's psychological mindedness toward himself or herself may not be so crucial. Nevertheless, the question of whether the ability assessed by the PMAP generalizes to the person's understanding of his or her own problems remains. Whether our measure's predictive ability would be as strong in the case of individual therapy is also open to question. The individual therapy patient is required to discuss his or her own problems. Discussion of other people's problems is discouraged. Typically, the therapist interprets such discussion as reflecting a defensive maneuver. In addition, it is not clear if the PMAP is applicable to therapies that utilize a nonpsychoanalytic theoretical approach. We argue that candidates for another approach to therapy should display behavior that is theoretically relevant to success with that approach.

A third aspect related to the issue of generalizability concerns the patient populations studied. The PMAP depicts a woman struggling with loss through divorce. This problem was particularly suited to the loss patients participating in the short-term group study. The issue of loss was also relevant to the day and evening treatment populations who suffer from serious long-term affective and personality disorders that often disrupt interpersonal relationships. We believe that problems associated with loss are ubiquitous and therefore relevant to all psychiatric populations.

A final issue regarding the generalizability of our findings concerns the measure's relevance for nonclinical populations. Clearly, it was developed for use with psychiatric populations; the second, third, and fourth studies were predictive studies that utilized such populations. Nevertheless, we believe that the measure would yield a valid assessment of psychological mindedness for nonclinical populations. Our belief is supported by the fact that the first study utilized a nonclinical population, and studies two and three found that level of psychological mindedness was not related to pretherapy levels of pathology. However, it is not clear whether the measure would predict anything of value if used with nonclinical populations. Ultimately, the generalizability of the PMAP remains an empirical question.

In addition to generalizability, the results of our studies raise another important issue. The discrepancy between the studies concerning the relationship between psychological mindedness and outcome is intriguing. As previously mentioned, in the second study, low psychologically minded patients who completed the short-term groups benefited as much as the highly psychologically minded patients. Explanations of that finding are perhaps premature given the small number of patients involved. Indeed, a major weakness of that study was the inability to test some relationships because so few of the low psychologically minded patients actually completed treatment. Nevertheless, future researchers are encouraged to investigate the interaction between psychological mindedness and different types of therapeutic process and its impact on outcome. Rather than reflecting a weakness of the PMAP, perhaps the inconsistent results involving outcome reflect meaningful differences among the clinical programs with which the PMAP was used.

An additional limitation of the PMAP relates to the manner in which we operationalized psychological mindedness. As previously described, the scale is a hierarchy whereby higher levels incorporate the scoring criteria from the scale's lower levels. We do not have empirical support for the hierarchy either in terms of the way the levels are ordered or in terms of conceptualizing the levels as reflecting one concept as opposed to several independent concepts. Further investigations need to address the validity of the hierarchy.

The PMAP has consistently predicted psychodynamic work. In terms of matching patients with a psychodynamically oriented therapy, we believe that the PMAP can be a useful clinical tool. Although video equipment requires a financial investment, the potential benefits for clinicians and patients are considerable. In that sense, the return on the investment may be substantial. At the very least, awareness of the criteria of high psychological mindedness may enable the clinician to listen for confirmation of the criteria while routinely interviewing potential group candidates.

To conclude, we are encouraged by the PMAP's utility to date. Our ideas for future research investigations include: adapting the PMAP for assessing the person's psychological mindedness toward the self, using the PMAP with patients referred for individual therapy, and investigating the validity of the hierarchy. We look forward to future attempts to expand the usefulness of our measure.

REFERENCES

American Psychiatric Association. (1980). *Diagnostic and statistical manual of mental disorders* (3rd ed.). Washington, DC: Author.

American Psychiatric Association. (1987). Diagnostic and statistical manual of mental disorders (3rd ed., Rev.). Washington, DC: Author.

Ammons, R. B., & Ammons, C. H. (1962). *The Quick Test: Provisional manual.* Missoula, MT: Psychological Test Specialists.

Appelbaum, S. A. (1973). Psychological mindedness: Word, concept, and essence. *International Journal of Psycho-Analysis, 54,* 35–46.

Appelbaum, S. A. (1977). *The anatomy of change.* New York: Plenum.

Budman, S. H., Demby, A., & Randall M. (1980). Short-term group psychotherapy: Who succeeds, who fails? *Group, 4,* 3–16.

de Carufel, F. L., & Piper, W. E. (1988). Group psychotherapy or individual psychotherapy. Patient characteristics as predictive factors. *International Journal of Group Psychotherapy, 38,* 169–188.

Derogatis, L. R. (1977). *SCL–90 administration, scoring and procedures manual I.* Baltimore: Johns Hopkins University Press.

Gough, H. G. (1957). *California psychological inventory.* Palo Alto, CA: Consulting Psychologists Press.

Horowitz, L., Rosenberg, S. E., Baer, B. A., Ureño, S., & Villaseñor, V. S. (1988). Inventory of interpersonal problems: Psychometric properties and clinical applications. *Journal of Consulting and Clinical Psychology, 56,* 885–892.

Horowitz, L. M., Rosenberg, S. E., & Kalehzan, B. M. (1992). The capacity to describe other people clearly: A predictor of interpersonal problems in brief dynamic psychotherapy. *Psychotherapy Research, 2,* 37–51.

Jackson, D. M. (1974). *Personality Research Form Manual.* New York: Research Psychologists Press.

Kernberg, O., Burstein, E., Coyne, L., Appelbaum, H., Horwitz, L., & Voth, H. (1972). Psychotherapy and psychoanalysis: Final report of the Menninger Foundation's psychotherapy research project. *Bulletin of the Menninger Clinic, 36,* 1–275.

Long, P. W. (1990). *Decisionbase.* Vancouver, BC: Christiana Enterprises.

McCallum, M. (1989). *A controlled study of effectiveness and patient suitability for short-term group psychotherapy.* Unpublished doctoral dissertation, McGill University, Montreal, Quebec, Canada.

McCallum, M., & Piper, W. E. (1987). *Manual for the Psychological Mindedness Assessment Procedure.* Unpublished manuscript.

McCallum, M., & Piper, W. E. (1990a). A controlled study of effectiveness and patient suitability for short-term group psychotherapy. *International Journal of Group Psychotherapy, 40,* 431–452.

McCallum, M., & Piper, W. E. (1990b). The Psychological Mindedness Assessment Procedure. *Psychological Assessment: A Journal of Consulting and Clinical Psychology, 2,* 412–418.

McCallum, M., & Piper, W. E. (1996). Psychological mindedness. *Psychiatry: Interpersonal and Biological Processes, 59,* 48–64.

McCallum, M., Piper, W. E., & O'Kelly, J. G. (in press). Predicting patient benefit from a group oriented, evening treatment program. *International Journal of Group Psychotherapy.*

Piper, W. E., Debbane, E. G., Bienvenu, J. P., & Garant, J. (1984). A comparative study of four forms of psychotherapy. *Journal of Consulting and Clinical Psychology, 52,* 268–279.

Piper, W. E., de Carufel, F. L., & Szkrumelak, N. (1985). Patient predictors of process and outcome in short-term individual psychotherapy. *Journal of Nervous and Mental Disease, 173,* 726–733.

Piper, W. E., Joyce, A. S., Azim, H. F. A., & Rosie, J. S. (1994). Patient characteristics and success in day treatment. *Journal of Nervous and Mental Disease, 182,* 381–386.

Piper, W. E., Joyce, A. S., Rosie, J. S., & Azim, H. F. A. (1994). Psychological mindedness, work and outcome in day treatment. *International Journal of Group Psychotherapy, 44,* 291–311.

Piper, W. E., & McCallum, M. (1988). *Manual for the Psychodynamic Work and Object Rating System.* Unpublished manuscript.

Piper, W. E., McCallum, M., & Azim, H. F. A. (1992). *Adaptation to loss through short-term group therapy*. New York: Guilford.

Piper, W. E., Rosie, J. S., Azim, H. F. A., & Joyce, A. S. (1993). A randomized trial of psychiatric day treatment for patients with affective and personality disorders. *Hospital and Community Psychiatry, 44*, 757–763.

Piper, W. E., Rosie, J. S., Joyce, A. S., & Azim, H. F. A. (1996). *Time-limited day treatment for personality disorders: Integration of research and practice in a group program*. Washington, DC: American Psychological Association.

Rosenbaum, R. L., & Horowitz, M. J. (1983). Motivation for psychotherapy: A factorial and conceptual analysis. *Psychological Theory, Research, and Practice, 20*, 346–354.

Ryan, E. R., & Cicchetti, D. V. (1985). Predicting quality of alliance in the initial psychotherapy interview. *Journal of Nervous and Mental Disease, 173*, 717–725.

Silver, D. (1983). Psychotherapy of the characterologically difficult patient. *Canadian Journal of Psychiatry, 28*, 513–521.

Smith, M. L., Glass, G. V., & Miller, T. I. (1980). *The benefits of psychotherapy*. Baltimore: John Hopkins University Press.

Tolor, A., & Reznikoff, M. (1960). A new approach to insight: A preliminary report. *Journal of Nervous and Mental Disease, 130*, 286–296.

Wallerstein, R. S., & Robbins, L. (1956). The psychotherapy research project of the Menninger Foundation. *Bulletin of the Menninger Clinic, 20*, 221–278.

Wolitzky, D. L., & Reuben, R. (1974). Psychological-mindedness. *Journal of Clinical Psychology, 30*, 26–30.

Woods, M., & Melnick, J. (1979). A review of group therapy selection criteria. *Small Group Behavior, 10*, 155–175.

Chapter 3

Assessing the Psychological Mindedness of Children and Adolescents

Robert L. Hatcher
Sherry L. Hatcher
University of Michigan

ORIGIN

Our interest in psychological mindedness began in the rich mix of clinical work and psychological research provided by the clinical psychology doctoral program at the University of Michigan. One of us (Robert) did his doctoral thesis on insight and self-observation in short- and long-term psychotherapy, and continues to be interested in the characteristics of patients that help them gain deeper understanding of themselves (R. Hatcher, 1981). The other (Sherry) has a longstanding interest in peer counseling and preventative mental health interventions with adolescents and college students (S. Hatcher, 1995). We both are practicing clinical psychologists, with daily interest in how our patients work to think about and understand themselves.

Psychological mindedness is a complex cognitive ability with special relevance to insight-oriented psychotherapy. The capacity to think psychologically about oneself, about other people, and about one's relationships to them is fundamental to the patient's ability to make use of therapies based on self-understanding. Psychodynamic clinicians recognized that understanding based on psychological mindedness is the means and the goal of their psychotherapeutic work (Blum, 1979). Until relatively recently, however, clinicians gave little attention to the question of psychological mindedness in children and adolescents. In her preface to a set of papers about insight, Anna Freud (1979) commented that "when it came to children, I merely classified their lack of insight with the absence of the numerous other characteristics which...distinguish the immature from the mature patient...(p. 3)". Kennedy (1979) was the first psychodynamic clinician to suggest a developmental line for children's capacity to think about and experience their internal worlds. She stressed that in addition to the cognitive capacity for understanding oneself or others, the capacity for insight depends on the child's ability to tolerate painful feelings and to not turn to externalizing methods for thinking about and dealing with internal states. She traced three stages in this developmental line. These stages include (a) "under 5s" with their limited capacity for self-observation of wishes and feelings, (b) latency children (5 to puberty), who have increased capacity for self-awareness, but rely heavily on external factors to explain and deal with internal states, and (c) adolescents, who have increased intellectual abilities to understand the self. Hoffman (1989), on the other hand, stressed that the capacity for self-understanding is a key element in the child's developing ability to tolerate painful affects. It seems likely that the growth of each of these features depends on that of the other, so that he child's increased capacity to tolerate feelings both contributes to and is aided by increased understanding of the meaning and nature of feelings.

Since the mid-1980s, academic psychologists have become greatly interested in the nature and development of the child's understanding of the mind (Astington, 1993; Wellman, 1990). Much of this research confirms and elaborates the psychodynamic views of Kennedy (1979) and Hoffman (1989). Two strands of this work are particularly relevant to the study of psychological mindedness: the development of children's "theory of mind" and children's growing understanding of emotions. In a series of ingenious experiments, theory of mind researchers have demonstrated that by about the age of 4 years, children come to understand a fundamental property of the mind: Minds create their own representations of reality, and these representations may differ from what really is—there are false beliefs about reality. Prior to age 4, children do not typically understand that a person, including themselves, could believe something that is not actually true. For example, a 3-year-old is told a story in which Sally has put a cupcake in a cupboard, but while Sally is at school, her mother moves the cupcake to the refrigerator. When Sally comes home from school, where will she look for the cupcake? Most 3-year-olds will answer, "in the refrigerator," because they do not understand, in fact cannot comprehend, that Sally has a "false belief" about the cupcake's location. Results like these indicate that under-4s do not understand that the mind actively creates and holds its own representations of reality. This discovery of the mind occurs in the framework of a "belief–desire" psychology, which may be a universal or innate human framework for psychological understanding. This naive or folk psychology assumes that people have desires that spur them to actions in the world, and these actions are based on beliefs about the nature of the world. Once the child develops an understanding of the representational activity of the mind, he or she can begin to predict the behavior of others based on inferences about their beliefs and desires. Pretend and deception become possible because the child understands that one can act on beliefs that are not in fact true.

These cognitive abilities are the bedrock of psychological mindedness, and children acquire them early in their development. Failure to develop these abilities is associated with catastrophic failure to understand the self and others. False-belief studies with autistic children demonstrate that they (a) lack this theory of mind, (b) are unable to imagine that others have minds of their own, and (c) cannot recognize the subjectivity of their own minds (Astington, 1993; Baron-Cohen, 1995). Many researchers believe that the emergence of theory of mind is genetically predetermined, although most believe that social experience can foster or inhibit its emergence and sophistication. Once the theory of mind capacity emerges, children complete their understanding of themselves and others with increasing sophistication. For example, by age 7, children have begun to recognize enduring traits (e.g., assertiveness, stubbornness) in themselves and others, motivational organizers that structure the person's behavior and sense of self. Over time, children's understanding of themselves and others is based less in terms of external events and momentary wishes and more in terms of internal, enduring beliefs and motivations (Wellman, 1990).

Also of special relevance to psychological mindedness is the child's growing understanding of mixed emotions (Carroll & Steward, 1984; Donaldson & Westerman, 1986; Harter & Buddin, 1987). The approaches of Carroll and Steward and Harter and Buddin are grounded in Piaget's work (1965, 1981), and show the child's growing cognitive capacity to understand the experiencing of increasingly complex feelings: first one feeling, then two same-valence feelings, then two opposite valence feelings to different targets, and then two simultaneously. Harter and Buddin's work grew out of their clinical experience with children's difficulty in acknowledging simultaneous positive and negative feelings. Harter and Buddin assessed the ability to conceptualize different combinations of feelings and targets in 126 children between ages 4 and 12 years (one half boys, one half girls) by showing a set of photographs of same-gendered children depicting a range of positive and negative emotions. Children chose photographs of either two same or two different valence feelings, placed on boards with line drawings to facilitate the questions asked (e.g., "How could you at the very same time have the first feeling about one thing and the second feeling about a different thing?"). A simple and highly reliable coding scheme was used to determine whether the child had satisfactorily explained how the feelings could be experienced as presented. Harter and Buddin demonstrated that at about 5 years of age, children hold the firm belief that only one emotion may be experienced at a time, and deny the possibility of having more than one feeling. As one of their subjects remarked, "It's hard to think of two feelings at the same time because you only have one mind." At about 7 years of age, children can acknowledge having two different positive feelings towards the same target (i.e., person or situation).

By almost 9 years of age, children can express same-valence feelings to different targets. By age 10,children can describe having opposite valence feelings at the same time, although only to different targets. A subject of this age remarked, "I was mad at my brother for hitting me, and pleased that my father gave me permission to hit him back." Finally, at mean age 11.3 years, children are able to describe opposite-valence feelings towards a single target: "I was happy that I got a present but mad that it wasn't what I wanted." Harter and Buddin found that children reached these levels of emotional understanding at considerably varying ages (standard deviations at each level averaged about 1.5 years). A study of a school-based intervention designed to enhance emotional competence showed no effect on 6- to 11-year-olds' ability to acknowledge simultaneous emotions (Greenberg, Kusche, Cook, & Quamma, 1995). Thus, care must be taken by clinicians not to overestimate the cognitive capacities of their child patients for understanding their mixed emotions. This study is relevant to the issue of psychological mindedness because of its focus on the child's understanding of his or her own feelings. Its scoring system is narrowly focused on the possibility of experiencing mixed feelings, however, and thus captures only a limited aspect of the idea of psychological understanding covered by the concept of psychological mindedness.

Carroll and Steward (1984) studied the relationship between Piagetian cognitive stages and children's ability to understand their own affective experience. They gave their subjects (thirty 4- to 5-year-olds and thirty 8- to 9-year-olds, one half boys, one half girls) a set of Piagetian intellectual tasks (sorting, classifying, and conservation tasks) together with a structured interview designed to "probe the child's affective understanding of the following five areas: the perception of feeling states (happy, sad, mad, and afraid) in the self and by others, the possibility of having more than one feeling at a time, and the possibility of changing feelings and hiding them" (p. 1487). The interviewer asked the child to demonstrate a feeling, and then asked, for example, "How do you know when you are feeling happy? How would I [the examiner] know that you were feeling happy? Can you feel sad and mad at the same time? Can feelings change? Can you hide your feelings? How? What happens?" A 4-point developmental coding scheme was developed on the basis of pilot data. Level 0 included "don't know" and no response. Level 1 responses were "characterized by the exclusive use of idiosyncratic and particularistic elements. No sense of internal feeling was conveyed." Level 1 also specifies self-perceptions defined primarily by situations rather than by inner states, and the idea that multiple feelings cannot occur simultaneously; hidden feelings are thought of in very concrete terms (e.g., "under the table"). Level 2 responses were "characterized by the use of multiple elements related idiosyncratically or by categories defined by specific examples of actions, behaviors, and/or expressions. No sense of inner processing of feelings was conveyed." At this level, self-perceptions of emotions refer to bodily states, multiple feelings are possible sequentially, and hidden feelings are imagined by simply not talking about them. Finally, Level 3 responses showed "the use of multiple elements with relations classified and/or ordered coherently, including a reference to self-reflective inner state" (p. 1488). At this level, children see common elements in themselves across situations, can imagine simultaneous feelings, and recognize that feelings can be unexpressed but still held inside. Carroll and Steward found strong differences in rated levels of understanding feelings between the 4- to 5-year-olds (23 of 30 at Level 1, 7 at Level 2) and the 8- to 9-year-olds (19 of 30 at Level 3, 10 at Level 2), and a partial correlation between affective and cognitive test scores of .40, $p < .001$.

Carroll and Steward's (1984) coding system recognizes the importance of the child's self-reflection and of the interior source of feelings, but does not include the idea of interacting internal states (as when, for example, an adolescent recognizes that an angry feeling towards a person is modulated by the caring feelings also held for the person), nor that there can be feelings that one is unaware of, that is, unconscious affective responses.

Donaldson and Westerman (1986) took a more psychodynamic approach to the experience of multiple affects by focusing on the child's developing understanding of ambivalence, in contrast to Carroll and Steward (1984) and Harter and Buddin (1987), whose studies included paired feelings of similar valence. Their developmental model reached beyond the idea, shared with the other investigators, of having two feelings at once for the same person or situation, to include the idea that "conflicting feelings interact with and modify one another," and the ability "to coordinate feelings provoked by the immediate situation with those related to enduring traits of the target and internal processes such as memories" (p. 656). Like Carroll and Steward, these researchers were interested in how children understand how feelings change. They proposed that as children mature, they would increasingly turn from external, situational explanations for changes in feelings, toward recognizing the role of internal processes in the emergence and control of feelings. Donaldson and Westerman studied 60 subjects (one half boys, one half girls): (a) twenty 4- to 5-year-olds, (b) twenty 7- to 8-year-olds, and (c) twenty 10- to 11-year-olds. Two stories were presented individually to the children, whose experience of conflicting feelings and ideas of how feelings change were probed. The Kitten Story—a child is given a kitten to replace one recently lost—assesses the ability to coordinate happy and sad feelings and the Puppy Story—a loved puppy destroys a toy the child built and liked a lot — tests the ability to coordinate anger and love. Donaldson and Westerman's scoring criteria were quite similar to Carroll and Steward's criteria, particularly at Levels 0, 1, and 2. Donaldson and Westerman's Level 2 specifies that the child realizes contradictory feelings can be experienced toward the same person, but adds the criterion that the child's understanding of the interaction of these felings does not include a way to reconcile them (e.g., in reference to the child in the Kitten Story, "some part of her body is happy and some part is sad").

Donaldson and Westerman's Level 3 includes recognition that ambivalent feelings influence each other (e.g., a bad feeling may be modulated by a good feeling). Feelings toward others are less linked to particular situations, so that the child can recognize that, although the puppy is annoying at the moment, it is also lovable in general.

Donaldson and Westerman (1984) also coded children's ideas of how sad and angry feelings change. The coding scheme ranges from the lowest level (Level 1) where only changes in circumstances will change feelings (e.g., only if the lost kitten returns), to Level 3, where negative feelings are produced by the child's own thoughts, memories, and attitudes (e.g., by remembering how lovable the puppy is). Their findings parallel those of the other researchers, demonstrating steady growth in understanding ambivalence and in understanding how feelings change, except that 14 of 20 of the 7- to 8-year-olds were able to acknowledge having mixed feelings toward the same object. Donaldson and Westerman attributed this difference to a more supportive interview method. However, this difference may be due to the fact that they examined the child's ideas about how others deal with ambivalent feelings. Unlike Carroll and Steward, they did not take the next step of asking the child to examine the story as a projective instrument, or to provide an example of their own, matching their explanation of the experience of the child in the story. Thus, the study does not indicate children's ability to understand their own ambivalence.

The studies described above were shaped by, and are indebted to, Piaget's ideas concerning the development of a wide range of cognitive capacities for understanding the world, and extend his initial work on the child's understanding of his or her own mind and the child's empathic understanding of others. Carroll and Steward's (1984) study included several Piagetian cognitive tasks to permit coordination of the child's developing understanding of his or her emotional and psychological world with the child's growing cognitive abilities. Donaldson and Westerman (1986) and Harter and Buddin (1987) based their categorization of increasingly complex and coordinated understanding of emotion on Piagetian understanding of mental development. The work of Damon and Hart (1982, 1988) and of Case (1985; Marini & Case, 1994) highlighted the possibility that the set of skills involved in psychological mindedness may be a developmentally achieved capacity based on the more general thrust of cognitive development demonstrated by Piaget. Marini and Case described the rationale behind this approach as follows. Case and other neo-Piagetians focused on two aspects of Piaget's thinking: (a) "the notion that adolescent thought is more abstract than earlier forms of thinking" and (b) "the notion that the process of abstraction involves the construction of a higher-order system, through the integration of two lower-order ones" (Marini & Case, 1994, p. 148). Thus, the hallmark of adolescent thought—complexity—should be evident in nonsocial reasoning about physical causality and linguistic relationships, and in reasoning about others' motives and attributes. Marini and Case administered a test of reasoning about physical causality (the balance beam task, which requires subjects to predict which way a balance beam with nine pegs would tip, depending on the placement of weights on the various pegs) and a "personality diagnosis" task. This task challenged subjects to predict the actions of protagonists in a series of stories involving increasingly complex descriptions of behavior. The most complex story describes a girl, Cathy, in a series of situations: (a) as assertive, (b) as accomodating, and (c) then as slipping and ruining her pants while she was returning home on the bus. The test question was "When she got off the bus a person approached her asking for directions. What do you think Cathy did? Why?" (p. 153). The responses of twenty subjects (gender not specified) at Grades 5, 7, 10, and 13 (for a total of 80 responses) were coded using a four-level coding scheme reflecting the subjects' ability to incorporate the traits and mood-altering experiences into their prediction of what the stories' protagonists would do. At Level 0, subjects "had to mention a personality trait (e.g., assertiveness) that took into account both the context and behavior of the main character." At Level 1, subjects had to abstract a trait from the character's behavior (e.g., assertiveness) and use it to predict behavior in the second situation. At Level 2, two traits had to be used to account for the character's behavior. At Level 3, both traits and mood-altering situations had to be used; subjects "had to show evidence of resolving the conflict between opposing tendencies by taking into account the effects of both of the traits and the most likely mood of the story character" (p. 152). A Level 3 response might be that Cathy hesitated when asked for directions because she was acommodating, but since she had delayed her return home to help others already, and she was upset that she had ruined her pants, her assertiveness won out and she declined to offer directions. Marini and Case reported interrater reliability of .94 for the coding of this relatively simple, structured story task. As expected, there was strong evidence of developmental progression in the personality diagnosis task with, for example, 30% of 7th graders, 75% of 10th graders, and 95% of 13th graders reaching Level 2. Marini and Case found an age-corrected correlation between the cognitive task and the personality diagnosis task of .51 ($p < .01$), similar to the .40 correlation found by Carroll and Steward (1984) between cognitive tests and a variant of psychological mindedness directed towards the self. Marini and Case's work is a good example of how psychological mindedness towards others could be assessed, although it does not examine psychological mindedness towards the self.

Our interests developed in the tradition of the studies of children's understanding affect and of others previously described. However, our interest was specifically the development of psychological mindedness in relation to the self and to others in conjunction with nonsocial aspects of cognitive development. We prepared measures of psychological mindedness toward the self and towards others, and of verbal and physical reasoning, and tested them in a sample of 179 children and adolescents, approximately one half boys, one half girls, including sixty 5th graders (mean age, 10.4 years), sixty 8th graders (mean age, 13.6 years) and fifty-nine 12th graders (mean age 17.7 years; R. Hatcher, S. Hatcher, Berlin, Okla, & Richards, 1990).

CONCEPTUAL DEFINITION

Psychological mindedness is the capacity to achieve psychological understanding of oneself and others. We view psychological mindedness as a complex capacity, acquired during the course of development. Psychological mindedness is built on both cognitive and emotional skills, and it can be seen as a term characterizing children's ability to make sense of themselves or the world in psychological terms. Further specification of this definition depends on how psychological understanding is defined, and different psychological theories, or different emphases within a general theory, could result in different conceptions of psychological mindedness. From a psychodynamic orientation, three lines of development in psychological mindedness are emphasized: (a) the growing understanding of internal, individual sources of motivation; (b) the developing ability to recognize the simultaneous presence of several, often conflicting motivations; and (c) the awareness of the use of self-deception to protect oneself against painful self-awareness. As noted, many researchers recognized a developmental progression in accounting for an individual's motivation beginning with external, situational causes, and proceeding toward increasingly complex, internal causes such as traits, attitudes, moods, wishes, and fears. The research previously described also shows that children develop the capacity to recognize the simultaneous presence of several affects; Marini and Case (1994) showed that adolescents can recognize several interacting motives in others. None of the studies described concerning affects included the idea that we protect ourselves against painful or frightening feelings, wishes or ideas by various defensive maneuvers, but this is an important aspect of psychodynamic self-understanding.

We also distinguish between psychological mindedness toward others and toward oneself. Understanding of others, we believe, is in some respects easier than understanding oneself, although understanding others requires the ability to conceptualize the mind of the other, and to create an empathic interpretation of the traits, attitudes, moods, wishes, fears, and so forth, of the other. Marini and Case (1994) demonstrated how, in the course of development, adolescents acquire the cognitive ability to create increasingly sophisticated interpretations of others' affective and motivational states. However, it is a different and less difficult task to see others' motives and affects than it is to see our own. For example, conflicts between different motives, or efforts to get free of painful affects, make it harder for us to see these motives and affects in ourselves than it is for others to see them in us. Thus we can develop a familiar and enduring picture of ourselves that protects us from seeing other, more conflictual features in ourselves. From a cognitive standpoint, reflexive self-awareness requires taking our own thought processes, motives, and feelings as objects of thought. In Piagetian terms, this requires formal operation on our formal operations (Piaget, 1976).

In addition to understanding psychological mindedness as a set of skills at a given level of development, we are also interested in how children achieve the capacity to understand others and themselves. We recognize that in a developmental framework, psychological mindedness will progress from the simple to the complex as the child matures. For example, younger children generally demonstrate unsophisticated ways of understanding themselves and others, often using stock descriptions (e.g., "he was nice because he's a nice guy") that show little capacity to think psychologically at all, much less to conceive of a complex inner mind. In our sample of sixty grade 5 boys and girls, approximately one half used these stock phrases to account for the behavior of a fairy tale character, and the others were able to demonstrate their own viewpoint (still using simple single traits) about psychological issues that the character faced. In a self-understanding task, one half the children were simply unable to see any link between a story they made up and their own personal psychology.

As children begin the transition to adolescence in about eighth grade (13 to 14 years of age), their capacity to think psychologically about themselves and others increases. Many are able to develop their own viewpoint about psychological issues they and others face, but very few achieve a model of the mind that recognizes the presence of interacting, internal motives (Marini & Case, 1994). Even these few, however, are unable to show an ability to think of themselves in this way. By the time adolescents reach grade 12, from one quarter to one half are able, at times, to think of others in the complex internal terms we associate with mature psychological mindedness. However, only about 15% of them demonstrate recognition of their own multiple, internal, and interacting motives, recognition we associate with the definition of psychological mindedness previously given.

OPERATIONAL DEFINITION

Our method for assessing psychological mindedness involves two different procedures, one to assess psychological mindedness toward others, the other toward the self.

Assessment of Psychological Mindedness Towards Others

Psychological mindedness toward others was assessed using two fairy tales as stimuli. Because we wanted to give the same stimuli to younger children and to late adolescents, it was necessary to find materials that could be understood by a wide age range. We selected two well-known fairy tales because they are familiar to younger children, but still contain a reasonably complex set of psychological issues. We also thought it unlikely that these stories would have been previously discussed from a psychological point of view. A description of the procedure follows.

The same procedure was followed for the two fairy tales, *Cinderella* and *The Emperor's New Clothes.* (Fairy tales were simplified one-page versions of these well-know stories.)The first story was read aloud twice by a research assistant to groups of 15–25 students. The stories were presented in counterbalanced design—one half of the groups heard *Cinderella* first, followed by questions relating to *Cinderella,* and one half heard *The Emperor's New Clothes* story first. During the readings, each child could follow the text of the fairy tales in their own booklet. After the reading, the research assistant posed the first of the three questions regarding the first story. For example, if *Cinderella* was read first, the assistant asked, "What kind of person is Cinderella? Describe her." The questions were also contained in the child's booklet, and the child was given 5 minutes to write his or her answer to the first question before the next one was read. The second question was, "Why was Cinderella so nice to people who were mean to her? Write some reasons why she acted that way." The third question was "Why were the stepsisters so mean to Cinderella? Write some reasons why they were so mean." The second story was presented in the same manner. The questions posed following *The Emperor's New Clothes* were as follows:

1. "What kind of person is the Emperor? Describe him."
2. "Why did he believe that he was wearing a beautiful new outfit? Write some reasons why he believed that."
3. "The little boy was the one to say that the emperor wasn't wearing any clothes. Why did he say it instead of a grown-up? Write some reasons why it was the little boy who spoke up."

The answers to the questions were rated separately, using a four-category rating scale (see Table 3.1) refined through pilot work with small samples of 5 subjects at each age level. The pilot work was designed to determine specifically how children would answer the questions, and to identify clear progressions in the child's descriptions of the fairy tale characters. Raters were trained to reliability using the pilot data in four 2-hour training meetings. It is likely that coding would be easier and more reliable with individual administration, where the examiner is free to ask the child to

TABLE 3.1

Fairy Tale Coding Scale: Psychological Mindedness Toward Others

Scale Category	Example
1. Unable to engage the task	"I don't know."
2a. Subject gives a direct quote or paraphrase of the story.	"They would think he was stupid if he told them he couldn't see it."
2b. Subject uses simple, stock phrases and ideas. These reflect "cliched" ideas that offer little new understanding beyond the story's own logic.	"She forgave him because she was nice [repeating the story's description]." "Two wrongs don't make a right."
3. Subject uses a different perspective that does not simply repeat the point of view of the story, but without recognizing the interacting motives or complex combinations seen at the next level.	"She was afraid of being punished" "She didn't want to act like her stepsisters." "Her parents taught her to be nice."
4. Subject gives an account using higher level, abstract concepts. Interacting psychological entities are recognized; concepts of internal conflict, need for self-deception are used; combinations of traits that work together are seen.	"He did not want to believe he was unfit to be emperor, and by believing he saw the cloth, he could believe he was fit to be emperor." "She was so shy and reserved that she was afraid of them."

Note. The scale is slightly modified from R. Hatcher, S. Hatcher et al., 1990. Reprinted with permission.

expand his or her answers so that a full sense of the child's understanding of the motives of the characters in the fairy tale could be elicited. Thus, some familiarity with the rating scales would be valuable for examiners. Furthermore, tape recording or transcribing the child's responses would yield more detailed and focused answers because the child would not be required to translate his or her answers into written words. However, the time and financial constraints of the relatively large number of subjects ($N = 179$) made individual administration unfeasible.

Assessment of Psychological Mindedness Toward Self

Psychological mindedness toward the self is assessed in a two-step process. First, the child is asked to write stories to two TAT-type cards. For our study we used two photographs. The first photograph shows an 8- to 10-year-old child and of indeterminate gender looking at a broken guitar. The second photograph shows a mother and three small children embracing in the foreground. In the background, a man sits at a table eating. These two evocative photographs were presented separately, and the child was asked to write a story about each one. The subjects were instructed to include a beginning, middle, and end in the story, and to tell what the people in the story are thinking and feeling. After both stories were written, the children were asked to reflect on their first story and write what they felt the story might tell about themselves, and to explain the links between the story and their ideas about what the story reveals about them. The same directions were given regarding the story written for the second picture. These questions are then rated on a six-item scale (see Table 3.2). Because the group

TABLE 3.2

Picture Story Coding Scale: Psychological Mindedness Toward the Self

Scale Category	Examples
1. The subject denies the relevance of the question	"This story does not relate to me at all."
2. The subject negates or denies a personal meaning of his or her response	"The character in this story is rebellious but this not true of me."
3a. The subject associates with the theme but does not reflect on his or her own thoughts, feelings or motives.	"I like war stories."
3b. The subject simply associates to a moral to the story without further reflection on himself or herself.	"I just have to find the good things in a situation."
4a. The subject straightforwardly attributes feelings to himself or herself in response to the task instructions.	"I am a caring person [as the character is described in the story]."
4b. The subject identifies with the character in the story with regard to one or more motivations for writing the story, but without seeing an interaction among them.	"I also feel that people don't like me."
5. The subject's self-observation contains a complex set of motives with interactions among them. The subject recognizes his or her ambivalence or a conflict between two motives.	"Like the girl in the story, I am jealous of my baby sister, even though I also love her."
6. The subject understands his or her defensive maneuvers. "I, too, want to hide it when I am angry at others so I always act agreeable."	

Note. Scale is slightly modified from R. Hatcher, S. Hatcher et al., 1990. Reprinted with permission.

administration method prevented clarifying questions from the administrator, rating was more difficult than it would be with individual administration.

PSYCHOMETRIC PROPERTIES

Reliability

Psychological Mindedness Toward Others. Scores for the fairy tales (three scores each, six scores total) were produced by sets of three raters. The mean interrater reliabilities between each rater pair and each score was $\kappa = .82$ (*Cinderella*) and $\kappa = .85$ (*Emperor*). Internal consistencies may be considered from two vantage points. First, the mean scores of the two fairy tales tasks can be compared through correlation. Here, $r = .79, p < .001, N = 179$. Second, the complete set of six scores (three from each task) may be viewed as a set of items assessing psychological mindedness toward others, whose internal consistency may be estimated by Cronbach's alpha (Cronbach, 1966). Here, $\alpha = .83$. These figures suggest that the fairy tales yield a satisfactorily reliable and internally consistent measure of psychological mindedness toward others.

Psychological Mindedness Toward Self. Scores for the question asked of each TAT-style card ("write what you think the story might tell about yourself") were produced by sets of three raters. Mean interrater reliability was $\kappa = .79$ for the first card and $\kappa = .69$ for the second. The correlation between the scores from the two cards was .62. With just two questions, this correlation is the best estimate of the internal consistency of the TAT method. The TAT-style assessment, consisting of only two scores, yields a less stable measure of psychological mindedness toward the self than does the six-item fairy-tale procedure, because any test's reliability is improved with more items (Kline, 1993).

We expect that psychological mindedness toward the self would be a more volatile and difficult capacity to satisfactorily assess because the task requires reflection on one's own personality and conflicts. Thus, a larger sample of these reflections would be needed to develop a measure with substantial internal consistency. We discuss this issue further in the concluding section.

Construct Validity There was no significant correlation between the measures of psychological mindedness to self and to others for five of the six combinations of grade level and gender in our sample of 179 children in 5th, 8th, and 12th grade (*r*s for 5th; 8th; and 12th-grade boys: -.30, .02, .26, respectively; for 5th and 8th grade girls, .13 and –.02). For 12th grade girls, $r = .47, p < .01$. Because there is good to moderate internal consistency for each measure and a reasonable range of scores, this failure to find a significant correlation is unlikely to be due to unreliable measurement. This finding raises interesting questions about the nature of these two forms of psychological mindedness. We note that McCallum and Piper's (1990) Psychological Mindedness Assessment Procedure (PMAP) assesses what we would call psychological mindedness towards others. The PMAP involves asking patients questions about a (single) videotaped interaction between a patient and therapist (portrayed by actors). This procedure appears to have the same rationale as our fairy tale procedure. McCallum and Piper found good predictive validity to productive work in a group therapy setting, where the work involves skills tapped by the PMAP, but they found no link to individual outcome. There may be reason to think that psychological mindedness toward the self would be a better predictor of individual outcome in treatments whose effect is presumed to be mediated by individual insight gained in a group setting.

We note that the girls in our sample scored higher than the boys on the measures of psychological mindedness towards others and towards self at all grade levels, with ANOVAs yielding $F(1, 178) = 12.24, p < .006$, and $F(1, 174) = 5.88, p < .01$, respectively. There is some evidence that the measures of psychological mindedness are related to more general measures of cognitive ability across age groups. Because there were significant differences between boys and girls on the psychological mindedness measures, these relations are examined separately. Partial correlations controlling for age were conducted between a composite measure of abstract reasoning ability (including spatial–logic and verbal reasoning) and the measures of psychological mindedness. For boys, the partial correlation between abstract reasoning and psychological mindedness to others is $r(12.3) = .29$, $p < .01$; to self, $r(12.3) = .24$, $p < .03$, $N = 83$. For girls, the partial correlation between abstract reasoning ability and psychological mindedness to others is $r(12.3) = .20$, $p = .054$, $N = 90$; to self, it is nonsignificant. These results suggest that psychological mindedness to others has a stronger link to established developmental cognitive markers than does psychological mindedness to self. This is not surprising, considering the difficulty of self-understanding and (as is be discussed later) the problem of sampling self-referential material. Marini and Case (1994), using individual administration of a spatial–logic task and a personality diagnosis task similar to our fairy tale task, found an age-corrected correlation of .51 in their sample of 80 5th through 12th graders.

RESEARCH USING THE MEASURE

Although there was a good deal of interest in our study from academic psychology, and some from clinicians, the scales have not been used in other research. A discussion of the study is presented in Cobb's (1992) textbook on adolescence.

The developmental hypothesis that empathy would increase following a training intervention was tested by teaching empathy to high school and college students using the concepts previously described. Enhanced teachability of empathy from early to later adolescence was demonstrated and the increased empathic sensibility occurred irrespective of gender (S. Hatcher et al., 1994).

SUMMARY

Our measures of psychological mindedness are reliable and demonstrate an interesting developmental line for psychological mindedness as a cognitive capacity. The measures can be administered in a group setting, although we recommend individual administration with inquiry and observer recording of the responses to make scoring of the results easier and more reliable. There is good evidence to suggest the usefulness of distinguishing between psychological mindedness directed toward the self and towards others, and we speculate that self-reflective thought is more relevant to change in reflectively based treatments than is other-directed thought.

Of special concern is the issue of eliciting good and representative samples of psychological mindedness, particularly directed toward the self. This issue could be addressed for psychological mindedness to the self by eliciting responses to more TAT-style cards. Our method elicits TAT-style stories that may be viewed as fantasy productions. Depending on the stimulus value of the card, and the relevance of the stimulus to the individual's own conflicts, the fantasy generated by the subject will be more or less likely to contain significant personal issues. To the extent that the fantasy is not personally relevant, the subject will have difficulty presenting a personal understanding of it, and the test will be less valid and reliable. Thus, including a range of cards would improve the reliability and validity of the test (Kline, 1993). On the other hand, we expect that the more conflictual these fantasies, the more difficult it will be to think in depth about them. For clinical and research purposes, we recommend the use of a range of picture stimuli that pull for a variety of personally relevant issues, such as depressive feeling, demands for social interaction, ambitious wishes, competitive situations, and so on. Depending on the use to be made of the results, our procedure could be adapted for use with standard TAT administration in a clinical psychological test battery, using a number of cards and assessing the person's conflict areas and the person's ability to reflect on them. As a standard test for pretherapy screening, we recommend using several cards to increase internal consistency.

The assessment of psychological mindedness directed toward others is more straightforward than is the assessment of psychological mindedness directed toward the self, as it does not require self-reflection. However, some subjects may find that the issues involved in the stimuli touch on painful issues existing between themselves and important others. The activation of conflict may make the task of recognizing others' motives more difficult. A valid assessment of this skill would require presenting the subject with a variety of personality qualities and situations for observation.

FUTURE DIRECTIONS

The methodology used to assess psychological mindedness in children is now available for further work, and the methods can be adapted for use in clinical settings. It will be especially useful in clinical settings that stress insight-oriented work. It is also potentially useful in preventive work and in community settings where both empathic concern for others and self-observational acumen can serve to facilitate interpersonal cooperation and tolerance.

Children's capacity for empathy, although related to the issue of psychological mindedness to others, may be distinguished from it. We view psychological mindedness as a more encompassing concept that is greater than the sum of its parts (empathy and self-observation). On the research side, the relationship of the construct of empathy to the construct of psychological mindedness should be further examined.

REFERENCES

Astington, J. W. (1993). *The child's discovery of the mind*. Cambridge, MA: Harvard University Press.

Baron-Cohen, S. (1995). *Mindblindness: An essay on autism and theory of mind*. Cambridge, MA: MIT Press.

Blum, H. P. (1979). The curative and creative aspects of insight. *Journal of the American Psychoanalytic Association, 27* (Suppl.), 41–70.

Carroll, J. J., & Steward, M. S. (1984). The role of cognitive development in children's understandings of their own feelings. *Child Development, 55*, 1486–1492.

Case, R. (1985). *Intellectual development: Birth to adulthood*. New York: Academic Press.

Cobb, N. J. (1992). *Adolescence: Continuity, change, and diversity*. Mountain View, CA: Mayfield.

Cronbach, L. J. (1951). Coefficient alpha and the internal structure of tests. *Psychometrika, 6*, 297–334.

Damon, W., & Hart, D. (1982). The development of self understanding from infancy through adolescence. *Child Development, 53*, 841–864.

Damon, W., & Hart, D. (1988). *Self-understanding in childhood and adolescence*. Cambridge, MA: Cambridge University Press.

Donaldson, S. K., & Westerman, M. A. (1986). Development of children's understanding of ambivalence and causal theories of emotions. *Developmental Psychology, 22*, 655–662.

Freud, A. (1979). The role of insight in psychoanalysis and psychotherapy-introduction. *Journal of the American Psychoanalytic Association, 27* (Suppl.), 3–8.

Greenberg, M. T., Kusche, C. A., Cook, E. T., & Quamma, J. P. (1995). Promoting emotional competence in school-aged children: The effects of the PATHS curriculum. *Development and Psychopathology, 7*, 17–136.

Harter, S., & Buddin, B. J. (1987). Children's understanding of the simultaneity of two emotions: A five-stage developmental acquisition sequence. *Developmental Psychology, 23*, 388–399.

Hatcher, R. (1981). Insight and self-observation. In S. Slipp (Ed.), *Curative factors in dynamic psychotherapy* (pp. 71–90). New York: McGraw-Hill.

Hatcher, R., Hatcher, S., Berlin, M., Okla, K., & Richards, J. (1990). Psychological mindedness and abstract reasoning in late childhood and adolescence: An exploration using new instruments. *Journal of Youth and Adolescence, 19*, 307–326.

Hatcher, S. (Ed.). (1995). *Peer programs on the college campus: Theory, practice, and "the voice of the peers."* San Jose, CA: Resource Publications.

Hatcher, S., Nadeau, M., Walsh, L., Reynolds, M., Galea, J., & Marz, K. (1994). The teaching of empathy for high school and college students: Testing Rogerian methods with the interpersonal reactivity index. *Adolescence, 29*, 961–974

Hoffman, L. (1989). The psychoanalytic process and the development of insight in child analysis: A case study. *Psychoanalytic Quarterly, 58*, 63–80.

Kennedy, H. (1979). The role of insight in child analysis: A developmental viewpoint. *Journal of the American Psychoanalytic Association, 27* (Suppl.), 9–28.

Kline, P. (1993). *The handbook of psychological testing*. New York: Routledge.

Marini, Z., & Case, R. (1994). The development of abstract reasoning about the physical and social world. *Child Development, 65*, 147–159.

McCallum, M., & Piper, W. E. (1990). The psychological mindedness assessment procedure. *Psychological Assessment, 2*, 412–418.

Piaget, J. (1976). *The grasp of consciousness*. Cambridge, MA: Harvard University Press.

Piaget, J. (1965). *The moral judgment of the child*. New York: Free Press.
Piaget, J. (1981). *Intelligence and affectivity: Their relationship during child development*. Palo Alto, CA: Annual Reviews.
Wellman, H. M. (1990). *The child's theory of mind*. Cambridge, MA: MIT Press.

Chapter 4

Alexithymia

Graeme J. Taylor
Helen L. Taylor
University of Toronto

The *alexithymia* construct encompasses a cluster of cognitive and affective characteristics that are virtually the obverse of several central features of psychological mindedness. The construct emerged from clinical observations over several decades that certain patients respond poorly to psychoanalysis and other insight-oriented psychotherapies because of a limited ability to describe and differentiate affects and to create fantasies. Such patients were variously labeled as infantile personalities (Ruesch, 1948), emotional illiterates (Freedman & Sweet, 1954), normopaths (McDougall, 1980b), normotics (Bollas, 1987) and anti-analysands (McDougall, 1980a). The formulation and subsequent validation of the alexithymia construct, however, has provided a precise definition of the cognitive–affective style of these patients, and permitted empirical investigation of the underlying significance of this style and its relationship with other personality traits (Taylor, 1994).

This chapter first reviews the origin and theoretical basis of the alexithymia construct, and then describes the psychometric properties of the Toronto Alexithymia Scale (TAS) and its most recent revision, the Twenty-Item Toronto Alexithymia Scale (TAS–20). Selected clinical and experimental research using these self-report scales is also reviewed, and a brief case vignette is presented to illustrate some implications of the construct and a clinical application of the TAS–20.

ORIGIN OF THE ALEXITHYMIA CONSTRUCT

The concept of alexithymia evolved from clinical observations that were made initially on patients suffering from classical psychosomatic diseases.[1] During the late 1940s, Ruesch (1948) and MacLean (1949) observed that many of these patients show an apparent inability to verbalize feelings. Ruesch noted also that such patients tend to be unimaginative and socially conforming, use direct physical action or bodily channels for emotional expression, and respond poorly to insight-oriented psychotherapy.

A few years later, Horney (1952) and Kelman (1952) reported similar characteristics in certain psychiatric patients whom they were finding difficult to treat psychoanalytically because of a lack of emotional awareness, paucity of inner experiences, minimal interest in dreams, concreteness of thinking, and externalized style of living. These psychiatric patients were prone to developing psychosomatic symptoms and often engaged in binge eating, alcohol abuse, or other compulsive behaviors, seemingly to avoid experiencing feelings of inner emptiness.

A group of French psychoanalysts working in the field of psychosomatic medicine subsequently reported a similar operational thinking style (which they referred to as *la pensée opératoire*) and mode of existence (*la vie opératoire*) among physically ill patients (Marty & de M'Uzan, 1963; Marty, de M'Uzan, & David, 1963). In the absence of an inner life of feelings and fantasies, these patients were preoccupied with physical symptoms and the minute details of external events, and they showed an affectless way of relating to other people.

The significance of these various reports was not fully appreciated until the early 1970s, when Shands (1975) and Nemiah and Sifneos (1970) began to systematically investigate the cognitive and affective style of patients suffering from one or more of the classical psychosomatic diseases. The results of their investigations seemed to confirm that many psychosomatic patients have a marked difficulty describing subjective feelings, an impoverished fantasy life, and a cognitive style that is literal, utilitarian, and externally orientated. Sifneos (1973) coined the term alexithymia (from the Greek: a = lack, lexis = word, thymos = emotion) to denote this cluster of cognitive and affective characteristics. He concluded that alexithymic patients should be treated with supportive rather than interpretive psychotherapy (Sifneos, 1975).

Quite independently, but almost simultaneously with the work of the psychosomatic researchers, Krystal (1968) and Krystal and Raskin (1970) were reporting similar characteristics in patients with posttraumatic states and in patients with substance use disorders. Wurmser (1974) also described deficits in the verbal affective expression and imaginal capacity of drug addicts, which he referred to as *hyposymbolization*. And in the field of eating disorders, Bruch (1973) observed that patients with anorexia nervosa lack an awareness of inner experiences and often are unable to describe their feelings. For these and related reasons, Bruch

[1]The so-called classical psychosomatic diseases are peptic ulcer, bronchial asthma, essential hypertension, thyrotoxicosis, ulcerative colitis, rheumatoid arthritis, and neurodermatitis. These seven diseases were selected for psychoanalytic investigation by Alexander (1950) and other pioneers in the field of psychosomatic medicine. At that time they were of uncertain etiology.

advised against attempting to give insight to eating disordered patients through interpretations of unconscious motivations; Krystal (1982) later concluded that "Alexithymia is possibly the most important single factor diminishing the success of psychoanalysis and psychodynamic psychotherapy" (p. 364).

With increasing interest in the concept, alexithymia was selected as the main theme of the 11th European Conference on Psychosomatic Research held in Heidelberg, Germany in 1976 (Brautigam & von Rad, 1977). The presentations and discussions at that conference facilitated general agreement for a more precise formulation of the alexithymia construct to include the following salient features: (a) difficulty in identifying and describing feelings; (b) difficulty in distinguishing between feelings and the bodily sensations that accompany emotional arousal; (c) constricted imaginal processes, as evidenced by a paucity of fantasies; and (d) an externally orientated cognitive style (Nemiah, 1977; Nemiah, Freyberger, & Sifneos, 1976; Taylor, 1984; Taylor, Bagby, & Parker, 1991). Although some so-called alexithymic individuals appear to contradict this definition of the construct because they experience chronic dysphoria or manifest outbursts of weeping or rage, intensive questioning usually reveals that "they know very little about their own feelings and, in most instances, are unable to link them with memories, fantasies, or specific situations" (Taylor et al., 1991, p. 155).

Several additional characteristics were associated with alexithymia, including a tendency toward social conformity, an infrequent recollection of dreams, a somewhat stiff wooden posture, and a lack of facial emotional expressiveness (Sifneos, 1988; Taylor, 1984). However, these characteristics are not always present in alexithymic individuals and are not part of the definition of the construct; indeed, as we describe later, social conformity and the ability to recall dreams did not emerge as essential features of alexithymia in the process of developing the TAS and validating the construct (Taylor, Bagby, Ryan, & Parker, 1990). Clinical experience suggests that it is the quality of dreams rather than their recall that distinguishes alexithymia (Levitan, 1989; Taylor, 1987).

Even without these additional characteristics, alexithymia is obviously a multifaceted construct, as is the psychological mindedness construct as broadly defined by Conte et al. (1990). Although the salient features (or subordinate concepts) of the alexithymia construct can be distinguished conceptually, they are related logically: The ability to identify and communicate feelings to others is contingent on an ability to distinguish one's feelings from the bodily sensations that accompany emotional states; and an externally orientated cognitive style reflects an absence of inner thoughts and fantasies, as well as a low range of emotional expressiveness. As we outline later, validational research should demonstrate that the subordinate concepts of the construct can be measured separately and that they are related empirically (Carver, 1989).

THEORETICAL BASIS OF ALEXITHYMIA

Although there is consensus about the definition of the alexithymia construct, there was controversy and debate over its theoretical basis. The main issue is whether the so-called alexithymic characteristics reflect developmental deficits, underlying psychoneurotic conflicts, or the influence of social and cultural factors on emotional expressiveness.

In their early clinical reports, Ruesch (1948) and MacLean (1949) attributed a difficulty in verbalizing feelings to a developmental arrest that resulted in an inability to symbolically represent emotions. A deficit model was also subsequently proposed by Marty and de M'Uzan (1963) and by Nemiah (1977) for understanding la pensée opératoire and alexithymia. In contrast, Horney (1952) and Kelman (1952) attributed a paucity of inner experiences and difficulty in communicating feelings to strong defenses against unconscious neurotic conflicts. In more recent contributions, Bruch (1985), Krystal (1988), and Robbins (1989) de-emphasized the role of neurotic conflicts and focused on arrests in affect development and other ego functions; Knapp (1981, 1983), however, adhered to a drive–conflict–defense model of the mind, attributing alexithymic characteristics entirely to the use of denial, repression, avoidance, reaction formation, and externalization.

Some critics argued that alexithymia is merely a social and cultural phenomenon rather than a personality trait, and that the formulation of the construct reflects the emphasis of Western psychotherapy on psychological mindedness (Kirmayer, 1987; Prince, 1987). There is no doubt that the verbal expression of emotion is influenced by prevailing cultural attitudes and by constraints imposed by certain languages (Leff, 1977). It seems less likely, however, that the constricted imaginal processes component of the alexithymia construct could be explained merely by cultural influences. Preliminary evidence that alexithymia is not a culture-bound construct is provided by reports of alexithymia among Japanese patients (Fukunishi, Saito, & Ozaki, 1992) and Indian patients (Sriram, Chaturvedi, Gopinath, & Shanmugam, 1987) and, as we outline later, by the successful crossvalidation of the TAS and TAS–20 in several different cultures.

Given the poor response of alexithymic patients to traditional psychodynamic psychotherapy (Krystal, 1982), and findings from recent empirical research (see Taylor, Bagby, & Parker, 1993), we favor a deficit model rather than a neurotic conflict model for conceptualizing alexithymia. It is important to recognize, however, that such a theoretical position does not exclude roles for conflict and primitive defenses, or constraints on verbal emotional expression imposed by certain languages. Indeed, as with other types of psychic deficit, the presence of alexithymia is likely to both initiate conflict and intensify ordinary developmental conflicts (Killingmo, 1989). Furthermore, primitive psychological defenses, such as splitting, denial, and externalization, are invariably associated with developmental failures and regressions (Dorpat, 1985). Although empirical investigation of this issue is in its early phases, studies using the TAS or TAS–20 found alexithymia to be associated with the use of immature and maladaptive defenses rather than neurotic defenses (Schaffer, 1993; Taylor, Bagby, & Parker, 1997; Wastell, 1993; Wise, Mann, & Epstein, 1991).

Our understanding of the theoretical basis of alexithymia was greatly helped by the contributions of Krystal (1974, 1988) and Lane and Schwartz (1987), who formulated models depicting an epigenetic sequence of affect development. Based on an integration of psychoanalytic concepts of symbol formation and Piaget's (1967) stages of cognitive development, Lane and Schwartz's model proposes a developmental sequence of five levels of emotional awareness ranging from a simple awareness of undifferentiated bodily sensations only (Level 1) to an awareness of complex blends of feelings and a capacity to appreciate the emotional experience of others (Level 5). The progressive elevation of emotions during early development from a sensorimotor level of experience to increasingly higher levels of cognitive processing is of major importance for affect regulation. The higher levels allow the older child and adult to evaluate their responses to both internal and external stimuli, and also to intentionally communicate emotions symbolically via language and images. In addition, the mental representation of affective experiences of the self interacting with others fosters the creation of memories, fantasies, and dreams, which further help in containing and modulating states of emotional arousal (Brown, 1993; Mayes & Cohen, 1992).

According to Lane and Schwartz's (1987) model, individual differences in the ability to identify and differentiate subjective feelings are explained by variations in the complexity of cognitive schemata and linguistic and other symbolic representations of emotions. Thus, alexithymic individuals are assumed to have suffered developmental arrests or regressions so that their emotions continue to be experienced at the lower levels of this hierarchical model of affect development. As a dimensional construct, severely alexithymic individuals are likely to focus on and amplify the physiological component of emotional arousal, or to employ action as an attempt to relieve unpleasant emotional tension. This is thought to contribute to their tendency to somatize, and to exhibit compulsive behaviors such as binge eating and substance abuse (Barsky & Klerman, 1983; Lane & Schwartz, 1987; Taylor, 1992). Individuals with mild or moderate alexithymia are still likely to manifest a limited emotional vocabulary and a proneness to undifferentiated states of unpleasant emotional arousal.

The salient features of the alexithymia construct are thought to reflect a deficit in the cognitive processing and regulation of emotions. This led to the suggestion (Taylor, 1994; Taylor et al., 1997) that the disorders with which alexithymia is most strongly associated be reconceptualized as disorders of emotion (affect) regulation. These conceptualizations of alexithymia are in advance of, but similar to, recent ideas of Salovey and

Mayer (Salovey, Hsee, & Mayer, 1993; Salavey & Mayer, 1989–90), who formulated the broader construct of *emotional intelligence*, which refers to "a set of skills hypothesized to contribute to the accurate appraisal and expression of emotion in oneself and others, the effective regulation of emotion in self and others, and the use of feelings to motivate, plan, and achieve in one's life" (p. 185).

We now consider self-report measures of alexithymia.

THE TORONTO ALEXITHYMIA SCALE

The TAS was developed by Taylor, Ryan, and Bagby (1985) using a combined rational and empirical approach to scale construction. Although several self-report alexithymia scales were already developed (including the MMPI Alexithymia Scale, the Schalling–Sifneos Personality Scale, and the Revised Schalling–Sifneos Personality Scale), these scales were developed without proper concern for contemporary standards of test construction (Golden, Sawicki, & Franzen, 1984; Nunnally, 1978). Not surprisingly, numerous studies showed that they lack adequate reliability and validity (Bagby, Parker, & Taylor, 1991; Bagby, Taylor, & Atkinson, 1988; Bagby, Taylor, & Ryan, 1986; Norton, 1989; Parker, Taylor, Bagby, & Thomas, 1991; Taylor & Bagby, 1988).

In constructing the TAS, Taylor et al. (1985) initially reviewed the literature on alexithymia and then defined five content areas thought to reflect the substantive domain of the construct. Based on these content areas, 41 self-descriptive statements were written to be rated on a 5-point Likert scale ranging from 1 (*strongly disagree*) to 5 (*strongly agree*) with one half of the items positively keyed and one half negatively keyed to control for response set. These items were administered to 542 undergraduate students. Following item analysis and exploratory factor analysis, 26 items were selected for the final version of the scale based on high item–total correlations, low correlations with a measure of social desirability, and significant loadings on factors theoretically consistent with the alexithymia construct.

The final 26-item TAS demonstrated adequate internal consistency (Cronbach's alpha = .79), a split-half reliability of .672, and good test–retest reliability over 1-week ($r = .82$, $p < .001$) and 5-week ($r = .75$, $p < .001$) intervals. Subsequent testing with an Indian dialect (Kannada) translation of the TAS yielded a 3-month test–retest reliability of .77 (Sriram, Chaturvedi, Gopinath, & Subbakrishna, 1987); a Finnish translation showed an 8-month test–retest reliability of .78 (Kauhanen, Julkunen, & Salonen, 1992b).

Factor analysis of the TAS using principal factor extraction with a varimax rotation produced a four-factor solution congruent with the theoretical conceptualization of alexithymia as a multifaceted construct. As outlined by Taylor et al. (1985), a scree test was performed, and the factors retained were those with an eigenvalue greater than 1. The four-factor solution accounted for 31.8% of the total variance. Factor 1, which accounted for 12.3% of the variance, comprised nine items referring to the ability to identify and describe feelings and to distinguish between feelings and the bodily sensations accompanying emotional arousal. Factor 2, accounting for 7.0% of the variance, comprised six items reflecting the ability to communicate feelings to other people. Factor 3, representing 6.4% of the variance, comprised five items assessing imaginal and daydreaming activity. Factor 4, accounting for 6.1% of the variance, comprised six items reflecting a preference for focusing on external events rather than on inner experiences. Although the first two factors (Difficulty Identifying and Distinguishing Between Feelings and Bodily Sensations, Difficulty Communicating Feelings) corresponded to the affective disturbance emphasized by Nemiah and Sifneos (1970); Factors 3 and 4 (Reduced Daydreaming, Externally Orientated Thinking) corresponded to the *pensée opératoire* initially described by Marty and de M'Uzan (1963). Social conformity did not emerge as a separate factor, and items referring to poor dream recall were eliminated on the basis of low item–total scale correlations or low item–factor scale correlations.

The four-factor structure of the TAS was subsequently crossvalidated in studies with both clinical and nonclinical populations (Bagby, Taylor, & Atkinson, 1988; Bagby, Taylor, Parker, & Loiselle, 1990) and was replicated with Finnish (Kauhanen et al., 1992b), Italian (Pasini, Delle Chiaie, Seripa, & Ciani, 1992), Kannada (Sriram, Chaturvedi, Gopinath, & Subbakrishna, 1987), and Spanish (Rodrigo & Lusiardo, 1992; Rodrigo, Lusiardo, & Normey, 1989) translations of the scale. The TAS showed adequate internal consistency in all of these studies.[2]

Some scale developers may question the findings of adequate estimates of internal consistency in a multifactorial scale. When evaluating the TAS, however, one must consider the theoretical conceptualization of alexithymia as a multifaceted construct composed of several logically related subordinate concepts. In measuring such a broad and multifaceted construct, "a scale can reach generally acceptable levels of internal consistency and homogeneity and still yield multiple factors" (Briggs & Cheek, 1986, p. 110).

Convergent and Discriminant Validity

The convergent and discriminant validity of the TAS were evaluated in college student samples in a series of studies examining the relationship of the scale with other personality measures. Given that the alexithymia construct is characterized in part by a paucity of inner experiences and an externally orientated cognitive style, it was expected that the TAS would

---

[2]The TAS is copyrighted by the American Psychosomatic Society, Inc. and is published in *Psychosomatic Medicine, 50*, 506–597, 1988.

correlate negatively with measures of psychological mindedness (i.e., responsiveness to inner needs, motives, and experiences of self) and need-for-cognition (i.e., the tendency to engage in effortful and analytical cognitive endeavors). In addition, given the reduced emotional expressiveness of alexithymic individuals and their limited engagement in imaginal activity, the TAS was expected to correlate negatively with a measure of anger expression and positively with a measure of minimally developed daydreaming. The TAS was expected not to correlate with measures of constructs theoretically unrelated to the alexithymia construct.

As anticipated, the TAS correlated negatively with the Psychological Mindedness (PY) scale of the California Psychological Inventory (Gough, 1969) ($r = -.334, p < .001$), negatively with the Need for Cognition Scale (Short Form, Cacioppo, Petty, & Kao, 1984) ($r = -.421, p < .001$) (Bagby et al., 1986), and negatively with the Anger-Expression Scale (Spielberger et al., 1985) ($r = -.35, p < .001$). The TAS also correlated positively (Bagby, Taylor, & Parker, 1988) with the Poor Attentional Control subscale ($r = .46, p < .001$) of the Short Imaginal Processes Inventory (Huba, Singer, Anhensel, & Antrobus, 1982). Discriminant validity of the TAS was demonstrated by an absence of correlations with several subscales of the Basic Personality Inventory (Jackson, 1974) including denial (which is equivalent to social desirability), interpersonal problems, alienation, and deviation (Bagby et al., 1986).

Overlapping with the constructs of alexithymia and psychological mindedness is the construct of *private self-consciousness* (see chap. 5), which was defined as the "habitual attendance to one's thoughts, motives, and feelings" (Turner, Scheier, Carver, & Ickes, 1978). In further testing of the convergent validity of the TAS, Loiselle and Dawson (1988) examined the relationship of the scale with the Private Self-Consciousness subscale (PSC) of the Self-Consciousness Scale (Fenigstein, Scheier, & Buss, 1975). In a sample of undergraduate university students, the TAS correlated negatively with the PSC ($r = -.23$, $p < .001$); as one might anticipate, this association was accounted for by the reduced daydreaming Factor 3 ($r = -.36$) and the externally orientated thinking Factor 4 ($r = -.47$) of the TAS.

Criterion Validity

The criterion validity of the TAS was supported by the discrimination of behavioral medicine outpatients designated alexithymic from those designated nonalexithymic on the basis of objectively rated clinical interviews (Taylor et al., 1988). Although alexithymia is generally regarded as a dimensional construct, data from this study were used to establish preliminary TAS cutoff scores to facilitate comparative studies among diverse populations. Individuals scoring ≥ 74 on the TAS are considered alexithymic; those scoring ≤ 62 are considered nonalexithymic.

Relationship with Measures of Ego Strength, Somatization, and Dysphoria

Given that alexithymic individuals are considered unresponsive to insight-oriented psychotherapies, it was expected that the TAS would correlate negatively with the MMPI Ego Strength scale (Es; Barron, 1953), a test that was designed to predict successful response to psychotherapy. The Es is also considered a useful predictor of personal adaptability and resourcefulness (Graham, 1987), characteristics said to be lacking in alexithymic individuals. In a sample of undergraduate university students, the TAS correlated negatively with the Es ($r = -.45$, $p < .001$; Bagby, Taylor, & Parker, 1988). Similarly, Taylor, Parker and Bagby (1990) found that among men with substance use disorders, those who scored in the alexithymic range on the TAS scored significantly lower on the Es than did those who scored in the nonalexithymic range.

Because of the alleged deficit in affect regulation and the tendency of alexithymic individuals to focus on and amplify the somatic component of emotional arousal (Barsky & Klerman, 1983; Lane & Schwartz, 1987), positive correlations were also expected between the TAS and measures of somatization and general dysphoria, including anxiety and depression. This was demonstrated in samples of college students and psychiatric outpatients, and in men with psychoactive substance dependence (Bagby, Taylor, & Atkinson, 1988; Bagby et al., 1986; Taylor, Parker, & Bagby, 1990; Taylor, Parker, Bagby, & Acklin, 1992).

Although several studies reported low or moderate magnitude positive correlations between the TAS and measures of anxiety and depression, we believe that these findings reflect the alexithymic individual's proneness to negative affectivity because of a reduced ability to modulate states of emotional arousal. Some investigators (e.g., Haviland, Hendryx, Cummings, Shaw, & MacMurray, 1991; Hendryx, Haviland, & Shaw, 1991) suggested that for some individuals, alexithymia may be a state phenomenon secondary to anxiety or depression. Findings from longitudinal studies, however, are more consistent with our view of alexithymia as a stable personality trait. For example, although Haviland, Shaw, Cummings, and MacMurray (1988) found the expected moderate positive correlation between TAS scores and Beck Depression Inventory (BDI) scores in a sample of newly abstinent male alcoholic inpatients, retesting after 3 weeks of treatment showed a significant reduction in BDI scores (Beck, Ward, Mendelson, Mock, & Erbaugh, 1961) but no significant change in the mean TAS score. Similarly, in a 1-year follow-up study of general hospital psychiatric outpatients, Salminen, Saarijarvi, Aairela, and Tamminen (1994) found no significant change in TAS scores for both men and women, although there was a significant reduction in psychological distress as measured by the Brief Symptom Inventory (Derogatis & Melisaratos, 1983).

The finding of positive correlations between the TAS and measures of depression also raised questions as to whether alexithymia and depression are overlapping, rather than distinct constructs, and whether the TAS is truly assessing a domain that is distinguishable from depression. Parker, Bagby, and Taylor (1991) addressed these questions using factor analysis. In a sample of undergraduate university students, factor analysis of a correlation matrix comprising items from both the TAS and the BDI yielded a four-factor, orthogonal solution, and with the factors corresponding closely with their respective construct: Factor 1 comprised items from the BDI; Factor 2 comprised items assessing the ability to identify and distinguish between feelings and bodily sensations, as well as the ability to describe feelings to others; Factor 3 comprised items assessing daydreaming and other imaginal activity; and Factor 4 comprised items assessing externally orientated thinking. A similar factor solution was obtained in a sample of psychiatric outpatients. These findings support the view that the TAS measures a construct distinct and separate from depression.

Limitations of the TAS

Although the TAS demonstrated psychometric properties superior to those of other self-report measures of the alexithymia construct (Bagby, Taylor, & Atkinson, 1988), further evaluation of the scale revealed several shortcomings (Bagby, Parker et al., 1994; Taylor, Bagby, & Parker, 1992). The shortcomings of the TAS include: (a) a high correlation between the first two factors, with several items loading on both factors; (b) items comprising Factor 3 (the daydreaming factor) each show low magnitude corrected item–total correlations with the full TAS (less the item); in some studies this factor correlated negatively with the first factor; (c) an apparent social desirability response bias for the daydreaming items or a high potential for subjects in nonEnglish speaking cultures to misinterpret the meaning of these items; and (d) the correlation between the third and fourth factors is lower than expected. These observations questioned the independence of the first two factors, and also suggested that the items assessing daydreaming have little theoretical coherency with the other facets of the alexithymia construct.

With these considerations in mind, and recognizing that the development of a scale is an ongoing process that may lead to further understanding and refinement of a construct as well as to revisions to the scale, Bagby, Parker et al. (1994; Bagby, Taylor, & Parker, 1994; Taylor et al., 1992) conducted a further series of studies that led to the introduction of a revised and improved version of the TAS.

THE TWENTY-ITEM TORONTO ALEXITHYMIA SCALE

To expand the item pool, 17 new items were written and added to the 26 items from the TAS. Seven of the new items assessed the imaginal processing facet of the alexithymia construct, five new items pertained to externally orientated thinking, and five new items pertained to communicating feelings to others. From this new pool of 43 items, Taylor et al. (1992) initially constructed a revised 23-item scale (the TAS–R), which demonstrated good internal consistency, convergent and discriminant validity, and a stable and replicable two-factor structure. However, subsequent testing of the factor structure of the TAS–R using confirmatory factor analyses indicated that a three-factor structure provided a better match to the data than a two-factor structure. A second revision of the scale was therefore attempted; it resulted in the development of the TAS–20.

In the development of the TAS–20, all items directly assessing daydreaming and other imaginal activity were eliminated because of low corrected item–total correlations or high correlations with a measure of social desirability (Bagby, Parker, & Taylor, 1994). The TAS–20 demonstrated good internal consistency (Cronbach's alpha = .81) in a university student derivation sample, and test–retest reliability over a 3-week interval ($r = .77, p < .01$). Adequate estimates of internal consistency were also found in psychiatric outpatient and university student samples (Bagby, Parker et al., 1994; Parker, Bagby, Taylor, Endler, & Schmitz, 1993).

Principal axis factoring yielded a three-factor structure for the TAS–20, theoretically congruent with the multifaceted alexithymia construct: (F1) difficulty identifying feelings and distinguishing them from bodily sensations that accompany emotional arousal; (F2) difficulty describing feelings to others; and (F3) externally orientated thinking. The stability and replicability of this three-factor structure were demonstrated with both clinical and nonclinical populations by the use of confirmatory factor analysis (Bagby, Parker et al., 1994; Parker, Bagby et al., 1993). Although the first two factors of the TAS–20 still correlated highly, a three-factor model provided a better fit to the data obtained from several different samples than did either a two-factor model or a unidimensional model. In fact, the parameter estimates for the relationships among the TAS–20 factors provided further evidence that the revised scale surmounts the limitations of the original TAS and that the three factors reflect separate, yet empirically related, facets of the alexithymia construct. More recent studies crossvalidated the three-factor structure in different cultures with translated versions of the TAS–20 including Finnish (J. Julkunen, personal communication, May 5, 1995), German (Parker, Bagby et al., 1993), Hindi (Pandey, Mandal, Taylor, & Parker, 1996), Greek (T. Anagnostopoulou, personal communication, April 6, 1995), Italian (G. Invernizzi & C. Bressi, personal communication, May 19, 1994), Japanese (I. Fukinishi, personal communication, May 3, 1995), Korean (Hyo Deog Rim, personal communication, October 19, 1995), Portuguese (S. Fortes, personal communication, April 4, 1995), Lithuanian (M. Beresnevaite, personal communication, February 2, 1996), and Swedish (S. Carlsson, personal communication, October 20, 1994).[3]

Convergent and Discriminant Validity

The superiority of the TAS–20 over the original TAS is also demonstrated by the strength of its correlations with measures of psychological mindedness and other closely related constructs. As previously reported by Taylor (1994) and by Bagby, Taylor et al. (1994), convergent validity of the TAS–20 was demonstrated by the findings of strong negative correlations with the Psychological Mindedness Scale (PMS) developed by Conte et al. (1990; see chap. 1, $r = -.68, p < .01$) and the Need for Cognition Scale (Short Form; NCS (Cacioppo et. al., 1984); $r = -.55$, $p < .01$) in a sample of undergraduate university students, and by a negative correlation with the Affective Orientation Scale (AOS (Booth-Butterfield & Booth-Butterfield, 1990); $r = -.37$, $p < .01$) in a mixed sample of normal adults and victims and perpetrators of verbal or physical abuse (Yelsma, 1996). Closely related to the construct of emotional intelligence (Salovey & Mayer, 1989–90), the AOS assesses the extent to which individuals are aware of their affects and use this information to guide communication behavior (Booth-Butterfield & Booth-Butterfield, 1990). In addition to the full scale, these data demonstrated the validity of the three TAS–20 factor scales. All three factors of the TAS–20 correlated significantly and negatively with the NCS, PMS, and AOS, although the magnitudes of the correlations were lower than for the composite score (Taylor, 1994). Such findings support the theoretical view that alexithymia is composed of at least three lower order concepts that are subsumed within the broader and more important superordinate construct (see Carver, 1989).

Psychological mindedness may be considered a component of the much broader *openness to experience* construct, which has been conceptualized as one of five basic dimensions of human personality, the Big Five (McCrae & Costa, 1985, in press; McCrae & John, 1992). The elements of the Openness to Experience dimension include active imagination, aesthetic sensitivity, attentiveness to inner feelings, preference for variety, intellectual curiosity, and independence of judgment. Consistent with the view that alexithymia reflects the obverse of psychological mindedness, in a university student sample the TAS–20 correlated negatively with the Openness to Experience factor ($r = -.49, p < .01$) of the NEO Personality Inventory (Costa & McCrae, 1985), and with the subscales assessing openness to feelings ($r = -.55, p < .01$), openness to ideas ($r = -.33, p < .01$), openness to

[3]Copyright on the TAS–20 is held by G. J. Taylor, R. M. Bagby, and J. D. A. Parker. The scale may be ordered from the senior author who can also provide further information about the translated versions.

aesthetics ($r = -.29, p < .01$), and openness to action ($r = -.24, p < .05$). In addition, and despite the absence of items on the TAS–20 that inquire directly about daydreaming or other imaginal activity, the TAS–20 also correlated negatively with the subscale assessing openness to fantasy ($r = -.30$, $p < .01$) (Bagby, Taylor et al., 1994).

Costa and McCrae (1987) argued that the evaluation of any new personality test should include an examination of its relationship with a standard taxonomy of personality traits. With this in mind, Bagby, Taylor et al. (1994) also examined the relationships between the TAS–20 and the other four basic dimensions of personality assessed by the NEO Personality Inventory—Neuroticism, Extraversion, Agreeableness, and Conscientiousness. Consistent with both the theoretical conception and clinical reports that alexithymic individuals are prone to experiencing undifferentiated states of unpleasant emotional arousal (Lane & Schwartz, 1987; Taylor, 1987), the TAS–20 correlated positively with Neuroticism ($r = .27, p < .05$) and with the subscales reflecting the tendency to experience the negative affects of anxiety ($r = .25, p < .05$), depression ($r = .36, p < .01$), and self-consciousness (i.e., shame and embarrassment; $r = .35, p < .01$). A positive correlation was also obtained with the subscale assessing vulnerability to stress ($r = .35, p < .01$). Within the domain of Extraversion, the TAS–20 correlated negatively with the Positive Emotions subscale ($r = -.36, p < .01$), a finding consistent with clinical reports that positive affects are not readily experienced by alexithymic individuals (Krystal, 1988; Sifneos, 1987). The finding of nonsignificant correlations with the dimensions of Agreeableness and Conscientiousness provided support for the discriminant validity of the TAS–20.

Although space does not permit full discussion, an examination of the correlations of the three TAS–20 factors with the broad dimensions of Neuroticism, Extraversion, and Openness, and the personality traits measured by the various subscales revealed a differential pattern of relationships that confirmed the importance of the factors and was theoretically congruent with the facet of the construct each factor measures (see Bagby, Taylor et al., 1994). Although a composite or total score of the TAS–20 correlates more strongly than factor scale scores with measures of closely related constructs (such as psychological mindedness, need for cognition, and affective orientation), not surprisingly, the factor scales correlate more strongly with measures more closely related to one or another facet of the alexithymia construct.

Concurrent Validity

The concurrent validity of the TAS–20 was assessed by examining its relationship with a modified version of the Beth Israel Hospital Psychosomatic Questionnaire (BIQ), which is an observer-rated measure of alexithymia (Apfel & Sifneos, 1979). A small sample of patients (N = 39) attending a behavioral medicine outpatient clinic were interviewed by one clinician, who was selected randomly from among three clinicians, all of whom rated the patient on the BIQ. As described in earlier reports (Bagby, Taylor et al., 1994; Taylor, 1994), the modified version of the BIQ comprised two six-item subscales—Affect Awareness and Operatory Thinking—that were scored using 7-point Likert rating formats ranging from 1 (*not true*) to 7 (*very true*). Strong positive correlations were obtained between the TAS–20 and the total BIQ ($r = .53$, $p < .01$) and its Affect Awareness ($r = .53$, $p < .01$) and Operatory Thinking ($r = .48$, $p < .01$) subscales, thus providing compelling evidence for both the concurrent validity of the TAS–20 and the consensual validity of the alexithymia construct (Bagby, Taylor et al., 1994). Factor 1 of the TAS–20 (Difficulty Identifying Feelings) correlated significantly with the total BIQ ($r = .57$) and the subscale assessing affect awareness ($r = .36$), and Factor 3 of the TAS–20 (Externally Orientated Thinking) correlated significantly with the total BIQ ($r = .30$) and the subscale assessing operatory thinking ($r = .30$). Factor 2, which reflects the inability to communicate feelings to others, showed strong correlations with both the Affect Awareness subscale ($r = .52$) and the Operatory Thinking subscale ($r = .58$).

The data from this study were also used to establish preliminary cutoff scores for the TAS–20 to facilitate comparative studies. Individuals scoring ≥ 61 are considered alexithymic; those scoring ≤ 51 are considered nonalexithymic. These cutoff scores provide more conservative estimates of the prevalence of alexithymia in clinical and nonclinical populations than do the cutoff scores recommended for the TAS.

CLINICAL AND EXPERIMENTAL RESEARCH

To date, most research using either the TAS or the TAS–20 explored the association of alexithymia with different psychiatric and medical disorders. A small number of studies were experimental and attempted to explore the neurobiological and developmental underpinnings of alexithymia, and provided further support for the validity of the construct. Space constraints permit only a brief overview of this research.

Clinical Studies

Several studies yielded empirical support for earlier clinical reports that many alcoholics and drug addicts manifest alexithymic characteristics. Although prevalence rates of alexithymia (based on the TAS cutoff score) range from 5% to 20% in college student and normal adult populations, rates of around 50% were found in U.S. and Canadian samples of recently abstinent substance dependent patients (Haviland, Shaw, MacMurray, & Cummings, 1988; Taylor, Parker et al., 1990). Using the TAS–20 cutoff score,

J.D.A. Parker (personal communication, September 20, 1994) calculated a similar rate of 51% of alexithymia for the Canadian sample, who had completed items for both the TAS and the TAS–20. In a more recent study with the TAS–20, however, Haviland, Hendryx, Shaw, and Henry (1994) reported a somewhat lower rate of 41.7% of alexithymia in a new sample of recently abstinent substance dependent patients. Although prevalence rates calculated from TAS–20 cutoff scores are also lower in normal populations (usually below 13%), other sample characteristics might influence the findings.

It was suggested that the high rates of alexithymia found in samples of recently abstinent substance abusers might be influenced by the high level of general dysphoria that typically accompanies abrupt withdrawal from alcohol or psychoactive drugs (Haviland, Shaw, Cummings et al., 1988). However, individuals with long periods of abstinence from psychoactive substances also have high rates of alexithymia based on TAS cutoff scores. For example, Ziolkowski, Gruss, and Rybakowski (1995) reported a rate of 48% of alexithymia in a group of alcoholic patients in Poland, and Delle Chiaie et al. (1994) reported a rate of 66.6% of alexithymia in a group of heroin addicts in Italy; the mean period of abstinence was 22 months in both of these studies. Rather than investigating a clinical population, Kauhanen, Julkunen, and Salonen (1992a) investigated a large community population of middle-aged men in Finland and found that both heavy acute intake of alcohol ("binge drinking") and long-term heavy use of alcohol were related linearly with scores on the TAS. The finding of a high rate of alexithymia among substance dependent individuals may partly explain why traditional psychoanalytic psychotherapy is considered by experienced clinicians to be generally unhelpful to alcoholic and drug dependent individuals (Bell & Khantzian, 1991; Krystal, 1982).

Patients with eating disorders are also well known for their lack of psychological mindedness and poor response to traditional psychoanalytic psychotherapy. Studies using the TAS reported high rates of alexithymia ranging from 40% to 61% in groups of patients with bulimia nervosa, and from 56% to 77% in groups of patients with anorexia nervosa (Bourke, Taylor, Parker, & Bagby, 1992; Cochrane, Brewerton, Wilson, & Hodges, 1993; de Groot, Rodin, & Olmsted, 1995; Jimerson, Wolfe, Franko, Covino, & Sifneos, 1994; Schmidt, Jiwany, & Treasure, 1993). Rates of only 5% and 7% of alexithymia were reported for two normal comparison groups (Bourke et al., 1992; de Groot et al., 1995). Following the development of the TAS–20, it was possible to recalculate the rate of alexithymia for the anorexic sample studied by Bourke et al. (1992); the prevalence remained high at 69% but, as expected, this was lower than the prevalence of 77% obtained with the less conservative cutoff score of the TAS.

Although the concept of alexithymia emerged from observations of patients with classical psychosomatic diseases, only a few studies investigated alexithymia in these patients and the prevalence rates were surprisingly lower than expected. Using an Indian dialect (Tamil) translation of the TAS, Fernandez, Sriram, Rajkumar, and Chandrasekar (1989) found a rate of only 27.5% of alexithymia in a group of patients with rheumatoid arthritis, which is lower than rates of 35% to 40% found in groups of general psychiatric outpatients (Taylor, Parker et al., 1992). Porcelli, Zaka, Leoci, Centonze, and Taylor (1995) used a validated Italian translation of the TAS–20 and found a prevalence of 35.7% of alexithymia in a group of outpatients with inflammatory bowel disease (ulcerative colitis and Crohn's disease) compared with a rate of 4.5% in a normal control group. In a study of Italian patients with essential hypertension, however, Todarello, Taylor, Parker, and Fanelli (1995) also used the TAS–20 and found a high rate of 55.3% of alexithymia, compared with lower rates of 32.7% in a psychiatric outpatient sample and 16.3% in normal controls. It appears that patients with diseases previously regarded as classical psychosomatic diseases are more psychologically heterogeneous than previously thought. Given that these diseases show a physiological heterogeneity as well (Weiner, 1977), we suspect future studies will demonstrate a wide range in the prevalence of alexithymia even among groups with the same disease.[4]

Although empirical research is challenging the view that alexithymia is strongly associated with diseases that were regarded previously as classical psychosomatic diseases, as noted earlier, several studies support the clinical observation that alexithymic individuals are prone to "functional" somatic symptoms. In addition to the previously mentioned findings of significant correlations between the TAS and measures of "functional" somatic complaints in groups of college students (Bagby et al., 1986; Bagby, Taylor, & Atkinson, 1988), the large Finnish epidemiological study of middle-aged men found a graded and statistically significant relationship between TAS scores and self-reported physical symptoms (Kauhanen, Julkunen, & Salonen, 1991). Other studies showed that psychiatric outpatients who score in the alexithymic range of the TAS score significantly higher than nonalexithymic psychiatric outpatients on several MMPI scales that collectively measure a diverse and extensive range of somatic symptoms and bodily concerns (Taylor, Parker et al., 1990, 1992). In addition, a high rate of alexithymia (53%) was reported in motor vehicle accident survivors who met DSM–III–R criteria for somatoform pain disorder (Cox, Kuch, Parker, Shulman, & Evans, 1994). Patients with chronic pain syndromes or other somatizing disorders are notorious for being difficult to treat with psychotherapy.

---

[4]It should be noted that most contemporary psychosomatic theorists no longer subscribe to the view held by Alexander (1950) and other pioneers in psychosomatic medicine that only certain diseases are "psychosomatic." As outlined in another contribution (Taylor, 1987), the term psychosomatic now refers not to a category of diseases, but to an approach to all medical illnesses and diseases. The traditional linear models of disease causality were largely replaced by biopsychosocial or dysregulation models derived from general systems theory (Taylor, 1992), in which alexithymia is conceptualized as one of several possible risk factors for the development of the disease.

Investigations of specific psychiatric populations with the TAS also provided support for earlier clinical reports of a strong association between alexithymia and posttraumatic stress disorder (PTSD). For example, Zeitlin, Lane, O'Leary, and Schrift (1989) found that in a sample of 25 male combat veterans with PTSD, 15 (60%) scored above the cutoff score for alexithymia on the TAS. Zeitlin, McNally, and Cassiday (1993) found that rape victims with a history of more than one episode of sexual assault scored more alexithymic on the TAS than did individuals with a single episode of rape. Krystal (1978, 1988) attributed the alexithymia secondary to trauma to affect regression involving dedifferentiation, deverbalization, and resomatization of affects.

Studies with specific psychiatric populations also provided empirical support for Freud's (1895/1962, 1898/1962) early distinction between the actual neuroses, which he regarded as somatic in origin and therefore unamenable to psychoanalytic therapy, and the *psychoneuroses*, which he attributed to psychic conflict that could be resolved by a psychoanalytic approach. Patients with panic disorder, a diagnosis encompassed by Freud's definition of *actual anxiety neurosis* (Nemiah, 1984), have high rates of alexithymia (47% to 67%) compared with low rates of alexithymia in patients with simple phobia (12.5%; Parker, Taylor, Bagby, & Acklin, 1993) and patients with obsessive–compulsive disorder (13%; Zeitlin & McNally, 1993).

Experimental Studies

The TAS was used to explore the hypothesis that a neurobiological dysfunction is the mechanism underlying alexithymia. In their study of male combat veterans with PTSD, Zeitlin et al. (1989) demonstrated that the efficiency of communication between the two cerebral hemispheres, "evaluated with a tactile finger localization task, was a significant predictor of the degree of alexithymia…independent of PTSD severity and IQ" (p. 1434). Using conjugate lateral eye movements as an index of hemispheric activation, Parker, Taylor, and Bagby (1992) found a significant relationship between left cerebral activation and alexithymia. These results are consistent with findings that individuals with a personality style of "inner attentiveness" (i.e., individuals who engage in fantasy and who are very aware of their affective states) were more likely to show right cerebral activation (Tucker, 1981).

Berenbaum and James (1994) used the TAS to examine the correlates and retrospectively reported antecedents of alexithymia. Their results suggest that the development of alexithymia is more conducive in families in which members are not permitted to act openly and express their feelings directly, or in which it is not possible to feel emotionally safe, and that high levels of alexithymia are associated with low levels of positive communication in the family.

The hypothesis that alexithymia reflects a reduced ability to cognitively process and modulate emotions was evaluated using a modified Stroop color-naming task (Parker, Taylor, & Bagby, 1993a). In the original version of the Stroop task (Stroop, 1935), subjects were required to name the color of ink in which items (meaningless rows of identical letters, or actual names of colors) are written, and to ignore the item content. Delays in color-naming (i.e., Stroop interference) occur when the items are the names of colors that conflict with the color in which they are written. It was subsequently found that any common word produces interference if the meaning of the word attracts the subject's attention despite his or her effort to attend to the color of the word. This is especially evident with words that induce emotional states or activate personally disturbing memories. Although emotion-activating (arousal) words would be expected to produce interference in both alexithymic and nonalexithymic individuals, Parker et al. (1993a) reasoned that alexithymic individuals should take significantly longer to color-name such words because of their reduced ability to cognitively process and thereby modulate each state of arousal. This was demonstrated in a sample of university students who were categorized into alexithymic and nonalexithymic groups on the basis of TAS–20 cutoff scores. Because the alexithymic and nonalexithymic groups did not differ significantly in their ability to color-name neutral words, the hypothesis that alexithymia reflects an impairment in the processing of emotional stimuli was supported.

Another experiment explored associations between alexithymia and deficits in the motor-behavioral domain of emotion response systems (Parker, Taylor, & Bagby, 1993b). After being asked to identify the emotions depicted in nine photographs of different posed facial emotional expressions, a sample of university students was categorized into high, moderate, and low alexithymia groups on the basis of TAS–20 scores. The high alexithymia group of students was significantly less able to recognize facial expressions of emotion than was the low alexithymia group.

CLINICAL APPLICATION OF THE TAS–20

Alexithymia has important clinical implications in both medical and psychiatric settings (Taylor, 1977, 1984, 1987; Taylor et al., 1991). These include the risk of overinvestigation and overtreatment, especially when physicians mistake the alexithymic patient's somatic complaints for undetected organic pathology, as well as countertransference and technical difficulties for clinicians who attempt to treat alexithymic patients with traditional psychodynamic psychotherapy. As previously noted, some therapists advise against the use of insight-oriented psychotherapies for alexithymic patients, and instead recommend supportive approaches (Freyberger, 1977; Sifneos, 1975). Other therapists have devised some modifications of individual psychodynamic psychotherapy, which may be combined with educational approaches and group therapy (Krystal, 1979; Taylor et al., 1991; Taylor et al., 1997; Swiller, 1988). An important clinical application of the TAS–20 might be its use as a screening device to identify probable alexithymic patients and thereby alert physicians and psychotherapists to potential treatment difficulties. The scale might also be used as an aid in assessing a therapeutic impasse and planning a more effective treatment strategy. This latter use of the scale is demonstrated in the following case vignette.

A 54-year-old divorced man was referred for consultation by his group psychotherapist who had observed that the patient had difficulty describing his feelings in the group and was unable to empathize with the feelings of other patients. This situation was generating considerable annoyance in the other patients and was leading rapidly toward a therapeutic impasse for the patient. The group therapist was unsure whether the patient's limitations reflected the use of neurotic defenses that should be confronted more vigorously and interpreted in the group, or whether they were manifestations of an alexithymic trait that required an alternative strategy such as an educational approach regarding emotional processing.

In consultation, the patient described a longstanding difficulty in expressing his emotions and in relating warmly to other people. He had been an only child and reported that his parents had rarely communicated positive emotions or showed physical affection. The patient indicated that he seldom recalled dreams or engaged in fantasies, and that he had no interests or hobbies that he regularly pursued. Indeed, when not working as an insurance salesman, he spent much of his time sitting around his home drinking alcohol. He had sought psychiatric treatment at the urging of his current girlfriend who was frustrated by his failure to become emotionally intimate.

The clinical impression of alexithymia was confirmed by a score of 75 on the TAS–20. Supplemental testing with the NEO Personality Inventory revealed a score in the low range on the Openness to Experience dimension, with very low scores on the scales assessing openness to fantasy, feelings, and aesthetic interests. Consistent with findings from the correlational studies described earlier, the patient also scored high on Neuroticism (indicating a proneness to negative affectivity) and extremely low on the positive emotions scale and the warmth scale of the Extraversion dimension.

These test results led to the recommendations that the therapist explain to the patient and the group some differences in the way people experience and process emotions, and adopt a modified psychotherapeutic approach to the patient that would incorporate techniques proposed by Krystal (1979) and Swiller (1988). These include helping the patient to recognize, differentiate, label, and gradually verbalize his own feelings. The patient could be helped to develop affect tolerance by being taught that states of unpleasant emotional arousal are self-limited in duration and intensity. Directing the patient's attention to behavioral expressions of emotions, such as sighs, gestures, and movements could also help connect him with feelings. The use of humour by the therapist, and engaging playfully with the patient, might expand the patient's imaginative life by prompting further development of his own capacity for playing with thoughts, ideas, and images. Candid feedback from other group members should be encouraged, to the extent that it does not threaten the patient's self-esteem, as this can help the patient learn about the impact of his lack of empathy on other people. At the same time, the patient's attention should be directed to communications between other group members that demonstrate more successful and sensitive ways of relating.

SUMMARY AND FUTURE DIRECTIONS

Alexithymia is a more precisely defined and more extensively validated construct than is the psychological mindedness construct. It can be reliably measured with either the TAS or the TAS–20, which are easy to administer and score. In contrast to other alexithymia scales, these measures were developed using a combined rational and empirical method of test construction. Consequently, the TAS and TAS–20 demonstrated psychometric properties superior to those of other self-report alexithymia scales, and enabled researchers to conduct meaningful empirical investigations of the construct with clinical and nonclinical populations. Major findings were the verification of earlier clinical reports that alexithymia is associated with a tendency to somatization, and that alexithymia is prevalent among patients with substance use disorders, eating disorders, and PTSD. Prospective longitudinal studies are needed, however, to determine the direction of causal relationships between alexithymia and these psychiatric disorders.

Most of the empirical studies reviewed in this chapter used the TAS to measure alexithymia. However, the shortcomings of this scale, surmounted by the revised 20-item version, make the TAS–20 the recommended scale for future research. The TAS–20 demonstrates higher levels of internal consistency and a more theoretically coherent factor structure than does the original scale. In the process of increasing the internal consistency of the TAS–20 and reducing social desirability response bias, items that assessed fantasy and other imaginal activity directly were eliminated. Nonetheless, this facet of the alexithymia construct appears to be assessed indirectly by the externally orientated thinking factor of the TAS–20, as evidenced by the finding of a strong negative correlation ($r = -.45$, $p < .01$) with the fantasy subscale of the Openness to Experience dimension of the NEO Personality Inventory (Bagby, Taylor et al., 1994).

A comparison of the relationships of the TAS and those of the TAS–20 with measures of psychological mindedness and related constructs provides additional support for recommending the TAS–20 in future research. The negative correlations between the TAS–20 and the NCS and PMS (Bagby, Taylor et al., 1994) are of greater magnitude than the negative correlations between the TAS and the NCS and PY scale of the CPI (Bagby et al., 1986). Indeed, the magnitude of the correlations of the TAS–20 with the NCS and PMS suggests that the TAS–20 should be a useful measure for patient selection and for predicting outcome of insight-oriented psychotherapies.

Individuals who score high on measures of need for cognition and psychological mindedness are likely to respond favorably to insight-oriented psychotherapies because they enjoy engaging in analytical cognitive endeavours, have access to their inner feelings, and have an interest in the meaning of their own behavior and that of others. However, the prospects for successful psychotherapy are greatly reduced for individuals who score high on measures of alexithymia, as such individuals are factually orientated and unanalytical in their thinking and are unable to elaborate on inner feelings and fantasies. Not surprisingly, the self-report Psychological Mindedness Scale successfully predicted outcome from psychodynamically oriented individual psychotherapy, as measured by the number of sessions attended, discharge ratings, improved psychosocial functioning, and decreased symptomatology (Conte et al., 1990). Patients with high alexithymia scores as measured by the interviewer-rated BIQ who were offered short-term psychodynamic psychotherapy had a higher drop out rate than did those offered systematic desensitization (Pierloot & Vinck, 1977). Given the relationships of the TAS–20 with the PMS and BIQ, we anticipate that TAS–20 scores also will be related to measures of the course and outcome of different therapies.

The finding of a strong inverse relationship between the TAS–20 and the Openness to Experience dimension on the NEO Personality Inventory is further indication that the TAS–20 might be a useful screening instrument in selecting patients for analytical psychotherapy. As Miller (1991) pointed out, openness to experience influences the patient's reactions to the therapist's interventions, in particular the ability to understand and accept psychodynamic interpretations. Outcome is also believed to be influenced by the therapist's personality and cognitive style (Langs, 1978). Research on the process and outcome of psychotherapy might benefit by assessing the level of alexithymia in therapists as well as in patients.

Although the TAS–20 meets the requirements of a measure suitable for clinical and research purposes, clinicians and researchers should not rely solely on this scale for distinguishing between high and low alexithymic individuals. In addition to administering the TAS–20, investigators should make a clinical judgment, perhaps based on two or more independent ratings of the BIQ. In our own clinical work (as demonstrated in the case vignette), we found it useful to administer the NEO Personality Inventory (Costa & McCrae, 1985) along with the TAS–20, and to examine scores on the fantasy and feelings subscales of the Openness to Experience dimension.

Given that alexithymia was attributed to deficits in the mental representation and verbalization of affects, some researchers may question whether the construct can be adequately assessed with a self-report scale. This might be explored in future research by also administering a projective measure such as the TAT or the Rorschach, and examining correlations with the length of the story responses to selected TAT cards (as an index of the ability to create fantasies) or with the set of alexithymia indices developed by Acklin and Bernat (1987).

Much more research is needed to further explore the developmental antecedents and neurobiological underpinnings of alexithymia, as well as the types of attachment patterns of alexithymic individuals. The results of such research should aid in the development of more effective psychotherapies or other treatments for individuals with medical and psychiatric disorders who are not psychologically minded.

REFERENCES

Acklin, M. W., & Bernat, E. (1987). Depression, alexithymia, and pain prone disorder: A Rorschach study. *Journal of Personality Assessment, 51*, 462–479.

Alexander, F. (1950). *Psychosomatic medicine*. New York: Norton.

Apfel, R. J., & Sifneos, P. E. (1979). Alexithymia: Concept and measurement. *Psychotherapy and Psychosomatics, 31*, 180–190.

Bagby, R. M., Parker, J. D. A., & Taylor, G. J. (1991). Reassessing the reliability and validity of the MMPI Alexithymia Scale. *Journal of Personality Assessment, 56*, 238–253.

Bagby, R. M., Parker, J. D. A., & Taylor, G. J. (1994). The Twenty-Item Toronto Alexithymia Scale—I. Item selection and cross-validation of the factor structure. *Journal of Psychosomatic Research, 38*, 23–32.

Bagby, R. M., Taylor, G. J., & Atkinson, L. (1988). Alexithymia: A comparative study of three self-report measures. *Journal of Psychosomatic Research, 32*, 107–116.

Bagby, R. M., Taylor, G. J., & Parker, J. D. A. (1988). Construct validity of the Toronto Alexithymia Scale. *Psychotherapy and Psychosomatics, 50*, 29–34.

Bagby, R. M., Taylor, G. J., & Parker, J. D. A. (1994). The Twenty-Item Toronto Alexithymia Scale—II. Convergent, discriminant, and concurrent validity. *Journal of Psychosomatic Research, 38*, 33–40.

Bagby, R. M., Taylor, G. J., Parker, J. D. A., & Loiselle, C. (1990). Cross-validation of the factor structure of the Toronto Alexithymia Scale. *Journal of Psychosomatic Research, 34*, 47–51.

Bagby, R. M., Taylor, G. J., & Ryan, D. P. (1986). Toronto Alexithymia Scale: Relationship with personality and psychopathology measures. *Psychotherapy and Psychosomatics, 45*, 207–215.

Barron, F. (1953). An ego-strength scale which predicts response to psychotherapy. *Journal of Consulting Psychology, 17*, 327–333.
Barsky, A. J., & Klerman, G. L. (1983). Overview: Hypochondriasis, bodily complaints, and somatic styles. *American Journal of Psychiatry, 140*, 273–283.
Beck, A. T., Ward, C. H., Mendelson, M., Mock, J., & Erbaugh, J. (1961). An inventory for measuring depression. *Archives of General Psychiatry, 12*, 57–62.
Bell, C. M., & Khantzian, E. J. (1991). Contemporary psychodynamic perspectives and the disease concept of addiction: Complementary or competing models? *Psychiatric Annals, 21*, 273–281.
Berenbaum, H., & James, T. (1994). Correlates and retrospectively reported antecedents of alexithymia. *Psychosomatic Medicine, 56*, 353–359.
Bollas, C. (1987). Normotic illness. In *The shadow of the object: Psychoanalysis of the unknown thought*. New York: Columbia University Press.
Booth-Butterfield, M., & Booth-Butterfield, S. (1990). Conceptualizing affect as information in communication production. *Human Communication Research, 16*, 451–476.
Bourke, M. P., Taylor, G. J., Parker, J. D. A., & Bagby. R. M. (1992). Alexithymia in women with anorexia nervosa: A preliminary investigation. *British Journal of Psychiatry, 161*, 240–243.
Brautigam, W., & von Rad, M. (Eds.). (1977). *Proceedings of the 11th European Psychosomatic Research Conference: Toward a theory of psychosomatic disorders*. Basel, Switzerland: Karger.
Briggs, S. R., & Cheek, J. M. (1986). The role of factor analysis in the development and evaluation of personality scales. *Journal of Personality, 54*, 106–148.
Brown, D. (1993). Affective development, psychopathology, and adaptation. In S. L. Ablon, D. Brown, E. J. Khantzian, & J. E. Mack (Eds.), *Human feelings: Explorations in affect development and meaning* (pp. 5–66). Hillsdale, NJ: Analytic Press.
Bruch, H. (1973). *Eating disorders. Obesity, anorexia nervosa and the person within*. New York: Basic Books.
Bruch, H. (1985). Four decades of eating disorders. In D. M. Garner & P. E. Garfinkel (Eds.), *Handbook of psychotherapy for anorexia nervosa and bulimia* (pp. 7–18). New York: Guilford.
Cacioppo, J. T., Petty, R. E., & Kao, C. F. (1984). The efficient assessment of need for cognition. *Journal of Personality Assessment, 48*, 306–307.
Carver, C. S. (1989). How should multifaceted personality constructs be tested? Issues illustrated by self-monitoring, attributional style, and hardiness. *Journal of Personality and Social Psychology, 56*, 577–585.
Cochrane, C. E., Brewerton, T. D., Wilson, D. B., & Hodges, E. L. (1993). Alexithymia in the eating disorders. *International Journal of Eating Disorders, 14*, 219–222.
Conte, H. R., Plutchik, R., Jung, B. B., Picard, S., Karasu, T. B., & Lotterman, A. (1990). Psychological mindedness as a predictor of psychotherapy outcome: A preliminary report. *Comprehensive Psychiatry, 31*, 426–431.
Costa, P. T., & McCrae, R. R. (1985). *The NEO Personality Inventory manual*. Odessa, FL: Psychological Assessment Resources.
Costa, P. T., & McCrae, R. R. (1987). Personality assessment in psychosomatic medicine: Value of a trait taxonomy. *Advances in Psychosomatic Medicine, 17*, 71–82.
Cox, B. J., Kuch, K., Parker, J. D. A., Shulman, I. D., & Evans, R. J. (1994). Alexithymia in somatoform disorder patients with chronic pain. *Journal of Psychosomatic Research, 38*, 523–527.
de Groot, J. M., Rodin, G., & Olmsted, M. P. (1995). Alexithymia, depression, and treatment outcome in bulimia nervosa. *Comprehensive Psychiatry, 36*, 87–94.
Delle Chiaie, R., Cianconi, P., Didonna, A., Saito, A., Regine, F., & Pancheri, P. (1994, August). *Alexithymia in opioid addicts. State dependent reaction or permanent trait?* Paper presented at the 20th European Conference on Psychosomatic Research, Gent, Belgium.
Derogatis, L. R. & Melisaratos, N. (1983). The brief symptom inventory: An introductory report. *Psychological Medicine, 13*, 595–605.
Dorpat, T. L. (1985). *Denial and defense in the therapeutic situation*. Northvale, NJ: Aronson.
Fenigstein, A., Scheier, M. F., & Buss, A. H. (1975). Public and private self-consciousness: Assessment and theory. *Journal of Consulting and Clinical Psychology, 4*, 522–527.
Fernandez, A., Sriram, T. G., Rajkumar, S., & Chandrasekar, A. N. (1989). Alexithymic characteristics in rheumatoid arthritis: A controlled study. *Psychotherapy and Psychosomatics, 51*, 45–50.

Freedman, M. B., & Sweet, B. S. (1954). Some specific features of group psychotherapy and their implications for selection of patients. *International Journal of Group Psychotherapy, 4,* 355–368.

Freud, S. (1962). On the grounds for detaching a particular syndrome from neurasthenia under the description "anxiety neurosis." In J. Strachey (Ed. and Trans.), *The standard edition of the complete psychological works of Sigmund Freud* (vol. 3, pp. 87–117). London: Hogarth Press. (Original work published 1895)

Freud, S. (1962). Sexuality in the aetiology of the neuroses. In J. Strachey (Ed. and Trans.), *The standard edition of the complete psychological works of Sigmund Freud* (Vol. 3, pp. 261–285). London: Hogarth Press (Original work published 1898)

Freyberger, H. (1977). Supportive psychotherapeutic techniques in primary and secondary alexithymia. *Psychotherapy and Psychosomatics, 28,* 337–342.

Fukunishi, I., Saito, S., & Ozaki, S. (1992). The influence of defense mechanisms on secondary alexithymia in hemodialysis patients. *Psychotherapy and Psychosomatics, 57,* 50–56.

Golden, C. J., Sawicki, R. F., & Franzen, M. D. (1984). Test construction. In G. Goldstein & M. Hersen (Eds.), *Handbook of psychological assessment* (pp. 19–37). New York: Pergamon.

Gough, H. G. (1969). *Manual for the California Psychological Inventory* (Rev. ed.). Palo Alto, CA: Consulting Psychologists Press.

Graham, J. R. (1987). *The MMPI: A practical guide* (2nd ed.). New York: Oxford University Press.

Haviland, M. G., Hendryx, M. S., Cummings, M. A., Shaw, D. G., & MacMurray, J. P. (1991). Multidimensionalty and state dependency of alexithymia in recently sober alcoholics. *Journal of Nervous and Mental Disease, 179,* 284–290.

Haviland, M. G., Hendryx, M. S., Shaw, D. G., & Henry, J. P. (1994). Alexithymia in women and men hospitalized for psychoactive substance dependence. *Comprehensive Psychiatry, 35,* 124–128.

Haviland, M. G., Shaw, D. G., Cummings, M. A., & MacMurray, J. P. (1988). Alexithymia: Subscales and relationship to depression. *Psychotherapy and Psychosomatics, 50,* 164–170.

Haviland, M. G., Shaw, D. G., MacMurray, J. P., & Cummings, M. A. (1988). Validation of the Toronto Alexithymia Scale with substance abusers. *Psychotherapy and Psychosomatics, 50,* 81–87.

Hendryx, M. S., Haviland, M. G., & Shaw, D. G. (1991). Dimensions of alexithymia and their relationships to anxiety and depression. *Journal of Personality Assessment, 56,* 227–237.

Horney, K. (1952). The paucity of inner experiences. *American Journal of Psychoanalysis, 12,* 3–9.

Huba, G. J., Singer, J. L., Anhensel, C. S., & Antrobus, J. S. (1982). *Short Imaginal Processes Inventory manual.* Port Huron, MI: Research Psychologists Press.

Jackson, D. N. (1974). *The Basic Personality Inventory.* London, Canada: Research Psychologist Press.

Jimerson, D. C., Wolfe, B. E., Franko, D. L., Covino, N. A., & Sifneos, P. E. (1994). Alexithymia ratings in bulimia nervosa: Clinical correlates. *Psychosomatic Medicine, 56,* 90–93.

Kauhanen, J., Julkunen, J., & Salonen, J. T. (1991). Alexithymia and perceived symptoms: Criterion validity of the Toronto Alexithymia Scale. *Psychotherapy and Psychosomatics, 56,* 247–252.

Kauhanen, J., Julkunen, J., & Salonen, J. T. (1992a). Coping with inner feelings and stress: Heavy alcohol use in the context of alexithymia. *Behavioural Medicine, 18,* 121–126.

Kauhanen, J., Julkunen, J., & Salonen, J. T. (1992b). Validity and reliability of the Toronto Alexithymia Scale (TAS) in a population study. *Journal of Psychosomatic Research, 36,* 687–694.

Kelman, N. (1952). Clinical aspects of externalized living. *American Journal of Psychoanalysis, 12,* 15–23.

Killingmo, B. (1989). Conflict and deficit: Implications for technique. *International Journal of Psychoanalysis, 70,* 65–79.

Kirmayer, L. J. (1987). Languages of suffering and healing: Alexithymia as a social and cultural process. *Transcultural Psychiatric Research Review, 24,* 119–136.

Knapp, P. H. (1981). Core processes in the organization of emotions. *Journal of the American Psychoanalytic Association, 9,* 415–434.

Knapp, P. H. (1983). Emotions and bodily changes: A reassessment. In L. Temoshok, C. Van Dyke, & L. S. Zegans (Eds.), *Emotions in health and illness: Theoretical and research foundations* (pp. 15–27). New York: Grune & Stratton.

Krystal, H. (1968). *Massive psychic trauma.* New York: International Universities Press.
Krystal, H. (1974). The genetic development of affects and affect regression. *Annual of Psychoanalysis, 2,* 98–126.
Krystal, H. (1978). Trauma and affects. *The Psychoanalytic Study of the Child, 33,* 81–116.
Krystal, H. (1979). Alexithymia and psychotherapy. *American Journal of Psychotherapy, 33,* 17–31.
Krystal, H. (1982). Alexithymia and the effectiveness of psychoanalytic treatment. *International Journal of Psychoanalytic Psychotherapy, 9,* 353–378.
Krystal, H. (1988). *Integration and self-healing: Affect, trauma, alexithymia.* Hillsdale, NJ: Analytic Press.
Krystal, H., & Raskin, H. (1970). *Drug dependence.* Detroit, MI: Wayne State University Press.
Lane, R. D., & Schwartz, G. E. (1987). Levels of emotional awareness: A cognitive developmental theory and its application to psychopathology. *American Journal of Psychiatry, 144,* 133–143.
Langs, R. J. (1978). Some communicative properties of the bipersonal field. *International Journal of Psychoanalytic Psychotherapy, 7,* 87–135.
Leff, J. (1977). The cross-cultural study of emotions. *Culture, Medicine, and Psychiatry, 1,* 317–350.
Levitan, H. (1989). Failure of the defensive functions of the ego in psychosomatic patients. In S. Cheren (Ed.), *Psychosomatic medicine: Theory, physiology, and practice* (Vol. 1, pp. 135–157). Madison, CT: International Universities Press.
Loiselle, C. G., & Dawson, C. (1988). Toronto Alexithymia Scale: Relationship with measures of patient self-disclosure and private self-consciousness. *Psychotherapy and Psychosomatics, 50,* 109–116.
MacLean, P. D. (1949). Psychosomatic disease and the "visceral brain." *Psychosmatic Medicine, 11,* 338–353.
Marty, P., & de M'Uzan, M. (1963). La "pensee operatoire" [Operational thinking]. *Revue Francaise de Psychanalyse, 27* (Suppl.), 1345–1356.
Marty, P., de M'Uzan, M., & David, C. (1963). *L'investigation psychosomatique* [Psychosomatic investigation]. Paris: Presses Universitaires de France.
Mayes, L. C., & Cohen, D. J. (1992). The development of a capacity for imagination in early childhood. *Psychoanalytic Study of the Child, 47,* 23–47.
McCrae, R. R., & Costa, P. T. (1985). Openness to experience. In R. Hogan & W. H. Jones (Eds.), *Perspectives in psychology: Theory, measurement, and interpersonal dynamics* (Vol. 1, pp.145–172). Greenwich, CT: JAI Press.
McCrae, R. R., & Costa, P. T. (in press). Conceptions and correlates of openness to experience. In S. R. Briggs & W. H. Jones (Eds.), *Handbook of personality psychology.* New York: Academic Press.
McCrae, R. R., & John, O. P. (1992). An introduction to the five-factor model and its applications. *Journal of Personality, 60,* 175–215.
McDougall, J. (1980a). The anti-analysand in analysis. In S. Lebovici & D. Widlocher (Eds.), *Psychoanalysis in France* (pp. 333–354). New York: International Universities Press.
McDougall, J. (1980b). *Plea for a measure of abnormality.* New York: International Universities Press.
Miller, T. R. (1991). The psychotherapeutic utility of the five-factor model of personality: A clinician's experience. *Journal of Personality Assessment, 57,* 415–433.
Nemiah, J. C. (1977). Alexithymia: Theoretical considerations. *Psychotherapy and Psychosomatics, 28,* 199–206.
Nemiah, J. C. (1984). Anxiety and psychodynamic theory. In L. Grinspoon (Ed.), *Psychiatry update: The American psychiatric association annual review* (Vol. 3, pp. 426–440). Washington, DC: American Psychiatric Press.
Nemiah, J. C., Freyberger, H., & Sifneos, P. E. (1976). Alexithymia: A view of the psychosomatic process. In O. W. Hill (Ed.), *Modern trends in psychosomatic medicine* (Vol. 3, pp. 430–439). London: Butterworths.
Nemiah, J. C., & Sifneos, P. E. (1970). Affect and fantasy in patients with psychosomatic disorders. In O. W. Hill (Ed.), *Modern trends in psychosomatic medicine* (Vol. 2, pp. 26–34). London: Butterworths.

Norton, N. C. (1989). Three scales of alexithymia: Do they measure the same thing? *Journal of Personality Assessment, 53*, 621–637.
Nunnally, J. C. (1978). *Psychometric theory* (2nd ed.). New York: McGraw-Hill.
Pandey, R., Mandal, M. K., Taylor, G. J., & Parker, J. D. A. (1996). Cross-cultural alexithymia: Development and validation of a Hindi translation of the Twenty-Item Toronto Alexithymia Scale. *Journal of Clinical Psychology, 52*, 173–176.
Parker, J. D. A., Bagby, R. M. & Taylor, G. J. (1991). Alexithymia and depression: Distinct or overlapping constructs? *Comprehensive Psychiatry, 32*, 387–394.
Parker, J. D. A., Bagby, R. M., Taylor, G. J., Endler, N. S., & Schmitz, P. (1993). Factorial validity of the 20-item Toronto Alexithymia Scale. *European Journal of Personality, 7*, 221–232.
Parker, J. D. A., Taylor, G. J., & Bagby, R. M. (1992). Relationship between conjugate lateral eye movements and alexithymia. *Psychotherapy and Psychosomatics, 57*, 94–101.
Parker, J. D. A., Taylor, G. J., & Bagby, R. M. (1993a). Alexithymia and the processing of emotional stimuli: An experimental study. *New Trends in Experimental and Clinical Psychiatry, 9*, 9–14.
Parker, J. D. A., Taylor, G. J., & Bagby, R. M. (1993b). Alexithymia and the recognition of facial expressions of emotion. *Psychotherapy and Psychosomatics, 59*, 197–202.
Parker, J. D. A., Taylor, G. J., Bagby, R. M., & Acklin, M. W. (1993). Alexithymia in panic disorder and simple phobia: A comparative study. *American Journal of Psychiatry, 150*, 1105–1107.
Parker, J. D. A., Taylor, G. J., Bagby, R. M., & Thomas, S. (1991). Problems with measuring alexithymia. *Psychosomatics, 32*, 196–202.
Pasini, A., Delle Chiaie, S., Seripa, S., & Ciani, N. (1992). Alexithymia as related to sex, age, and educational level: Results of the Toronto Alexithymia Scale in 417 normal subjects. *Comprehensive Psychiatry, 33*, 42–46.
Piaget, J. (1967). *Six psychological studies*. New York: Random Press.
Pierloot, R., & Vinck, J. (1977). A pragmatic approach to the concept of alexithymia. *Psychotherapy and Psychosomatics, 28*, 156–166.
Porcelli, P., Zaka, S., Leoci, C., Centonze, S., & Taylor, G. J. (1995). Alexithymia in inflammatory bowel disease. A case-control study. *Psychotherapy and Psychosomatics, 64*, 49–53.
Prince, R. (1987). Alexithymia and verbal psychotherapies in cultural context. *Transcultural Psychiatric Research Review, 24*, 119–136.
Robbins, M. (1989). Primitive personality organization as an interpersonally adaptive modification of cognition and affect. *International Journal of Psychoanalysis, 70*, 443–459.
Rodrigo, G., & Lusiardo, M. (1992). Factor structure of a Spanish version of the Toronto Alexithymia Scale. *Psychotherapy and Psychosomatics, 58*, 197–201.
Rodrigo, G., Lusiardo, M., & Normey, L. (1989). Alexithymia: Reliability and validity of the Spanish version of the Toronto Alexithymia Scale. *Psychotherapy and Psychosomatics, 51*, 162–168.
Ruesch, J. (1948). The infantile personality. *Psychosomatic Medicine, 10*, 134–144.
Salminen, J. K., Saarijarvi, S., Aairela, E, & Tamminen, T. (1994). Alexithymia — state or trait? One-year follow-up study of general hospital psychiatric consultation outpatients. *Journal of Psychosomatic Research, 38*, 681–685.
Salovey, P., Hsee, C. K., & Mayer, J. D. (1993). Emotional intelligence and the self-regulation of affect. In D. M. Wegner & J. W. Pennebaker (Eds.), *Handbook of mental control* (pp. 258–277). Englewood Cliffs, NJ: Prentice Hall.
Salovey, P., & Mayer, J. D. (1989–90). Emotional intelligence. *Imagination, Cognition and Personality, 9*, 185–211.
Schaffer, C. E. (1993). *The role of adult attachment in the experience and regulation of affect*. Unpublished doctoral dissertation, Yale University.
Schmidt, U., Jiwany, A., & Treasure, J. (1993). A controlled study of alexithymia in eating disorders. *Comprehensive Psychiatry, 34*, 54–58.
Shands, H. C. (1975). How are "psychosomatic" patients different from "psychoneurotic" patients? *Psychotherapy and Psychosomatics, 26*, 270–285.
Sifneos, P. E. (1973). The prevalence of alexithymic characteristics in psychosomatic patients. *Psychotherapy and Psychosomatics, 22*, 255–262.
Sifneos, P. E. (1975). Problems of psychotherapy of patients with alexithymic characteristics and physical disease. *Psychotherapy and Psychosomatics, 26*, 65–70.

Sifneos, P. E. (1987). Anhedonia and alexithymia: A potential correlation. In D. C. Clark & J. Fawcett (Eds.), *Anhedonia and affect deficit states* (pp. 119–127). New York: PMA Publishing Corporation.

Sifneos, P. E. (1988). Alexithymia and its relationship to hemispheric specialization, affect, and creativity. *Psychiatric Clinics of North America, 11*, 287–292.

Spielberger, C. D., Johnson, E. H., Russell, S. F., Crane, R. J., Jacobs, G. A., & Worden, T. J. (1985). The experience and expression of anger: Construction and validation of an anger expression scale. In M. A. Chesney & R. H. Rosenman (Eds.), *Anger and hostility in cardiovascular and behavioural disorders* (pp. 5–30). New York: McGraw-Hill.

Sriram, T. G., Chaturvedi, S. K., Gopinath, P. S., & Shanmugam, V. (1987). Controlled study of alexithymic characteristics in patients with psychogenic pain disorder. *Psychotherapy and Psychosomatics, 47*, 11–17.

Sriram, T. G., Chaturvedi, S. K., Gopinath, P. S., & Subbakrishna, D. K.(1987). Assessment of alexithymia: Psychometric properties of the Toronto Alexithymia Scale (TAS)—A preliminary report. *Indian Journal of Psychiatry, 29*, 133–138.

Stroop, J. R. (1935). Studies of interference in serial verbal reactions. *Journal of Experimental Psychology, 18*, 643–662.

Swiller, H. I.(1988). Alexithymia: Treatment utilizing combined individual and group psychotherapy. *International Journal of Group Psychotherapy, 38*, 47–61.

Taylor, G. J. (1977). Alexithymia and the countertransference. *Psychotherapy and Psychosomatics, 28*, 141–147.

Taylor, G. J. (1984). Alexithymia: Concept, measurement, and implications for treatment. *American Journal of Psychiatry, 141*, 725–732.

Taylor, G. J. (1987). *Psychosomatic medicine and contemporary psychoanalysis*. Madison, CT: International Universities Press.

Taylor, G. J. (1992). Psychoanalysis and psychosomatics: A new synthesis. *Journal of the American Academy of Psychoanalysis, 20*, 251–275.

Taylor, G. J. (1994). The alexithymia construct: Conceptualization, validation, and relationship with basic dimensions of personality. *New Trends in Experimental and Clinical Psychiatry, 10*, 61–74.

Taylor, G. J., & Bagby, R. M. (1988). Measurement of alexithymia: Recommendations for clinical practice and future research. *Psychiatric Clinics of North America, 11*, 351–366.

Taylor, G. J., Bagby, R. M., & Parker, J. D. A. (1991). The alexithymia construct: A potential paradigm for psychosomatic medicine. *Psychosomatics, 32*, 153–164.

Taylor, G. J., Bagby, R. M., & Parker, J. D. A. (1992). The revised Toronto Alexithymia Scale: Some reliability, validity, and normative data. *Psychotherapy and Psychosomatics, 57*, 34–41.

Taylor, G. J., Bagby, R. M., & Parker, J. D. A. (1993). Is alexithymia a non-neurotic personality dimension? A response to Rubino, Grasso, Sonnino and Pezzarossa. *British Journal of Medical Psychology, 66*, 281–287.

Taylor, G. J., Bagby, R. M., & Parker, J. D. A. (1997). *Disorders of affect regulation: Alexithymia in medical and psychiatric illness*. Cambridge: Cambridge University Press.

Taylor, G. J., Bagby, R. M., Ryan, D. P., & Parker, J. D. A. (1990). Validation of the alexithymia construct: A measurement-based approach. *Canadian Journal of Psychiatry, 35*, 290–297.

Taylor, G. J., Bagby, R. M., Ryan, D. P., Parker, J. D. A., Doody, K. F., & Keefe, P. (1988). Criterion validity of the Toronto Alexithymia Scale. *Psychosomatic Medicine, 50*, 500–509.

Taylor, G. J., Parker, J. D. A., & Bagby, R. M. (1990). A preliminary investigation of alexithymia in men with psychoactive substance dependence. *American Journal of Psychiatry, 147*, 1228–1230.

Taylor, G. J., Parker, J. D. A., Bagby, R. M., & Acklin, M. W. (1992). Alexithymia and somatic complaints in psychiatric outpatients. *Journal of Psychosomatic Research, 36*, 417–424.

Taylor, G. J., Ryan, D. P., & Bagby, R. M. (1985). Toward the development of a new self-report alexithymia scale. *Psychotherapy and Psychosomatics, 44*, 191–199.

Todarello, O., Taylor, G. J., Parker, J. D. A., & Fanelli, M. (1995). Alexithymia in essential hypertension and psychiatric outpatients. A comparative study. *Journal of Psychosomatic Research, 39*, 987–994.

Tucker, D. M. (1981). Lateral brain function, emotion, and conceptualization. *Psychological Bulletin, 89*, 19–46.

Turner, R. G., Scheier, M. F., Carver, C. S., & Ickes, W. (1978). Correlates of self-consciousness. *Journal of Personality Assessment, 42,* 285–289.

Wastell, C. A. (1993). *In defense of feelings: The role of defenses in modulating affect reactions to trauma.* Unpublished doctoral dissertation, Macquarie University, New South Wales, Australia.

Weiner, H. (1977). *Psychobiology and human disease.* New York: Elsevier.

Wise, T. N., Mann, L. S., & Epstein, S. (1991). Ego defensive styles and alexithymia: A discriminant validation study. *Psychotherapy and Psychosomatics, 56,* 141–145.

Wurmser, L. (1974). Psychoanalytic considerations of the etiology of compulsive drug use. *Journal of the American Psychoanalytic Association, 22,* 820–843.

Yelsma, P. (1996). Affective orientations of perpetrators, victims, and functional spouses. *Journal of Interpersonal Violence, 11,* 141–161.

Zeitlin, S. B., Lane, R. D., O'Leary, D. S., & Schrift, M. J. (1989). Interhemispheric transfer deficit and alexithymia. *American Journal of Psychiatry, 146,* 1434–1439.

Zeitlin, S. B., & McNally, R. J. (1993). Alexithymia and anxiety sensitivity in panic disorder and obsessive-compulsive disorder. *American Journal of Psychiatry, 150,* 658–660.

Zeitlin, S. B., McNally, R. J., & Cassiday, K. L. (1993). Alexithymia in victims of sexual assault: An effect of repeated traumatization? *American Journal of Psychiatry, 150,* 661–663.

Ziolkowski, M., Gruss, T., & Rybakowski, J. K. (1995). Does alexithymia in male alcoholics constitute a negative factor for maintaining abstinence? *Psychotherapy and Psychosomatics,* 63, 169–173.

Chapter 5

Self-Consciousness and Its Relation to Psychological Mindedness

Allan Fenigstein
Kenyon College

ORIGINS OF THE CONCEPT

The psychological concept of *self-consciousness* refers to a relatively stable personality tendency to direct attention and thought toward oneself. Originally developed by Fenigstein, Scheier, and Buss (1975), the notion of self-focused attention as an individual difference variable was essentially an outgrowth of Duval and Wicklund's (1972) theory of self-awareness.

The essence of self-awareness theory was the identification of a fundamental distinction between attention directed inward toward the self versus attention directed outward toward the environment. Although the self may be regarded as an object of attention much like any other perceivable object, the theory implicitly acknowledged the psychological uniqueness and personal importance of the self. A great deal of research subsequently supported the self's special status: Knowledge about the self is especially elaborate and well-organized, and is more readily brought to mind, compared to other knowledge domains (e.g., Kihlstrom et al., 1988; Klein & Loftus, 1988; Markus, 1977; Rogers, Kuiper, & Kirker 1977). Events cannot help but be perceived from the self's own perspective, and thus the self provides an especially important interpretive framework for making judgments about events (e.g., Fenigstein & Abrams, 1993; Greenwald, 1980); and the self, virtually by definition, is of extraordinary hedonic relevance (e.g., Jones & Davis, 1965); that is, events that affect us personally are almost always more psychologically significant than events affecting only others. Recognition of these special qualities suggests, indeed almost demands, that attention directed toward the self has different, and often more important, psychological consequences than attention toward anything else. As a result, several different theories and approaches were developed in an attempt to examine and understand these effects (e.g., Buss, 1980; Carver & Scheier, 1981; Duval & Wicklund, 1972; Gibbons, 1990; Hull & Levy, 1979).

When treating self-directed attention as a social psychological variable, the various versions of self-awareness theory all agree that momentary stimulus conditions may guide whether one's attention becomes primarily focused away from or back toward oneself. Distracting events or engaging activities that require conscious effort ordinarily draw attention toward those stimuli and away from the self. By contrast, stimuli that reflect or suggest an aspect of the self, such as mirrors, the sound of one's own voice or heartbeat, or the presence of an observing audience—that is—cues that make one aware of oneself as an object in the world, direct attention back toward the self.

SELF-CONSCIOUSNESS AS A PERSONALITY CHARACTERISTIC

Inevitably, researchers working with the theory of self-awareness began to suspect that self-focused attention, in addition to being influenced by experimental manipulations, may also result from fairly stable dispositional tendencies that differ considerably among individuals. Fenigstein et al. (1975, p. 522) speculated that "some persons constantly think about themselves, scrutinize their behavior (or appearance), and mull over their thoughts—to the point of obsessiveness"; for others, the "absence of self-consciousness is so complete that they have no understanding of either their own motives or of how they appear to others (p. 522)." These personality differences were identified in terms of the *trait* of *self-consciousness* the relatively permanent tendency of individuals to direct more or less attention to the self. *Self-awareness*, in contrast, refers to the psychological *state* of being attentive to the self, whether as a result of transient situational variables, chronic dispositions, or both.

After determining that no psychometric instrument existed to assess individual differences in self-consciousness, Fenigstein et al. (1975) constructed their own measure, called the Self-Consciousness Scale (SCS). In designing the scale, several basic content areas were first identified as relevant to the concept of self-consciousness, and items were then generated, largely on the basis of their face validity, to sample these domains: (a) preoccupation with one's own past, present, or future behavior; (b) awareness of one's own attributes, both positive and negative; (c) sensitivity to inner feelings; (d) introspective behavior; (e) a tendency to visualize oneself; (f) awareness of one's own appearance and style of presentation; and (g) concern over the appraisal of others. Starting with an initial pool of 38 different questionnaire items, numerous psychometric refinements resulted in a final 23-item inventory (see Table 5.1).

TABLE 5.1

Items and Factor Loadings of the Self-Consciousness Scale

	Factor Loading[a]		
	Private Self-Consciousness	*Public Self-Consciousness*	*Social Anxiety*
Private:			
I'm always trying to figure myself out. (1)	.65		
Generally, I'm not very aware of myself. (3)[b]	−.48		
I reflect about myself a lot. (5)	.73		
I'm often the subject of my own fantasies. (7)	.45		
I never scrutinize myself. (9)[b]	−.51		
I'm generally attentive to my inner feelings. (13)	.66		
I'm constantly examining my motives. (15)	.62		
I sometimes have the feeling that I'm off somewhere watching myself. (18)	.43		
I'm alert to changes in my mood. (20)	.55		
I'm aware of the way my mind works when I work through a problem. (22)	.46		
Public:			
I'm concerned about my style of doing things. (2)		.47	
I'm concerned about the way I present myself. (6)		.65	
I'm self-conscious about the way I look. (11)		.61	
I usually worry about making a good impression. (14)		.72	
One of the last things I do before I leave the house is to look in the mirror. (17)	.51		
I'm concerned about what other people think of me. (19)		.73	
I'm usually aware of my appearance. (21)		.60	
Social anxiety:			
It takes me time to overcome my shyness in new situations. (4)			.76
I have trouble working when someone is watching me. (8)		.26	.45
I get embarrased very easily. (10)			.70
I don't find it hard to talk to strangers. (12)[b]			−.66
I feel anxious when I speak in front of a group. (16)	.21		.46
Large groups make me nervous. (23)			.69

Note. From Fenigstein et al. (1975). The numbers in parentheses indicate the sequence of items on the scale.

[a]Only factor loadings greater than .20 are listed.

[b]Item was reversed for scoring.

PRIVATE AND PUBLIC SELF-CONSCIOUSNESS

One of the most significant and heuristic findings to emerge from repeated factor analyses of the SCS was that self-consciousness, although originally thought of as a single, global dimension, actually had two distinct components, one private and one public (Fenigstein et al., 1975). *Private self-consciousness* identified a tendency to be aware of the covert, internal aspects of self, and to be particularly attentive to one's inner thoughts and feelings. *Public self-consciousness,* in contrast, involved an awareness of and interest in the outwardly displayed manifestations of self, such as appearance, social behavior, and the impression made on others. Persons with this characteristic were thought to be especially cognizant of how the self was being viewed by others. A third factor measured by the SCS, *social anxiety,* correlated significantly with public self-consciousness, $r(452) = .21$; p .05 (Fenigstein et al., 1975), and may best be regarded as an occasional byproduct of public self-consciousness (e.g., Buss, 1980; Leary, 1983). Because social anxiety does not deal directly with the notion of self-focused attention, it is not immediately relevant to the present discussion, and will receive little further attention.

In addition to the extensive factor analytic evidence confirming that the private and public self-consciousness dimensions were factorially distinct, the correlation between the two subscales was consistently shown to be relatively weak, usually below .30 (Fenigstein et al., 1975; see also reviews by Carver & Scheier, 1981; Wicklund & Gollwitzer, 1987), again indicating that the two dimensions, to a large extent, function independently of each other; the presence of one neither precludes nor necessitates the other.

Differentiating between the private and public self is arguably one of the most fundamental and significant distinctions made by humans. Readily recognized aspects of human behavior, such as pretense and impression management (e.g., Goffman, 1959), would seem to imply an important psychological difference between the "inner" self that is understood to be real or genuine by the person, and is largely beyond any conscious control, and the "outer" self that is presented to and perceived by others, and often involves an element of deliberate disingenuousness (e.g., Schlenker, 1980). Some social theorists claimed this distinction to be a recent sociohistorical phenomenon; Baumeister (1986), for example, suggested that only within the past few centuries has the realization emerged that private aspects of the self can be separate and distinct from public behavior and appearances. However, evolutionary theorists, who place great emphasis on deceit and its detection as a fundamental element in the evolution of the human mind (e.g., Tooby & Cosmides, 1990), would argue that being able to differentiate between another's real and apparent motives occupies a prominent position in the long span of human evolutionary history.

In effect, Fenigstein et al. (1975) found that the distinction between the private and public self may also serve as the basis of two separate individual difference dimensions. Some persons, when directing attention toward the self, may be more prone to focus on and think about private self matters, such as personal feelings of self-worth, one's cognitive faculties, bodily and emotional states, a sense of one's inner being, and one's future hopes and desires. For others, the public aspects of self, such as appearance, dress, and style of behavior, along with thoughts and feelings concerning the recognition or regard received from others, is more salient and of greater interest, and thus more likely to draw the individual's attention.

Although separating the private and public aspects of self, in retrospect, appears theoretically and empirically justifiable, this division was not considered during the early stages of scale development. Fenigstein et al.'s (1975) original conception, based on the work of Duval and Wicklund (1972), was of a unitary, homogeneous disposition to be self-attentive, and that conception guided the initial creation of scale items. Only after repeated samples and analyses demonstrated there was no such unitary factor did the notion of two different kinds of self-consciousness begin to emerge. And only then was it realized that distinguishing between the inner, personal aspects of the self and the self as a social entity, a distinction of longstanding value in psychology (e.g., Erikson, 1956; James, 1890; Jung, 1957) was rediscovered and empirically validated, this time with the aid of a personality measure.

ADMINISTERING THE SELF-CONSCIOUSNESS SCALE

Self-consciousness is operationally defined by the SCS, a 23-item self-report questionnaire that measures two different kinds of dispositional self-consciousness (see Table 5.1). Subjects are asked to respond to each item on the scale in terms of its self-descriptiveness, on a 5-point rating scale ranging from 0 (*extremely uncharacteristic of me*) to 4 (*extremely characteristic of me*), with 2 (*neither characteristic nor uncharacteristic of me*) as the midpoint or neutral response. The scale typically requires fewer than 10 minutes to complete.

As indicated in Table 5.1, 10 of the items assess private self-consciousness. These items are summed (after ratings for the two inverted items are reversed) to yield a Private Self-Consciousness score, ranging from a low of 0 to a high of 40, with a mean score close to 26, and a standard deviation near 5.0, for the original sample of 432 college students on whom the scale was standardized (Fenigstein et al., 1975). The Public Self-Consciousness score is derived by adding together the seven items that relate to that dimension; this score ranges from 0 to 28, with the original college sample yielding a mean score of about 19 and a standard deviation close to 4.0. There were no significant gender differences on either private or public self-consciousness for the original sample. Some researchers, on occasion, employ a Total Self-Consciousness measure, effectively ignoring the distinction between attention to the private and public selves, by adding the scores of the two subscales together.

That private and public self-consciousness are separable and relatively independent dimensions means that scores on one have little relation to scores on the other. For research or diagnostic purposes, no difficulties arise from the fact that the SCS can identify those who are high on both kinds of self-consciousness, high on one and low on the other, or low on both.

RELIABILITY AND VALIDITY OF THE SELF-CONSCIOUSNESS SCALE

The SCS was shown to have good reliability over time, with test–retest correlations (N = 84) over a 2-week period of .80 for the scale as a whole, and .84

and .79 for the public and private self-consciousness subscales, respectively, suggesting the existence of relatively stable personality tendencies toward self-focused attention in a college population (Fenigstein et al., 1975).

Several studies provided evidence of convergent validity for the scale. Turner, Scheier, Carver, and Ickes (1978) showed that private self-consciousness correlated with other psychological measures to which it is theoretically related, such as thoughtfulness, reflectiveness, and the use of visual imagery in dealing with personal problems. Public self-consciousness was found to relate to several variables which suggest an awareness of oneself as an object of awareness to others, such as social anxiety (as measured by the Self-Consciousness Scale, Fenigstein et al., 1975), shyness (Schlenker & Weigold, 1990), sociability (Turner et al., 1978), and self-monitoring, the tendency of persons to manage their public impressions (Fenigstein, 1979; Turner et al., 1978).

Carver and Glass (1976) offered evidence of discriminant validity: as expected, neither private nor public self-consciousness related to measures of intelligence, need for achievement, test anxiety, or impulsivity. In addition, Turner et al. (1978) found that both subscales were unrelated to a measure of social desirability. These findings are all consistent with theoretical conceptions that regard self-consciousness as a relatively pure attentional tendency; attention may be directed toward aspects of the self that are positive or negative, but by themselves, neither public nor private self-consciousness have a reliable relationship with any specific value-laden content.

THE SELF-ATTENTIONAL ASPECTS OF SELF-CONSCIOUSNESS

A question of fundamental importance to the construct validity of the SCS is whether the two different types of self-consciousness, conceptualized as personality dimensions, in fact involve self-focused attention. Although both subscales have a good deal of face validity, that is, the relevant questionnaire items explicitly deal with attention to aspects of the self that are either covert and psychologically private, or public and socially observable, a more definitive response requires the use of independent sources of evidence.

Research concerning the self-attentional properties of private self-consciousness was straightforward, consistent, and noncontroversial, and is dealt with here only briefly. Carver and Scheier (1978), in one of the initial attempts at construct validation, showed that high, compared to low, privately self-conscious persons were more likely to respond to a sentence completion task with self-focused responses, that is, responses that clearly focused on the self with little or no regard for the external world. Private self-conscious persons, for example, were more likely to complete the sentence stem, "It's fun to dream about…," with a self-focused response such as "my success," than with an external world focused response such as "giving a party for friends"; the effect for public self-consciousness, however, failed to reach significance. Consistent with the idea of heightened attention to one's inner traits or characteristics, several studies have demonstrated easier access to, that is, better memory for, that information as a function of private self-consciousness (e.g., Hull & Levy, 1979; Nasby, 1985; Turner, 1980). Finally, individual differences in private self-consciousness have often yielded precisely the same effects as have differences in self-awareness arising from the presence of a mirror (e.g., Froming, Walker, & Lopyan, 1982; Scheier & Carver, 1977), strongly suggesting that both sets of effects can be explained in terms of self-attention. In general, even self-awareness theorists who were skeptical of the dispositional approach (e.g., Gibbons, 1990; Wicklund & Gollwitzer, 1987) seem to regard the experience of private self-consciousness as virtually synonymous with that of self-directed attention.

Those same theorists, however, expressed serious misgivings about the essential nature of public self-consciousness, questioning whether that construct has anything to do with attention toward the self. Gibbons (1990), for example, argued that directing attention toward the self as a social object involves an external rather than a self orientation, in which the person's primary focus is on what others think of the self. The involvement of "others" or the possibility of an "external" perspective, however, need not compromise the fundamental self-focus of public self-consciousness. Other persons play a critical role in a number of important theories of self (e.g., Cooley, 1902; Mead, 1934), yet their inclusion in no way diminishes the central theoretical focus on the self. As for the notion of an external orientation, Duval and Wicklund (1972), in their original formulation of the theory, explicitly defined self-awareness in terms of an external perspective, likening it to a process of figuratively coming outside oneself and retrospectively looking back on the self. In other words, using the mind's eye to view oneself from the outside (i.e., imagining the public aspects of the self) is entirely consistent with the concept of self-focused attention (e.g., Hass, 1984).

Gibbons' (1990) assumption that the thought processes and concerns of the publicly self-conscious person emphasizes others, rather than the self, as if attention is somehow focused away from the self, is also misguided. The concept of public self-consciousness was always explicitly conceptualized in terms of a focus on inner experience, although the content of that experience is concerned with the public aspects of oneself (Fenigstein et al., 1975; Fenigstein, 1987). Consciousness of a "public" self certainly implies a tacit awareness of others, but those others are of interest or importance only insofar as the imagined object of their thoughts is oneself. That is, what is most salient to the publicly self-conscious person is not others, but rather those aspects of the self that are potentially being viewed or thought about by others (Fenigstein et al., 1975). Research indicating that public self-consciousness is related to such other-oriented issues as self-presentation (e.g., Fenigstein, 1979; Turner & Peterson, 1977) or concerns about the impressions made on others (e.g., Carver & Scheier, 1981) is entirely consistent with the idea that the attention of the publicly self-conscious person is primarily directed inward toward those aspects of the self that render the self a social object.

Although the use of a sentence-completion task, perhaps because of its impersonal and undifferentiated nature, offered only equivocal support for the self-attentional properties of public self-consciousness (Carver & Scheier, 1978), other more appropriate measures provide substantial evidence of construct validity. Franzoi and Brewer (1984), for example, in a naturalistic study of ongoing thought, found that publicly self-conscious persons were especially likely to think about themselves as social objects who were being observed by others. The trait of public self-consciousness was also associated with either better memory for, or memory biased in favor of, personal information specific to the socially observable aspects of self, such as one's physical characteristics and the impression made on others (e.g., Nasby, 1989; Turner, Gilliland, & Klein, 1981). Finally, a number of studies showed that public self-consciousness results in effects similar to those induced by stimuli that heighten attention to the visible aspects of self, such as an observing audience or a videotape camera (e.g., Fenigstein, 1979, 1984; Froming & Carver, 1981; Hass, 1984). Thus, there is considerable evidence converging on the idea that publicly self-conscious individuals attend to and think about those aspects of self that are observable to, and have a direct effect on, others.

THEORY AND RESEARCH ON PRIVATE AND PUBLIC SELF-CONSCIOUSNESS

The concept of self-consciousness derives much of its appeal from the assertion that self-directed attention has unique, significant, and—not surprisingly, given the multifaceted (e.g., public vs. private) nature of self—highly varied psychological consequences. This chapter suggests, however, that despite the multiplicity of findings associated with self-awareness, a few basic psychological processes may serve to integrate the diverse effects of both private and public self-consciousness: All such effects derive from the experience of systematically attending to particular aspects of the self. The consequences of this self-directed attention, for both types of self-consciousness, may be conceptualized largely in terms of: (a) increased knowledge or cognizance of those self-aspects, (b) a heightening of the subjective value or importance of those self-aspects, and (c) an increase in the intrusiveness of those self-aspects into other realms of thought. Despite this conceptual overlap, the specific psychological outcomes of these attentional processes, as they apply to the public and private self, are often quite different and sometimes even at odds with each other in their specific manifestations. These outcome differences once again reinforce the validity of the distinction between consciousness of the private and public self.

The research in this area is voluminous; the Self-Consciousness Scale (Fenigstein et al., 1975) has been one of the most widely cited personality measures since its development (and all of the self-consciousness research discussed in this chapter is based on that scale). Rather than attempt a comprehensive review of the literature (e.g., Gibbons, 1990; Scheier & Carver, 1983), much of which is not entirely relevant to the focus of this volume, a brief overview of the major implications of self-consciousness is presented, followed by a closer examination of those self-consciousness effects bearing directly on the question of psychological mindedness.

Private Self-Consciousness

One of the more obvious consequences of attending to an object is that more information about that object is gained or made available. When attention is focused on one's private thoughts or feelings, cognizance of those thoughts or feelings is increased, as evidenced by studies showing that self-descriptions tend to be more detailed and extensive (e.g., Franzoi, 1983; Nasby, 1985; Turner, 1978) and correspond more closely with actual behavior (e.g., Scheier, Buss, & Buss, 1978; Underwood & Moore, 1981) as a result of private self-consciousness. Even bodily sensations become more clearly experienced under these conditions, as evidenced by research showing that subjects are less susceptible to placebo effects, that is, to misinformation regarding internal sensations (e.g., Scheier, Carver, & Gibbons, 1979).

Not only are internal sensations recognized more clearly, but affective reactivity to these events is also apparently heightened as a function of private self-consciousness. In reaction to both positive and negative emotional stimuli, subjects high in private self-consciousness, compared to those low on that dimension, reported more intense affective responses (Scheier, 1976; Scheier & Carver, 1977). (It is still unclear, however, whether the effect of private self-consciousness on affect is direct, i.e., due to an objective increase in physiological responding, or indirect, i.e., the result of a heightening of the subjective psychological experience.)

Several studies, using a variety of approaches, suggest that heightened awareness of private thoughts and feelings increases the subjective importance of those self-aspects. Cheek and Briggs (1982), for example, found that privately self-conscious persons tend to construct their identity out of the unique, idiosyncratic, and relatively private elements of their existence, rather than through any social connection with others. Similarly, Fenigstein and Vanable (1993) found that private self-consciousness was more closely associated with a measure of private self-esteem, evaluating how highly one valued oneself, than with a measure of public self-esteem, assessing the extent to which persons believed they were valued by others.

Self-awareness is associated with a self-evaluation process involving a comparison between whatever aspect of self is most critical in a given situation and appropriate standards of behavior (e.g., Duval & Wicklund, 1972; Wicklund, 1975). However, research on self-consciousness showed that in many circumstances, several different, often opposing, standards may be operating. When a conflict exists between one's own goals or standards and the needs or desires of others, privately self-conscious persons tend to be responsive to, and act in accordance with, their own personal beliefs or values, irrespective of social pressure from others (e.g., Froming & Carver, 1981; Greenberg, 1982; Scheier, 1980).

Another indication of the self's subjective importance is its relative availability (Tversky & Kahneman, 1973), that is, the ease with which the self, as a cognitive entity, comes to mind and becomes implicated in subsequent judgments. Private self-consciousness, by focusing attention toward the self, heightens the self's salience, thereby increasing its availability. This effect has been well-documented with respect to causal attributions. When making judgments about the causes of an event, responsibility may be attributed either externally, to others or to situational influences, or internally, to the self. Several studies found that as private self-consciousness increases, judgments become biased toward the inclusion of the self, and the self is more likely to be seen as causally responsible for events (e.g., Buss & Scheier, 1976; Fenigstein & Carver, 1978).

Although the relationship between self-focus and self-attribution is robust (e.g., Duval & Wicklund, 1973; Fenigstein & Carver, 1978) and appealing in its parsimony, its generality is moderated by several considerations. Focusing on the self also heightens the need to protect self-esteem (e.g., Greenwald, 1980), and this need is often effected through the avoidance of blame. In situations where self-involvement is high, that is, where the outcome is likely to have significant impact on one's sense of self, self-focus has been shown to actually lower the sense of personal responsibility for negative or unsuccessful outcomes (e.g., Federoff & Harvey, 1976). Other research found that in order to heighten self-attributions of responsibility, self-attention needs to be specifically directed toward a sense of oneself as a causal agent. When Fenigstein and Levine (1984) induced subjects to focus on the self as weak and powerless, as opposed to strong and potent, attributions to the self were significantly lessened. Thus, attributional judgments do not relate to self-attention in any simple fashion, but rather depend on what aspects of self are activated by that attention, and the kinds of attributions that best serve those self-aspects.

Public Self-Consciousness

Public self-consciousness is defined as the tendency to direct attention toward the self as a social object, and its effects may be understood as the outcome of a process of attending to those aspects of the self that are observable to others or that constitute one's public identity. Attending to the public aspects of self should make one more knowledgeable about that domain. Accordingly, persons high in public self-consciousness, compared to those low on that dimension, were shown to have easier access to information about the externally displayed aspects of self (e.g., Nasby, 1989; Turner et. al., 1981), and were more cognizant of their appearance and of the public impressions they thought they were conveying (e.g., Miller & Cox, 1982; Tobey & Tunnell, 1981).

There is also evidence that habitual attention to the public aspects of self increases the extent to which those aspects are valued as personally important: Persons high in public self-consciousness, compared to those low on that dimension, were more responsive to the perceived esteem of others than to a personal sense of self-esteem (Fenigstein & Vanable, 1993), and emphasized self aspects that related to their social existence, such as physical characteristics and group affiliations, over those aspects of self that were more private in nature in constructing their identity (Cheek & Briggs, 1982).

Although privately self-conscious persons show little awareness of or consideration for the opinions or desires of others (e.g., Ellis & Holmes, 1982), those who are publicly self-conscious are very cognizant of themselves as objects of attention to others. As a result, they are more responsive to the perceived needs and expectations of others, as evidenced by their susceptibility to conformity pressures (e.g., Froming & Carver, 1981), and their willingness to act in ways they think others will approve, regardless of their own private beliefs (e.g., Greenberg, 1982; Scheier, 1980).

Self-attention, in this case to the self as a social object, again heightens the self's salience and availability, and one of the effects of public self-consciousness is to increase the extent to which the self becomes implicated into the assumed thoughts of others. As a result of their own awareness of themselves as objects of attention to others, publicly self-conscious persons readily assume that others are also aware of, and attending to, them. This bias in social inference, involving an assumed knowledge of what others are thinking, has a number of interesting implications.

To the extent that publicly self-conscious persons are preoccupied with how they are seen by others, they may be susceptible to the belief that they actually are the object of observation by others. Fenigstein and Vanable (1992), for example, found that as public self-consciousness increased, persons were more likely to feel as if they were being watched, even in the absence of any evidence to that effect. These heightened feelings of observability or conspicuousness may also underlie the social anxiety or inhibition that often accompanies public self-consciousness (e.g., Buss, 1980; Fenigstein et al., 1975; Gibbons, 1990).

Awareness of your own observability to others can also result in the (not altogether illogical) assumption that others are very much aware of your presence and thus are likely to be acting with you in mind. In one study (Fenigstein, 1979), for example, individuals were ignored by a group of confederates who were engaged in conversation among themselves. This was intended as an ambiguous social experience, in that the groups' behavior may or may not have been relevant to the self. Persons low in public self-consciousness presumably viewed the group's interest in each other as having little or nothing to do with them, and were largely unaffected by the experience. However, high publicly self-conscious persons, being very cognizant of the others' awareness of them, could not avoid the (in this case, accurate) inference that they were deliberately being shunned; this personalistic interpretation (e.g., Jones & Davis, 1965) resulted in a very strong negative reaction to the group.

Other studies (e.g., Fenigstein, 1984; Fenigstein & Vanable, 1992) confirmed the general tendency of persons high in public self-consciousness to make self-referent interpretations of others' behavior and (mis)construe their actions as being targeted toward the self. For example, Fenigstein (1984) found that persons high in public self-consciousness, when faced with the possibility that either they or another had been picked to participate in a demonstration, exaggerated the likelihood that they were the chosen one. These studies all suggest an increase in the subjective importance of the self, with that importance being expressed, in the case of public self-consciousness, in terms of the extent to which the self is thought to be a prominent part of others' thinking.

The heightened importance of the self in the thinking of publicly self-conscious persons is also illustrated by the tendency to use the self's thinking as a basis for making judgments about the thinking of others. In a series of studies involving a variety of attitudes, behaviors, and causal inferences, Fenigstein and Abrams (1993) had subjects answer questions, both from their own perspective and from the perspective of hypothetical others in the same situation. Public self-consciousness, by heightening the salience of one's own perspective, consistently increased the assumption that others thought and acted in the same way as the self. That is, when making inferences about the attitudes of others, or when making judgments about another's causal perspective, subjects who were especialy aware of themselves as social objects used their own thoughts as a basis for generating inferences about the thoughts of others.

This research suggests that although persons who are publicly self-conscious are especially aware of themselves as social objects to others, that does not necessarily imply accurate (i.e., empathic) knowledge of others' thoughts or feelings. Instead, these persons tend to be egocentrically biased, that is, biased by their own thinking, in the social inferences they make. As public self-consciousness heightens awareness and the cognitive availability of the self as a social entity, that self is more likely to be implicated into the assumed thoughts of others, resulting in a broad range of self-centered social–cognitive biases. Specifically, publicly self-conscious persons are prone to (a) exaggerate the extent to which they occupy the thoughts of others, (b) transform ambiguous or insignificant events into ones that appear to have personal relevance for the self, (c) overperceive the self as the cause or target of other's actions, and (d) attribute or project their own thoughts and behaviors onto others.

SELF-CONSCIOUSNESS AND PSYCHOLOGICAL MINDEDNESS

Psychological mindedness is defined as the tendency to try to understand or explain behavior in psychological terms (e.g., Wolitzky & Reuben, 1974). That is, the psychologically-minded individual does not simply accept behavior at face value, but rather views that behavior with an eye toward gaining insight into the underlying needs, wishes, or motives behind it. Although some theorists (e.g., McCallum & Piper, 1990) conceptualize psychological mindedness specifically in terms of receptivity to psychoanalytic explanations such as unresolved intrapsychic conflicts, others define it as a more general preference to engage in psychological accounts of behavior (e.g., Farber, 1989).

The concept of psychological mindedness is of special interest to clinicians because of the assumption that an individual inclined toward psychological accounts of behavior would be more amenable to the therapeutic process, or at least more receptive to a therapist's insights or interpretations of behavior; presumably, a person that is not psychologically minded, given his or her lack of interest in or understanding of psychological mechanisms, would be a relatively poor candidate for insight-oriented therapy.

Some theorists (e.g., Farber, 1989) regard self-consciousness, especially toward the inner, covert aspects of the self, as synonymous with or closely related to the construct of psychological mindedness, in that they both involve an interest in the inner workings of one's mind. However, a careful examination of these two dimensions reveals some important differences (e.g., Wolitzky & Reuben, 1974). In particular, although self-awareness suggests a tendency to think about ongoing psychological events, those thoughts are characterized, not so much by their attempt at explaining behavior as by the fact that the object of explanation is the self. Nevertheless, it may be of some interest to explore how attention toward the self relates to psychological mindedness.

What, then, are the implications of self-consciousness for the notion of psychological mindedness, specifically in terms of the therapeutic situation? Although no research has directly examined how these two variables relate to each other, some preliminary understanding of their relationship may be gained by identifying some issues that are relevant to both self-consciousness and psychological mindedness, and on which their effects may be expected to converge. In particular, psychological mindedness is posited to relate to (a) heightened awareness of ongoing mental processes, (b) greater amenability to the therapeutic process, resulting, presumably in better therapeutic outcomes, and (c) enhanced receptivity to the therapist's insights. Because self-consciousness also has implications for each of these issues, it may be of interest to compare the findings of the self-consciousness research with the expected effects of psychological mindedness. To the extent that psychological mindedness and self-consciousness are related to each other, their effects should be similar. It should be noted that because much of the research on self-consciousness was conducted in nonclinical settings, some of the following analyses may include speculations based on extrapolations from those studies.

SELF-CONSCIOUSNESS AND AWARENESS OF MENTAL PROCESSES

Franzoi and Brewer (1984) found that persons high in private self-consciousness, given their attention to internal thoughts and feelings, were more likely to disclose private information to friends. Presumably, as cognizance of and interest in these phenomena increases, so does the likelihood of their being discussed with others. To the extent that this kind of disclosure is essential to the therapeutic process, private self-consciousness, by providing valuable psychological insights, may facilitate meaningful give-and-take between patient and therapist.

However, an important distinction needs to be made between process and content, as they refer to the therapeutic enterprise. Although self-consciousness may indeed promote the process of therapy, whereby client and therapist discuss psychological concepts such as motives and needs in an attempt to gain an understanding of the underlying causes of behavior, that process needs to be distinguished from the content of that discussion, which refers to the specific insights the patient makes as a result of that process. Before concluding that an awareness of internal psychological processes is therapeutic, it must first be asked whether the insights identified are valid—do they represent reality? In this regard, it is important to understand that psychological mindedness refers to a preference, rather than an ability, for psychological explanations; that is, to engage in behavioral accounts making use of concepts such as motives or defensive strategies, although clearly an indication of psychological mindedness, says little about whether or not those explanations are correct.

Does self-focused attention, directed toward past or present psychological events, facilitate accurate insight? Not necessarily, according to several lines of evidence. As was shown in research on public self-consciousness, thinking about how one is viewed by others does not always translate into an understanding of the perspective of others (e.g., Fenigstein, 1984; Fenigstein & Abrams, 1993; Fenigstein & Vanable, 1992). Instead, preoccupation with oneself as a public object of attention often leads to exaggerated assumptions about the role of the self in other's thoughts. This research suggests that thinking about the self, rather than clarifying knowledge about it, sometimes has the effect of heightening the self's availability or subjective importance, resulting in a biasing of mental judgments.

Public self-consciousness, although directing attention inward toward one's own thoughts, involves an added layer of complexity, in that those thoughts involve assumptions about the self-relevant thoughts of others. That added complexity may not allow a fair test of the effects of self-attention on self-insight. Less complex and perhaps more germane to the present issue is research suggesting that private self-consciousness, by focusing attention on private thoughts or feelings, offers more accurate information about those phenomena (e.g., Nasby, 1985; Scheier et al., 1978; Turner, 1978). This conclusion, however, is tempered by several considerations. For example, although some research argues that private self-consciousness clarifies the experience of internal sensations (e.g., Scheier et. al., 1979), other research suggests that, contrary to the notion of mere clarification, the effect of focusing attention on emotional states is to intensify, that is, to change, them (e.g., Scheier & Carver, 1977).

Questions may also be raised about the extent to which self-consciousness facilitates insight into the self's causal role. As opposed to increasing accuracy, some research suggests that self-focused attention, by heightening the self's salience or importance, results in biased judgments of causality involving either exaggerated self-attributions (e.g., Buss & Scheier, 1976; Fenigstein, 1979), or causal judgments serving primarily to protect self-esteem (e.g., Federoff & Harvey, 1976).

Research showing that self-directed attention heightens the accuracy of self-reports (e.g., Gibbons, 1990; Scheier et al., 1978), presumably because privately self-conscious individuals know themselves better, is also open to question; in particular, there is an alternative explanation for this "veridicality" effect. Among the most well-established findings in the self-awareness literature is research showing that self-awareness increases adherence to appropriate (as defined by the situation) or conventional standards of behavior (e.g., Duval & Wicklund, 1972; Wicklund & Duval, 1971). For example, Scheier, Fenigstein, and Buss (1974) found that in a laboratory study of aggression, where men had the opportunity to deliver painful shocks to women in clear violation of conventional standards of behavior, self-directed attention as induced by a mirror significantly reduced aggression in comparison to a no-mirror control group. In the context of a psychological study asking subjects to provide self-reports of behavior, it may be that self-consciousness, rather than providing insight into the self, simply motivates subjects to adhere to an implicit situational standard, and to be more careful and deliberate in their responses.

Other research questioned the reliability of the veridicality effect. Osberg and Schrauger (1986), for example, argued that one of the more objective ways to define self-insight is to view it as the ability to translate relevant self-knowledge into accurate predictions about one's future behavior in well-defined circumstances. Those with a greater understanding of their mental and emotional processes ought to be more successful in recognizing how those processes will direct subsequent behavior. In general, their research found that self-predictions of future behavior, compared to the judgments of external evaluators, had only modest accuracy. More relevant to the present discussion, however, were findings showing that private self-consciousness had the effect of decreasing the validity or accuracy of self-predictions.

Thus far, it has been suggested that although self-consciousness may appear to facilitate insight into one's own mental and emotional experiences, the research in support of that claim is inconsistent and equivocal. However, before asking whether self-attention can facilitate self-insight, an even more basic question is whether such insight is possible. Nisbett and Wilson (1977) convincingly argued and demonstrated that access to higher order mental processes is poor, thus limiting one's ability to know the causes of, or, the psychological processes underlying or explaining, one's thoughts and behavior. Although this argument generated controversy and challenge (e.g., Ericsson & Simon, 1980; Hixon & Swann, 1993; Smith & Miller, 1978), there remains considerable evidence in support of the contention that many mental phenomena are not open to insight (e.g., Nisbett & Bellows, 1977; Wilson, 1985). Research showed, for example, that persons' estimates of the degree of correlation between their own moods and several predictor variables (such as weather or amount of sleep) was no more accurate (as judged by the actual correlation between reported mood and a given predictor) than were the estimates made by a control group of subjects relying entirely on "armchair" speculations about the relation between mood and various predictors (Wilson, Laser, & Stone, 1982). That is, actors are no better at identifying the causes of their own behavior than are random observers, despite the fact that observers have no access to the private, inner workings of the actors' minds.

In subsequent studies on "thoughtfulness" (e.g., Wilson, 1990; Wilson, Dunn, Kraft, & Lisle, 1989), subjects were explicitly asked to think about (i.e., to direct attention toward), the reasons or explanations for their feelings or attitudes, a kind of laboratory simulation of the psychological mindedness often exercised in a therapy session. These studies consistently found that this form of thoughtfulness produced greater changes in feelings or attitudes than occurred when little thought was given to them. That is, when thought or attention is directed inward, although it may focus on some "core truth" or "insight" regarding the source of feelings, it is just as likely to highlight some tangential, but momentarily salient, idea, resulting in new thoughts about and a change in attitude. This inability to differentiate between real and experimentally manipulated causal explanations again suggests that people have relatively poor access to their higher order mental processes, and that directing attention to these processes does little to provide a clearer, more insightful understanding of them.

Extrapolating from this research to the clinic, where persons are asked, not only to provide a clearer picture of existing self-information, but to uncover new insights about the self, scepticism about the accuracy of those insights can only be greater. When asked to examine the workings of their own minds, clients may have little difficulty in offering accounts of psychological phenomena. But these introspections, rather than being based on valid therapeutic insights, may simply reflect broadly shared cultural theories about psychological cause and effect (e.g., Nisbett & Wilson, 1977), or may rely on salient and persuasive suggestions by the therapist that were subtly incorporated into the client's thought processes, and were subsequently recognized as plausible psychological explanations.

A number of examples have now been identified of what amounts to the psychological equivalent of the Heisenberg principle: Self-observation seems to change the nature of whatever aspect of self is being observed. That is, when attention or thoughtful scrutiny is directed toward psychological phenomena such as ongoing affect (e.g., Scheier & Carver, 1977), causal judgments for one's behavior (Duval & Wicklund, 1973), the reasons underlying one's attitudes or feelings (e.g., Wilson, 1990), or the idea of oneself as a social object (e.g., Fenigstein, 1984), this "looking inward," rather than having a simple clarifying or elucidating effect, instead tends to significantly alter whatever aspect of the self is being thought about, essentially by altering the salience or subjective importance of that aspect. Thus, although self-directed attention may facilitate the process of engaging in a search for the causes of one's own behavior, and although it may appear to facilitate insight into those causes, one must be sceptical about the accuracy or value of the insights gained.

SELF-CONSCIOUSNESS, MENTAL HEALTH, AND PSYCHOPATHOLOGY

To the extent that psychological mindedness facilitates the therapeutic process, and that self-consciousness mediates that relationship, another important question to be asked is whether self-consciousness itself has any implications for improving or debilitating psychological functioning. Although the validity of the insights derived from self-awareness were questioned, a heightened cognizance of mental events may still be of therapeutic value to the extent that they help provide psychological explanations, albeit inaccurate ones, for behavior. That is, the understanding gained from these explanations may be illusory, but nonetheless beneficial in fostering a sense of control and an appreciation of the meaning of behavior (e.g., Heider, 1958). In other words, the more people think they know about themselves, the more they may feel they are in a position to exercise meaningful control over their behavior, and that could be an important prerequisite of mental health (e.g., Langer, 1983).

On the other hand, a number of different approaches to psychopathology suggest that a heightened awareness of self may be psychologically dysfunctional. Some theorists argue, for example, that self-scrutiny invariably leads to self-criticism and negative affect. Self-awareness, by focusing attention on personal shortcomings (e.g., Brockner, 1979), or by attuning the self to inner contradictions (e.g., Scheier & Carver, 1980), or by preventing people from ignoring or escaping unpleasant or threatening truths about themselves (e.g., Baumeister, 1991; Gibbons, 1990), may produce decrements in mood or self-esteem. Others argue that self-focused attention is inextricably linked to greater awareness of, and rumination about, specifically dysphoric emotions, which then heighten the individual's distress (e.g., Wood, Saltzberg, & Goldsamt, 1990). Although there is relatively little research suggesting that self-consciousness has positive consequences for mental health, there has been a virtual explosion of research in recent years emphasizing self-focused attention as a means of explaining various disordered behaviors, including anxiety, depression, and paranoia (e.g., Ingram, 1990; Pyszczynski, Greenberg, Hamilton, & Nix, 1991).

Anxiety

Numerous studies support the idea that heightened attention to the self promotes anxiety (e.g., Izard, 1972; Sarason, 1972; Wine, 1982). Although private self-focus increases awareness of and responsiveness to affective stimuli generally (e.g., Scheier & Carver, 1977), the effect is especially robust in the case of negative affect (e.g., Csikszentmihalyi & Figurski, 1982; Gibbons, 1990). In part, this may be because the ordinary stream of consciousness is largely made up of unfinished intentions, and attention to these thoughts is likely to provoke discomforting emotions such as anxiety, fear, sadness, and anger (Singer, 1988). In addition to the amplification of negative affect, self-focus may also exacerbate anxiety by increasing negative thinking (e.g., Beck & Clark, 1988), fostering ruminative and nonproductive coping responses (Beck & Emery, 1985), and contributing to performance deficits (Carver, Peterson, Follansbee, & Scheier, 1983).

An important insight into the relationship between self-attention and anxiety was provided by Izard's (1972) analysis of emotion suggesting that anxiety in a performance context almost always involves an element of self-evaluation, along with the concomitant concern and apprehension that self-evaluation produces. Self-awareness is also conceptualized in terms of a real or imaginary evaluative audience, composed of the self or others, who in effect are watching the self-aware person perform (Carver & Scheier, 1981; Duval & Wicklund, 1972; Fenigstein & Vanable, 1992). Thus, to the extent that self-evaluation is dependent on self-awareness, self-focused attention may be a crucial component of the performance interference associated with anxiety. This effect may be especially strong when there is also a negative outcome expectancy (e.g., Carver & Scheier, 1981). In that case, attention is unlikely to be directed toward the task at hand, but instead may be directed further inward, resulting in excessive and ruminative self-preoccupation, as occurs in the case of test anxiety (Wine, 1982) and sexual spectatoring (Barlow, 1986).

Depression

Several parallels were noted between the characteristics of depression and those of private self-focused attention, such as low self-esteem, self-blaming tendencies, and difficulty in engaging in self-deceptive or positive illusions (e.g., Musson & Alloy, 1988). In addition, studies consistently show positive correlations between measures of self-focus and those of depression (e.g., Ingram, Lumry, Cruet, & Sieber, 1987; Smith & Greenberg, 1981). These findings inspired several theoretical models of depression according self-focused attention a central role (e.g., Greenberg & Pyszczynski, 1986; Lewinsohn, Hoberman, Teri, & Hautzinger, 1985).

Pyszczynski and Greenberg (1987), argued that a reciprocal relationship exists between self-focus and depression, resulting in an ever-increasing, perseverative cycle: Depressed persons engage in higher levels of self-directed attention than do nondepressed persons (e.g., Ingram et al., 1987); and self-focus helps to maintain the various affective, cognitive, and behavioral consequences associated with depression. This cycle is often set in motion by the loss of a central source of self-worth, which establishes a depressed state and focuses the victim's attention on a sense of self incapable of restoring self-worth. That self-focus, by heightening negative thinking (e.g., Pyszczynski, Hamilton, Herring, & Greenberg, 1989), negative affect (Wood, Saltzberg, Neale, Stone, & Rachmiel, 1990), self-blame and low self-esteem (e.g., Pyszczynski, Holt, & Greenberg, 1987), and performance deficits (e.g., Strack, Blaney, Ganellen, & Coyne, 1985), serves to exacerbate the depression. In addition to these links, Wood, Saltzberg, Neale et. al., (1990) point out that depressed persons also tend to use coping responses that resemble the characteristics of self-awareness: both involve systematically observing behavior and being overly preoccupied with feelings. Self-focus then, by fostering rumination about moods and problems, may interfere with more productive, problem-focused coping, thus heightening and prolonging the depression.

Paranoia

The idea that paranoia is related to self-consciousness has a long history (e.g., Cameron, 1943; Kraepelin, 1915; Shapiro, 1965). More recently, research by Fenigstein (e.g., Fenigstein, 1984, 1994; Fenigstein & Vanable,

1992) consistently found relationships between public self-consciousness and measures of paranoia. As a result of directing one's own attention toward the self, the person may come to believe that others are also directing attention toward him or her. That is, self-consciousness, by heightening the salience and subjective importance of the self, and overinvolving the self in the social inference process, may contribute to the distinctly paranoid tendency to perceive oneself as the target of others' thoughts and actions. That misperception, whereby, for example, the laughter of others in the distance comes to be seen as a personal embarrassment, is commonly referred to as an idea (or delusion) of reference, and may be regarded as one of the hallmark characteristics of paranoid thinking (e.g., Cameron, 1943; Magaro, 1980; Millon, 1981; Swanson, Bohnert, & Smith, 1970).

Because paranoia is marked by serious, self-referential distortions in the way in which others' actions are perceived and interpreted, its specific relation to public self-consciousness, in which attention is directed toward those aspects of the self that are potentially observable by others, is not surprising. As suggested earlier, awareness of one's own observability to others can easily induce a feeling of visibility or conspicuousness (e.g., Fenigstein & Vanable, 1992), resulting in the (not altogether illogical) paranoid assumption that others are watching you or are very much aware of your presence, and thus are likely to be acting with you in mind (e.g., Fenigstein, 1979). It is not unreasonable at that point to engage in paranoid interpretations of others' behavior, transforming insignificant and irrelevant events into ones that appear to have personal relevance for the self, so that for example, the appearance of a stranger on the street is taken as an indication that one is being watched or plotted against (e.g., Fenigstein, 1984).

Although the research on self-consciousness and paranoia was largely concerned with direct effects on paranoid behavior, self-focus may also be related to paranoia through some critical mediating mechanisms. In particular, to interpret events as if they were intentionally directed toward the self is to engage in personalistic thinking (Heider, 1958; Jones & Davis, 1965). This thinking, in which another's behavior is explained in terms of their personal intent or dispositions, may offer some critical insights into many of the interpersonal dynamics of paranoia. For example, paranoids rarely accept the idea that bad things just happen (e.g., Millon, 1981; Shapiro, 1965). Instead, they are inclined to regard the negative event itself as evidence for another's malevolent intentions toward them. Given the attribution of intent, minor slights become major insults, and eventually, the accumulation of such occurrences constitutes evidence for a view of the world as a hostile and threatening place. Other manifestations of paranoia then become comprehensible: suspicion and guardedness; selective attention to signs of trickery or exploitation; misinterpretation of apparently harmless events as malevolent; readiness to take offense and counterattack;

and blaming others for all of one's difficulties. As a result, hostilities become intensified, suspicions are confirmed, and enemies are found everywhere.

Another mechanism, through which self-focus may relate to paranoia, is by interfering with the ability to take another's perspective. One of the basic elements of the thinking of paranoid persons is their utter inability to understand the motivations and perspectives of others (e.g., Millon, 1981) or to examine behavior from any context other than their own (e.g., Shapiro, 1965). Self-focused attention by, in effect, locking persons into their own perspective, may contribute to this diminished capacity for considering other viewpoints. Fenigstein and Abrams (1993) found that attention focused toward the public aspects of self, by heightening the salience of one's own perspective, consistently increased the assumption that others thought and acted in the same way as the self. That is, the narrowness and rigidity of paranoid thought—the failure to examine events critically or in a broader context, the extreme selectivity in processing information, and the unwillingness to consider alternative perspectives—may, in part, result from the self-focused style of thought that characterizes paranoia.

There is a good deal of evidence that public self-consciouness is associated with a variety of effects that are remarkably similar to those observed in paranoia. In particular, as a result of their own preoccupation with themselves as social objects, persons high in public self-consciousness have difficulty avoiding the personalistic inference that others are acting with them in mind or that events in some way are targeted toward them. Given that such egocentric, self-referential inferences are one of the defining characteristics of paranoid thought, this research suggests a strong relationship between self-consciousness and paranoid ideation.

Although the prevailing wisdom in clinical psychology has been that accurate self-knowledge is a prerequisite of mental health, and that self-consciousness may, to some extent, underlie or mediate that self-knowledge, the research reviewed suggests that for individuals suffering from anxiety, depression, or paranoia, whatever the therapeutic benefits of self-awareness, those benefits are more than likely to be offset by the debilitating psychological consequences of self-focused attention.

SELF-CONSCIOUSNESS AND RECEPTIVITY TO THERAPEUTIC SUGGESTIONS

A final and fundamental issue arising with respect to psychological mindedness is whether self-consciousness renders an individual more receptive to a therapist's insights or interpretations of behavior. The speculative answer is a highly tentative yes; that is, self-conscious clients may, in fact, be likely to find themselves in agreement with their therapist, but that agreement may reflect conformity processes more than a genuine meeting of the minds.

In any therapeutic situation, there are a great many psychological influences that operate to encourage the patient's acceptance of the therapist's insights. Self-insight is often established as a significant therapeutic goal for the client, and proximity to that goal is often judged by the extent to which a client's insights fall in line with those of the therapist. As a result, acceptance of the therapist's insights, in and of itself, may be taken as an indication of progress by the client. In addition, that acceptance may serve as confirmation of the therapist's acumen, and presumably would be regarded as a positive outcome by the therapist. Thus, independent of the actual therapeutic benefits of agreeing with the therapist's insights, such agreement is a highly desirable goal for both the client and the therapist, and both are motivated to achieve it.

In the presence of this salient and consensually accepted behavioral standard, the implications of a considerable body of research on self-consciousness are clear: self-directed attention should heighten awareness of that standard, and increase conformity to it (e.g., Carver & Scheier, 1981; Duval & Wicklund, 1972). This effect should operate irrespective of whether self-consciousness is private or public because standards are not in conflict: the client's personal standard of gaining insight is concordant with the standard represented by the therapist, and responsiveness to either one should facilitate the patient's agreement with the therapist's interpretations.

SUMMARY AND CONCLUSIONS

In summary, an examination of the nature of self-consciousness raises serious questions about the therapeutic value of any such self-directed attention. Research on self-consciousness offers little support for the notion that self-attention or self-reflection can actually facilitate insight into psychological phenomena; even if there are any benefits to an awareness of ongoing mental processes, they must be weighed against the debilitating effects of the self-preoccupation, rumination, and dysphoria that often accompany self-consciousness; and acceptance by the patient of the therapist's insights must be at least partly regarded as an artifactual outcome of the effects of self-consciousness on persuasibility and conformity to consensual standards of behavior.

Thus we are left with several tentative conclusions about the relationship between psychological mindedness and self-consciousness. To the extent that psychological mindedness involves a tendency to direct attention toward the inner, psychological aspects of the self, that does not bode well for the posited therapeutic value of psychological mindedness. On the other hand, if such therapeutic benefits are validated, the present review suggests that such beneficial effects are unlikely to be mediated by any self-consciousness that may be associated with psychological mindedness.

REFERENCES

Barlow, D. (1986). Causes of sexual dysfunction: The role of anxiety and cognitive interference. *Journal of Consulting and Clinical Psychology, 54,* 14–48.

Baumeister, R. F. (1986). *Identity: Cultural change and the struggle for self.* New York: Oxford University Press.

Baumeister, R. F. (1991). *Escaping the self: Alcoholism, spirituality, masochism, and other flights from the burden of selfhood.* New York: Basic Books.

Beck, A. T., & Clark, D. A. (1988). Anxiety and depression: An information processing perspective. *Anxiety Research, 1,* 23–36.

Beck, A. T., & Emery, G. (1985). *Anxiety disorders and phobias: A cognitive perspective.* New York: Basic Books.

Brockner, J. (1979). The effects of self-esteem, success–failure, and self-consciousness on task performance. *Journal of Personality and Social Psychology, 37,* 1732–1741.

Buss, A. H. (1980). *Self-consciousness and social anxiety.* San Francisco: Freeman.

Buss, D. M., & Scheier, M. F. (1976). Self-awareness, self-consciousness, and self-attribution. *Journal of Research in Personality, 10,* 463–468.

Cameron, N. (1943). The development of paranoic thinking. *Psychological Review, 50,* 219–233.

Carver, C. S., & Glass, D. C. (1976). The self-consciousness scale: A discriminant validity study. *Journal of Personality Assessment, 40,* 169–172.

Carver, C. S., Peterson, L. M., Follansbee, D. J., & Scheier, M. F. (1983). Effects of self-directed attention on performance and persistence among persons high and low in test anxiety. *Cognitive Theory and Research, 7,* 337–354.

Carver, C. S., & Scheier, M. F. (1978). Self-focusing effects of dispositional self-consciousness, mirror presence, and audience presence. *Journal of Personality and Social Psychology, 36,* 324–332.

Carver, C. S., & Scheier, M. F. (1981). *Attention and self-regulation: A control theory approach to human behavior.* New York: Springer-Verlag.

Cheek, J. M., & Briggs, S. R. (1982). Self-consciousness and aspects of identity. *Journal of Research in Personality, 16,* 401–408.

Cooley, C. H. (1902). *Human nature and the social order.* New York: Scribner's.

Csikszentmihalyi, M., & Figurski, T. J. (1982). Self-awareness and aversive experiences in everyday life. *Journal of Personality, 50,* 15–28.

Duval, S., & Wicklund, R. A. (1972). *A theory of objective self-awareness.* New York: Academic Press.

Duval, S., & Wicklund, R. A. (1973). Effects of objective self-awareness on attributions of causality. *Journal of Experimental Social Psychology, 9,* 17–31.

Ellis, R. J., & Holmes, J. G. (1982). Focus of attention and self-evaluation in social interaction. *Journal of Personality and Social Psychology, 43,* 67–77.

Ericsson, K. A., & Simon, H. A. (1980). Verbal reports as data. *Psychological Review, 87,* 215–251.

Erikson, E. H. (1956). The problem of ego identity. *Journal of the American Psychoanalytic Association, 4,* 56–121.

Farber, B. A. (1989). Psychological-mindedness: Can there be too much of a good thing? *Psychotherapy, 26,* 210–217.

Federoff, N. A., & Harvey, J. H. (1976). Focus of attention, self-esteem, and the attribution of causality. *Journal of Research in Personality, 10,* 336–345.

Fenigstein, A. (1979). Self-consciousness, self-attention, and social interaction. *Journal of Personality and Social Psychology, 37,* 75–86.

Fenigstein, A. (1984). Self-consciousness and the overperception of self as a target. *Journal of Personality and Social Psychology, 47,* 860–870.

Fenigstein, A. (1987). On the nature of public and private self-consciousness. *Journal of Personality, 55,* 543–554.

Fenigstein, A. (1994). Paranoia. In V. S. Ramachandran (Ed.), *Encyclopedia of human behavior* (Vol. 3, pp. 401–410). San Diego, CA: Academic Press.

Fenigstein, A., & Abrams, D. (1993). Self-attention and the egocentric assumption of shared perspectives. *Journal of Experimental Social Psychology, 29,* 287–303.

Fenigstein, A., & Carver, C. S. (1978). Self-focusing effects of heartbeat feedback. *Journal of Personality and Social Psychology, 36,* 1241–1250.
Fenigstein, A., & Levine, M. (1984). Self-attention, concept activation, and the causal self. *Journal of Experimental Social Psychology, 20,* 231–245.
Fenigstein, A., Scheier, M. F., & Buss, A. H. (1975). Public and private self-consciousness: Assessment and theory. *Journal of Consulting and Clincal Psychology, 43,* 522–527.
Fenigstein, A., & Vanable, P. A. (1992). Paranoia and self-consciousness. *Journal of Personality and Social Psychology, 62,* 129–138.
Fenigstein, A., & Vanable, P. A. (1993). *Private and public self-esteem: The effects of self-consciousness.* Unpublished manuscript, Kenyon College, Gambier, OH.
Franzoi, S. L. (1983). Self-concept differences as a function of private self-consciousness and social anxiety. *Journal of Research in Personality, 17,* 275–287.
Franzoi, S. L., & Brewer, L. C. (1984). The experience of self-awareness and its relation to level of self-consciousness: An experiential sampling study. *Journal of Research in Personality, 18,* 522–540.
Froming, W. J., & Carver, C. S. (1981). Divergent influences of private and public self-consciousness in a compliance paradigm. *Journal of Research in Personality, 15,* 159–171.
Froming, W. J., Walker, G. R., & Lopyan, K. J. (1982). Public and private self-awareness: When personal attitudes conflict with societal expectations. *Journal of Experimental Social Psychology, 18,* 476–487.
Gibbons, F. X. (1990). Self-attention and behavior: A review and theoretical update. In L. Berkowitz (Ed.), *Advances in experimental social psychology* (Vol. 23, pp. 249–303). New York: Academic Press.
Goffman, E. (1959). *The presentation of self in everyday life.* Garden City, NY: Doubleday.
Greenberg, J. (1982). Self-image versus impression management in adherence to distributive justice standards: The influence of self-awarenes and self-consciousness. *Journal of Personality and Social Psychology, 44,* 5–19.
Greenberg, J., & Pyszczynski, T. (1986). Persistent high self-focus after failure and low self-focus after success: The depressive self-focusing style. *Journal of Personality and Social Psychology, 50,* 1039–1044.
Greenwald, A. G. (1980). The totalitarian ego: Fabrication and revision of personal history. *American Psychologist, 35,* 603–618.
Hass, R. G. (1984). Perspective taking and self-awareness: Drawing an E on your forehead. *Journal of Personality and Social Psychology, 46,* 788–798.
Heider, F. (1958). *The psychology of interpersonal relations.* New York: Wiley.
Hixon, J. G., & Swann, W. B. (1993). When does introspection bear fruit? Self-reflection, self-insight, and interpersonal choices. *Journal of Personality and Social Psychology, 64,* 35–43.
Hull, J. G., & Levy, A. S. (1979). The organizational functions of self: An alternative to the Duval and Wicklund model of self-awareness. *Journal of Personality and Social Psychology, 37,* 756–768.
Ingram, R. E. (1990). Self-focused attention in clinical disorders: Review and a conceptual model. *Psychological Bulletin, 107,* 156–176.
Ingram, R. E., Lumry, A. E., Cruet, D., & Sieber, W. (1987). Attentional processes in depressive disorders. *Cognitive Theory and Research, 11,* 351–360.
Izard, C. (1972). *Patterns of emotion: A new analysis of anxiety and depression.* New York: Academic Press.
James, W. (1890). *The principles of psychology* (Vol. 1). New York: Holt, Rinehart & Winston.
Jones, E. E., & Davis, K. E. (1965). From acts to dispositions: The attribution process in person perception. In L. Berkowitz (Ed.), *Advances in experimental social psychology* (Vol. 2, pp. 219–266). New York: Academic Press.
Jung, C. G. (1957). *The undiscovered self.* New York: New American Library.
Kihlstrom, J. F., Cantor, J., Albright, J., Chew, B., Klein, S., & Niedenthal, P. (1988). Information processing and the study of the self. In L. Berkowitz (Ed.), *Advances in experimental social psychology* (Vol. 21, pp. 145–178). New York: Academic Press.
Klein, S. B., & Loftus, J. (1988). The nature of self-referent encoding: The contributions of elaborative and organizational processes. *Journal of Personality and Social Psychology, 55,* 5–11.

Kraepelin, E. (1915). *Psychiatrie: Ein Lehrbuch* [Psychiatry: A Textbook] (7th ed.). Leipzig, Germany: Barth.
Langer, E. (1983). *The psychology of control*. Beverly Hills, CA: Sage.
Leary, M. R. (1983). *Understanding social anxiety: Social, personality, and clinical perspectives*. Beverly Hills, CA: Sage.
Lewinsohn, P. M., Hoberman, H., Teri, L., & Hautzinger, M. (1985). An integrative theory of depression. In S. Reiss & R. Bootzin (Eds.), *Theoretical issues in behavior therapy* (pp. 331–359). New York: Academic Press.
Magaro, P. A. (1980). *Cognition in schizophrenia and paranoia: The interpretation of cognitive processes*. Hillsdale, NJ: Lawrence Erlbaum Associates.
Markus, H. (1977). Self-schemata and processing information about the self. *Journal of Personality and Social Psychology, 35*, 63–78.
McCallum, M., & Piper, W. E. (1990). The psychological mindedness assessment procedure. *Psychological Assessment: A Journal of Consulting and Clinical Psychology, 2*, 412–418.
Mead, G. H. (1934). *Mind, self, and society*. Chicago: University of Chicago Press.
Miller, L. C., & Cox, C. L. (1982). For appearance's sake: Public self-consciousness and makeup use. *Personality and Social Psychology Bulletin, 8*, 748– 751.
Millon, T. H. (1981). *Disorders of personality*. New York: Wiley.
Musson, R. F., & Alloy, L. B. (1988). Depression and self-directed attention. In L. B. Alloy (Ed.), *Cognitive processes in depression* (pp. 193–220). New York: Guilford.
Nasby, W. (1985). Private self-consciousness, articulation of the self-schema, and recognition memory of trait adjectives. *Journal of Personality and Social Psychology, 49*, 704–709.
Nasby, W. (1989). Private and public self-consciousness and articulation of the self-schema. *Journal of Personality and Social Psychology, 56*, 117–123.
Nisbett, R. E., & Bellows, N. (1977). Verbal reports about causal influences on social judgments: Private access versus public theories. *Journal of Personality and Social Psychology, 35*, 613–624.
Nisbett, R. E., & Wilson, T. D. (1977). Telling more than we can know: Verbal reports on mental processes. *Psychological Review, 84*, 231–259.
Osberg, T. M., & Schrauger, J. S. (1986). Self-prediction: Exploring the parameters of accuracy. *Journal of Personality and Social Psychology, 51*, 1044–1057.
Pyszczynski, T., & Greenberg, J. (1987). Self-regulatory perseveration and the depressive self-focusing style: A self-awareness theory of the development and maintenance of depression. *Psychological Bulletin, 102*, 122–138.
Pyszczynski, T., Greenberg, J., Hamilton, J. C., & Nix, G. (1991). On the relationship between self-focused attention and psychological disorder: A critical reappraisal. *Psychological Bulletin, 110*, 538–543.
Pyszczynski, T., Hamilton, J. C., Herring, F. H., & Greenberg, J. (1989). Depression, self-focused attention, and negative memory bias. *Journal of Personality and Social Psychology, 57*, 351–357.
Pyszczynski, T., Holt, K., & Greenberg, J. (1987). Depression, self-focused attention, and expectancies for future positive and negative events for self and others. *Journal of Personality and Social Psychology, 52*, 994–1001.
Rogers, T. B., Kuiper, N. A., & Kirker, W. S. (1977). Self-reference and the encoding of personal information. *Journal of Personality and Social Psychology, 35*, 677–688.
Sarason, I. G. (1972). Experimental approaches to test anxiety: Attention and the uses of information. In C. D. Spielberger (Ed.), *Anxiety: Current trends in theory and research* (Vol. 2, pp. 381–403). Orlando, FL: Academic Press.
Scheier, M. F. (1976). Self-awareness, self-consciousness, and angry aggression. *Journal of Personality, 44*, 627–644.
Scheier, M. F. (1980). Effects of public and private self-consciousness on the public expression of personal beliefs. *Journal of Personality and Social Psychology, 39*, 514–521.
Scheier, M. F., Buss, A. H., & Buss, D. M. (1978). Self-consciousness, self-report of aggressiveness, and aggression. *Journal of Research in Personality, 12*, 133–140.
Scheier, M. F., & Carver, C. S. (1977). Self-focused attention and the experience of emotion: Attraction, repulsion, elation, and depression. *Journal of Personality and Social Psychology, 35*, 625–636.
Scheier, M. F., & Carver, C. S. (1980). Private and public self-attention, resistance to change, and dissonance reduction. *Journal of Personality and Social Psychology, 39*, 390–405.

Scheier, M. F., & Carver, C. S. (1983). Two sides of the self: One for you and one for me. In J. Suls & A. G. Greenwald (Eds.), *Psychological perspectives on the self* (Vol. 2, pp. 123–157). Hillsdale, NJ: Lawrence Erlbaum Associates.

Scheier, M. F., Carver, C. S., & Gibbons, R. X. (1979). Self-directed attention, awareness of bodily states, and suggestibility. *Journal of Personality and Social Psychology, 37*, 1576–1588.

Scheier, M. F., Fenigstein, A., & Buss, A. H. (1974). Self-awareness and physical aggression. *Journal of Experimental Social Psychology, 10*, 264–273.

Schlenker, B. R. (1980). *Impression management: The self-concept, social identity, and interpersonal relations*. Monterey, CA: Brooks/Cole.

Schlenker, B. R., & Weigold, M. F. (1990). Self-consciousness and self-presentation: Being autonomous versus appearing autonomous. *Journal of Personality and Social Psychology, 59*, 820–828.

Shapiro, D. (1965). *Neurotic styles*. New York: Basic Books.

Singer, J. L. (1988). Sampling ongoing consciousness and emotional experience: Implications for health. In M. J. Horowitz (Ed.), *Psychodynamics and cognition* (pp. 297–346). Chicago: University of Chicago Press.

Smith, E. R., & Miller, F. D. (1978). Limits on perception of cognitive processes: A reply to Nisbett and Wilson. *Psychological Review, 85*, 355–362.

Smith, T. W., & Greenberg, J. (1981). Depression and self-focused attention. *Motivation and Emotion, 5*, 323–331.

Strack, S., Blaney, P. H., Ganellen, R. J., & Coyne, J. C. (1985). Pessimistic self-preoccupation, performance deficits, and depression. *Journal of Personality and Social Psychology, 49*, 1076–1085.

Swanson, D. W., Bohnert, P. J., & Smith, J. (1970). *The paranoid*. Boston: Little, Brown.

Tobey, E. L., & Tunnell, G. (1981). Predicting our impressions on others: Effects of public self-consciousness and acting, a self-monitoring subscale. *Personality and Social Psychology Bulletin, 7*, 661–669.

Tooby, J., & Cosmides, L. (1990). On the universality of human nature and the uniqueness of the individual: The role of genetics and adaptation. *Journal of Personality, 58*, 17–67.

Turner, R. G. (1978). Self-consciousness and speed of processing self-relevant information. *Personality and Social Psychology Bulletin, 4*, 456–460.

Turner, R. G. (1980). Self-consciousness and memory of trait terms. *Personality and Social Psychology Bulletin, 6*, 273–277.

Turner, R. G., Gilliland, L., & Klein, H. M. (1981). Self-consciousness, evaluation of physical characteristics, and physical attractiveness. *Journal of Research in Personality, 15*, 182–190.

Turner, R. G., & Peterson, M. (1977). Public and private self-consciousness and emotional expressivity. *Journal of Consulting and Clinical Psychology, 45*, 490–491.

Turner, R. G., Scheier, M. F., Carver, C. S., & Ickes, W. (1978). Correlates of self-consciousness. *Journal of Personality Assessment, 42*, 285–289.

Tversky, A., & Kahneman, D. (1973). Availability: A heuristic for judging frequency and probability. *Cognitive Psychology, 5*, 207–232.

Underwood, B., & Moore, B. S. (1981). Sources of behavioral consistency. *Journal of Personality and Social Psychology, 40*, 781–785.

Wicklund, R. A. (1975). Objective self-awareness. In L. Berkowitz (Ed.), *Advances in experimental social psychology* (Vol. 8, pp. 233–275). New York: Academic Press.

Wicklund, R. A., & Duval, S. (1971). Opinion change and performance facilitation as a result of objective self-awareness. *Journal of Experimental Social Psychology, 7*, 319–342.

Wicklund, R. A., & Gollwitzer, P. M. (1987). The fallacy of the private-public self-focus distinction. *Journal of Personality, 55*, 492–523.

Wilson, T. D. (1985). Strangers to ourselves: The origins and accuracy of beliefs about one's own mental states. In J. H. Harvey & G. Weary (Eds.), *Attribution in contemporary psychology* (pp. 9–36). New York: Academic Press.

Wilson, T. D. (1990). Self-persuasion via self-reflection. In J. Olson & M. P. Zanna (Eds.), *Self-inference processes: The Ontario Symposium* (Vol. 6, pp. 43–67). Hillsdale, NJ: Lawrence Erlbaum Associates.

Wilson, T. D., Dunn, D. S., Kraft, D., & Lisle, D. J. (1989). Introspection, attitude change, and attitude–behavior consistency: The disruptive effects of explaining why we feel the way we do. In L. Berkowitz (Ed.), *Advances in experimental social psychology* (Vol. 19, pp. 123–205). Orlando, FL: Academic Press.

Wilson, T. D., Laser, P., & Stone, J. (1982). Judging the predictors of one's own mood: Accuracy and the use of shared theories. *Journal of Experimental Social Psychology, 18*, 537–556.

Wine, J. D. (1982). Evaluation anxiety: A cognitive-attentional construct. In H. W. Krohne & L. C. Laux (Eds.), *Achievement, stress, and anxiety* (pp. 207–222). Washington, DC: Hemisphere.

Wolitzky, D. L., & Reuben, R. (1974). Psychological-mindedness. *Journal of Clinical Psychology, 30*, 26–30.

Wood, J. V., Saltzberg, J. A., & Goldsamt, L. A. (1990). Does affect induce self-focused attention? *Journal of Personality and Social Psychology, 58*, 899–908.

Wood, J. V., Saltzberg, J. A., Neale, J. M., Stone, A. A., & Rachmiel, T. B. (1990). Self-focused attention, coping responses, and distressed mood in everyday life. *Journal of Personality and Social Psychology, 58*, 1027–1036.

Chapter 6

Personal Intelligence

Lee Crandall Park
Johns Hopkins University, Baltimore
Thomas Joseph Park
University of Illinois at Chicago

Personal intelligence refers to information-processing capacities about psychological characteristics of self and others. Gardner (1983) described two kinds of personal intelligence. *Intrapersonal intelligence* is defined as a capacity for "access to one's own feeling life—one's range of affects or emotions: the capacity instantly to effect discriminations among these feelings and, eventually, to label them, to enmesh them in symbolic codes, to draw upon them as a means of understanding and guiding one's behavior" (p. 239). More recently Gardner (1993a, 1993b) stated that having an accurate model of oneself, which is necessary for effective decision making, is also an essential element of intrapersonal intelligence. *Interpersonal intelligence* is defined as "the ability to notice and make distinctions among other individuals and, in particular, among their moods, temperaments, motivations, and intentions" (1983, p. 239). This intelligence includes the "capacity to place one's self into the skin of specific other individuals" (p. 250). Such capacity can involve the ability to understand and predict the behaviors of others, to work appropriately and cooperatively with others, as well as to empathize—that is, to accurately experience the feelings and motivations of another person from the perspective of that other person (1983, 1993b).

Gardner first identified personal intelligence in his landmark book, *Frames of Mind: The Theory of Multiple Intelligences* (1983). He defined human intelligence as: "The ability to solve problems, or to fashion products that are valued in one or more cultural or community settings." (1993b, pp. 7, 15–16). Gardner provided detailed evidence that there are at least six relatively independent or modular categories of intelligence: linguistic, musical, logical–mathematical, spatial, bodily–kinesthetic, and personal. He identified these intelligence constructs using specific prerequisites and criteria including: (a) evidence for basic information-processing mechanisms that are activated by certain kinds of internally or externally presented information, (b) isolation of a function by brain damage, (c) the existence of exceptional individuals, (d) a distinctive developmental history; (e) evolutionary history and evolutionary plausibility, and (f) human and primate experimental evidence (Gardner 1983, 1985, 1993b). Gardner conjectured that there may be specific subunits of these intelligences as well as additional intelligences. Although personal intelligence, the ability to know oneself and others, is considered to be the most advanced of the intelligences, regulating the other categories of intelligence to some extent, researchers find it difficult to study. To our knowledge, only one rudimentary scale exists for measuring it in a clinical setting.

Gardner reasoned that the expression of personal intelligence, probably to a greater degree than other intelligences, is markedly vulnerable to cultural and caregiver influences, requiring appropriate life experiences for full and healthy development. It is probable, for instance, that a skill for consistent, accurate empathy in adulthood requires a history of healthy reinforcement and education during the developing years (Brothers, 1989; Damon, 1990; Hunt, 1990) regardless of an exceptional inborn talent for experiencing others.

The theory of multiple intelligences generated considerable interest and debate. In general, educators have been in favor of the theory because the concept of modularity is in alignment with their experience that each individual has his or her own unique combination of talents and liabilities, and can greatly benefit from identification of these characteristics (Chion-Kenney, 1994). In contrast, psychometricians emphasize the concept of a unitary general intelligence or g factor that can be measured for everyone using a standardized test such as the Wechsler Adult Intelligence Scale (WAIS; Fraser, 1995; Herrnstein & Murray, 1994).

In the following sections, we provide an explanatory evolutionary history for personal intelligence, and argue that this form of intelligence is not simply a passive talent but involves very active information-gathering mental activities based on instinct. We discuss possible advantages and disadvantages of personal intelligence, and we provide examples of the molding, and at times perversion, of personal intelligence by interpersonal and cultural influences. Finally, we show how these concepts may apply to borderline personality disorder (BPD) and narcissistic personality disorder (NPD), including a discussion of our recent clinical study of BPD using an exploratory measure to estimate personal intelligence.

PERSONAL INTELLIGENCE: BIOLOGICAL ROOTS

Evolution and Social Intelligence

Gardner (1983, 1994) emphasized that a proposed intelligence becomes much more plausible if evolutionary antecedents can be identified. A hallmark of primate evolution is the capacity for a complex social life (Brothers, 1989; Cheney & Seyforth, 1990; Goodall, 1986; Lovejoy, 1981; Ristau, 1991). This faculty, termed social intelligence, involves impressive precursor characteristics of personal intelligence (Brothers, 1990). Small (1990) summarized studies demonstrating primate social intelligences as "a knack for functioning as a social group, day in and day out, a special kind of intelligence—a social acumen calling for a good memory, the ability to recognize and categorize others and the capacity to act on that knowledge" (p. 40).

In a fascinating example of research in this area, Cheney and Seyfarth (1990) demonstrated the ability of vervet monkeys to maintain and recognize complex social relationships involving kinship, friendship and dominance rank, to form social bonds, to work collaboratively, to remember many details about one another and about rules, and to act accordingly. For example, when a mother vervet monkey hears the recorded distress cry of her infant, she turns to look in the direction of the sound, but other females in the group look at the mother.

Evidence for the development of social intelligence in primates suggests that until the appearance of more recent hominoids, social intelligence was only a rudimentary form of personal intelligence, focused on behavioral information about others but not on examination of minds of either self or others. For instance, Cheney and Seyfarth (1990) demonstrated that vervets are able to acquire sophisticated social knowledge and to make use of limited abstract concepts, yet they do not show evidence of perceiving the mental states of others or of examining their own mental states.

The emergence of personal intelligence appears to be a recent development, probably coinciding with the enormous increase in size and complexity of the human brain during the Pleistocene epoch. Brain size doubled from 700 cc in early Homo two million years ago, to 1400 cc in Homo sapiens. This period was associated with the development of behaviors requiring increasingly sophisticated uses of social intelligence including bonding, food sharing, warning patterns for predator avoidance, group hunting and scavenging, and language development (Andrews & Stringer, 1993; Fisher, 1982; Leakey & Lewin, 1992; Lovejoy, 1981; Stanley, 1992). Perhaps most significant for personal intelligence were the developing patterns of physical and psychological bonding. Lovejoy (1981) proposed that a major characteristic of physical bonding was increasingly strong biological–sexual fidelity. The rationale for this development is that the bonded pair could more adequately provide for a family group that included extremely helpless offspring. Such bonding appears to have been a necessary precursor for intense personal relationships involving intimacy, empathy, and a sense of responsibility (Fisher, 1982). It was postulated that this was an aspect of an accelerated evolutionary brain–human environment feedback loop that promoted the capacity for differentiated feelings, for grasp of the individual differences of others, and for a developing sense of self (Wills, 1993). It was even suggested that such aspects of social intelligence may have been the major factors contributing to the development of consciousness, giving evolutionary advantage to individuals who could thereby better grasp the intentions, thoughts, and feelings of others (Humphrey, 1976).

The prime function of speech and language is to communicate precise information from one individual to another; its development was closely tied to the unique expansion of social intelligence in our species (Andrews & Stringer, 1993; Pinker, 1994). Speech occurs at a rate of about 15 to 25 sounds per second, permitting a data transmission rate three to ten times faster than for any other primate (Lieberman, 1991). There is much evidence supporting Chomsky's theory (1975) that the brain has an inbuilt capacity for syntax and that we are uniquely programmed for language acquisition when raised in a language-using culture. The brain mechanisms that developed for language facilitated the development of other crucially important capacities such as planning ahead, skillfully influencing others, enhanced memory, potential for sophisticated abstract concepts, and the ability to examine our own mental processes (Lieberman, 1991). Language is a major vehicle for learning and using symbol systems, which is essential for effective expression of personal intelligence in one's culture.

Social intelligence was studied in humans prior to Gardner's introduction of the concept of personal intelligence (Sternberg & Smith; 1985; Taylor & Cadet, 1989; Walker & Foley, 1973; Wyer & Srull, 1989). The range of definitions is varied and includes (a) abilities to understand, to get along with, to deal with others; (b) abilities to make use of prior knowledge about people; and (c) abilities to accurately perceive the feelings and motivations of people (Hunt, 1928; Moss & Hunt, 1927; Strang, 1930; Thorndike, 1920; Wedeck, 1947). Sternberg and Smith (1985) described testing instruments developed to measure social intelligence in humans, including photographs of individuals and of couples who may or may not be emotionally involved with one another, self and observer ratings of interpersonal sensitivity, and tests for nonverbal sensitivity. None of these approaches were shown to reliably measure individual differences in social intelligence. Because of the complex factors involved in developing testing instruments and the subtleties involved in tuning into self and others, relatively intimate and longitudinal knowledge of a subject may be necessary for such characteristics to be studied effectively.

Instinctual Underpinnings of Personal Intelligence

There are strong indications that personal intelligence is based on instinct and, further, that it evolved by natural selection as an aspect of built-in reasoning processes for solving specific adaptive problems. An instinct involves both competence for a behavior and the urge to carry it out. For example, a spider is both able to spin a web and is compelled to do so

(Pinker, 1994). Primate studies demonstrated that social intelligence is inextricably linked with the urge to collect and respond to pertinent information, (e.g., Goodall, 1986). The gathering, emotional coloration, and interpretation of social information were of such compelling significance for the evolution of primates that there must be instinctual underpinnings to these processes (Brothers, 1990; Damasio, 1994). The human urge to employ personal intelligence is easily observed in the urge to gossip, to follow soap operas, to read self-help books and so forth (Barkow, Cosmides, & Tooby, 1992). We further postulate that the greater the personal intelligence of an individual, the stronger is the associated urge to utilize it.

Barkow, Cosmides, and Tooby (1992) argued that along with competence for and urge to engage in social exchange (their term for characteristics of social intelligence), the urge is channeled in circumscribed ways as *reasoning instincts* targeted to resolve specific adaptive problems such as recognizing emotions, interpreting social situations correctly, choosing to act altruistically, preventing danger, bonding, selecting a mate, competing, maintaining status, and deceiving (Buss, 1995; Edgar, 1993; Wright, 1995). For each type of problem there is an innate "special purpose" and "domain-specific" neural reasoning module with an algorithm for solving that particular problem. Premack and Premack (1995) even described a possible "theory of mind" reasoning module, apparently unique to humans. It programs us, beginning in infancy, to have the perception that there must be a cause for movement existing within an object if that object seems to move spontaneously, and that this cause has perception, intent, and goals.

Cosmides and Tooby (1992) wrote that the human "adapted mind" probably operates with hundreds or even thousands of such programs or reasoning modules, almost all of them unidentified and unstudied. They challenge the "Standard Social Science Model," that the reasoning capacities of the human mind are essentially general-purpose and content-independent. When considered along with Gardner's proposals, doubts are raised about the extent of general-purpose intelligence and general-purpose reasoning abilities, two characteristics traditionally valued as particularly human (Barrow, 1995; Pinker, 1994).

Cosmides and Tooby (1992) are pioneers in the new field of evolutionary psychology, which holds that to understand our reasoning instincts, we must study the conditions during the 2 million year Pleistocene epoch when members of our genus were hunter–gatherers. Apparently the operation of the human brain has not changed measurably since this period during which behaviors associated with sophisticated personal intelligence emerged. Only 10,000 years ago humans were still hunter–gatherers, and the dramatic development of civilization since then was based on the same brain. That is, there is fossil and other evidence for cultural, but not biological, evolution (Gould, 1994). For instance, consider the development of mathematics, written language, and pottery. Schmandt-Besserat (1992) and others compiled strong evidence that these skills developed from the simple use of clay tokens as counters for items of trade, such as animals and grain. Once these tokens were "invented," it took a few thousand years before humans grasped the symbolic potential of tokens, with their various shapes and marks, and developed mathematical concepts and written language. There is no need to postulate any physical evolution in these developments. To illustrate, if a newborn Cro-Magnon infant of 40,000 years ago could be placed in a modern environment, he or she would demonstrate no distinguishable psychological or developmental characteristics from a newborn infant of today. An important implication is that primitive reasoning patterns are still quite active in modern Homo sapiens, although they may often be hidden from us by explanatory rationalizations.

Other possible reasoning modules for solving social problems in a hunter–gatherer environment could include loyalty to the group, follow-the-leader, herd or clannish characteristics, dominance, control, appropriation, aggression, and us versus them characteristics (Calvin, 1991; Premack & Premack, 1995). In some situations, two or more such mechanisms activated in an individual could work at cross-purposes (Pinker, 1994). In addition, such biologically based constraints or imperatives could overwhelm rational thinking (Barkow et al., 1992). The power of built-in mental programs over otherwise good reasoning capabilities is suggested by a recent study of chimpanzees taught to recognize Arabic numerals (Boysen & Berntson, 1995). Chimp A was presented with two plastic numerals representing the amount of candy to be received by herself and by Chimp B, and she was to point to the number that was for Chimp B. Chimp A was able to reliably select the lower number. However, if the plastic numbers were replaced with pieces of candy, Chimp A would reliably select the plate with the most candy and then become quite upset when that plate was given to Chimp B. If the candy were replaced again with plastic numbers, Chimp A could again make the correct decisions. It appears that Chimp A could make reasoned decisions, but that a more basic neural module for taking food overruled the understanding of the game when actual food was involved. Analogously, LeDoux (1993) argued that some humans may have dominant subcortical pathways that react quickly to perceived danger, overruling any cortex-based insights or decisions.

Many inexplicable situations in historical and modern times can suddenly make sense if we consider this "adapted mind" approach (Drozdiak, 1995; Premack & Premack, 1995; Tuchman, 1984; Wright, 1995). For instance, humans seem to have a powerful urge to find a leader and then to cooperate and follow. In Bosnia and Rwanda, follow-the-leader, herd and us-versus-them patterns frequently overwhelmed rational self-interest and humane concerns for others, including children, even in intermarried families who had recently lived peacefully side by side.

As we discuss later, these issues are very relevant to our studies of borderline patients. Patients and their parents vary in definite ways regarding perceptive talents, the urge to gain access to these talents, and the degree to which they may be governed by rigid inborn algorithms or instead are potentially able to experience themselves and their human environment in a flexible and rational manner.

PERSONAL INTELLIGENCE: INTERACTIONS OF NATURE AND ENVIRONMENT

The Development of Personal Intelligence: Pros and Cons

The significance of social intelligence for the evolutionary success of primates is clear. However, some of the unique characteristics of personal intelligence in humans may have developed as chance products of rapid brain evolution, raising the possibility that there could be characteristics that are potentially maladaptive. Wills (1993) argued that the very mechanisms involved in rapid evolution could also permit maladaptive changes, that is, the substantial brain grown after birth has allowed for major caregiver and other environmental effects on brain development, creating an increasingly complex gene–culture feedback loop (Huttenlocher, 1979; Wolpaw, Schmidt, & Vaughan, 1991). Gould (1986) also cautioned against assuming that evolutionary changes always occur as benefits and states that many human behaviors are "side consequences of the building of the human brain" (p. 9).

The pros and cons of personal intelligence can be reviewed by considering the capacity for empathy, a particularly human characteristic that can require exceptional integration of both intra- and interpersonal intelligence. Empathy and altruism are proposed to be interrelated, instinct-based aspects of human nature. The *empathy–altruism hypothesis* holds that when a human accurately experiences distress or need in another person from the perspective of that other person, there is a built-in urge to reduce that distress, an urge paralleling the magnitude of the empathic emotion (Batson & Shaw, 1991). Although the theory of multiple intelligences defines capabilities that are neither prosocial nor antisocial, a genetic basis for empathy–altruism could provide humans with an intelligence including benevolent intuitiveness and helpfulness to others. Oliner and Oliner (1988) examined characteristics of individuals who risked their lives to save Jews from the Holocaust. They found it was not circumstances, religiosity, or even attitudes about Nazis, that best distinguished rescuers from nonrescuers but rather a characteristic he termed *extensivity*, that is, the recognition of and caring for the state of others when this extends beyond one's own group, along with associated altruistic behaviors involving risk and cost without expectation of external rewards. This example provides a clue to a potential evolutionary benefit of such integration of self- and other-awareness; that is, the ability to evaluate social situations becomes increasingly independent of algorithms for us-versus-them, follow-the-leader, and so forth. The highest personal intelligence could be seen as the relative capacity to surmount more primitive and instinctive programs, affects, and biases and to view ourselves and others with a unique degree of observational accuracy and rational reasoning (Gardner, 1983; Salovey & Mayer, 1990).

Did these particular characteristics have evolutionary advantage, particularly in dangerous Pleistocene times, or did they simply appear when the mind became sufficiently complex? As Shakespeare demonstrated in Hamlet, consciousness, self-reflection, and preoccupation about others can breed self-doubt and hesitation when action would save the day. Competitive and predatory individuals responding to a situation on a more programmed basis would have the advantage of speed of reaction as well as being able to act in more immediate self-interest.

Farber (1989) has reviewed the literature concerning potential disadvantages of psychological mindedness, which he defined (1985) as "the disposition and ability to reflect on the meaning and motivation of behavior, thoughts, and feelings in oneself and others" (p. 170), a definition similar to Gardner's definition of personal intelligence. The possible negative consequences of psychological mindedness reviewed by Farber include inhibition of spontaneity and action, self-doubt, guilt, emotional detachment, distress, anxiety, depression, and somatic symptoms. Farber found that high psychological mindedness can contribute to lower self-esteem and to others perceiving such individuals as withholding their feelings. He suggests that psychological mindedness brings a heightened awareness of the painful aspects of existence. In line with this, there are some data supportive of "depressive realism," the proposal that depressed individuals can assess reality more accurately than can nondepressed individuals (Ackerman & DeRubeis, 1991). (There are additional data suggesting that depressed subjects tend to have more accurate judgments only about others and not about themselves.) Nesse (1991) argued that suffering can be an important natural aspect of recognizing and responding successfully to environmental problems. In contrast, Gould (1989) provided an argument for rejoicing in self-awareness, even of knowledge that there may be no apparent meaning or purpose for our existence.

We suspect that the negative consequences of high personal intelligence or psychological mindedness may involve aspects of parenting. Historically, parenting involved indoctrination along with discouragement of autonomy, as discussed by Alice Miller (1983) and illustrated by the Ten Commandments, which speak only to respecting parents and not at all to respecting children. The higher the personal intelligence of a child, the more likely the child will be rejected or punished for having independent, perceptive observations and questions. This, in turn, could lead to a sense of badness for having core mental processes that cannot be stifled. If this is a common occurrence in the general population, then it is likely that any group of individuals with high psychological mindedness and with talents for assessing interpersonal reality will also tend to show higher average scores on measures of depression and low self-esteem.

Parenting is a prime example for considering the difficulty evaluating pros and cons of high personal intelligence in view of the likelihood that quality of parenting significantly affects expression of this intelligence. The higher an infant's capacity for perceptivity of self and others, the more essential could be a good caregiver environment for development of this talent. This concept is compatible with some of Suomi's research (1991). He selectively bred Rhesus monkeys to be "high reactive," that is, very fearful and anxious in new and challenging situations. These monkeys are also highly aware of their environment from birth (S.J. Suomi, personal communication, July 19, 1991), which may be analogous to a human capacity for high interpersonal intelligence. Such monkeys tend to maintain an anxious pattern and reach a relatively marginal adult adjustment. However, when raised by exceptionally nurturing foster mothers, such monkeys become the most socially skilled and dominant members of their peer groups. This finding is an indication that these monkeys are not inherently defective, but have an acute sensitivity to their environment resulting in their becoming defective or exceptional adults depending on whether they are raised with the special care that nurtures their unusual talent.

"High reactive" easily distressed infants made up about 20% of the 4-month-old infant population studied by Kagan (1994). The majority of these children develop an inhibited temperament and as adults may be at higher risk for anxiety disorders and depression. Might a significant number of these children been born highly perceptive and aware of their environment, comparable to Suomi's subjects, requiring a special caregiver environment for healthy development of their perceptive gifts (Davis, Luce, & Kraus, 1994)? Analogously, Boyce et al. (1995) suggested there may be a subset of children with "heightened sensitivity to the character of the social world" who have exceptional vulnerability in high stress, unsupportive interpersonal environments but who develop exceptional resilience in low stress, nurturing environments.

Defective and Perverse Manifestations of Personal Intelligence

In this section, we discuss defective aspects of personal intelligence that could be either inborn or environmentally induced. Two clinically defined personality disorders that appear to be directly linked to defective aspects of personal intelligence are narcissistic personality disorder (NPD) and borderline personality disorder (BPD). The Diagnostic and Statistical Manual of Mental Disorders (DSM–IV; American Psychiatric Association, 1994) includes the following characteristics for NPD: (a) a grandiose sense of self-importance, (b) a belief that they are special in a very superior way, and (c) a sense of entitlement. All of these indicate an inaccurate sense of self, that is, a defective intrapersonal intelligence. In addition, these individuals (a) lack empathy, (b) have a penchant for envy, and (c) are interpersonally exploitative, indicating a defective interpersonal intelligence.

DSM–IV includes the following characteristics for BPD: (a) severe identity disturbance, (b) a markedly unstable self-image or sense of self, and (c) chronic feelings of emptiness, indicating a defective intrapersonal intelligence. These individuals also exhibit (a) frantic efforts to avoid real or imagined abandonment and (b) a pattern of unstable and intense interpersonal relationships characterized by alternation between extremes of idealization and devaluation, indicating defective interpersonal intelligence.

There are a number of possible causes of defective personal intelligence. First, it is likely that considerable variability can exist from individual to individual in degrees of inborn personal intelligence considering that evolutionary development of such uniquely human characteristics was rapid and recent (Simons, 1989; Wills, 1993). Such genetic variability would allow for some newborns to have much less and others much more than the usual capacity for perceptiveness about self and others. In addition, atavistic genes that were silenced during evolution of personal intelligence could become activated in some individuals (Cantu & Ruiz, 1985).

Second, it is likely that personal intelligence is made up of multiple modular subunits that work together, with the potential that there could be defective or missing subunits as well as poor coordination between such elements. Certainly, modularity is the case in other perceptual systems such as the visual system where many different brain subsystems analyze features such as color, movement, form, and depth (Gazzaniga, 1989; Kosslyn & Koenig, 1992). Characteristics of intrapersonal intelligence that could have modular representations in the brain and vary from individual to individual include abilities to access a range of emotions, to discriminate among emotions, to use emotions to understand oneself, and to have a model of oneself that facilitates decision making. Characteristics of interpersonal intelligence could include abilities to distinguish moods, temperaments, motivations, and intentions of others, as well as capacity for warmth and empathy. In addition, there could be variations in other kinds of reasoning modules suggested by Cosmides and Tooby (1992) and by Premack and Premack (1995). For instance, autistic individuals may have a defective theory of mind mechanism, whereas retarded individuals with Williams Syndrome demonstrate abilities suggesting that such a mechanism is selectively spared (Brothers, 1990; Frith, 1993; Karmiloff-Smith, Klima, Bellugi, Grant, & Baron-Cohen, 1995).

A third major cause of defective personal intelligence may be its high vulnerability to interpersonal and cultural influences during the developing years. Pathological manifestations of personal intelligence resulting from such influences can be considered "perversions" of the instinctual urge to express this intelligence, as with perversions of other instincts such as sex and hunger (eg., bulimia and anorexia) (Welldon, 1988). Factors involved include (a) attachment and phase requirements (Bowlby, 1988; Kohut, 1971), (b) "goodness of fit" between a child's temperament and his or her human environment (Thomas & Chess, 1984), (c) constitutional and maturational irregularities (Greenspan, 1992), and (d) outright abuse and neglect (Cicchetti & Carlson, 1989; Storr, 1990). Because of the unique brain development after birth in humans, it is extremely difficult to differentiate inborn defects from those hardwired after harmful environmental events during the early months and years of life (Teicher, Ito, Glod, Schiffer, & Gelbard, 1994).

With these three types of influence in mind, we speculated about sources of defective personal intelligence in NPD and BPD. It is our impression that patients diagnosed as having NPD frequently have inborn deficiencies in personal intelligence, in particular in the capacity for empathy. Some NPD patients also seem to be strongly motivated by fixed, exploitative frames of mind suggesting the possibility of dominating inborn reasoning algorithms. In addition, many have had childhood experiences that seem to have imperilled the healthy use of the positive capabilities they did have.

Borderline individuals, on the other hand, frequently exhibit characteristics suggesting they have a high inborn personal intelligence, with clear childhood experiences accounting for perverse manifestations such as persuasive, complex projective identification (described below). Finally, individuals with these disorders can have overlapping characteristics. For instance, Kernberg (1975) described "narcissistic personalities functioning on a borderline level," individuals who may have been born with high overall personal intelligence but who may also have specific defects in their personal intelligence (e.g., exceptional ability to detect intentions and vulnerabilities of others but without empathy), and/or extremely chaotic backgrounds, and/or who may have introjected characteristics of very intrusive, cold parents. Such individuals, who lack or suppress empathy, can be very powerful, and/or dangerous, such as Adolf Hitler and Charles Manson (Hartmann, 1991).

Projective identification, a uniquely human phenomenon, is of particular relevance for personal intelligence (Gabbard & Wilkinson, 1994; Kernberg, 1986; Ogden, 1982). Definitions of projective identification vary somewhat, but in general they include the view that it involves an interpersonal transaction in which one person induces specific feelings in a second person, with the second person unaware that feelings are being coerced, that is, believing that he or she "owns" the feelings. Such feelings are not generated *de novo*, rather a receptive potential must already be present in the second person that has been perceived (out of awareness) by the initiator. Projective identification probably occurs frequently in everyone and can be a positive way of revising attitudes when we can allow others to contain and alter or "launder" our projections, and then reintroject such modified states back to us (Ogden, 1994; C.G., Schulz, personal communication, May 5, 1995).

Projective identification has been a particular topic of interest in the treatment of borderline patients because this process can often persuade therapists, even experienced therapists, to become enmeshed in distressing anxiety, guilt, and anger, and even to feel overwhelmed by feelings of passionate attachment to patients. An exceptional degree of personal intelligence appears to be involved because at times such patients accurately perceive subtle or hidden feelings of the therapist and then facilitate intensification of these feelings until the therapist behaves in a specific fashion that can even be irrational, all usually occurring without the therapist (or the patient) aware of the coercive dynamics.

There are various theories to explain projective identification. One holds that it reflects an inborn mechanism or a faculty to promote attachment, in line with theories of Bowlby (1988) and Kohut (1971). For instance, the infant cries not just from distress or to simply generate a response, but, at a much more powerful level, to directly coerce caring feelings and behaviors from caregivers that the latter experience as originating from within themselves. Some of the literature suggests that the coercive projective identification of borderline patients reflects an inherent pathology of such a characteristic. This view would require careful research to evaluate inborn defects versus caregiver effects (Dunn & Plomin, 1990).

It seems unlikely that an infant has an inborn capacity for more than rudimentary projective identification. For example, the "distress cry" can have an impact without the detection of specific emotions in a given individual by the infant (MacLean, 1985; Morgan, 1995; van der Kolk, 1987a). Projective identification as manifested by borderline patients appears to reflect a remarkable, albeit pathological, skill that must have been learned through a great deal of interactive experience with caretakers exhibiting certain characteristics and behaviors, as we discuss later.

An important issue to study is the occurrence of defective personal intelligence in the care of offspring. Did personal intelligence and the intrusive power of language develop primarily through social interactions of adults and, if so, what does this say about childrearing? There is not good evidence that personal intelligence involves a particular knack for knowing how to understand and care for infants. Miller (1983) discussed *poisonous pedagogy*, the history of severely harmful childrearing practices that encouraged stamping out a child's individuality and sense of self. Traditional religions have tended to promote adult power and control over children. Books on how to raise children are purchased in great numbers by insecure parents who will believe the popular fad of the day, from very strict schedules to almost complete abdication of structure. None of this suggests that personal intelligence involves special inborn directedness for knowing how to be or what to do.

There has been a general assumption that humans have a basic instinct, characteristic of all primates, for the care of offspring that existed long before the development of personal intelligence. Welldon (1988) found that parenting was not studied with appropriate objectivity because of a deep bias to believe in this maternal instinct and to idealize motherhood (Hrdy, 1995). This bias has inhibited the consideration that instincts can be attenuated in primates as well as become perverted in expression (Bard, 1995; Harlow, 1964). Drawing on extensive clinical experience, Welldon argued that perverted parenting is the product of defective and abusive experiences in the childhood of the parent. These experiences fashion a perverted parental personal intelligence that may suppress or misdirect any primal parenting instinct to serve private purposes damaging to the child (Fonagy et al., 1995). Miller (1981) also wrote about perverted parenting, including parents who try to make their children care for them as their own parents did not, a complete reversal of the appropriate parental role. In addition, some parents try so hard to be different from their own self-centered parents that they are hopelessly unable to set any limits, thereby fostering self-centered children (Sherman, 1994). As we discuss later, the very capacities we have for observing and perceiving our peers and for infiltrating psychological boundaries by gesture and speech, can be used with enormous destructiveness to the minds of children.

Finally, some ethological theories emphasize the negative manifestations of human social intelligence in deeply rooted patterns of aggression, manipulation and deception. One view is that these behaviors reflect instinct-based, essential characteristics of human nature (Alexander, 1989; Byrne, 1991; Davies, 1981; Lorenz, 1966; Storr, 1972). The more prevalent view is that these behaviors, are not usually the result of instincts specifically for such behaviors but reflect the enormous developmental plasticity of humans, who are "polymorphously educable" (Montagu, 1978), and whose follow-the-leader and us-versus-them mental programs can be bent or perverted to align with cultural belief systems and the goals of charismatic leaders (Benedict, 1934; Gould, 1988; Leakey & Lewin, 1992). Dramatic illustrations of submission to a charismatic leader are the mass murders and suicides of fanatical religious groups and Nazi Germany. Examples of extreme culturally enforced patterns include: (a) children who participate in robbery and brutal murder of strangers without the slightest distress and yet seem otherwise perfectly normal psychologically (Bruce, 1968); (b) brutal warriors who can be cultured, sensitive, and artistic (Forgey, 1988); (c) grotesquely deformed feet as highly erotic objects (Levy, 1992); (d) marriage as a very hostile struggle for dominance (Lindholm & Lindholm, 1979); and (e) culturally designated group homosexuality in adolescence to be followed by heterosexuality in adulthood (Herdt, 1981).

PERSONAL INTELLIGENCE IN BORDERLINE PERSONALITY DISORDER

Our interest in personal intelligence developed in the course of work with patients diagnosed with BPD (Park, Imboden, Park, Hulse, & Unger, 1992). Subsequent consideration of personal intelligence in patients diagnosed with narcissistic personality disorder occurred secondarily as a result of findings from our BPD research. Accordingly, the remaining sections of this chapter focus mainly on BPD and on our study of personal intelligence in borderline patients.

In this section, we discuss the clinical picture of BPD, the evolution of concepts about this syndrome, and our rationale for examining personal intelligence in these patients. BPD has been of considerable research interest in recent decades because of the frequency of the condition in clinical populations, its severity, its etiologic mystery, and the power of the patients to elicit emotional involvement of therapists and hospital staffs. With regard to severity, approximately 10% of patients commit suicide, usually relatively early in the illness (Stone, 1990b). Until recently it was thought the condition was essentially incurable, but several long-term studies demonstrated that by 15 years after initial clinical contact, two thirds of surviving patients are no longer borderline and are functioning normally or with only minimal symptoms (Frances, 1990; Stone, 1990b).

An epidemiological study found that BPD occurred in approximately 2% of a sample of the general population, with 73% being women (Schwartz, Blazer, George,& Winfield, 1990). Fifty percent of borderline respondents had used some form of outpatient mental health service in the prior 6 months and 19.5% had an inpatient hospitalization in the prior year. Furthermore, BPD is reported to occur in over 10% of psychiatric outpatients, in about 20% of inpatients, and in more than 60% of inpatients in settings with a predominance of personality disorders (Kass, Skodol, Charles, Spitzer, & Williams, 1985; Widiger & Frances, 1989; Zanarini, Frankenberg, Chauncey, & Gunderson, 1987).

It is probable that the enormous suffering of these patients drives such a high percentage to seek professional help. The great majority of BPD patients are chronically depressed and one third experience posttraumatic stress disorder (Gunderson & Sabo, 1993). Other frequent comorbid diagnoses are anxiety, phobic, substance abuse, and eating and panic disorders. Severe symptomatology can pervade multiple areas of functioning, including relationships, sense of self, mood, and behavior. Patients can live in almost constant psychic pain, burdened by self-hate, intense and painful relationships, potentially damaging impulsiveness, and chronic dysphoria that can progress quickly to severe and suicidal depression. Their severely damaged sense of self can be manifested in burdensome confusion about who they are, what they value, what they want in life, and sometimes even about their sexual orientation. At times they experience dissociative states (Shearer, 1994; Spiegel, 1994). They tend to long desperately for intimacy with others and yet experience great interpersonal distrust. They often make commitments to emotionally unreliable people (Celani, 1994). When interpersonally stressed, they easily become confused and enraged, thereby distancing others while simultaneously experiencing extreme feelings of emptiness and abandonment.

Many borderline patients appear to have a heightened perceptivity of the feelings and motives of others. This ability is frequently manifested in the manipulative induction of feelings like those the patients themselves experience, that is, projective identification. For clinicians who treat these patients psychotherapeutically, the most striking personality feature is this flavor of the therapist–patient relationship. The ability of these patients to access and then strongly influence private emotions engenders the classical, perhaps pathognomonic, countertransference problems and special treatment relationships (Zanarini, Gunderson, Frankenburg, & Chauncey, 1990).

We are particularly interested in elucidating the nature of this perceptive talent, which has not been the subject of indepth investigation. The psychological powers and intuitive perceptions of borderline patients are briefly explained in the literature as manifestations of pathology, a skill that is peculiar in some way, or a learned response to certain kinds of childhood stress.

We reviewed the clinical literature for examples of intuitive capabilities and interpersonal powers of these patients, including a review of the countertransference literature for evidence of therapist reactions to patients who detect private or hidden emotions. Adler (1985) and Gunderson (1989) discussed the frequency with which hospitalized borderline patients evoke seriously disruptive staff conflicts in which one or more staff members passionately protect the patient as a "helpless waif" requiring nurturance, and who are quite hostile to other staff members who feel helplessly enraged at the same patient as an "angry manipulator" requiring severe limits (Gunderson, 1989, p. 2757). The capabilities of borderline patients in catalyzing such psychological firestorms is remarkable considering they are in institutions managed by experienced professionals who know and make the rules.

Masterson (1976) describes borderline patients as "exquisitely sensitive to the daily emotional state of the therapist, to his tone of voice and nonverbal messages conveyed by gestures and body posture" (p. 104). Carter and Rinsley (1977), Krohn (1974), and Shapiro (1978) describe borderline patients as having a peculiar perceptiveness for subtle and unconscious feelings, impulses, and thoughts of other people. Krohn (1974) gave an example of a borderline patient who had the "uncanny capacity to recognize some very private impulses and judgments within other people" (p. 145). "He would regularly put into words private associations of the therapist just as the therapist was having them" (p. 146). Another patient manifested an "uncanny responsiveness to the most subtle, unconscious content in others" (p. 154). "The therapist of the borderline is often suddenly surprised to hear the patient voice what the therapist comes to recognize as very private conflicts. It is as if the therapist has suddenly been dealt a very deep, confronting interpretation by the patient" (p. 161). Krohn referred to this intuitive capacity as borderline empathy. Stone (1985) found that borderline patients can have the ability to sense and to respond empathically to hidden feeling of individuals for whom they care.

Discussing countertransference, Kernberg, Selzer, Koenigsberg, Carr, and Applebaum (1989) stated: "Uncannily, borderline patients seem to sense the therapist's vulnerability and may choose the exact moment when the therapist wishes the patient dead to announce a suicide plan" (p. 75). Gabbard and Wilkinson (1994) stated that borderline patients "possess an uncanny ability to tune into the therapist's vulnerabilities and to exploit them" (p. 5) to produce guilt. The problem of boundary violations in the treatment of BPD, particularly patient–therapist sexual contact, was addressed by Gutheil (1989): "What may be less universally acknowledged is that patients with borderline personality disorder possess the ability, as it were, to seduce, provoke, or invite therapists into boundary violations of their own in the countertransference" (p. 600). Averill et al. (1989) proposed that borderline patients vulnerable to such abuse may have particular "projective or sending power" (p. 391) which transmits unconscious fantasies and neediness with special impact.

Two published controlled studies found evidence of perceptiveness in borderline patients. In the first, Ladisich and Feil (1988) assessed empathy in 20 borderline patients, 20 neurotic patients, and 19 patients who had a history of schizophrenia. These were inpatients in 11 therapy groups of 4 months duration, each group having six members and a therapist. Empathy was defined as an accurate sensing or perceiving of other peoples' feelings or qualities, and was measured using the 139-item Lazare–Klerman Trait Scale (LKTS; Lazare, Klerman, & Armor, 1966), the 40 item Giessen Test (GT; Beckmann & Richter, 1972), and a 21 item Unpleasant Person Hierarchy Test (UPHT) based on the Empathy Test by Kerr (1965). Patients rated themselves and other group members both at the beginning and termination of the group therapy program. The group therapists also rated the patients. Empathy was assessed by calculating how accurately a person could rate others' ratings of themselves. The borderline patients scored significantly higher than did the neurotic and schizophrenic groups and were as good as the therapists, who presumably had more knowledge of the patients. These results apparently were unexpected, and the authors proposed a possible relationship of high empathy in BPD to vulnerability for psychosis.

In the second study, Frank and Hoffman (1986) compared two groups of patients, 10 borderline and 14 neurotic, using the Profile of Nonverbal Sensitivity (brief exposure PONS; Rosenthal, Hall, DiMatteo, Rogers, & Archer, 1979). They demonstrated significantly higher nonverbal sensitivity in the borderline group, which they felt provided empirical evidence for the concept of borderline empathy, the apparent ability of borderlines to accurately tune in to the internal state of others. They therefore suggested an empathic ability in BPD, but they also proposed that the empathy is a "borderline" or pathology-based type that developed as a way of contending with maternal emotional neglect. In a subsequent paper, Hoffman and Frank (1987) presented some correlations from the same study that were consistent with the additional possibility of a constitutional vulnerability contributing to the nonverbal sensitivity. However, the literature indicates that the capacity for empathy and perceptiveness involves an inborn talent (Brothers, 1989; Davis et al., 1994; Neubauer & Neubauer, 1990; Rushton, Fulker, Neale, Nias, & Eysenck, 1986), rather than being an inborn weakness, a vulnerability to psychosis, or a manifestation of childhood stress per se.

The findings and observations discussed have only recently led to studies designed to evaluate their possible etiologic significance. A review of the history of BPD research reveals why such studies were so late in coming (Park, 1994). The condition was not identified until fairly recently and was originally thought to be a variant of or "borderline" to schizophrenia, hence the name. Seminal research by Gunderson in the 1970s identified objective diagnostic criteria that engendered many studies involving large populations of borderline patients (Gunderson, 1982). These studies revealed that BPD was not a variant of psychotic illness, leading to labeling of the condition as a personality disorder of unknown etiology. Once it became clear that the etiology of BPD could not be understood from findings about schizophrenia, numerous etiologic theories were advanced including proposals that BPD is a variant of depressive illness, that there are various neurobiological vulnerabilities, and that BPD is engendered by factors in childhood such as parental separations and loss, family conflict, and parental psychopathological behaviors toward offspring including neglect, overinvolvement, and overprotection (Gunderson & Zanarini, 1989; Zanarini, Gunderson, Marino, Schwartz, & Frankenburg, 1989). A complicating issue has been clinicians' reactions to the personal discomfort these patients evoke. With their perceptive talent imbedded in the service of self-protection, neediness, control, and rage, borderline patients have been negatively viewed by many clinicians as deliberate manipulators who are unreliable, will not respond to treatment, are unpredictably suicidal, and who are troublemakers to be avoided if possible. "Borderline" became a pejorative word that labeled disliked patients, leading to misdiagnoses that further delayed an understanding of the syndrome (Frances, First, & Pincus, 1995).

Although there were clinical reports of serious abuse during the childhoods of borderline patients, the first controlled studies of abuse histories did not reach print until the late 1980s (Herman, Perry, & van der Kolk, 1989; Links, Steiner, Offord, & Eppel, 1988; Zanarini et al., 1989). These and many subsequent studies revealed an enormous amount of physical and sexual abuse reported by a majority of borderline patients. The patients did not seem to recognize their experiences as abusive or to report them spontaneously (Shengold, 1989). Zanarini et al. (1989) investigated the occurrence of caregiver verbal or psychological abuse, defined as chronically devaluative or blaming statements and found that it was by far the most common form of abuse (other than neglect, which they did not categorize as abuse), occurring in 72% of 50 borderline patients. Psychological abuse was the only form of abuse distinguishing the BPD group from each of the control groups with a probability of error of less than 5%. Similarly, Stone (1990a) found that 73% of 15 BPD patients reported a history of intense verbal abuse with physical and sexual abuse occurring at a lesser frequency. In spite of its prevalence among borderline patients, researchers did not focus on the verbal abuse, targeting instead the less frequent histories of physical and sexual abuse. However, we proposed that the critical etiological finding was the psychological abuse, and we expected an even higher frequency would be found if more categories of psychological abuse were examined (Park et al., 1992). Further, the enduring damage from physical and sexual abuse to the body stems from the accompanying abuse of the mind (Garbarino, Guttman, & Seeley, 1986; Hart & Brassard, 1987). Subsequent to completion of our study, Gallagher, Flye, Hurt, Stone, and Hull (1992) reported on the recollected histories of various degrees of verbal abuse in a sample of 22 borderline women, with 86% acknowledging significant degrees of such abuse.

Mental health experts and participants in the child abuse and neglect movement have focused increasingly on psychological or emotional abuse and neglect, as it may be the most insidious, prevalent, and destructive form of childhood abuse (Garbarino et al., 1986; Hart & Brassard, 1987; McGee & Wolfe, 1991). For instance, one can imagine a physically abused child still experiencing inner psychological freedom to have his or her own thoughts and feelings, but psychological freedom could be largely eliminated if the assault is directed to the thoughts and feelings themselves (Stolorow & Brandchaft, 1987). Such head-on confrontation is actually an attack on the core machinery of a child's personal intelligence, because it obstructs and damages the capacity to know and understand oneself and others, including even the capacity to know that one has been abused (Fonagy et al., 1995; Hart & Brassard, 1987; Shengold, 1989). Interference with, as well as neglect of, this developmental requirement may be a necessary condition for most adolescent and adult psychopathology (Park, 1992). Developmental literature and longitudinal studies, as well as primate research, provide convincing evidence that it is not the characteristics of children, such as defects and vulnerabilities, that should be considered as the predominant factors actively engendering adult psychopathology, but rather a defective caregiver or cultural environment that is misaligned with the child's psychological characteristics and requirements (Bowlby, 1988; Byne & Parsons, 1993; Greenspan, 1992; Lidz, 1990; Tienari et al., 1991; Rorty, Yager, & Rossotto, 1994; Vaillant, 1977; Werner, 1989).

We summarized salient features of BPD and searched for a pattern. Those features are:

1. The extreme suffering, self-hate, anger, identity disturbance, emptiness, and fear of abandonment.
2. Frequent co-occurrence of chronic depression and posttraumatic stress disorder, as well as dissociative experiences suggesting possible relationship to dissociative identity disorder.
3. General history of severe, pervasive psychological abuse as well as frequent history of physical and sexual abuse.
4. The chronic, intense, failed search for intimacy, along with great distrust.
5. Evidence of perceptive talents, a capacity for empathic response, and the perversion of these charactertistics.

It seemed likely, based on the aforementioned characteristics, that chronic and severe assault throughout childhood on self-esteem and on detected autonomous mental processes of the child must be the essential source of the syndrome. This could provide an explanation for items 1–3 but would not fully account for items 4 or 5.

The perceptive talents and the enduring search for intimacy are perplexing. Childhood rejection, abuse, and invalidation frequently result in an impoverished mental life, in diminished perceptivity, empathy, and introspection, in abusive behaviors, and probably in diminished psychological mindedness (Alverez, Schonbar, & Farber, 1993; Bowlby, 1984; Cichetti & Carlson, 1989; Goleman, 1995; Hunt, 1990; Montagu, 1978; Ressler & Shachtman, 1992; Shengold, 1989; van der Kolk, 1987b). We asked ourselves why borderlines characteristically persist in a lifelong search for self-understanding and love, why they retain the capacity for caring about others, why they are so psychologically minded that they return again and again for psychotherapeutic help despite prior failed treatment, why borderline mothers are so often intensely preoccupied with being good mothers, and why most borderline patients recover after years of troubled self-examination. We concluded that there must be an inborn cognitive characteristic at work here, because nothing in their deprived childhood could account for this staying power (Park et al., 1992; Shengold, 1989).

Miller's book (1981) about abused, gifted children also alerted us to the possibility of an inborn characteristic. By "gifted" she referred to: "an amazing ability to perceive and respond intuitively" (p. 8); "lively people who are especially capable of differentiated feelings" (p. 9); "attentive, lively, sensitive" (p. 10); "great intensity of feelings, depth of experience, curiosity, intelligence, quickness, and ability to be critical" (p. 97). She described examples of extreme suffering of people who were apparently gifted and also psychologically abused by caregivers, the same pattern we found in our borderline patients.

DEVELOPMENT OF A SCALE FOR ESTIMATING PERSONAL INTELLIGENCE

Gardner's (1983) theory and description of personal intelligence provided us with a conceptual framework for the study of individual differences in perceptive talents. He argued that, as with other forms of intelligence, personal intelligence varies and includes exceptional individuals. Our first hypothesis was that BPD patients have high personal intelligence, albeit expressed in perverse ways. Our second hypothesis was that childhood psychological abuse engendered this perversion. There was also a third hypothesis that high personal intelligence in borderline patients is biologically based.

We did not find a suitable instrument for directly assessing personal intelligence (Costa & McCrae, 1990; Park et al., 1992; Salovey & Mayer, 1990). Gardner (1983) pointed out that there has been a lack of studies of personal intelligence, perhaps due to the difficulty of study and to the high degree of personal involvement required. Therefore, the first task of our study was to develop a scale to estimate personal intelligence in a clinical setting, which in our case was office-based private practice. Research in this area is in its infancy, and we want to emphasize that our scale is a very preliminary attempt to assess personal intelligence.

The first two items of our four-item personal intelligence scale were designed to detect perceptual competence or an urge to access and use it, the latter in line with the concept that personal intelligence is instinct based. The two items are: (1) Intense preoccupation with and/or talented access to one's feelings; and (2) Intense preoccupation with and/or sense of the feelings of others. According to our hypotheses, borderline patients can have high personal intelligence that is expressed in perverse ways. We think that one of the reasons for such perversion was the need to conceal and disguise their perceptive abilities from dangerous caregivers, who would become extremely threatening when intuitive responses made them uneasy or angry. The children would then learn to feel profoundly bad for experiencing their own natural feelings and perceptions and try to prevent them from occurring, thereby perverting their intrapersonal intelligence. In addition, Fonagy et al. (1995) proposed that borderline individuals actively refused to develop a competent theory of mind about self and others in order to obstruct accurate perceptions about the minds of uncaring, hostile, and malevolent caregivers, which allowed them to maintain a sense of empathic, caring qualities in them. This would be very damaging for the development of skills involving interpersonal intelligence. Inhibitions and distortions of both intra- and interpersonal intelligence could be expected to limit the frequency of easily observed incidents of talented access to self and others in a clinical setting. Therefore, we additionally rated "intense preoccupation" on assumptions that in spite of such major interferences with natural perceptions, a strong instinctual urge to understand self and others would remain quite discernable in the form of intense preoccupation with these themes, with high intensity reflecting high personal intelligence (see prior discussion of instinctual underpinnings of personal intelligence). Because we were looking for serious efforts to gain understanding, we attempted to exclude observable indications of other kinds of preoccupation, such as hypervigilance focused primarily on detecting signals of potential danger from others without significant interest in understanding them, inquisitiveness, competitive efforts to gain attention, or a burden of symptomatic distress and strong affects. We did not develop specific guidelines for such differentiation in this study, relying instead on clinical impressions. We believe that serious effort to understand something typically has a very different flavor from defensive hypervigilance, prying, attention-gaining behaviors, or simply preoccupation with symptoms and distressing feelings. We hope to develop a more standardized way of evaluating these characteristics.

Examples of preoccupation about self include patients who were besieged by and obsessed about feelings that they were bad or evil. Such individuals could not experience inner permission to enjoy themselves, such as the patient who eagerly bought a fish tank and then obsessed for several months about why he could not bring himself to put fish in it. Examples of talented access to one's feeling were rather infrequent early in therapy but tended to become more common in later stages. One example was a librarian who began therapy enraged, hating herself, suicidal, and obsessing about her incompetence in both her personal and work environments. After several years of therapy, and while caring for chronically ill babies and small children in a volunteer job, she validated for herself that she could experience deep, varied, and empathically accurate emotions of concern, tenderness, and love, feelings that had a very positive effect on the children and their caregivers (in sharp contradiction to her mother's malicious attacks on such characteristics). This development was accompanied by a dramatic transformation at work from an odd, ostracized workhorse to an administrative leader.

With regard to preoccupation about others, an extreme example was the patient who spent a great deal of time lying in bed, intensely ruminating over the most minimal interactions with others, often developing paranoid-tinged themes about their meanings. There were many examples of patients showing a sense of the feelings of others. One patient sensed her therapist's unexpressed feelings of pessimism, acknowledging later that she used this perception to make him feel as hopeless as possible. A male patient brought a gun to a therapy session following a meeting during which the therapist privately decided it was time to explicitly discuss the mother's extreme malevolence. Two female patients would invariably know surprisingly early in relationships when males were in their sexual power.

The third item (3) of our scale required at least three perceptive intuitions or insights about others expressed during therapy. These were especially noted at times when patients were relatively calm and if they demonstrated a knack for reading the therapist's private emotions or thoughts. Such examples had to be clear and understandable to at least two members of the research team. One patient helped her therapist to correct his approach by saying, seemingly out of the blue, "It doesn't help me if you feel sorry for me. It throws me off and I can't help trying to make you feel that way even more. It's like an addiction, to make you have a feeling for me."

The fourth item (4) consisted of two parts: capacity for empathic concern for important others is clearly evident at times, and grandiosity, devaluation, and envy are not pervasive. Item 4 was based on the assumption that high personal intelligence generally would be associated with high empathy and low grandiosity. Capacity for empathy was frequently manifested in our patients, including concern for the welfare of parents, children, spouses, and friends.

The second part of item 4 involved overall clinical impressions as well as specific examples. Grandiosity, devaluation, and envy were judged to be pervasive if they were detected frequently and in many contexts, and were highly resistant to change or insight. One patient presented interactions with her teenage son in which she enticed the autonomy-striving son into being vulnerable and would then make the perfect subtle confusing statement. She manifested such behaviors repeatedly, always "forgetting" discussions about their inappropriateness.

Our study patients were outpatients seen in private practice. Clinical records of 107 patients were reviewed, and in addition to being diagnosed according to DSM–III–R, patients were also classified according to the number of criteria they met for BPD (American Psychiatric Association, 1987; Frances, Clarkin, Gilmore, Hurt, & Brown, 1984). We identified 23 patients (18 females, 5 males) who met the DSM–III–R definition of BPD, that is, five to eight criteria. Twenty of these patients received concomitant Axis I, primarily affective, diagnoses. We identified 38 control patients (23 females and 15 males) who had personality disorders other than BPD and who met two or fewer DSM–III–R diagnostic criteria for BPD. Twenty-two of these patients had Axis I diagnoses. Of the 38 control patients, 4 (11%) were diagnosed with cluster A, 10 (26%) with cluster B, and 24 (63%) with cluster C personality disorders. (Seven patients were diagnosed as personality disorder not otherwise specified but were easily classified by cluster.) The average age was 32 years for the borderline group and 39 years for the controls. The study patients were of above-average socioeconomic status. For instance, 21 of the borderline patients and 33 of the controls attended college at some point during therapy or were college graduates. All study patients were Caucasian except for one borderline patient (African American) and one control (Asian American). Diagnoses of study patients were made on a consensus basis by two psychiatrists without an additional reliability check.

All of the BPD patients and 36 of the controls received individual psychotherapy, primarily a combination of supportive and exploratory therapy, with the majority seen every 1 or 2 weeks. Six borderline and 3 control patients participated in group psychotherapy. Treatment duration of at least 6 months was specified because it was assumed brief contact would be unlikely to reveal some of the characteristics we were studying, particularly disguised personal intelligence and history of psychological abuse. It is possible that this requirement selected for a particular subtype of borderline patient. For instance, Hurt and Clarkin (1990) identified three subsets of DSM–III BPD criteria that characterize different groups of borderline patients: impulse, affective, and identity clusters. Rockland (1992) suggested that patients in the impulse cluster (including especially self-damaging acts and impulsive behaviors) and the affective cluster (including especially intense and unstable affects and relationships) would be much more likely to be treatment dropouts in longer term dynamic therapies, whereas patients in the identity cluster (including especially chronic feelings of emptiness, identity disturbance and intolerance of being alone) would more likely be introspective and psychologically minded, and therefore respond well to longer term dynamic therapy and stay in treatment. Also, 16 of the borderline patients met only five criteria for BPD and 17 had never been hospitalized, factors Rockland considers positive for dynamic therapy.

The four personal intelligence items were rated dichotomously by consensus for each of the 61 study patients. The three raters were psychiatrists, each with at least 20 years of postresidency psychotherapy experience. Two of the raters had prior extensive experience in clinical psychopharmacological or other clinical research. The raters were not blind to diagnoses because two of them had rated the diagnoses. Ratings were derived primarily from notes made during as well as immediately after therapy sessions. The notes were written before the study was designed, and before patients were reviewed by raters for DSM classification of personality disorders. A score of 0 to 4 was given to each patient according to how many of the four criteria were met, and we arbitrarily defined patients with scores of 3 (in any combination) or all 4 as having high personal intelligence, which we have termed "giftedness."

Applying our assignment of patients who scored 3 or 4 as gifted, 17 of the 23 BPD patients (74%) met at least three criteria. A significantly smaller proportion of the controls met at least three criteria (13/38:34%), $x^2 = (1, N = 61) = 7.52, p < .01$.

A comparison of borderlines and controls for each of the four checklist items revealed that Item 2 was the most discriminating (Table 6.1). Ninety-six percent (22/23) of borderlines versus 45% (17/38) of controls were judged as having intense preoccupation with and/or sense of the feelings of others. Clinically, the characteristics of Item 2 are prominently manifested in the powerful vicissitudes of projective identification as well as in the intense, repetitive search for empathy and intimacy in relationships, including those with therapists.

Item 1 was less discriminating, with 100% of borderlines versus 66% (25/38) of controls being judged as having intense preoccupation with and/or talented access to one's feelings. Item 1 could have been less discriminating because both borderlines and controls selected themselves as being self-preoccupied by seeking therapy.

Item 3 was also less discriminating than Item 2, with 61% (14/23) of borderlines versus 32% (12/38) of controls expressing at least three perceptive intuitions or insights about others. The long-term experience of the therapists with borderline patients may have made them particularly alert to boundaries and projective identification, such that manifestations of group differences were blunted regarding observations of therapists' vulnerabilities. Item 4 did not discriminate between the two groups: 65% (15/23) borderlines versus 66% (25/38) controls. It may have been inappropriate to combine empathy and grandiosity in one item.

Distinguishing a person's personal intelligence capacity versus inability to make use of it can be very difficult. One of the most difficult patients to evaluate met seven criteria for BPD but also met four criteria for NPD. Although she suffered greatly, she could also be quite insensitive and even cruel to her husband, her children, and others. She appeared to have a high capacity to intuitively grasp the vulnerabilities of others in order to play on them and dominate them, but she also appeared to have almost no capacity for empathy. We assumed that an extremely harsh childhood environment may have stifled some of her inborn intuitive capacities. This seemed to be born out after several years of intensive psychotherapy when the patient was finally willing and able to consider her harsh mental processes. She could see she was capable of being quite perceptive of how others felt and

TABLE 6.1
Patients' Scores on Items from Personal Intelligence Scale

	Items			
Patient group	1	2	3	4
BPD (*N* = 23)	23 (100%)	22 (96%)	14 (61%)	15 (65%)
Control (N = 38)	25 (66%)	17 (45%)	12 (32%)	25 (66%)
Difference (%)	34%	51%	29%	1%

could even empathize, but then in a "nanosecond" she would immediately refuse to empathize so that she could feel superior and in control and could play with them like a "cat with a mouse." This patient's mother was described as extremely cold, envious, manipulative, and vengeful. The patient stated that her mother could react with "venomous rage" if the patient demonstrated perceptive insights about herself and others, particularly about the mother. In this setting the patient learned to be just as harsh as the mother, but with the added ability that for "nanoseconds" she could use her perceptive abilities to tune into the inner states of others with remarkable accuracy. This patient is still in therapy and is experiencing an ability to have "real feelings" with increasing frequency. However, she still does not know if the cruel part of her will give up the safety and harsh pleasures of being immune to empathy and caring.

We reviewed histories of both the borderline and control groups for evidence of childhood abuse. We found that 100% of borderline patients reported at least two of five types of chronic, severe psychological abuse, versus only 32% (12/38) of the controls [$x^2 = (1, N = 61) = 24.70, p < .001$]. (Borderline patients also reported physical and sexual abuse more frequently than did controls, but this difference was not statistically significant.) Perhaps the most important finding of the study was that 74% (17/23) of the BPD patients were rated as both gifted and psychologically abused versus 13% (5/38) of the controls [$x^2 = (1, N = 61) = 20.38, p < .001$].

We also investigated patients' perceptions of parental personality characteristics and found that 91% (21/23) of the BPD patients described a dominant, unempathic parent versus 37% (14/38) of the controls [$x^2 = (1, N = 61) = 15.22, p < .001$]. This parent, usually the mother (18/21), tended to be extremely controlling, exploitive, unempathic, limited or lacking in expression of warmth, and frequently quite hostile towards detectible autonomous behaviors, observations and thoughts, even signs of pleasure, in the child, with the other parent usually neglectful or ineffective.

In summary, the study results were quite compatible with the first hypothesis that borderline patients frequently have high personal intelligence with a talent or gift for self- and other-perceptiveness. There was also strong evidence of severe psychological abuse, compatible with the second hypothesis that such abuse engenders the perversion of high personal intelligence in borderline patients. The study did not directly address the third hypothesis that high personal intelligence in borderline patients is biologically based. However, indirect evidence from the study may point by default to the likelihood of an inborn characteristic because the known environmental factors cannot account for our findings and actually work against them. In other words, it has been repeatedly reported that severe and chronic abuse characteristically dulls traits reflecting personal intelligence, yet paradoxically our study patients retained them to a high degree. As discussed earlier, such traits are also frequently revealed in the clinical BPD literature in descriptions of unusual interpersonal powers, perceptiveness about therapists' feelings and motives, intense preoccupation with emotions of self and others, very active mental life, capacity for empathy, intense search for intimacy, and indications of psychological mindedness. Nevertheless, although our personal intelligence scale's items seem to assess stable characteristics, full elucidation of biological components will require other kinds of investigations such as longitudinal and twin studies.

As a result of our preliminary findings, we plan to carry out more refined studies to examine our working hypothesis that the classical borderline syndrome can be engendered by the interaction of high personal intelligence (nature), and severe, chronic psychological abuse (nurture), without the necessity for any other etiological variables such as inborn defects. (We believe this to be a major but not the only possible developmental path to BPD.) We now believe that as children these patients learned to express their needs in a decentered, yet intuitive, way that could gain attention as a substitute for love or cause a disturbance as an expression of anger, in a manner that was not significantly dangerous because the parents (and the children) did not understand the perceptive level at which they were being coerced and provoked. Viewed as a learned capacity that perversely serves the urgent requirements of attachment, autonomy, rage, and pleasure in a dangerous environment, it makes sense why projective identification is a major characteristic of the borderline syndrome. The perversion of high personal intelligence can explain why borderlines appear to have characteristics suggestive of psychological mindedness, yet paradoxically have been considered poor candidates for dynamic psychotherapy or even for staying in treatment, and also can explain why these patients are frequently disturbing to therapists.

The highly controlling, exploitative, and unempathic characteristics of the dominant parents of our borderline patients led us to the posthoc conclusion that these parents had substantial characteristics of pathological narcissism, with many of them probably meeting the full criteria for NPD. Furthermore, these parents' harsh demands for unquestioned allegiance to self-centered, inflexible guidelines, and goals, their apparent inability to achieve meaningful new learning about self and others or even to tolerate alternative views, and the frequent absence of sufficiently explanatory childhood experiences of their own, suggested to us that the parents might have low inborn personal intelligence and be strongly governed by the kind of primitive algorithms proposed by Cosmides and Tooby (Barkow et al., 1992). The accuracy and intrusive power of language as a psychological weapon opened the door for these parents to directly abuse their children's perceptual mental machinery.

We will investigate the possibility that individuals who develop BPD and NPD tend to be at extremes of personal intelligence, with psychopathology frequently reflecting complex interactions of parents at one extreme and offspring at the other. A multidisciplinary approach to the study of social perceptivity and childrearing involving psychiatry, clinical psychology, and cognitive, comparative, developmental, and social psychology, should provide valuable insights about child development, as well as about human nature and its vicissitudes.

There were a number of weaknesses in this study that can occur in long-term clinical research, including small sample size, limited testing instruments, raters who were not blind to diagnosis or to each others' ratings, and associations that cannot prove causal relationships (Frances, 1990). Data were retrospectively derived from subjective reports and were potentially biased by both observers and patients. However, some of the results were statistically strong.

We wish to reemphasize that personal intelligence is a rather new concept that has not been studied in patient populations except as it might be an element in other measures discussed in this volume. Our personal intelligence scale is a rudimentary exploratory measure that distinguished BPD patients from control patients, but we cannot be certain that we were actually measuring personal intelligence. The next step in the study of personal intelligence should be the development and subsequent reliability and validity testing of a more sophisticated scale.

SUMMARY AND FUTURE DIRECTIONS

The concept of personal intelligence may lead to hypotheses for evolutionary, biological factors in psychological mindedness. Although definitions of psychological mindedness vary (Conte et al., 1990; Dollinger, Reader, Marnett, & Tylenda, 1983; Farber, 1985; Hall, 1992; McCallum & Piper, 1990), they are all quite compatible with the proposal that high psychological mindedness can be based on high personal intelligence.

It is important to integrate concepts and descriptions of personal intelligence and psychological mindedness, as well as to identify those elements that are particularly relevant to psychotherapy. A major task is to determine when limitations in personal intelligence are based on neglect, abuse, and faulty learning, and are therefore presumably changeable, and when limitations are based on inborn defects, and are therefore presumably unchangeable. If childhood environment stifles and distorts the development of aspects of this intelligence, is there permanent impairment or can there be degrees of improvement or recovery? Warnes (1986) discussed such issues as they apply to alexithymic, or nonpsychologically minded individuals.

Developmental, sociological, and biological research have demonstrated the complex connectedness of nature and nurture (Bowlby, 1988; Moran, 1994; Plomin, 1994; Werner, 1989; Wolpaw et al., 1991; Wright, 1995). Early stress and trauma can provoke disturbed gene expression and brain development, temperamental changes, and serious physical illness, including even cancer, and can also severely impede long-term recovery from perinatal physical and behavioral problems (Bowlby, 1984, 1988; Kotulak, 1993; Siegel, 1989; Teicher et al., 1994; Werner, 1989). Such findings suggest a necessity for extreme caution in evaluating sources and changeability of apparently inborn or biological defects in humans.

The concept of personal intelligence has profound implications not only for psychotherapy and for parenting but also for the education of children. Children are born with various potentials and learn to make use of them selectively through childhood experiences, including formal education. Gardner (1993a) made clear, for instance, that personal intelligence is a capacity that does not include an inborn sense of right and wrong and can express itself in dramatically differing ways, such as the interpersonal intelligences of Ghandi or Mandela versus Stalin.

Learning how to know oneself and others may be one of the most important skills for a child to develop (Damon, 1990; Goleman, 1995), yet it is not effectively addressed by most educational systems, much less the consideration that there can be significant individual variation in the inherent capacity to know. Consider the child with low capacity for empathy but with a special capacity to perceive characteristics about others that can be manipulated for that child's own ends. What happens when such a child grows up without any help to understand about self and others? Would such a person have a better ability to be empathic if he or she had been helped in school to grasp concepts such as putting oneself in another's place or that emotionally based responses may have accompanying explanatory thought patterns that are not rational? On the other hand, what happens when a sensitive, perceptive child has not been helped to understand that others can disguise insensitivity as well as predatory intentions?

Gardner (1993b, 1994) is at the forefront of the development of a multiple intelligences approach for teaching children. The goal is to identify and work with each child's unique combination of abilities and liabilities, focusing on interactive learning programs incorporating hands-on characteristics such as apprenticeship and children's museums. Also, many schools are discovering the advantages of programs for emotional literacy and for conflict resolution such as peer counseling, in which students learn to evaluate, moderate, and dispense decisions about disruptive student behaviors such as fighting. In private and large public schools, the majority of students volunteer to participate in such programs and they tend to become very involved. The benefits of these programs include learning to question one's own feelings and impulses, thinking more perceptively about the feelings and motives of others, and a measurable decrease in serious student problems and conflicts. Additionally, such activities can provide important clues for identifying troubled children and dysfunctional home environments.

It is essential to further study the proposals that we are born with varying capacities for knowing ourselves and others, and that the skills for utilizing such capacities must be learned. We need to continue exploring the dimensions of personal intelligence, develop reliable ways to measure them, and provide effective educational and therapeutic approaches for individuals whose life experiences have left such capacities neglected or damaged. The development of methods to assess and maximize a child's personal intelligence in both the home and school may be critical for mental health, for career success, for the health and strength of society, and possibly for the long-term survival of our species.

ACKNOWLEDGMENTS

Our database is from an earlier published study (Park et al., 1992). We thank Mary Woodfill Park and Stephanie Suzanne Reynolds for library and database searches and for editorial review.

REFERENCES

Ackerman, R., & DeRubeis, R. J. (1991). Is depressive realism real? *Clinical Psychology Review, 11*, 565–584.

Adler, G. (1985). *Borderline psychopathology and its treatment*. Northvale, NJ: Aronson.

Alexander, R. (1989). The evolution of the human psyche. In P. Mellars & C. Stringer (Eds.), *Origins and dispersal of modern humans* (pp. 455–513). Princeton, NJ: Princeton University Press.

Alverez, J. R., Schonbar, R. A., & Farber, B. A. (June, 1993). *Psychological mindedness: A test of Alice Miller's hypothesis*. Paper presented at the meeting of the Society for Psychotherapy Research, Pittsburgh, PA.

American Psychiatric Association. (1987). *Diagnostic and statistical manual of mental disorders* (3rd ed., Rev.). Washington, DC: Author.

American Psychiatric Association. (1994). *Diagnostic and statistical manual of mental disorders* (4th ed.). Washington, DC: Author.

Andrews, P., & Stringer, C. (1993). The primates' progress. In S. J. Gould (Ed.), *The book of life* (pp. 219–251). New York: Norton.

Averill, S. C., Beale, D., Benfer, B., Collins, D. T., Kennedy, L., Myers J., Pope, D., Rosen, I., & Zoble, E. (1989). Preventing staff-patient sexual relationships. *Bulletin of the Menninger Clinic, 53*, 384–393.

Bard, K. A. (1995). Parenting in primates. In M. H. Bornstein (Ed.), *Biology and ecology of parenting* (pp. 27–58). Mahwah, NJ: Lawrence Erlbaum Associates.

Barkow, J. H., Cosmides, L., & Tooby, J. (Eds.). (1992). *The adapted mind: Evolutionary psychology and the generation of culture*. New York: Oxford University Press.

Batson, C. D., & Shaw, L. L. (1991). Evidence for altruism: Toward a pluralism of prosocial motives.*Psychological Inquiry, 2*, 107–122.

Beckmann, D., & Richter, H. E. (1972). *Giessen Test (GT)*. Bern, Switzerland: Hans Huber.

Benedict, R. (1934). *Patterns of culture*. Boston: Houghton Mifflin.

Bowlby, J. (1984). Violence in the family as a disorder of the attachment and caregiving systems. *American Journal of Psychoanalysis, 44*, 9–27.

Bowlby, J. (1988). Developmental psychiatry comes of age. *American Journal of Psychiatry, 145*, 1–10.

Boyce, W. T., Chesney, M., Alkon, A., Tschann, J. M., Adams, S., Chesterman, B., Cohen, F., Kaiser P., Folkman, S., & Wara, D. (1995). Psychobiologic reactivity to stress and childhood respiratory illness: Results of two prospective studies. *Psychosomatic Medicine, 57*, 411–422.

Boysen, S. T., & Berntson, G. G. (1995). Responses to quantity: Perceptual vs. cognitive mechanisms in chimpanzees *(Pan troglodytes)*. *Journal of Experimental Psychology: Animal Behavior Processes, 21*, 82–86.

Brothers, L. (1989). A biological perspective on empathy. *American Journal of Psychiatry, 146*, 10–19.

Brothers, L. (1990). The social brain: A project for integrating primate behavior and neurophysiology in a new domain. *Concepts in Neuroscience, 1*, 27–51.

Bruce, G. (1968). *The stranglers: The cult of thuggee and its overthrow in British India*. New York: Harcourt Brace.

Buss, D. M. (1995). Evolutionary psychology: A new paradigm for psychological science. *Psychological Inquiry, 6*, 1–30.

Byne, W., & Parsons, B. (1993). Human sexual orientation: The biologic theories reappraised. *Archives of General Psychiatry, 50*, 228–239.

Byrne, R. W. (1991, May). Brute intellect. *Sciences*, pp. 42–47.

Calvin, W. H. (1991). *The throwing madonna: From nervous cells to hominid brains*. New York: Bantam.

Cantu, J. M., & Ruiz, C. (1985). On atavism and atavistic genes. *Annales De Genetique, 28*, 141–142.

Carter, L., & Rinsley, D. B. (1977). Vicissitudes of "empathy" in a borderline adolescent. *International Review of Psychoanalysis, 4*, 317–326.

Celani, D. P. (1994). *The illusion of love*. New York: Columbia University Press.

Cheney, D. L., & Seyfarth, R. M. (1990). *How monkeys see the world: Inside the mind of another species*. Chicago: University of Chicago Press.

Chion-Kenney, L. (1994, May 3). How we learn: The multiple intelligences teaching approach. *The Washington Post*, p. B5.

Chomsky, N. (1975). *Reflections on language*. New York: Pantheon.

Cicchetti, D., & Carlson, V. (Eds.). (1989). *Child maltreatment: Theory and research on the causes and consequences of child abuse and neglect*. Cambridge, MA: Cambridge University Press.

Conte, H. R., Plutchik, R., Jung, B. B., Picard, S., Karasu, T. B., & Lotterman, A. (1990). Psychological mindedness as a predictor of psychotherapy outcome: A preliminary report. *Comprehensive Psychiatry, 31*, 426–431.

Cosmides, L., & Tooby, J. (1992). Cognitive adaptations for social exchange. In J. H. Barkow, L. Cosmides, & J. Tooby (Eds.), *The adapted mind: Evolutionary psychology and the generation of culture* (pp. 163–228). New York: Oxford University Press.

Costa, P. T., & McCrae, R. R. (1990). Personality disorders and the five-factor model of personality. *Journal of Personality Disorders, 4*, 362–371.

Damasio, A. R. (1994). *Descartes' error: Emotion, reason, and the human brain*. New York: Grosset–Putnam.

Damon, W. (1990). *The moral child: Nurturing children's natural moral growth*. New York: Free Press.

Davies, N. (1981). *Human sacrifice*. New York: Dorset Press.

Davis, M. H., Luce, C., & Kraus, S. J. (1994). The heritability of characteristics associated with dispositional empathy. *Journal of Personality, 62*, 369–391.

Dollinger, S. J., Reader, M. J., Marnett, J. P., & Tylenda, B. (1983). Psychological mindedness, psychological construing, and the judgment of deception. *Journal of General Psychology, 108*, 183–191.

Drozdiak, W. (1995, July 2). Noted jurist (Richard Goldstone) says bias contains 'seeds of genocide'. *The Washington Post*, p. A24.

Dunn, J., & Plomin, R. (1990). *Separate lives: Why siblings are so different*. New York: Basic Books.

Edgar, B. (1993). What's behind the human mind? *Anthroquest, 47*, 10–11.

Farber, B. A. (1985). The genesis, development, and implications of psychological mindedness in psychotherapists. *Psychotherapy, 22*, 170–177.

Farber, B. A. (1989). Psychological mindedness: Can there be too much of a good thing? *Psychotherapy, 26*, 210–217.

Fisher, H. E. (1982). *The sex contract: The evolution of human behavior*. New York: William Morrow.

Fonagy, P., Steele, M., Steele, H., Leigh, T., Kennedy, R., Mattoon, G., & Target, M. (1995). Attachment, the reflective self, and borderline states. In S. Goldberg & J. Kerr (Eds.), *John Bowlby's attachment theory: Historical, clinical and social significance* (pp. 233–278). New York: Analytic Press.
Forgey, B. (1988, October 30). Daimyo: First rays of a rising sun. *The Washington Post*, pp. G1, G3, G5.
Frances, A. (1990). Forward. In M. H. Stone (Ed.), *The fate of borderline patients* (pp. Vii–ix). New York: Guilford.
Frances. A., Clarkin, J. F., Gilmore, M., Hurt, S. W., & Brown, R. (1984). Reliability of criteria for borderline personality disorder: A comparison of DSM–III and the diagnostic interview for borderline patients. *American Journal of Psychiatry, 141*, 1080–1084.
Frances, A., First, M. B., & Pincus, H. A. (1995). *DSM–IV guidebook.* Washington, DC: American Psychiatric Press.
Frank, H., & Hoffman, N. (1986). Borderline empathy: An empirical investigation. *Comprehensive Psychiatry, 2*, 387–395.
Fraser, S. (Ed.). (1995). *The bell curve wars*. New York: Basic Books. Frith, U. (1993). Autism. *Scientific American, 268*, 108–114.
Frith, U. (1993). Autism. *Scientific American, 268, 108–114.*
Gabbard, G. O., & Wilkinson, S. M. (1994). *Management of countertransference with borderline patients*. Washington, DC: American Psychiatric Press.
Gallagher, R. E., Flye, B. L., Hurt, S. W., Stone, M. H., & Hull, J. W. (1992). Retrospective assessment of traumatic experiences (RATE). *Journal of Personality Disorders, 6*, 99–108.
Garbarino, J., Guttman, E., & Seeley, J. (1986). *The psychologically battered child: Strategies for identification, assessment, and intervention*. San Francisco: Jossey-Bass.
Gardner, H. (1983). *Frames of mind: The theory of multiple intelligences.* New York: Basic Books.
Gardner, H. (1985). The centrality of modules. *The Behavioral and Brain Sciences, 8*, 12–14.
Gardner, H. (1993a). Introduction to the tenth anniversary edition. In H. Gardner, *Frames of mind* (pp. ix–xxvi). New York: Basic Books.
Gardner, H. (1993b). *Multiple intelligences theory: The theory in practice*. New York: Basic Books.
Gardner, H. (1994, June). *Multiple intelligences theory: Implications for practice.* Paper presented at the Symposium on Multiple Intelligences in Practice, Washington, DC.
Gazzaniga, M. (1989). Organization of the human brain. *Science, 245*, 947–952.
Goleman, D. (1995). *Emotional intelligence*. New York: Bantam.
Goodall, J. (1986). *The chimpanzees of Gombe: Patterns of behavior.* Cambridge, MA: Harvard University Press.
Gould, S. J. (1986). Gould shoots down firmly held beliefs about evolution at annual meeting. *Psychiatric News, 21*, 9.
Gould, S. J. (1988, December). Ten thousand acts of kindness: Who occupies the driver's seat of human history? *Natural History*, pp. 12–17.
Gould, S. J. (1989, April). Tires to sandals: As we strive to understand nature, do we seek truth or solace? *Natural History*, pp. 8–15.
Gould, S. J. (1994, September). Lucy on the Earth in stasis. *Natural History*, pp. 12–20.
Greenspan, S. I. (1992). *Infancy and early childhood: The practice of clinical assessment and intervention with emotional and developmental challenges.* Madison: International Universities Press.
Gunderson, J. G. (1982). Empirical studies of the borderline diagnosis. In L. Grinspoon (Ed.), *Psychiatry 1982: The American Psychiatric Association annual review* (pp. 415–437). Washington, DC: American Psychiatric Press.
Gunderson, J. G. (1989). Borderline personality disorder. In T. B. Karasu (Ed.), *Treatments of psychiatric disorders: A task force report of the American Psychiatric Association* (pp. 2749–2759). Washington, DC: American Psychiatric Association.
Gunderson, J. G., & Sabo, A. N. (1993). The phenomenological and conceptual interface between borderline personality disorder and PTSD. *American Journal of Psychiatry, 150*, 19–27.
Gunderson, J. G., & Zanarini, M. C. (1989). Pathogenesis of borderline personality. In A. Tasman, R. E. Hales, & A. J. Frances (Eds.), *American psychiatric press review of psychiatry*, (Vol. 8, pp. 25–48). Washington, DC: American Psychiatric Press.
Gutheil, T. G. (1989). Borderline personality disorder, boundary violations, and patient-therapist sex: Medicolegal pitfalls. *American Journal of Psychiatry, 146*, 597–602.

Hall, J. A. (1992). Psychological mindedness: A conceptual model. *American Journal of Psychotherapy, 46*, 131–140.

Harlow, H. F. (1964). Early social deprivation and later behavior in the monkey. In A. Abrams, H. H. Garner, & J. E. P. Toman (Eds.), *Unfinished tasks in the behavioral sciences* (pp. 154–173). Baltimore: Williams & Wilkins.

Hart, S. N., & Brassard, M. R. (1987). A major threat to children's mental health: Psychological maltreatment. *American Psychologist, 42*, 160–165.

Hartmann, E. (1991). *Boundaries in the mind: A new psychology of personality*. New York: Basic Books.

Herdt, G. H. (1981). *Guardians of the flutes: Idioms of masculinity*. New York: McGraw–Hill.

Herman, J. L., Perry, J. C., & van der Kolk, B. A. (1989). Childhood trauma in borderline personality disorder. *American Journal of Psychiatry, 146*, 490–495.

Herrnstein, R. J., & Murray, C. (1994). *The bell curve: Intelligence and class structure in American life*. New York: Free Press.

Hoffman, W., & Frank, H. (1987). Borderline empathy and borderline pathology: Constitutional considerations. *Comprehensive Psychiatry, 28*, 412–415.

Hrdy, S. B. (1995). Natural-born mothers. *Natural History, 104*, 30–42.

Humphrey, N. K. (1976). The social function of intellect. In P. P. G. Bateson & R. A. Hinde (Eds.), *Growing points in ethology* (pp. 303–317). New York: Cambridge University Press.

Hunt, M. (1990) *The compassionate beast: What science is discerning about the humane side of humankind*. New York: William Morrow.

Hunt, T. (1928). The measurement of social intelligence. *Journal of Applied Psychology, 12*, 317–334.

Hurt, S. W., & Clarkin, J. F. (1990). Borderline personality disorder: Prototypic typology and the development of treatment manuals. *Psychiatric Annals, 20*, 13–18.

Huttenlocher, P. R. (1979). Synaptic density in human frontal cortex: Developmental changes and effects of aging. *Brain Research, 163*, 195–205.

Kagan, J. (1994). *Galen's prophecy: Temperament in human nature*. New York: Basic Books.

Karmiloff-Smith, A., Klima, E., Bellugi, U., Grant, J., & Baron-Cohen, S. (1995). Is there a social module? Language, face processing, and theory of mind in individuals with Williams Syndrome. *Journal of Cognitive Neuroscience, 7*, 196–208.

Kass, F., Skodol, A., Charles, E., Spitzer, R. L., & Williams, J. B. W. (1985). Scaled ratings of DSM-III personality disorders. *American Journal of Psychiatry, 142*, 627–630.

Kernberg, O. F. (1975). *Borderline conditions and pathological narcissism*. New York: Aronson.

Kernberg, O. F. (1986). *Severe personality disorders*. New Haven, CT: Yale University Press.

Kernberg, O. F., Selzer, M. A., Koenigsberg, H. W., Carr, A. C., & Applebaum, A. H. (1989). *Psychodynamic psychotherapy of borderline patients*. New York: Basic Books.

Kerr, W. A. (1965). *The empathy test*. Munster, IN: Psychometric Affiliates.

Kohut, H. (1971). *The analysis of the self*. New York: International Universities Press.

Kosslyn, S. M., & Koenig, O. (1992). *Wet mind: The new cognitive neuroscience*. New York: Free Press.

Kotulak, R. (1993, August). Children's brains may change in response to stress. *The Washington Post*, pp. 11–12.

Krohn, A. (1974). Borderline "empathy" and differentiation of object representations: A contribution to the psychology of object relations. *International Journal of Psychiatry, 3*, 142–165.

Ladisich, W., & Feil, W. B. (1988). Empathy in psychiatric patients. *British Journal of Medical Psychology, 61*, 155–162.

Lazare, A., Klerman, G. L., & Armor, D. J. (1966). Oral, obsessive and hysterical personality patterns: An investigation of psychoanalytic concepts by means of factor analysis. *Archives of General Psychiatry, 14*, 624–630.

Leakey, R., & Lewin, R. (1992). *Origins reconsidered: In search of what makes us human*. New York: Doubleday.

LeDoux, J. (1993, May). Emotions and rationality. *Psychiatric Times*, p. 19.

Levy, H. S. (1992). *The lotus lovers: The complete history of the curious erotic custom of footbinding in China*. New York: Prometheus Books.

Lidz, T. (1990). Optimism in treatment of schizophrenia still premature, says expert. *Psychiatric News*, pp. 26, 33.

Lieberman, P. (1991). *Uniquely human: The evolution of speech, thought and selfless behavior.* Cambridge, MA: Harvard University Press.

Lindholm, C., & Lindholm, C. (1979, October). Marriage as warfare: The Pakhtun of Pakistan. *Natural History*, pp. 11–20.

Links, P. S., Steiner, M., Offord, D., & Eppel, A. (1988). Characteristics of borderline personality disorder: A Canadian study. *Canadian Journal of Psychiatry, 33*, 336–340.

Lorenz, K. (1966). *On aggression*. New York: Harcourt Brace.

Lovejoy, C. O. (1981). The origin of man. *Science, 211*, 341–350.

MacLean, P. D. (1985). Brain evolution relating to family, play and the separation call. *Archives of General Psychiatry, 42*, 405–417.

Masterson, J. F. (1976). *Psychotherapy of the borderline adult: A developmental approach*. New York: Brunner/Mazel.

McCallum, M., & Piper, W. E. (1990). The psychological mindedness assessment procedure. *Psychological Assessment: A Journal of Consulting and Clinical Psychology, 2*, 412–418.

McGee, R. A., & Wolfe, D. A. (1991). Psychological maltreatment: Toward an operational definition. *Development and Psychopathology, 3*, 3–18.

Miller, A. (1981). *Prisoners of childhood: How narcissistic parents form and deform the emotional lives of their gifted children*. New York: Basic Books.

Miller, A. (1983). *For your own good: Hidden cruelty in childrearing and the roots of violence*. New York: Farrar, Straus & Giroux.

Montagu, A. (Ed.). (1978). *Learning non-aggression: The experience of non-literate societies*. New York: Oxford University Press.

Moran, M. (1994). Psychiatrist (Stanley Greenspan) takes swing at 'bell curve'. *Psychiatric News, 29*, 1, 16.

Morgan, E. (1995). *The descent of the child: Human evolution from a new perspective*. New York: Oxford University Press.

Moss, F. A., & Hunt, T. (1927). Are you socially intelligent? *Scientific American, 137*, 108–110.

Nesse, R. M. (1991, December). What good is feeling bad? The evolutionary benefits of psychic pain. *The Sciences*, pp. 30–37.

Neubauer, P. B., & Neubauer, A. (1990). *Nature's thumbprint: The new genetics of personality*. New York: Addison-Wesley.

Ogden, T. H. (1982). *Projective identification and psychotherapeutic technique*. Northvale, NJ: Aronson.

Ogden, T. H. (1994). The analytic third: Working with intersubjective clinical facts. *International Journal of Psychoanalysis, 75*, 3–19.

Oliner, S. P., & Oliner, P. (1988). *The altruistic personality: Rescuers of Jews in Nazi Europe*. New York: Free Press.

Park, L. C. (1992). Psychiatry ignoring child abuse and neglect movement. *Psychiatric News, 27*, p. 14.

Park, L. C. (1994). Does this patient need psychiatric referral? Borderline personality disorder is serious, life-threatening, and fairly common, yet it goes unrecognized by most physicians. *Hospital Medicine, 30*, 36–42.

Park, L. C., Imboden, J. B., Park, T. J., Hulse, S. H., & Unger, H. T. (1992). Giftedness and psychological abuse in borderline personality disorder: Their relevance to genesis and treatment. *Journal of Personality Disorders, 6*, 226–240.

Pinker, S. (1994). *The language instinct*. New York: William Morrow.

Plomin, R. (1994). Nature, nurture, and social development. *Social Development, 3*, 37–53.

Premack, D., & Premack, A. J. (1995). Origins of human social competence. In M. S. Gazzaniga (Ed.), *The cognitive neurosciences* (pp. 205–218). Cambridge, MA: MIT Press.

Ressler, R. K., & Shachtman, T. (1992). *Whoever fights monsters*. New York: St. Martin's Press.

Risteau, C. A. (1991). *Cognitive ethology: The minds of other animals*. Hillsdale, NJ: Lawrence Erlbaum Associates.

Rockland, L. H. (1992). *Supportive therapy for borderline patients: A psychodynamic approach*. New York: Guilford.

Rorty, M., Yager, J., & Rossotto, E. (1994). Childhood sexual, physical, and psychological abuse in bulimia nervosa. *American Journal of Psychiatry, 151*, 1122–1126.

Rosenthal, R., Hall, J. A., DiMatteo, M. R., Rogers, P. L., & Archer, D. (1979). *Sensitivity to nonverbal communication: The PONS test*. Baltimore: Johns Hopkins University Press.

Rushton, J. P., Fulker, D. W., Neale, M. C., Nias, D. K. B., & Eysenck, H. J. (1986). Altruism and aggression: The heritability of individual differences. *Journal of Personality and Social Psychology, 50*, 1192–1198.
Salovey, P., & Mayer, J. D. (1990). Emotional intelligence. *Imagination, Cognition and Personality, 9*, 185–209.
Schmandt-Besserat, D. (1992). *Before writing, Volume I: From counting to cuneiform*. Austin: University of Texas Press.
Schwartz, M., Blazer, D., George, L., & Winfield, I. (1990). Estimating the prevalence of borderline personality disorder in the community. *Journal of Personality Disorders, 4*, 257–272.
Shapiro, E. R. (1978). The psychodynamics and developmental psychology of the borderline patient: A review of the literature. *American Journal of Psychiatry, 135*, 1305– 1315.
Shearer, S. L. (1994). Dissociative phenomena in women with borderline personality disorder. *American Journal of Psychiatry, 151*, 1324–1328.
Shengold, L. (1989, November). Patients abused as children must overcome denial, repetition of past. *Psychiatric Times*, pp. 39–40.
Sherman, C. (1994, July). Overindulgence can lead to aggression and panic in children. *Clinical Psychiatry News*, p. 13.
Siegel, B. S. (1989). *Peace, love and healing*. New York: Harper & Row.
Simons, E. L. (1989). Human origins. *Science, 245*, 1343–1350.
Small, M. F. (March, 1990). Political animal: Social intelligence and the growth of the primate brain. *Sciences*, pp. 36–42.
Spiegel, D. (1994). *Dissociation: Culture, body and mind*. Washington, DC: American Psychiatric Press.
Stanley, S. M. (1992). An ecological theory for the emergence of homo. *Paleobiology, 18*, 237–257.
Sternberg, R. J., & Smith, C. (1985). Social intelligence and decoding skills in nonverbal communication. *Social Cognition, 3*, 168–192.
Stolorow, R., & Brandchaft, B. (1987). Developmental failure and psychic conflict. *Psychoanalytic Psychology, 4*, 241–253.
Stone, M. H. (1985). Disturbances in sex and love in borderline patients. In Z. Defries, R. C. Friedman, & R. Corn (Eds.), *Sexuality: New perspectives* (pp. 159–186). Westport, CT: Greenwood Press.
Stone, M. H. (1990a). Abuse and abusiveness in borderline personality disorder. In P. S. Links (Ed.), *Family environment and borderline personality disorder* (pp. 131–148). Washington, DC: American Psychiatric Press.
Stone, M. H. (1990b). *The fate of borderline patients: Successful outcome and psychiatric practice*. New York: Guilford.
Storr, A. (1972). *Human destructiveness*. New York: Basic Books.
Storr, A. (1990). *Churchill's black dog, Kafka's mice and other phenomena of the human mind*. New York: Balantine.
Strang, R. (1930). Measures of social intelligence. *American Journal of Sociology, 36*, 263–269.
Suomi, S. J. (1991). Early stress and adult emotional reactivity in rhesus monkeys. In Ciba Foundation Symposium 156, *The childhood environment and adult disease* (pp. 171–188). Chichester: Wiley.
Taylor, E. H., & Cadet, J. L. (1989). Social intelligence, a neurological system? *Psychological Reports, 64*, 423–444.
Teicher, M. H., Ito, Y., Glod, C. A., Schiffer, F., & Gelbard, H. A. (1994). Early abuse, limbic system dysfunction, and borderline personality disorder. In K. R. Silk (Ed.), *Biological and neurobiological studies of borderline personality disorder* (pp. 177–207). Washington, DC: American Psychiatric Press.
Thomas, A., & Chess, S. (1984). Genesis and evolution of behavior disorders: From infancy to early adult life. *American Journal of Psychiatry, 141*, 1–9.
Thorndike, E. L. (1920). Intelligence and its uses. *Harper's, 140*, 227–235.
Tienari, P., Kaleva, M., Lahti, I., Lasky, J. Moring, J., Naarala, M., Sorri, A., Wahlberg, K. E., & Wynne, L. (1991). Adoption studies on schizophrenia. In C. Eggers (Ed.), *Schizophrenia and youth: Etiology and therapeutic consequences* (pp. 442–451). Berlin: Springer-Verlag.
Tuchman, B. W. (1984). *The march of folly: From Troy to Vietnam*. New York: Knopf.
Vaillant, G. E. (1977). *Adaptation to life*. Boston: Little, Brown.

van der Kolk, B. A. (1987a, April). Psychobiology of attachment/separation. *Psychiatric Times*, pp. 1, 4–5.

van der Kolk, B. A. (1987b). *Psychological trauma*. Washington, DC: American Psychiatric Press.

Walker, R. E., & Foley, J. M. (1973). Social intelligence: Its history and measurement. *Psychological Reports, 33*, 839–864.

Warnes, H. (1986). Alexithymia, clinical and therapeutic aspects. *Psychotherapy and Psychosomatics, 46*, 96–104.

Wedeck, J. (1947). The relationship between personality and "psychological ability." *British Journal of Psychology, 37*, 133–151.

Welldon, E. V. (1988). *Mother, madonna, whore: The idealization and denigration of motherhood*. New York: Guilford.

Werner, E. E. (1989). Children of the garden island. *Scientific American, 260*, 106–111.

Widiger, T. A., & Frances, A. J. (1989). Epidemiology, diagnosis, and comorbidity of borderline personality disorder. In A. Tasman, R. E. Hales, & A. J. Frances (Eds.), *American psychiatric press review of psychiatry* (Vol. 8, pp. 8–24). Washington, DC: American Psychiatric Press.

Wills, C. (1993). *The runaway brain: The evolution of human uniqueness*. New York: Basic Books.

Wolpaw, J. R., Schmidt, J. T., & Vaughan, T. M. (Eds.) (1991). *Activity-driven CNS changes in learning and development*. New York: New York Academy of Sciences.

Wright, R. (1995, March). The biology of violence. *New Yorker*, pp. 68–77.

Wyer, R. S., Jr., & Srull, T. K. (Eds.) (1989). *Advances in social cognition, Volume II: Social intelligence and cognitive assessments of personality*. Hillsdale, NJ: Lawrence Erlbaum Associates.

Zanarini, M., Frankenburg, F., Chauncey, D., & Gunderson, J. G. (1987). The diagnostic interview for personality disorders: Interrater and test-retest reliability. *Comprehensive Psychiatry, 28*, 467–480.

Zanarini, M. C., Gunderson, J. G., Frankenburg, F. R., & Chauncey, D. L. (1990). Discriminating borderline personality disorder from other Axis II disorders. *American Journal of Psychiatry, 147*, 161–167.

Zanarini, M. C., Gunderson, J. G., Marino, M. F., Schwartz, E. O., & Frankenburg, F. R. (1989). Childhood experiences of borderline patients. *Comprehensive Psychiatry, 30*, 18–25.

Chapter 7

Psychological Mindedness as "Reading Between the Lines"

Stephen J. Dollinger
Southern Illinois University at Carbondale

The concept of psychological mindedness is rich, with much importance within psychotherapy and relevance to personality psychology. Because it is so rich, it is open to many possible operationalizations as Hall (1992) documented and as this volume exemplifies. The approach I and my students take is to conceptualize psychological mindedness as the ability "to read between the lines" of what a person does or says. Following Hall's distinction between interest and ability, this working definition would have to be broadened to include both the ability to search beneath the surface of human behavior as well as the interest in doing so. Although therapists often regard psychological mindedness as an attribute of self-inquiry rather than one of person-perception (e.g., Abramowitz & Abramowitz, 1974), we take the position that perception of self and other makes a worthwhile empirical question: Are insight into others and insight into the self related? For example, are those who see through another's defense of rationalization themselves more or less disposed to recognize their own rationalization and then less likely to use this defense? In its broadest sense, I believe that psychological mindedness encompasses social–cognitive skills and an interest in things psychological, in its narrowest sense, an ability and willingness to penetrate self-protective defenses toward insight and understanding.

My research program on such issues, the topic of this chapter, was prompted by clinical experience and developed by its inclusion of concepts from developmental, cognitive, and social–personality psychology. The initial concern was an interest in knowing how child clients perceived me and how my clients might be perceived by their peers. (This issue is underscored today when seeing some contemporary television "role models" such as Bart Simpson and Beavis and Butt-head as they encounter psychotherapists!)

Thus, we started with two surveys of children's knowledge of and interest in psychology. From these initial inquiries, the research then progressed to a series of studies on a specific kind of reading between the lines, an understanding of defense mechanisms. Insight into one's own defenses is a usual hallmark of psychological mindedness regardless of one's definition, because defenses are barriers to self-understanding (Appelbaum, 1973; McCallum & Piper, 1990). However, as interpersonal phenomena, defenses are inherently interesting. This is because logic does not suffice to provide an explanation; some kind of psycho-logic is needed. From the defense-understanding work, the research program turned to the study of a more discrete kind of reading between the lines, recognizing the affective script underlying protocols of word associations. This chapter considers each topic chronologically as the research program developed.

CHILDREN'S APTITUDES AND ATTITUDES

In an effort to appraise children's concepts of psychology, my graduate school mentor and I surveyed over 1,300 children from Grades 5 through 12 (Dollinger & Thelen, 1978). Although most of the data do not bear directly on our immediate purposes, we found knowledge of and attraction to psychology were generally unrelated. The career of psychologist fit with other helping professions in children's conceptual schemata. In a factor analysis of career attractiveness ratings, psychologist loaded on a factor with school counselor, school teacher, and clergyperson. More noteworthy were children's answers to an open-ended question, "what kinds of problems do you think clinical psychologists help people with?" Children primarily conceptualized psychological problems as social or interpersonal in nature (e.g., family, marital). More than did younger subjects, older subjects cited problems internal to the person such as emotions and thoughts (Dollinger, Thelen, & Walsh, 1980); younger subjects were more likely to cite observable acts (e.g., smoking, fighting). Thus, ideas of "psychological problem" seem to follow the external to internal or surface to depth course found in self-conceptions (e.g., Mohr, 1978) and social cognition generally (Flavell, 1977).

READING BETWEEN THE DEFENSES

My first doctoral student and therapy supervisee, Beth McGuire, reported on some clinical observations that shaped the direction of our research. Her client's comments to another child, overheard by other children in a classroom setting, involved blatant rationalization. This intriguing observation prompted us to examine the literature on children's understanding of defenses and to design a study. The extant literature provided some clues as to how children evaluated and understood various forms of child deviance (e.g., Coie & Pennington, 1976; Maas, Marecek, & Travers, 1978; Marsden, Kalter, Plunkett, & Barr-Grossman, 1977), and how children understood disguised motives relevant to defenses (Berzonsky, 1973; Chandler, Paget, & Koch, 1978; Whiteman, 1967). Based on the literature and this client, we devised seven stories and accompanying line drawings to illustrate self-blame, projection, denial, and other defenses (Dollinger & McGuire, 1981). We presented our stories to 34 children spanning the entire age range of a private alternative elementary school. (Relative to public schools, this school had a more child-centered philosophy and it attracted both gifted children and those with behavior problems. The school attracted relative few children from impoverished homes.) The stimuli can be exemplified by the displacement story:

> Alex wanted to go and play with his friends after school one day. But his mom said, "No Alex, first you have to do your homework and feed Rover." Alex was mad but he didn't say anything. He just went to his room and did his homework. As he put away his book, Rover came up to him looking very hungry and nudging him with his nose. Alex said, "You're a bad dog," and pushed him away with his knee.

Children were asked to retell the story (scored for number of "information units" recalled) and to explain why the story characters responded as they did. Explanations were reliably coded into 4 levels:

1. Vague and irrelevant answer—child is taken in by defense,
2. Simple explanation referring just to affect or immediate stimulus
3. Some tying together of affect and behavior
4. Perceptive tying together of affect, behavior, and situation.

The children were also administered a perspective-taking task to assess their cognitive egocentrism (Chandler, 1973). In this task, subjects viewed a Picture Arrangement cartoon (e.g., the Little King from the Wechsler Adult Intelligence Scale [WAIS]) and they were asked merely to tell the story depicted in its correct sequence. Next, one or two significant cartoon frames were removed, changing the story. Then, the experimenter introduced a puppet and the child was asked to retell the story from the puppet's perspective. This final retelling was scored for the intrusion of information from the child's perspective. Higher scores indicated a more egocentric perspective.

Not surprisingly, we found that (a) defense understanding was related to age and to verbal memory, (b) some defenses, notably displacement, were more easily "seen through" by the children, and (c) most importantly, good perspective-takers were better at seeing through defenses than were their more egocentric peers. This finding was extended by Rosenthal and Simeonsson (1990), who showed that hospitalized emotionally disturbed adolescents had less adequate understanding of some defenses than did normal peers.

A subsequent study showed that children evaluated defenses in different ways and, by Grade 5, perceived defenses in gender-stereotypic ways (Dollinger, Staley, & McGuire, 1981). Here, our stimuli consisted of a common story of four youngsters (denoted by letters rather than names) on a softball team who responded to the loss of a championship game in different ways. The first denied any concern about the loss, another projected by blaming cheaters on the other team, a third self-blamed for the loss, and a fourth (control) character was described as being appropriately sad. Fifth and sixth graders from a public elementary school ($N = 76$) evaluated the story characters on various dimensions. Although all characters were rated very low on happiness, the control character was perceived as highest on goodness, smartness, and likability, suggesting that most defenses are negatively evaluated. Projection was rated lower on these qualities than were denial and self-blame. Children perceived the projecting or externalizing character as male and the self-blaming character as female, a stereotypic pattern that is consistent with other studies on self-reported defense preferences among adolescents and adults (Cramer, 1979, 1988).

For her dissertation, Beth McGuire (1982) turned to the issue of children's defense usage whereas Arlinda Staley and another student, Brian Thomson, addressed the question of how defense understanding and use correlate. This is an important question, regardless of one's theoretical approach to psychological mindedness. In general, dynamically oriented clinicians would view defenses as unconscious and, when brought to consciousness, less likely to be used; therefore, a negative correlation would be predicted between understanding of a defense and use of that defense. Social-learning oriented clinicians might view defenses as learned coping mechanisms; from this orientation, use and understanding might be more positively related to each other. (For example, rationalization might be viewed as a kind of cognitive restructuring, which could be desirable as long as it reduced anxiety.)

To measure defense preference, Staley (1985) used the Gleser and Ihilevich (1969) Defense Mechanisms Inventory (DMI) along with portions of our earlier defense understanding task. Sixty-seven adolescents (75% African American) participated. Results for girls were inconclusive for the DMI defense categories of turning against self, turning against object, and projection: The preference to use each defense and understanding of that same defense was correlated near zero. Results for boys were more perplexing: correlations were –.44, $p < .01$ for turning against self, +.22, *ns*, for turning against object, and +.38, $p < .01$ for projection. Thus, depending on the defense and gender, different theories received slight support. Taking the boys' and girls' results together, the study did not offer strong support for either a psychodynamic or social learning viewpoint.

Thomson (1986) explored the same issue with 86 children from Grades 3 to 6 using a multiple-choice version of a denial understanding task (patterned after the Tolor and Reznikoff [1967] Insight Test) and use of denial measured by the Lie Scale for Children (Sarason, Davidson, Lighthall, Waite, & Ruebush, 1960). Again, results were perplexing. The correlation between use of denial and understanding of denial was +.21 for boys, −.22 for girls, both $p < .10$.

One later project revised the defense understanding task for use with adults and tested its relation to other measures of psychological mindedness (Dollinger, Reader, Marnett, & Tylenda, 1983). This attempt was also an unsuccessful one in that defense understanding failed to correlate with six other relevant measures. Among the measures failing to correlate were the Adjective Check List (ACL) intraception scale, two California Psychological Inventory (CPI) psychological mindedness scales, one of the Guilford social intelligence tests, a psychological-construing (personality description) task (Craig & Boyle, 1979; Livesley & Bromley, 1973; Peevers & Secord, 1973), and a new measure later termed the Word Association Implications Test (WAIT). This test, described later, was to become a major focus in subsequent work.

In general, then, our program on children's defense understanding addressed provocative questions but with some frustratingly inconclusive results. The strongest conclusions that can be made are that defense understanding consistently correlates with age and verbal intelligence, (Dollinger & McGuire, 1981; Staley, 1985; Thomsen, 1986) and that defenses are perceived differently and defense use has some noteworthy gender-typing effects (Dollinger et al., 1981; McGuire, 1982; Staley, 1985). In retrospect, it is also clear that the program had gone in the direction of studying psychological mindedness via understanding of others rather than self-insight.

SAGACITY, ACUMEN, AND THE WORD ASSOCIATION IMPLICATIONS TEST (WAIT)

About the time that my students and I were developing the WAIT, I read Scheibe's (1979) thought-provoking book, *Mirrors, Masks, Lies, and Secrets* (see also Scheibe, 1978). Drawing from a wide range of sources from within and outside psychology, Scheibe suggested a number of conceptual categories for thinking about the question of penetrating defenses (or in his terms, *human predictability*). First, Scheibe suggested that people can predict one another's behavior by three modes: *sagacity, acumen* and *authority*. (The last, also termed *control*, is inherent in the roles of the psychoanalyst and laboratory experimenter but does not really concern us in the research program.) Sagacity entails some of the skills one associates with scientific psychology—keen observation plus careful study and understanding of the stimulus–stimulus and stimulus–response connections that give one person a predictive advantage over another. As Scheibe (1979) wrote, "the sagacious mind knows which among the myriad properties of things are the ones worth noticing—the ones having an essential attribute enabling the observer to reach some useful conclusion...sagacious predictions combine good observation and careful reasoning" (p. 14). Acumen, by way of contrast, entails a more empathic understanding of another; it "carries the sense of penetration, of the power to pass through barriers or defenses" (p. 39).

Being easily known and predicted puts a person at a strategic disadvantage. Thus, people have tools for preventing others from knowing the self too well. Scheibe offers four categories (or metaphors) of tools by which penetration is avoided. These concepts provide the book's title. The mirror metaphor as a tool for avoiding another's penetration is best illustrated by two things: the therapist's one-way mirror (which allows him or her to observe without being observed) and the therapist's nondirective style of mirroring a patient's response. (Word association itself involves a mirroring of the stimulus in the sense that the response usually reflects some logical link to the stimulus. Of course, responses that are less stimulus-bound may be more revealing of the person's conscious and unconscious processing.) Masks involve various kinds of false selves. Lies or misrepresentations are common tactics in strategic interaction. Finally, the secret is a major tool of information management both defensively and offensively; its most dramatic form in psychology is the notion of the unconscious—secrets a person keeps from the self.

As we began to move beyond defense understanding in creating new reading-between-the-lines tasks, Freud's use of free association served as a prototype for the recognition of hidden meanings and reading between the lines. In devising a new task, the word association technique was thought to have several points in its favor. First, associations are brief, discrete units that can be influenced by the experimental context, including the person's cognitive set (Cramer, 1968). Thus, the implications of word associations can be manipulated experimentally by controlling the imaginary context of a respondent immediately prior to his or her assessment. Second, the brevity of word associations means that many more test protocols can be judged in a given unit of time, as compared with, the longer thematic material in interviews, inkblot, or Thematic Apperception Test (TAT) methods. Because more judgments are made, the test length is increased which, from a psychometric standpoint, is likely to improve the reliability of the measure. Third, word associations are easily grasped by subjects as young as age 12; little training is required to comprehend the basic activity. Fourth, the technique is analogous to methods in past clinical use (Rapaport, Gill, & Schafer, 1968). However, because the procedure is less common than it once was, it is a novel task for most practicing clinicians.

The WAIT builds on the classic classroom demonstration of how word associations can be influenced by a simple suggestion of guilt (e.g., Potkay, 1974), which can itself be traced to earlier clinical and laboratory studies (notably that of Jung, 1910, but see also Henke & Eddy, 1909; Yerkes & Berry, 1909). The method also borrows from methods used by early criminologists (Larson, 1932), from the induction of fantasy scripts in early experimental neurosis research (Huston, Shakow, & Erickson, 1934), and more contemporary work on the guilty-knowledge technique of lie detection (Lykken, 1978). Thus, the basic premise is that persons who have imagined commission of a crime may show guilty knowledge of that act through their word associations, even (or especially) when they attempt to suppress evidence of that guilty affect and knowledge. Thus, the WAIT involves a kind of psychological line-up in which subject-judges attempt to discern which "suspect" in a line-up has fantasized a particular affect-inducing script, specifically a theft of $20.

To create the WAIT, we invited 30 undergraduate volunteers to come into our clinic for a videotaped word association test. Prior to the taping, each was asked to imagine one of five scripts (see details to follow). The WAIT presents the suspects' videotaped or transcribed word association protocols to subject-judges whose task is to detect the thief within the 10 sets of 3 suspects. Each suspect responded to 20 word association stimuli and 6 of these words were selected to touch on aspects of the thief script so that thief suspects, despite their efforts to keep their identity hidden, might inadvertently telegraph their guilt through associations, reaction times, or affect. The method provides a brief, face valid analogue in which the criterion (and therefore the true meaning of the associations) can be experimentally established. This is because the suspects were randomly assigned to receive the fantasy scripts. (Although the WAIT involves detection of a crime, we regard the method as a clinical analogue because the key evidence to be used by judges is the verbal and affective leakage of information a person may be attempting to suppress.)

Particulars of the WAIT

The WAIT presents the word associations of 30 undergraduate suspects who imagined different scenarios prior to taking a word association test. There was 1 target suspect in each of 10 3-person triads who fantasized the following thief script:

> You are in a pizza parlor frequented by students. While waiting for your companion to return from the restroom, you notice a group leaving from the table next to your booth. One of the people in the group has dropped his wallet on the floor between the table and your booth. Since no one seems to notice it, you pick it up and find a $20 bill. You decide to keep it. A minute later, the person returns and looks around the table. He then asks if you noticed a wallet anywhere, and says that he lost his wallet. You reply, "No I

> haven't seen it, but I hope you find it." Then he checks with the proprietor and leaves. You feel somewhat guilty but try to think about your "good fortune." But the thought keeps coming back to you, "I am a thief ... I am a thief ... I am a thief." It's hard to shake off that thought.

The four control scripts involved (a) observing another person steal a book, (b) preparing mentally to respond to a false accusation of plagiarism, (c) falling asleep in the library, and (d) earning a grade of A and not having to take a final exam. All were considered affect-inducing stories with which college students could easily identify. Scripts (A) and (B) each related to 3 of the 20 word association stimuli in some fashion, but scripts (C) and (D) were not related to the words. In any case, subject-judges were only informed of the thief script. Five of the 10 judgment triads matched a "thief" with suspects who received the (A) and (B) scripts. The other 5 thieves were matched with suspects who received the (C) and (D) scripts.

After imagining the randomly-assigned script, the suspects participated individually in a word association test. The stimulus-response word association list included a number of stimuli related to the critical script including the words *steal*, *pizza*, *thief*, *money*, *wallet*, and *guilty*. Suspects were videotaped with their consent. Their responses were later transcribed into a booklet version of the task.

The task, then, involved identification of the critical target person—the thief—by either watching the videotape or examining the transcription showing the word associations of the 3 suspects in a given line-up. With one judgment per line-up, the WAIT yields scores from 0 to 10. Based on the binomial expansion and assuming 1 in 3 odds for each judgment, individuals who score 7 or more correct judgments (hits) perform beyond the chance level of 3.3 hits (i.e., 1:3 odds per judgment x 10 judgments, $p < .02$). Thus, 7 or more hits is regarded as skilled performance on the WAIT.

In our standard procedure, we introduce the task by describing its construction, inviting subjects to imagine their own word associations to the stimulus words, reading and hearing the thief script, imagining their associations after knowledge of the script, and then reading and judging the 10 WAIT protocols. A sample protocol from the booklet version is shown in Table 7.1.

Sagacious Reading Between the Lines

Dollinger and Riger (1984) selected several tasks as markers of sagacity and acumen to predict WAIT performance. Following Scheibe's description and examples of sagacity, we used a simple digit cancellation task as a measure of alert observation and effort. Thus, subjects were given a sheet of paper showing numerals typed in nearly random order and they were given 4 minutes to cross out as many target numerals (e.g., 2s preceded by 9s) as they could find. (Although this was our key marker of sagacity, later

TABLE 7-1

Sample Item of the Word Association Implications Test (Suspect 2 is the Thief)

	Responses		
Stimulus	*Suspect 1*	*Suspect 2*	*Suspect 3*
Green	Red	Blue	Red
Class	School	Room	School
Steal	Metal	Thief	Iron
Sing	Song	Song	Dance
Dead	Alive	Alive	Alive
Student	Work	Teacher	Class
Pizza	Hungry	Pizza Parlor	Tacos
Happy	Good	Sad	Sad
Thief	Rob	Beggarman	Prison
Window	Break	Windowpane	Break
Friendly	Nice	Nice	Happy
Money	Green	Coins	Green
Cook	Restaurant	Frying pan	Good
Grade	A	Report card	A
Cold	Winter	Hot	Hot
Wallet	Leather	Money	Money
Dance	Ballet	Music	Sing
Village	People	People	People
Lake	Sailboat	Water	Water
Guilty	Innocent	Crime	Innocent

research further elaborated on the multiple aspects of this complex concept. For example, we examined their expert knowledge of which clues were worthy of their vigilant attention.) To operationalize acumen, we used the defense understanding task (as in Dollinger et al., 1983), the Hogan (1969) Empathy Scale, plus a game-strategy task (Sutton-Smith & Roberts, 1967) as a measure of ability to think about the others' thoughts. Hogan's Empathy Scale is a measure of the disposition to consider the consequences of one's actions for another. It is empirically derived from the CPI and MMPI item sets. The game strategy task was used because Scheibe explicitly considered the perspective-taking and "mind-reading" of strategic games as a kind of acumen. Finally, we also asked subjects to rate their use of various cues in the suspects (e.g., their tone of voice, reaction times, word associations, facial expressions) and in themselves (e.g., reasoning, empathy, gut reactions, ESP).

Results suggested that the WAIT requires sagacity more than acumen. Across two slightly different instructional conditions, empathy and game strategy tended to correlate negatively with the WAIT ($r = -.24, p < .10$ and $r = -.30, p < .05$, respectively). Defense understanding was a nonsignificantly correlate. Thus, acumen did not seem to be involved in the WAIT. However, two findings suggested that sagacity was involved. First, the digit cancellation task correlated significantly with WAIT scores ($r = .33, p < .01$). Second, supplementary ratings showed that the best judges claimed to just use the suspects' word associations ($r = .53, p < .001$) and to depend on their own reasoning ($r = .27, p < .05$). From supplementary studies of the stimulus videotape (Dollinger, 1985), we learned that facial expressions and reaction times were not diagnostic of thief status but word association meanings could be diagnostic. For example, the response *parlor* to the stimulus word *pizza* proved to be much more frequently given by thief than foil suspects, $\phi = .71$, $p < .001$. Because good judges on the WAIT were more vigilant and claimed to use just the word associations, they seemed intuitively to know which clues to look for—a clear indication of better sagacity. Poor judges claimed to use combinations of all available information ($r = -.38$, $p < .01$); thus they tended to think like the self-deluding clinician of the preclinical versus statistical debate era who thinks he or she can outperform actuarial information by combining all sorts of complex information in a configural way.

Building on the Dollinger and Riger investigation, we conducted a series of four projects including one study with social welfare majors (therapists in training) and one study of high school students (Dollinger, 1985). Drawing on Scheibe's descriptions, we hypothesized that tasks requiring sagacity rather than acumen should be more easily trainable. The major issue in these four studies was whether WAIT judgment could be improved by training. A secondary issue was whether the videotaped version of the WAIT and the paper-and-pencil (transcript) version yielded similar findings. (The videotape required about 1 hour to administer because each set of three word association protocols took about 6 minutes, including about 1 minute for making judgments; the booklet version, with 3 suspects' responses juxtaposed on a page, took about 20 minutes)

These studies used increasingly complex training methods ranging from imagining one's own responses as if one were a thief, to explicit guides in which clues were diagnostic. We also created a diagnostic clue recognition task to see whether subjects began to perceive valid clues (like *pizza:parlor*). Across four studies, the conclusion can be stated simply. Training rarely improved judgment and complex training was in fact detrimental. However, subjects who, after making judgments on the WAIT, could recognize responses that were diagnostic of the thief did achieve more accurate judgments. The results were remarkably similar for the two versions of the WAIT, and the performance of students in high school was not noticeably different from those in college.

Recalling Scheibe's description of sagacity as involving vigilant attention (as well as expert knowledge), we were struck by the informal observation that, with the paper-and-pencil WAIT, some subjects circled ostensible clues whereas others made annotations on their booklet. These observations led to a study in which vigilance was operationalized as a dependent variable (Dollinger, Greening, & Tylenda, 1985). We did this by measuring the number of judgments on which such notes were made (0–10). We also manipulated vigilance as an independent variable by directing some subjects to circle clues, inviting it as a strategy for others, and making no mention of it to a third group of subjects. Last, we gave the clue recognition task noted previously. Surprisingly, whereas the instructional set did affect clue recognition, it did not directly improve WAIT hit rates.

In a supplementary internal analysis, vigilance was operationalized as above- or below-median frequency of the circling of clues. Subjects were crossclassified on this variable and on knowledge of clues on the recognition task (above or below median). Only 19% of the subjects low in vigilance and knowledge were skilled judges on the WAIT as compared with 45% of the subjects high in either vigilance or knowledge or both (interaction yielded $p < .01$). This result suggested further support for Scheibe's concept of sagacity and its application to the WAIT.

An additional internal analysis was conducted in the Dollinger et al. (1985) study to examine which clues were being circled by those vigilant judges with good and poor hit rates. This analysis supported the knowledge component of sagacity by demonstrating that (a) good judges were attending to a variety of valid clues, (b) good judges recognized the most valid clue (*pizza:parlor*) more quickly than did bad judges whereas bad judges seemed increasingly oblivious to it, and (c) bad judges were actually vigilant to clues that might be leading them exactly in the wrong direction. For example, 76% of bad judges circled the clue *money:green* as compared to 27% of good judges. Although this clue was valid and could therefore help make a judgment, it was valid as a contradiagnostic clue being given more frequently by nonthief than thief suspects (Dollinger, 1985). Because most adults tend to reason by looking for confirming rather than disconfirming evidence (Snyder & Campbell, 1980)—which is admittedly dubious—the bad judges were attending to information that probably led away from accurate judgment. A later study of judges' reasoning about clues confirmed these impressions and suggested that bad judges may overgeneralize, make arbitrary inferences, ignore baserate information, and generally think in a pseudopsychological (or what they think of as psychological) manner (Dollinger, Fisher, Thomas, & Houshmand, 1992).

Schema for Clues

Two facts about the WAIT together create a paradox: (a) subjects cannot be easily trained to be good judges on the WAIT, and yet (b) clue knowledge predicts good judgment. This paradox might be resolved if some subjects incidentally acquire a knowledge structure of what is relevant, that is, a schema of how people's word associations are influenced by the thief script. We refer to such knowledge as schemata rather than simple recall of word associates because subjects are thought to store knowledge in concept structures that may take several forms and can be tapped by various methods. This knowledge seems to involve relations between the thief script, word stimuli and responses.

Dollinger and McMorrow (1991) appraised this schema by having subjects write a short essay to a probe about clues. Subjects were told that, in past research, thieves tended to respond with *parlor* to the word *pizza* but nonthieves responded with an ingredient (e.g., *cheese*). They were asked to explain why that might have been. Essays were reliably grouped by two judges (88% agreement before discussion) into five categories

1. No explanation,
2. statement of one's ignorance,
3. variety of implausible responses,
4. suggestions that their script prompted thieves to think about the location of their guilty act,
5. Level 4 answers plus a recognition that the baserate response, including that of nonthieves, would probably involve gustatory associations.

Groups 4 and 5 (pooled) exceeded Groups 1–3 on their WAIT performance, showing better understanding of how the script could affect word associations.

Over a series of studies, we developed a more efficient task that asked subjects to specify which clues they recalled as being diagnostic and contradiagnostic to the six critical stimulus words. They were shown the key stimulus words (*steal*, *pizza*, *thief*, *money*, *wallet*, and *guilty*) and asked to list responses that they regarded as diagnostic of the thief. We devised a scoring key for this newer schema task by crediting answers significantly diagnostic of suspect status (such as *pizza:parlor*; Dollinger, 1985). Then we added idiosyncratic clues given by the thief that seemed conceptually related to the thief script (e.g., *pizza:money*). Most of these consisted of words that actually appeared in the thief script and had a near-zero probability of occurrence among foils (e.g., *money:thief*). Nearly synonymous terms (e.g., *steal:thief*) were not credited nor were associations that were "primaries" (most frequent response) for both thief and foil suspects (e.g., *wallet:money*).

Three studies tested the relation of this schema task to WAIT judgment, all yielding confirmatory findings (Dollinger, Levin, & Robinson, 1991). Dollinger (1994) replicated this relationship by reanalyzing earlier studies using a preliminary scoring system of the schema task. Pooling across studies yielded a correlation between hit rate and schema scores of $r = .47$, $p < .001$ at the level of individual subjects ($N = 293$). By aggregating all subjects who attained a given hit rate, 10 groups of subjects were formed, that is, those who attained exactly 1, 2, 3,...10 correct judgments. (No subjects failed to get at least 1 correct.) The average schema scores for these groups were then obtained. A clear ascending pattern of average schema scores showed the superior performance of those who were the best judges. For example, the average schema scores of those with 1, 4, 7, and 10 correct judgments were .25, 2.94, 5.33 and 9.50, respectively (see Dollinger, 1994 for complete data). A rank-order correlation between the 10 hit-rate levels and the average schema scores was computed; this yielded an aggregate level correlation (rho) of .99, $p < .001$.

Dollinger et al. (1991, Study 2) tested the notion that clue schemata are implicitly acquired, using a test–retest design. Thus, subjects completed the schema task before judging any protocols, after one set of 10 judgments, and after another set of 10 (counterbalancing the standard and alternate sets). Results showed that subjects could generate almost no schematic responses before judging protocols. This supports the concept that these schema are incidentally–acquired while doing the task. Performance on the schema task correlated not only with preceding WAIT judgments but also with improvements to successive judgments. Thus, performance seems to be largely a function of incidental acquisition of schemata. Generalizing beyond this task, we might speculate that psychological mindedness is implicitly acquired through interactions with people; it is a skill or set of skills that may be difficult to teach.

Other Correlates of the WAIT

Dollinger et al. (1991, Study 3) tested whether inductive reasoning, in which the person must infer a general rule from the particular case, correlated with WAIT scores. This study used a version of a letter sets task, in which the subject must infer a rule governing the logic behind sets of letters (nonsense syllables) and then determine the set that does not conform to this rule. This task correlated $r = .40, p < .001$ with the WAIT, suggesting that inductive reasoning may be involved in the WAIT. Additionally, this study showed that subjects who viewed the WAIT more as play than work did better, $r = .29$, and those who viewed it more like a game than a test did better, $r = .27$ (both $p < .05$), presumably because they viewed the task more heuristically than algorithmically. The multiple R predicting WAIT scores from schemata, inductive reasoning, and these two indicators of subjects' task perception was $R = .71$, $p < .001$.

Subjects in the Dollinger and McMorrow (1991) study previously noted also provided access to college admission test data (the ACT) and took tests of reasoning and reading ability, specifically the Similarities Test of the WAIS and a practice Miller Analogies Test (Sternberg, 1981), plus the Nelson–Denny Reading Inventory (Brown, Bennett, & Hanna, 1981). Good judges surpassed their less skilled peers on Similarities, replicating the letter sets finding just noted. More importantly, because these tests are partitioned into component skill areas, we can learn from the Nelson–Denny and ACT more specific information about who achieves better hit rates on the WAIT. For example, the Nelson–Denny Interpretive Reading subsection was much more strongly related to the WAIT than was the Literal Comprehension subsection. Additionally, the humanities reading passages discriminated good and bad WAIT judges, whereas the science section did not (social science was marginally related). Turning to the ACT, the English and Social Studies scales discriminated good and bad WAIT judges, whereas the Mathematics and Natural Sciences scales did not. Thus, the WAIT may require knowledge acquired in the study of social studies and the humanities. This results seem to fit with the idea that the WAIT involves some *psychological* mindedness (in view of the social studies correlate) and reading between the lines (in view of the interpretive reading correlate).

Despite such correlates, and the point that women tend to do better on standardized tests in English but men in mathematics (findings which in fact held true in our sample), gender differences are minimal in the WAIT (Dollinger, 1992).

SELF-FOCUS, OVERCONFIDENCE, AND ILLUSORY CORRELATION

Although the preceding results comprise the most important findings on the WAIT, several additional studies bear on supplementary issues of clinical interest. First, whereas self-insight certainly requires attention to the self, understanding of others may require that attention be directed away from the self. Particularly in an interactive context, anxious self-awareness may interfere with recognition of important material. One can easily imagine, for example, the novice clinician whose anxiety over being observed by the supervisor leads to a failure to hear the client's real agenda. As an analogue task, the WAIT allowed a test of this notion.

Dollinger, Greening, and Lloyd (1987) assigned subjects to either a standard (nonevaluative) or an experimental anxiety-provoking–evaluative context. Subjects were pretested on the Test Anxiety (Sarason, 1972) and Self-Consciousness Scales (Fenigstein, Scheier, & Buss, 1975). Then for one half, permission was requested to remove the covering on a one-way mirror so that they (ostensibly) might be videotaped while doing the WAIT for later review by a "team of experts" at judging body language. This manipulation was intentionally a broad one, hoping to induce test anxiety in those so prone, and public self-consciousness in those so prone. Although the personality variables and personality x condition effects were nonsignificant, the experimental condition exerted a significant detrimental effect on WAIT scores. It also led subjects to be less vigilant as indicated by fewer instances of circling clues while processing the information. Samuel and Dollinger (1989) replicated and extended this study by separating the mirror and videotape manipulation into two separate variables crossed in a factorial design. Again, personality did not effect WAIT scores but the presence of the mirror undermined performance. Thus, self-focused attention appears to interfere with recognition of implications.

Overconfidence

As with many kinds of subjective skills, people may believe that they are more psychologically minded or better at knowing the truth about others than are most people (Dollinger, Tylenda, Reader, & Marnett, 1984). Certainly, overconfidence in one's clinical judgment is a potential problem for professional psychologists (e.g., Oskamp, 1965). Does this emerge on the WAIT? We tested this possibility in a study using the videotaped version of the WAIT. In this study (Greening & Dollinger, 1985) we asked subjects to indicate their confidence as they made each judgment. One half of the subjects were given guidelines on possible clue information that might aid their judgment. The issue then is one of the confidence–accuracy calibration: When subjects are 50% confident are they 50% accurate? Overall, the correlation between mean confidence (across 10 judgments) and number of hits was near-zero regardless of whether additional information was provided. However, when aggregating across the subjects and classifying judgments according to confidence intervals, we found hit rates did rise appropriately with increases in confidence. For example, pooled across conditions, when subjects expressed confidence in the 33%–39% range, they were 44% accurate (i.e., 48 of 110 such judgments were correct). Hit rates associated with increasing confidence ranges (40%–49%, 50%–59%, 60%–69%, etc.) generally did increase: 54%, 47%, 62%, 64%, 69%, 72%, and, for the 100% confidence level, 86%. The generally positive connection of confidence and accuracy suggests that, as a group, subjects have fairly good metacognition about their inferences. However, people also tended to be poorly calibrated when their confidence exceeded 70%.

Illusory Correlation

Clinical judgment is potentially subject to illusory correlations or the perception of covariation between signs and diagnoses even when these classes of events are unrelated (Chapman & Chapman, 1967, 1969). Might this happen in the WAIT? We addressed this question by studying the schemata for clues of 164 subjects who examined WAIT protocols in which a suspect was always identified as the thief (Dollinger, Greening, & Radtke, 1994). Approximately, one fourth of the subjects received veridical diagnoses—the suspect labeled as the thief did in fact read the thief script. Another group received seven veridical diagnoses (plus three incorrect ones). A third group received three veridical diagnoses and a fourth group received no veridical diagnoses. After studying the WAIT booklet with these "judgments" provided, subjects then took the schema task. Although the last group (zero true information) was notably lower in their incidental learning of clues, as they should have been, Groups "3," "7," and "10" did not differ. This lack of effect strongly suggests the possibility of illusory correlation.

LIMITATIONS AND FUTURE DIRECTIONS

After 10 years of research on the WAIT, the factors contributing to successful "reading between the lines" on this task are fairly clear. However, the task itself has several limitations. First, it is clearly an analogue task that has limited real-world utility. This suggests one direction for future study—might it have some validity for success in clinical or counseling psychology graduate study? More likely is the possibility that it will be useful to introduce graduate students to some of the processes involved in clinical judgment. Another limitation is the fact that it is noninteractive, a possibility that gives a decided advantage to sagacity over acumen (Scheibe, 1979). Thus, another possible direction is to devise an interactive version of the WAIT to determine whether the standard form, in fact, could serve as a valid proxy for a more interactive task.

CONCLUSIONS

Studies on the WAIT suggest five main conclusions about people's ability to read between the lines of what another says. First, this skill requires a sagacious mind, that is, a knowledge of what to look for and attention to just those clues. As part of sagacity, judgment also requires good reasoning. Second, this knowledge of what to look for seems to be implicitly acquired while making the judgments; it is not easily taught. Third, given these components of sagacity, it is not surprising that intellectual measures predict performance on our test of reading between the lines. In particular, it seems that interpretive rather than literal comprehension is required, in keeping with the notion of reading between the lines. It is also interesting that humanities and social science competence better predicts this skill than does mathematical or natural science competence. Researchers often hope to minimize the role of intelligence as a factor in psychological mindedness or general intelligence as a factor in social intelligence (e.g., Appelbaum, 1973). However, our results suggest that intellectual competence does play a role. Obviously it is possible to imagine or recall anecdotal examples that contradict this generalization; clinical experience suggests that intelligence can be used in the service of self-deception. Perhaps, however, it is generally a positive predictor of psychological mindedness about others. Fourth, reading between the lines of another's behavior seems to benefit from a more relaxed and playful mental state. Perceiving the situation as evaluative or self-focusing is not conducive to accurate reading between the lines but having a sense of playfulness (rather than work) is. Fifth, the results remind us of the need for psychologists to maintain an attitude of humility about their own inferences and judgments about others. The person hoping to perceive and know the truth about another must avoid the pitfalls of overconfidence, illusory correlation, and overinterpretion of the data.

ACKNOWLEDGMENTS

The author is grateful to Drs. Stephanie Clancy Dollinger and Leilani Greening for their comments on this chapter.

REFERENCES

Abramowitz, S. I., & Abramowitz, C. V. (1974). Psychological mindedness and benefit from insight-oriented group therapy. *Archives of General Psychiatry, 30*, 610–615.

Appelbaum, S. A. (1973). Psychological mindedness: Word, concept and essence. *International Journal of Psycho-analysis, 54*, 35–46.

Berzonsky, M. D. (1973). Some relationships between children's conceptions of psychological and physical causality. *Journal of Social Psychology, 90*, 299–309.

Brown, J. I., Bennett, J. M., & Hanna, G. (1981). *The Nelson-Denny Reading Test*. Chicago: Riverside.

Chandler, M. J. (1973). The Picture Arrangement subtest of the WAIS as an index of social egocentrism: A comparative study of normal and emotionally disturbed children. *Journal of Abnormal Child Psychology, 1*, 340–349.

Chandler, M. J., Paget, K. F., & Koch, D. A. (1978). The child's demystification of psychological defense mechanisms: A structural and developmental analysis. *Developmental Psychology, 14*, 197–205.

Chapman, L. J., & Chapman, J. P. (1967). Genesis of popular but erroneous psychodiagnostic observations. *Journal of Abnormal Psychology, 72*, 193–204.

Chapman, L. J., & Chapman, J. P. (1969). Illusory correlation as an obstacle to the use of valid psychodiagnostic signs. *Journal of Abnormal Psychology, 74*, 271–280.

Coie, J. D., & Pennington, B. F. (1976). Children's perceptions of deviance and disorder. *Child Development, 47*, 407–413.

Craig, G., & Boyle, M. E. (1979). The recognition and spontaneous use of psychological descriptions by young children. *British Journal of Social and Clinical Psychology, 18*, 207–208.

Cramer, P. (1968). *Word association*. New York: Academic Press.

Cramer, P. (1979). Defense mechanisms in adolescence. *Developmental Psychology, 15*, 476–477.

Cramer, P. (1988). The Defense Mechanism Inventory: A review of research and discussion of the scales. *Journal of Personality Assessment, 52*, 142–164.

Dollinger, S. J. (1985). Sagacious judgment via word association. *Journal of Personality and Social Psychology, 49*, 1738–1752.

Dollinger, S. J. (1992). *Gender differences in the WAIT: A review of 10 studies*. Unpublished manuscript, Southern Illinois University at Carbondale.

Dollinger, S. J. (1994). Individual differences on the Word Association Implications Test: Incidental learning of schemata. *Personality and Individual Differences, 17*, 703–706.

Dollinger, S. J., Fisher, D., Thomas, D., & Houshmand, S. (1992). *Do poor judges of implications read too little or too much "between the lines?"* Unpublished manuscript, Southern Illinois University at Carbondale.

Dollinger, S. J., Greening, L., & Lloyd, K. (1987). The "mirror" and the "mask": Self-focused attention, evaluation anxiety, and the recognition of psychological implications. *Bulletin of the Psychonomic Society, 25*, 167–170.

Dollinger, S. J., Greening, L., & Radtke, R. (1994). *Illusory correlation and the WAIT: Reading too much between the lines*. Submitted for publication.

Dollinger, S. J., Greening, L., & Tylenda, B. (1985). Psychological-mindedness as "reading between the lines": Vigilance, locus of control, and sagacious judgment. *Journal of Personality, 53*, 603–625.

Dollinger, S. J., Levin, E. L., & Robinson, A. E. (1991). The Word Association Implications Test. *Journal of Personality Assessment, 57*, 368–380.

Dollinger, S. J., & McGuire, B. (1981). The development of psychological mindedness: Children's understanding of defense mechanisms. *Journal of Clinical Child Psychology, 10,* 117–121.

Dollinger, S. J., & McMorrow, M. A. (1991). Individual differences in "reading between the lines": The word association implications test. *American Journal of Psychology, 104,* 395–411.

Dollinger, S. J., Reader, M. J., Marnett, J. P., & Tylenda, B. (1983). Psychological-mindedness, psychological-construing, and the judgment of deception. *Journal of General Psychology, 108,* 183–191.

Dollinger, S. J., & Riger, A. L. (1984). On penetrating the "mask": The role of sagacity and acumen in a word association-clinical judgment task. *Journal of Personality and Social Psychology, 46,* 145–152.

Dollinger, S. J., Staley, A., & McGuire, B. (1981). The child as psychologist: Attributions and evaluations of defensive strategies. *Child Development, 52,* 1084–1086.

Dollinger, S. J., & Thelen, M. H. (1978). Children's perceptions of psychology. *Professional Psychology, 9,* 117–126.

Dollinger, S. J., Thelen, M. H., & Walsh, M. (1980). Children's conceptions of psychological problems. *Journal of Clinical Child Psychology, 9,* 191–194.

Dollinger, S. J., Tylenda, B., Reader, M. J., & Marnett, J. P. (1984). Self-ascribed psychological-mindedness: A self-serving bias in "penetrating the mask." *Journal of Social Psychology, 124,* 127–129.

Fenigstein, A., Scheier, M. F., & Buss, A. H. (1975). Public and private self-consciousness: Assessment and theory. *Journal of Consulting and Clinical Psychology, 43,* 522–527.

Flavell, J. H. (1977). *Cognitive development.* Englewood Cliffs, NJ: Prentice-Hall.

Gleser, G. C., & Ihilevich, D. (1969). An objective instrument for measuring defense mechanisms. *Journal of Consulting and Clinical Psychology, 33,* 51–60.

Greening, L., & Dollinger, S. J. (1985). Confidence at recognizing psychological implications. *Bulletin of the Psychonomic Society, 23,* 311–313.

Hall, J. A. (1992). Psychological-mindedness: A conceptual model. *American Journal of Psychotherapy, 66,* 131–140.

Henke, F. G., & Eddy, M. W. (1909). Mental diagnosis by the association reaction method. *Psychological Review, 16,* 399–409.

Hogan, R. (1969). Development of an empathy scale. *Journal of Consulting and Clinical Psychology, 33,* 307–316.

Huston, P. E., Shakow, D., & Erickson, M. H. (1934). A study of hypnotically induced complexes by means of the Luria technique. *Journal of General Psychology, 11,* 65–97.

Jung, C. G. (1910). The association method. *American Journal of Psychology, 21,* 219–269.

Larson, J. A. (1932). *Lying and its detection.* Chicago: University of Chicago Press.

Livesley, W. J., & Bromley, D. B. (1973). *Person perception in childhood and adolescence.* London: Wiley.

Lykken, D. T. (1978). Uses and abuses of the polygraph. In H. L. Pick, Jr., H. W. Leibowitz, J. E. Singer, A. Steinschneider, & H. W. Stevenson (Eds.), *Psychology: From research to practice* (pp. 171–191). New York: Plenum.

Maas, E., Marecek, J., & Travers, J. R. (1978). Children's conceptions of disordered behavior. *Child Development, 49,* 146–154.

Marsden, G., Kalter, N., Plunkett, J. W., & Barr-Grossman, T. (1977). Children's social judgments concerning emotionally disturbed peers. *Journal of Consulting and Clinical Psychology, 45,* 948.

McCallum, M., & Piper, W. E. (1990). The psychological mindedness assessment procedure. *Psychological Assessment: A Journal of Consulting and Clinical Psychology, 2,* 412–418.

McGuire, B. A. (1982). *Defense preferences from middle childhood to middle adolescence.* Unpublished doctoral dissertation, Southern Illinois University at Carbondale.

Mohr, D. M. (1978). Development of attributes of personality identity. *Developmental Psychology, 14,* 427–428.

Oskamp, S. (1965). Overconfidence in case-study judgments. *Journal of Consulting Psychology, 29,* 261–265.

Peevers, B. H., & Secord, P. F. (1973). Developmental changes in attribution of descriptive concepts to persons. *Journal of Personality and Social Psychology, 27,* 120–128.

Potkay, C. R. (1974). Using the word association test "to catch a thief." *Professional Psychology, 5*, 446–447.

Rapaport, D., Gill, M. M., & Schafer, R. (1968). The word association test. In R. R. Holt (Ed.), *Diagnostic psychological testing* (rev. ed.; pp. 231–267). New York: International Universities Press.

Rosenthal, S. L., & Simeonsson, R. J. (1990). Comprehension of defense mechanisms in emotionally disturbed adolescents. *Acta Paedopsychiatrica, 53*, 253–260.

Samuel, V., & Dollinger, S. J. (1989). Self-focused attention and the recognition of psychological implications. *Journal of Psychology, 123*, 623–625.

Sarason, I. G. (1972). Experimental approaches to test anxiety: Attention and the uses of information. In C. D. Spielberger (Ed.), *Anxiety: Current trends in research and theory* (Vol. 2, pp. 381–403). New York: Academic Press.

Sarason, S., Davidson, K., Lighthall, F., Waite, R., & Ruebush, B. (1960). *Anxiety in elementary school children*. New York: Wiley.

Scheibe, K. E. (1978). The psychologist's advantage and its nullification: Limits of human predictability. *American Psychologist, 33*, 869–881.

Scheibe, K. E. (1979). *Mirrors, masks, lies, and secrets*. New York: Praeger.

Snyder, M., & Campbell, B. (1980). Testing hypotheses about other people: The role of the hypothesis. *Personality and Social Psychology Bulletin, 6*, 421–426.

Staley, A. A. (1985). *Sex differences in children's use and understanding of defensive strategies*. Doctoral dissertation, Southern Illinois University at Carbondale, 1985. *Dissertation Abstracts International, 47*(7), 3128B.

Sternberg, R. J. (1981). *Barron's how to prepare for the MAT* (3rd ed.). Woodbury, NY: Barron's Educational Services.

Sutton-Smith, B., & Roberts, J. M. (1967). Studies of an elementary game of strategy. *Genetic Psychology Monograph, 75*, 3–42.

Thomson, B. K. (1986). *An examination of the relationship between children's understanding and use of denial*. Unpublished doctoral dissertation, Southern Illinois University at Carbondale.

Tolor, A., & Reznikoff, M. (1967). Relation between insight, repression sensitization, internal-external locus of control, and death anxiety. *Journal of Abnormal Psychology, 72*, 426–430.

Whiteman, M. (1967). Children's conceptions of psychological causality. *Child Development, 38*, 143–155.

Yerkes, R. M., & Berry, C. S. (1909). The association reaction method of mental diagnosis [Tatbestandsdiagnostik]. *American Journal of Psychology, 20*, 22–37.

Chapter 8

Social Perspective Taking

Rosanne Menna
University of Toronto
Nancy J. Cohen
C. M. Hincks Centre, Toronto

Social cognition is a summary term referring to the cognitive mechanisms individuals apply to understanding social situations (Staub & Eisenberg, 1981). In this chapter, we examine one aspect of social cognition, the concept of *social perspective taking,* a construct similar to psychological mindedness. Social perspective taking refers to the ability to free oneself of one's own view and to recognize and understand the thoughts, feelings, and motives of the self and others (Shantz, 1983). Similarly, psychological mindedness was defined as the capacity to achieve psychological understanding of thoughts, feelings, and motives of the self and others (Hatcher, Hatcher, Berlin, Okla, & Richards, 1990). We start by discussing the construct of social perspective taking, delineating its historical roots and theoretical bases. Then, we go on to describe one current method of measuring social perspective taking, the Interpersonal Negotiation Strategies Interview (INS; Selman, 1981; Selman, Beardslee, Schultz, Krupa, & Podorefsky, 1986; Selman & Demorest, 1984), its theoretical base, administration, scoring, psychometric properties, and application. Factors influencing social perspective taking and the interface between social perspective taking and components of object relations theory are also discussed. The chapter concludes with consideration of the clinical implications of social perspective taking research and possible directions for future investigation. Throughout the chapter, a developmental framework is used to trace the growth of social perspective taking capacity from early childhood to adulthood.

ORIGINS AND THEORETICAL BASIS

Social perspective taking has its roots in Mead's (1934) theory, in which the ability to take another person's role is considered to be a fundamental process in the socialization of the self, and in Piaget's theory of cognitive development in which social perspective taking arises from the ability to decenter (Piaget, 1965, 1970). Information-processing theories contributed to understanding the component skills underlying the elements of social perspective taking (Crick & Dodge, 1994; Rubin & Krasnor, 1986; Yeates & Selman, 1989).

Most of the early research in the area of social perspective-taking ability stems from Piaget's demonstration of the emergence of integrated patterns of cognitive functioning throughout development and across the various domains of space, number, causality, logical classification, and relations (Flavell, Botken, Fry, Wright, & Jarvis, 1968; Inhelder & Piaget, 1958; Miller, Kessel, & Flavell, 1970; Piaget, 1972; Selman & Byrne, 1974). Of most relevance here are Piaget's experiments with children that required them to think about how objects would be perceived by others. Together with his earlier work on children's understanding of the rules of games and how they communicate with one another, Piaget proposed the concepts of *egocentrism* and *decentration*. Egocentrism refers to the lack of differentiation between the self and other. Decentration refers to the ability to consider multiple perspectives of a situation. Subsequently, these concepts were applied to the social domain, with the introduction of the construct of social perspective taking (Selman, 1980; Selman & Byrne, 1974). Selman and colleagues further defined and refined this construct. More specifically, Selman (1980) defined the concept of social perspective taking as including:

> ...a developing understanding of how human points of view are related and coordinated with one another and not simply what social or psychological information may appear to be like from an alternative individual's perspectives as in the construct of role-taking. (p. 22)

Selman and colleagues applied this definition to specific areas of the social world including moral development, friendship formation, and interpersonal negotiations. They also have been the only investigators to study the developmental course of social perspective taking from early childhood to adulthood (Beardslee, Schultz, & Selman, 1987; Selman, 1976, 1980; Yeates, Schultz, & Selman, 1991). In other literature on social perspective-taking ability, this skill is believed to be acquired in early childhood (Shantz, 1983). However, Selman (1980) found that perspective taking has stage-like properties reflecting increasing differentiation and integration of the social perspectives of self and other that continues to develop into adolescence and adulthood.

Selman's work is of critical importance in understanding the development of the ability to take others' perspectives (Selman, 1980, 1981; Selman et al., 1986). It showed that children's reasoning in each social domain develops from an uncoordinated, individualistic understanding to an understanding that coordinates two perspectives, and then to an understanding that individual perspectives must be viewed in reference to a more complex social system.

In more recent work, Selman and colleagues examined the development of social perspective taking in the domain of interpersonal negotiation strategies (INS; Selman, 1980; Selman & Demorest, 1984; Yeates & Selman, 1989). Selman's model of interpersonal negotiation strategies builds on his earlier work, and focuses on the ways individuals deal with one another in a variety of contexts. Specifically, the INS model addresses how people coordinate their understanding of others' thoughts, feelings, and motives in conjunction with their own in attempting to balance inner and interpersonal conflicts.

The INS model posits that interpersonal understanding proceeds through a series of stages that reflect increasing differentiation and integration of the social perspectives of self and other (Selman, 1980; Selman & Demorest, 1984; Selman et al., 1986). Selman argued that this understanding varies developmentally, with social perspective taking becoming increasingly more sophisticated. As children become aware of the perspectives of others, they incorporate this information into their decision-making process and produce higher level strategies based on their new ability to coordinate perspectives. The developmental progression of perspective taking begins with a simple egocentric judgment (the self's own viewpoint is the same as the others) between the ages of 3 and 5 years. This gives way to a self-reflective level between the ages of 6 and 8 years, in which the individual recognizes the self as the possible focus of others' perspectives. Then between 9 and 15 years of age there is a mutual or second-person perspective, which is characterized by the ability to recognize the perspective of self and other even though they are not in relation to one another. Finally, moving into adulthood, there is the understanding that there is a network of perspectives binding individuals into a social system. The lower levels' perspective taking are not replaced by the higher levels'; the lower levels are still present and may appear under certain conditions.

A general limitation of the initial formulation of the cognitive–structural approach is that, whereas it sets out the sequence of development, it typically does not specify how social–cognitive competencies are translated into actual behavior in specific contexts (Yeates & Selman, 1989). It is important to know whether hypothesized shifts in social perspective taking are actually related to behavior. To address this, an information processing or functional component of social perspective taking was proposed to specify the means by which variations in social behavior occur (Dodge, 1986; Rubin & Krasnor, 1986; Selman & Schultz, 1988; Yeates & Selman, 1989).

In the social information-processing or functional tradition, researchers examined the properties of social behavior and proposed a number of models of social competence and interpersonal problem solving (Dodge, 1980; Rubin & Krasnor 1986; Selman et al., 1986; Spivack, Platt, & Shure, 1976; Spivack & Shure, 1982). For example, Spivack and Shure (1982) showed that the ability to generate a variety of solutions to hypothetical social problems is an important component of social problem solving that is related to behavioral adjustment in children and adolescents. Specifically, they found that socially adjusted children and adolescents were more likely to consider the possible consequences of a particular course of action before engaging in the behavior. Spivak and Shure suggested that the ability to generate a variety of solutions to social problems is a developmental prerequisite for more mature social problem solving. Taking a different approach, Dodge (1986) proposed a model to explain the requisite cognitive processing steps involved in skilled social behavior. These steps include the encoding of social cues, interpretation of those cues, mental search for possible responses to the situation, evaluation of consequences and selection of a response, and enactment of the chosen response. Although Spivack and Shure and Dodge acknowledged developmental issues in the study of social information processing, their models focus primarily on perceptual and processing skills and ignore the developmental trajectories of the skills (Yeates & Selman, 1989).

Yeates and Selman (1989) examined the variations in social perspective taking developmentally, and introduced a functional component analysis into the INS model. The functional analysis they described is similar to those described by other researchers documenting the social problem-solving process (e.g., Crick & Dodge, 1994; Dodge, 1986; Spivack, Platt, & Shure, 1976; Spivack & Shure, 1982, 1985). In particular, Yeates and Selman identified four sequential problem-solving steps in the social problem-solving process: defining the problem, generating alternative strategies, selecting and implementing specific strategies, and evaluating outcomes. Within each of these steps, responses can be further classified to represent the four developmental levels of social perspective-taking ability described earlier. The addition of a functional component analysis to the INS model provides information on the variations in the developmental level of perspective taking across the specific steps in the social problem-solving process, something lacking in the models proposed by Dodge (1980, 1986) and Spivack and Shure (1982, 1985). This approach allows for the examination of social perspective taking across the social problem-solving process. For example, one can identify the level of perspective taking at each of the four problem-solving steps.

In addition to incorporating both a developmental component and a functional component, Yeates and Selman (1989) specified an action component in the INS model. The action component is intended to describe the interpersonal orientation of the social problem-solving strategies taken at each level in the coordination of social perspectives. The strategies are classified to depict the relative priority given to achieving one's own needs (referred to as *self-transforming*) as opposed to another's (referred to as *other-transforming*). By combining developmental level and interpersonal orientation, Yeates and Selman found a means to demonstrate how strategies that appear different in action because they reflect opposite interpersonal orientations (e.g. self-transforming as opposed to other-transforming) can reflect similar levels of perspective taking.

This review is necessarily brief. For more comprehensive reviews on social cognition, see Crick and Dodge, 1994; Higgins and Bargh, 1986; Shantz, 1983. For a review and assessment of the development of INS in action see Selman and Demorest, 1984; Yeates, Schultz and Selman, 1990, 1991.

MEASUREMENT OF SOCIAL PERSPECTIVE TAKING

Although a variety of perspective taking measures were used, only one is discussed in this chapter: the INS interview. This semistructured interview was developed by Selman (1981) to tap children's understanding of social perspective taking during social conflicts. As discussed earlier, the INS interview not only addresses the development of the coordination of perspectives but also the development of action and the relation between interpersonal action and interpersonal thought. Children were shown to improve on the INS measure following both clinical and school-based interventions and thus it has demonstrated potential for clinical application (Selman, 1980; Selman & Demorest, 1984; Yeates & Selman, 1989).

The INS interview is comprised of a number of hypothetical dilemmas presenting conflict situations between a protagonist and a significant other. The protagonist in these dilemmas either wants something from the significant other or must react to the other's efforts to gain something from the protagonist. The name of the protagonist is consistent with the gender of the child. The following is an example of one of the hypothetical dilemmas used (Schultz, Yeates, & Selman, 1989):

> Randy and Tom are friends. They have just been assigned to work together on a project in school and only have two days to finish the project. They meet after school and Randy says he wants to start working on the project right away, but Tom wants to play softball first.

The dilemmas may occur during school but are not restricted to school situations. The children and adolescents are asked to listen to the brief dilemmas and, after each, to answer questions posed in a semistructured interview. These dilemmas include conflicts with peers and with authority figures who are both familiar and unfamiliar protagonists. The previous example is of a conflict with a familiar peer. Alternatively, it is possible to ask individuals to generate and discuss conflicts that occur in their daily lives. The semistructured interview includes probes to elicit the individual's ability to understand the conflict, generate solutions, and evaluate the outcomes. A complete interview includes four to eight dilemmas and typically takes 30 to 60 minutes to administer. The interview is audiotaped and transcribed for scoring. Directions for the administration are presented in the INS scoring manual. Responses to questions for each protocol are scored using a detailed INS scoring guide (Schultz et al., 1989). The scoring guide provides instructions and examples required for coding subjects' responses on overall level of perspective taking, across the problem-solving steps, and on interpersonal orientation.

As discussed earlier, a functional analysis entails the breakdown of responses into four sequential problem-solving steps. Responses at each step (i.e., definition of the problem, action proposed, justification provided, and evaluation of outcomes) are scored separately for level of perspective taking. The global strategy level in the INS model is the average of these scores across the different dilemmas. Although a detailed description of scoring (Schultz et al., 1989) is beyond the scope of this chapter, it can be summarized as follows. The responses are scored for (a) structural level, (b) functional steps, and (c) interpersonal orientation.

Structural Level

As discussed earlier, the structural level depicts the developmental level at which the subject's response reflects a consideration of the social perspectives between the protagonist and the significant other (i.e., in the earlier example between Randy and Tom). Responses are classified according to the level of perspective taking underlying them. The structural analysis focuses on the form of the strategy or strategies the subject suggests using to resolve the conflict. The development of interpersonal negotiation strategies progresses through a series of four levels described in detail later. These four levels were developed to capture the developmental progression of perspective taking. The score ranges from 0 to 3 and reflects the level of sophistication with which social perspectives are coordinated. Each progression in level follows an increasing differentiation and integration in the capacity to view oneself as situated in a broader social context that involves multiple perspectives (Selman, 1980; Selman et al., 1986). The four levels are:

ø. egocentric and undifferentiated,
1. subjective and unilateral,
2. self-reflective and reciprocal,
3. third-person and mutual.

More specifically, Level 0 strategies imply a lack of the coordination of the perspectives of the person and the actor in the consideration of the particular problem. At this level, the physical and psychological characteristics of those involved are not clearly differentiated. The possibility that another person may interpret the same behavior differently is not recognized. Strategies classified as Level 0 are primarily impulsive, physicalistic strategies (e.g., impulsive reactions).

The key conceptual advance from Level 0 to Level 1 is the clear differentiation of physical and psychological characteristics (Schultz et al., 1989). Level 1 strategies reflect recognition that each person has a unique and subjective psychological life. Also, the subjective perspective of others is thought to be directly observable. These strategies do not coordinate the perspectives of two individuals. For example, strategies classified as Level 1 may include one-way commands and simple and unchallenging accommodations in terms of the perspective of and impact on one person.

Strategies classified as Level 2 are based on an understanding of both the self and the other as capable of reflecting and having opinions and behaviors that influence each other or the situation. These strategies indicate an ability to take a second-person perspective on one's thoughts and actions, along with the realization that others can do so as well. The perspectives of self and other are both appreciated in that some kind of interaction which is mutually influential is evident. However, they are still not coordinated in relation to one another. For example, strategies classified as Level 2 may include strategies that focus on exchanges (e.g., discussing ideas, seeing two points of view).

Level 3 strategies reflect an integration of the interests of the other and the self as viewed from a third-person or social systems perspective. The strategies displayed suggest that the subject is reflective about the interactive system embedded in a larger social context. For example, the strategies may involve compromise, dialogue, and the recognition and development of various priorities (e.g., friendship). The strategies indicate an understanding that concern for various priorities over time relates to the solution of any immediate problem.

Functional Analysis

The responses are also examined using a functional component analysis. As described earlier in the chapter, a functional component analysis depicts the steps involved in social problem-solving. The four sequential problem solving steps are characterized as follows:

1. defining the problem,
2. generating alternative strategies,
3. selecting and implementing a specific strategy,
4. evaluating outcomes.

The relation between the structural and functional analysis is that the problem situation is divided into a series of steps that describe problem solving and, consequently, each step is scored for level of perspective taking, therefore providing a more detailed analysis of the social problem-solving process. The comments of two children referred to a children's mental health clinic indicate the difference in their understanding of other's points of view. Each child was asked to define the problem to the dilemma presented earlier.

Example 1: A 10-year-old's understanding:

Question: What is the problem here? Why is that a problem?
Answer: The problem is you only have 2 days and you should work before you play. (Why?) Because if they don't finish it they are gonna fail.

Example 2: A 12-year-old's understanding:

Question: What is the problem here? Why is that a problem?
Answer: They have to work on the project together and Randy wants to start right away, but Tom wants to play softball. (Why is that a problem?) Because if they have to work on it together, they have to be at the same place and they both have to work on it, not just one of them. (At the same time you mean?) Yeah.

The 10-year-old fails to consider that Randy and Tom may not have the same point of view regarding the situation. However, the 12-year-old is aware that both Randy and Tom have a distinct point of view. The 12-year-old's answer coordinates the points of view of Randy and Tom in a plausible way and takes both person's points of view into account.

Interpersonal Orientation

The responses generated for steps 2 (generating alternative strategies) and 3 (selecting and implementing a specific strategy) are scored for interpersonal orientation. These responses are categorized to reflect the priority given to achieving one's own as opposed to the other's needs. There are three scoring categories: (a) self-transforming, (b) other-transforming, and (c) collaborative. Self-transforming strategies are those in which the self's or the protagonist's needs are seen as secondary relative to the other's needs. The self is changed in some way in order to meet the needs of the other. Strategies classified as other-transforming are those in which the self's needs are considered primary and attempts are made to change the perspective of the other to meet the needs of the self. Collaborative strategies are those in which an attempt is made to balance the needs of both the self and other by equally considering the perspectives of both. Strategies that are not collaborative and cannot be clearly classified as self-transforming or other-transforming are coded as indeterminate. This classification system demonstrates how strategies that appear different in terms of overt action can reflect similar levels of perspective taking.

PSYCHOMETRIC PROPERTIES OF THE INS

Reliability

The psychometric properties of the INS interview were shown to be good with the exact agreement between raters' global social perspective-taking scores ranging from 75% to 91% (Schultz & Selman, 1989; Yeates et al., 1990). The interview was used across a range of ages and with both normal and clinical samples. In a study with elementary and junior high school children, Yeates et al. (1990) reported 75% agreement among raters with a correlation between overall INS score of $r = .89$, $p < .05$. They also found that the interrater correlations for average scores at each step across four dilemmas ranged from .74 to .87. In a study that included children between the ages of 11 and 19 years at risk for affective disorders, a Pearson product-moment correlation of .94 was obtained for the global scores between raters (Beardslee et al., 1987). In addition, good INS test–retest reliability was demonstrated in various school-based and clinical intervention studies (Selman & Demorest, 1984; Yeates et al., 1990). For instance, Yeates et al. (1990) reported a significant correlation for overall INS perspective taking scores across a 4-month interval ($r = .69$, $p < .05$).

Validity

Validity studies were conducted to examine the developmental sequence of the INS and the relations between the INS levels and social and personality functioning. A variety of studies demonstrated that developmental variations in social perspective taking are positively related to age (Gurucharri & Selman, 1982) and IQ (Beardslee et al., 1987; Selman et al., 1986). Furthermore, interpersonal negotiation strategies in thought are related to personality factors such as level of object relations and preferred defense mechanisms (Schultz & Selman, 1989). Moreover, Selman and colleagues demonstrated that social perspective-taking ability is related to broader aspects of social adjustment. For example, Selman (1980) compared children's social perspective-taking skills with their understanding of friendship and found that children who responded at a high level to perspective-taking problems were also likely to have more sophisticated ideas about friendship. In addition, Yeates et al. (1991) demonstrated that the capacity for perspective coordination is related to measures of social status. In a sample of public school children, they found that overall level of social perspective-taking development was related to peer nominations elicited from the childrens' classmates. This provides some evidence for the ecological validity of the instrument. Taken together, these findings suggest that social perspective taking is related to aspects of psychological and behavioral functioning.

POTENTIAL PROBLEMS OF SOCIAL PERSPECTIVE TAKING RESEARCH

A limitation in most studies of social perspective taking is that generalizability to real world thinking is uncertain (Keating, 1990; Keating,

Menna, & Matthews, 1992; Menna, 1994; Menna & Keating, 1993). The studies discussed here used standardized measures of social perspective taking asking subjects how a protagonist would respond in a hypothetical situation. Although measures like the INS offer important information with regard to social perspective-taking skills, they ignore the variability in perspective taking that might occur during the solution of real-world problems.

In an attempt to address this issue, Menna and Keating (1993) examined adolescents' and young adults' perspective taking ability (i.e., cognitive complexity) in response to real-world tasks. Subjects were interviewed to examine their understanding of stress and coping in their own lives (i.e., worries and daily life stresses). The responses were then scored for level of cognitive complexity, that is, an adaptation of Selman's (1980; Selman et al., 1986) scoring of levels of perspective taking. Menna and Keating found that when considering real-world problems, younger adolescents reported more simplistic, self-focused responses, whereas young adults were more likely to recognize a third-person perspective. Specifically, the young adults were better able to differentiate the self's perspective from that of the other and to understand stressful encounters as reciprocal. These findings are consistent with Selman's (1980) finding that during adolescence, individuals further develop their ability to perceive the point of view of others and to analyze their own and others' behaviors and emotions (Selman, 1980; Selman et al., 1986). Menna and Keating's work is noteworthy because they applied the construct of social perspective taking to examine how individuals deal with stressful dilemmas in their own lives.

In our current work, we are comparing social perspective-taking ability in relation to solutions of hypothetical dilemmas with social perspective taking ability in relation to solutions of *real-world dilemmas*. We defined real-world dilemmas as the problems children report that cause them to worry or feel stress. In a sample of 7- to 14-year-olds, in addition to the INS, we are examining children's social perspective-taking ability concerning their own real-world dilemmas (Menna & Cohen, 1995). To this end, children are interviewed to elicit their understanding of the daily hassles and worries in their own lives. A coding system to identify childrens' perspective taking strategies, which is based on Selman's work, was developed. The following case examples are taken from this ongoing work. The examples demonstrate some of the types of responses given by children referred to a children's mental health center to the INS interview and to their own real-life dilemmas. These children are functioning at a level appropriate for their age and grade level and the hypothetical dilemmas administered are similarly appropriate for their age and grade level.

Matt was 14 years old when he was referred to the center by his probation officer because of conduct and behavior problems both in and outside school, and for antisocial problems. Matt was administered a battery of tests to assess his speech and language performance, intellectual functioning, and reading and school achievement. In addition to this testing, Matt was administered the INS interview and also asked to identify his daily stresses and worries and to discuss them. The psychological testing revealed that Matt had overall average intelligence and was functioning at grade level. Matt's responses to the hypothetical INS dilemmas were most often at an impulsive and physicalistic level of reasoning. For example, Matt's best solution to the Randy and Tom dilemma presented earlier was as follows:

Matt: Tommy better work or he's going to beat the hell out of him.
Interviewer: (Why?)
Matt: To teach him a lesson.

The same level of responses were given by Matt when he was asked to discuss his real dilemmas. Matt gave noninteractive, impulsive, and primitive physicalistic strategies for dealing with his problems. For example, his response when discussing a recent conflict with his friends was: "I tell them, or ask them to stop. If they don't, I walk away and sit about 10 feet away from them." In both of these instances, Matt's strategies for dealing with social conflict were devoid of any intent to communicate reciprocally or collaboratively. Compared to peers his own age, Matt's overall score is low. Most children Matt's age would be employing more mature reciprocal strategies, which sometimes include collaborative social perspective-taking.

The second example illustrates a higher level of reasoning when dealing with social conflicts. John was 12-years-old when he was referred to the center by his teacher and other school personnel because of emotional problems. John's intellectual functioning was average and academically he was performing at grade level. John's responses to the hypothetical dilemmas were most often at a reciprocal level of reasoning. For example, John's best solution to the dilemma presented earlier was as follows:

Randy could just say—he could also agree with Tom and just say, right, like I'll go and play softball and play with you, and then after we'll come in and we'll do the project. This will make Tom happy and not get into a fight with him.

In this example, John suggested a collaborative approach to the problem. However, lower level responses were given by John when he was asked to discuss his real-life problems. John reported having difficulty with his teacher, stating "she is unfair." His response to a reported conflict with his teacher was coded as impulsive. John's response to the conflict was as follows: "I just walk out and the next day they can't say anything to me or sometimes if I don't feel like fighting and I am tired that day, I just go down to the office." John's response to his real problem suggested a lack of coordination of the perspectives of his teacher with the problem he was having. Obtaining responses in the two situations demonstrated that John was able to generate a repertoire of strategies. However, when dealing with his conflict with his teacher, John employed a unilateral strategy and avoided reciprocal or mutual communication. John believed that the teacher had the problem. He did not take ownership for any part of the problem, whereas in the example with Randy and Tom, John viewed the problem as shared.

This example also provides us with information regarding the level of strategies children employ when dealing with conflicts with peers as opposed to dealing with conflicts with adults. As mentioned earlier, Selman et al. (1986) observed that the overall level of the suggested strategy and the level of each functional step are sensitive to contextual variations. As seen in this example, John's overall social perspective-taking competence level was higher in dilemmas in which the conflict was with a peer rather than with an adult.

The way we think about the self and other is influenced by previous social experience (Chandler & Helm, 1984; Piaget, 1965). For example, individuals who differentiated between self and other and who approached an interpersonal situation with a third-person perspective were more likely to report experiencing high social support (Menna, 1994). The individuals who reported low support were more likely to generate physicalistic or subjective, self-focused responses in the particular context. The findings can be interpreted two ways. One interpretation is that social support may foster the development of self from other differentiation. A second interpretation is that individuals may be able to access more support as a result of being able to make self-from other-differentiations. Felner, Farber, and Primavera (1983) suggested that perceived social support, the appraisal that one is supported, is in part a function of the availability of social networks. However, it also depends on the interpersonal skills (e.g., self-from other-differentiation) in accessing and maintaining supportive relationships. So, John's response to the conflict with his teacher also may be a function of his prior social experiences. John's interactions and solutions to his difficulties at home may be very much like those seen at school. John's social exchanges may not be set up so as to foster self-from other-differentiation. Thus, John's perspective-taking skills depend, in part, on the kinds of social experiences he has had.

FACTORS INFLUENCING SOCIAL PERSPECTIVE TAKING

A variety of factors influence social perspective-taking ability, including cognitive capacity, affect, and context (i.e., the type of relationship, such as peer vs. authority figure). With respect to cognitive capacity, the shift from unidimensional perspective taking to a differentiation and coordination of perspectives is related to other changes in cognitive functioning. These developmental shifts in cognitive capacity may be due to the automatization of problem solving and biological maturation (Case, 1985, 1992). As children develop, they can perform more mental operations on tasks because the mental space required to perform more complex tasks has increased due to increases in operational efficiency (Case, 1985, 1992; Miller, 1989). Practice enables children to become automatic at performing basic tasks; as a result, automatic processes require less memory capacity, thus freeing up more mental operating space for more complex tasks. In addition to automaticity, biological maturation is an important contributor to developmental shifts in cognitive capacity. Case (1985, 1992) speculated that degree of myelinization may be related to operational efficiency. As children develop, the degree of myelinization increases and, as a result, operational efficiency and capacity increases. Shifts in cognitive capacity are also affected by increases in experiential knowledge and by improved attentional capacities (Crick & Dodge, 1994). Therefore, as children mature, they become capable of representing several different dimensions of a problem, whereas previously they could focus on only one. This ability to generate and consider several different representations of information creates the opportunity for conceptual reorganization and thus, more mature social perspective-taking ability.

Although cognitive processes influence social perspective-taking ability directly, they also interact with affective factors to influence problem solving in most situations (Oatley, 1992). At times, the ability to differentiate and integrate the needs of the self and the other may be dominated by affect, that is, by one's needs to satisfy various wishes, fears, and defenses at that particular time. The avoidance or blocking of feelings may inhibit problem solving on particular tasks. In contrast, the recognition of feelings may facilitate performance and lead to the emergence of new and more adaptive responses (Oatley, 1992; Simon, 1967).

Variations in perspective coordination were also obtained as a function of contextual factors. Children give higher level strategies in contexts involving familiar as opposed to unfamiliar participants and in contexts involving children as opposed to adults (Selman et al., 1986; Selman & Demorest, 1984).

RELATION BETWEEN SOCIAL–COGNITIVE AND OBJECT RELATIONS THEORIES

The integration of social–cognitive theory with other theories of interpersonal relationships and particularly object relations theory was attempted in recent years (Schultz & Selman, 1989; Stuart et al., 1990; Westen, 1992). The joint examination of these theoretical approaches has potential value for understanding the development of interpersonal functioning. Although the databases are different, both approaches focus on the nature of representation of the self and others, as well as the cognitive and affective processes that influence these representations. Moreover, both approaches have as their central theme an understanding of the maturity of interpersonal relationships, which is of interest to clinicians. The following studies illustrate the potential utility of applying both object relations and social cognitive theories to future empirical research and diagnostic assessment.

Schultz and Selman (1989) used object relations theory in an attempt to understand the relation between an individual's level of interpersonal understanding and the level reflected in actual behavior during social interactions. They have begun to identify personality factors, such as defensive style and unconscious representations, that may explain the gap between level of interpersonal understanding and actual behavior. In this study, adolescents were administered the INS interview to measure social perspective taking and self-reported interpersonal orientation, and a revised version of the Defense Mechanism Inventory (DMI; Gleser & Ihilevich, 1969) to measure preferred defense mechanisms. Responses were coded for interpersonal orientations. That is, the coding system was designed to characterize the orientation (i.e., as self-transforming as opposed to other-transforming) of the action taken when responding to the dilemmas. Also, in order to assess maturity of object representations of self and other, subjects were asked to give spontaneous descriptions of their mother, father, and self (Blatt, Chevron, Quinlan, & Wein, 1981). Each of the descriptions were scored using Blatt's (1974) object representation system. In this system, the responses are scored for conceptual level of object relations development, that is, the cognitive developmental sequence in the formation of mental representations of self and others. By employing this system, Schultz and Selman (1989) were able to characterize four aspects of the subject's object representation. Object representations were coded for differentiation, accuracy, articulation, and integration. Each of these was assessed for object relational development, where high scores indicate higher levels of object relations. Schultz and Selman found that the object representation level significantly correlated with level of social perspective taking. This suggests that object representation represents a personality structure where higher levels of object representtion support more mature social perspective-taking ability. They also found that preferred defense mechanisms and levels of object representation predicted level of self-reported action (i.e., interpersonal orientation), even when controlling for INS perspective-taking levels. They suggested that when there is a difference in the maturity of levels of social thought and self-reported action, the gap between them may be attributed in part to psychodynamic processes. That is, delays in personality development may lead to the selection of less sophisticated strategies in conflictual interactions (Yeates et al., 1990).

Westen (1992) attempted to integrate social cognition and object relations theories to understand the relation between mental representation and interpersonal behavior. He suggests that the comparison of groups with known interpersonal pathology (e.g., depression, borderline personality disorder) with one another as well as with groups of normal subjects on measures of object relational and social–cognitive processes can provide a clearer understanding of the psychological processes that mediate actual behavior.

Traditionally, object relations theorists interpreted the interpersonal functioning (i.e., the development of the ability to differentiate one's own perspective from the perspective of others) of patients with borderline personality disorder as a less mature level of functioning (Kernberg, 1975). Findings of Westen and colleagues suggest different explanations for the developmental level of interpersonal functioning (Stuart et al., 1990; Westen, Lohr, Silk, Gold, & Kerber, 1990). They devised a finer measuring instrument that combined constructs from both the social–cognitive and object relations theories. Before describing the findings from the studies, it is important to note that the construct of social perspective taking was adapted to develop coding systems reflecting perspective coordination, or what object theorists refer to as *interpersonal cognitive complexity*. Stuart et al. (1990) compared Rorschach responses of subjects with a diagnosis of borderline personality disorder with subjects diagnosed as having major depressive disorder and with normal subjects on a measure of the cognitive–developmental level (i.e., perspective-taking coordination) of subjects' attributions of intention. They applied Blatt, Brenneis, Schimek, and Glick's (1976) measure of object-relational maturity to score the Rorschach protocols. Subjects with a diagnosis of borderline personality disorder produced significantly more advanced cognitive–developmental (i.e., more mature perspective coordination) responses as assessed by Blatt et al.'s (1976) object relations measure. They also found that subjects with a diagnosis of borderline personality disorder produced more malevolent responses than did either normal subjects or those with a diagnosis of major depressive disorder.

In an attempt to further delineate these findings, Westen et al. (1990) constructed a scale based on the assumption that cognitive and affective components may be inaccessible to introspection due to motivational factors and lack of cognitive access. The measure was designed to assess the following four dimensions: (a) complexity of representations of people (i.e., perspective coordination), (b) affective tone of relationship paradigms, (c) capacity for emotional investment in relationships and moral standards, and (d) understanding of social causality. Each of these dimensions was assessed using a 5-point continuous scale where a score of 5 represented the highest level of functioning (Westen et al., 1990). Using this scale, Westen et al. found that borderline subjects had significantly higher mean scores on cognitive complexity (i.e., perspective-taking coordination), emotional investment, and social causality than did the comparison groups. These results indicate that although subjects with a diagnosis of borderline personality disorder are capable of more complex social cognition (i.e., mature social perspective taking) than subjects with a diagnosis of major depressive disorder or normal comparison subjects, they use this capacity to manage what they perceive as an "aggressive, hostile object world." Westen (1992) suggested that the attributions that patients with borderline personality disorder make regarding people's behavior, thoughts, and feelings are distorted by their own motivational and defensive processes. What is apparent here is that the skills for accurately identifying rather than evaluating the situation are lagging. This lends further support to Schultz and Selman's (1989) suggestion that personality factors may mediate social reasoning and actual behavior. Moreover, in this instance, the developmental findings and constructs from social–cognitive theory (i.e., perspective taking) provided object relations theorists with additional information regarding the psychological functioning of a clinical population. Both Westen et al.'s and Schultz and Selman's (1989) studies provide preliminary findings that suggest the potential utility of applying an integrated understanding of object relations and social cognition theories to empirical questions. Furthermore, in this instance, the application of a coding system like Westen et al's (1990), Selman et al.'s (1986) functional analysis, and Dodge's (1986) social processing system helped tease apart these differences.

RESEARCH ON CLINICAL POPULATIONS

Social–cognitive lags are associated with atypical social and affective development (Quiggle, Garber, Panak, & Dodge, 1992; Yeates et al., 1990) and a growing body of research is examining this relation (e.g., Lochman & Dodge, 1994). Nevertheless, there has been limited investigation of clinical samples and the bulk of research on social perspective taking was done with normal populations.

In one of the few studies involving emotionally disturbed children, Selman and colleagues found that these children lagged behind in the acquisition of social perspective-taking skills relative to control children their own age (Selman, 1981; Selman et al., 1986; Selman & Demorest, 1984). In particular, results from a longitudinal study comparing behaviorally and emotionally disturbed boys to male peers matched for age, race, socioeconomic status (SES), and IQ suggested that the sequence of progression through INS levels was the same for both groups. However, the development of the clinic-referred children lagged behind that of the control group. In addition, relatively low levels of social perspective taking on the INS were related to the self-reported use of physical and avoidant strategies to resolve conflict. Selman and colleagues also observed that immature levels of social perspective ability were associated with poor peer relations (Selman, 1981; Selman, Jaquette, & Lavin, 1977). Selman (1981) compared conceptions of friendship and actual behavior of emotionally disturbed clinic-referred children with peers and found that children who displayed lower levels of perspective taking ability had difficulties forming and maintaining friendships. Beardslee et al. (1987) found that the psychosocial functioning (a composite score reflecting self-reported and mother's rating of behaviors in interpersonal situations) of adolescents whose parents had an affective disorder was related to adolescents' overall level of perspective taking ability. Moreover, their findings suggested that a high global INS level was associated with good psychosocial functioning, whereas a low global INS level was associated with poor psychosocial functioning. Taken together, these studies suggest that INS levels are related to actual social behavior and adjustment.

These studies of clinical samples did not examine social perspective taking in relation to specific symptom patterns. Cohen, Kershner, and Wehrspann (1985) compared social perspective taking skills in clinically identified school-aged children whose behavior fit into clusters of internalizing or externalizing symptom patterns using the classification system based on the Achenbach Child Behavior Checklist (Achenbach, 1978). In this study, two social perspective-taking tasks were used, the Chandler Social Perspective Taking Task and the Selman Friendship Interview. The Chandler Task measured the logical operations required for perspective taking, whereas the Selman Friendship Interview, like the INS, measured the coordination of social perspectives. Cohen et al. found that boys with internalizing symptoms showed significantly more mature perspective taking responses than did boys with externalizing symptoms. As well, there was an association between cognitive maturity and several personality characteristics such that the children with higher self-esteem, a greater internal locus of control, and more adaptive coping styles showed a more mature understanding of the perspectives of another.

Cohen is examining children's social perspective-taking ability in a clinical sample of 7- to 14-year-olds using the INS interview as part of her ongoing work (Cohen, 1992–1996). Based on the Child Behavior Checklist (Achenbach, 1991), the children were classified into three clinical subgroupings: (a) children with externalizing symptoms, (b) children with internalizing symptoms, and (c) those who are comorbid (both internalizers and externalizers). The preliminary findings suggest that the clinically referred children exhibit the same developmental sequence as do Selman et al.'s (1986) normal children, but have lower social perspective-taking scores. This developmental lag in social perspective-taking ability may place the clinically referred children at greater risk for continuing maladaptive outcomes (e.g., poor peer relations). Analyses of these interview protocols continue and the relations between the INS levels and a broader range of both social and emotion measures (e.g., coping style, real-world reasoning, and emotion decoding) will be examined when the data are complete (Menna & Cohen, 1995).

Research on clinical populations may be important in order to understand the etiology of some atypical social behaviors. If the etiology is associated with social cognitive delays this also may provide direction for treatment.

CLINICAL IMPLICATIONS

Developmental social-cognitive researchers suggested that examination of the development of social perspective-taking ability may provide a useful complement to the traditional diagnostic evaluations of childhood psychopathology (Selman & Schultz, 1988; Yeates et al., 1991).

Examining social perspective-taking ability can provide clinicians with information regarding a client's representations of social situations. Specifically, information regarding an individual's developmental level of social perspective-taking competence can serve several functions. First, measures of social perspective-taking ability provide the clinician with another way of assessing an individual's capacity for self-observation and insight (i.e., a process akin to psychological mindedness) (Selman & Schultz, 1988). For instance, examples of responses from the INS and real-world protocols presented earlier illustrated the particular difficulties that may contribute to maladjustment. A client like Matt who deals with interpersonal conflicts primarily with unilateral strategies, such as one-way assertions and physicalistic responses, may not be well suited for traditional insight-oriented psychotherapy, at least at the beginning of intervention.

Second, assessment of social perspective-taking ability provides a developmental approach to formulating therapeutic interventions. A developmental perspective, like the one provided by the INS, may provide important information regarding the entry point for therapy by pinpointing the structural level of a person's representation of his or her world. For instance, Matt may benefit initially from supportive psychotherapy or behavioral intervention, as he does not have the self-reflective capacities required for insight-oriented therapies. Moreover, a developmental approach allows a clinician to judge whether a client's representational world, in this case social perspective-taking competence, has matured over time. The application of the INS interview or the INS coding system to real-world events also provides clinicians with the opportunity to use the social perspective-taking dimensions to code session transcripts and to document increases in complexity of representations over the course of therapy and follow-up. Selman and Demorest (1984), for example, observed weekly 1-hour pair therapy sessions with two young boys over the course of 2 school years. A transcript and narrative analysis was used to identify all the INS levels each child used within each session. The strategies were charted to show the total distribution of strategies and trends in the use of various strategies over time. By using this method of analysis, the authors were able to document a trend from unilateral strategies toward increased use of reciprocal strategies. Selman and Demorest made the point that regardless of intervention, this developmental method allows clinicians to classify behavior and to identify an individual's range of possibilities, limitations, and developmental growth.

CONCLUSIONS

Research on social cognition advanced our understanding of how individuals process information about their social world. Social–cognitive theorists provided a developmental framework that is often lacking in other conceptual frameworks. One aspect of social cognition, social perspective taking, is discussed in this chapter. We present an overview of the relevant literature on both normal and clinical samples. We provide a brief review of exploratory work integrating object relations and social–cognitive theories in order to explain the discrepancies and interactions between the complexity of social problem solving and actual behavior. This exploratory work is especially important because social problem solving and action are often found to be unrelated (Schultz & Selman, 1989; Shantz, 1983). Also, this work offers considerable promise for both theory and intervention. Furthermore, we present the INS measure, which provides clinicians and researchers with a developmental continuum of social–cognitive development (Beardslee et al., 1987). As Selman and his colleagues noted, understanding both diagnostic and developmental factors (e.g., social perspective taking) is potentially important in selecting appropriate interventions. The assessment of the level of social–cognitive capacity using the INS measure provides clinicians and researchers with the opportunity to trace the growth of social perspective-taking capacity through intervention. Although there is considerable normative developmental literature on social perspective taking that promotes the application of these data to understanding maladaptive behavior, there is a paucity of research on clinical populations. This points to much needed future research. In terms of clinical applications, social–cognitive developmental information could have a profound influence on clinical decision making and treatment monitoring. Recent attempts to integrate social–cognitive and psychodynamic theories hold promise of enriching both theoretically driven research and clinical practice. The availability of a methodology (the INS interview) to study social perspective taking should facilitate this process.

ACKNOWLEDGMENTS

The preparation of this chapter was completed while Rosanne Menna was a Research Fellow at the C. M. Hincks Centre. Research described in the chapter was funded by grants to Nancy J. Cohen from Health Canada (NHRDP Grants # 6606–4835 and # 6606–3502).

REFERENCES

Achenbach, T. M. (1978). The child behavior profile: I. Boys aged 6–11. *Journal of Consulting and Clinical Psychology, 46,* 478–488.

Achenbach, T. M. (1991). *Manual for the Child Behavior Checklist 14–18 and 1991 Profile.* Burlington: University of Vermont.

Beardslee, W. R., Schultz, H. H., & Selman, R. L. (1987). Interpersonal negotiation strategies, adaptive functioning, and DSM–III diagnoses in adolescent offspring of parents with affective disorders: Implications for the development of mutuality in relationships. *Development Psychology, 23,* 807–815.

Blatt, S. J. (1974). Levels of object representation in anaclitic and introjective depression. *Psychoanalytic study of the child, 29,* 107–157. Blatt, S. J., Brenneis, C. B., Schimek, J. G., & Glick, M. (1976). Normal development and psychopathological impairment of the concept of the object on the Rorschach. *Journal of Abnormal Psychology, 35,* 364–373.

Blatt, S. J., Brenneis, C. B., Schimek, J. G., & Glick, M. (1976). Normal development an psychopathological impairment of the concept of the object on the Rorschach. *Journal of Abnormal Psychology, 35,* 364–373.

Blatt, S. J., Brenneis, C. B., Schimek, J. G., & Glick, M (1976). Normal development and psychopathological impairment of the concept of the object on the Rorschach. *Journal of Abnormal Psychology, 35,* 364–373.

Blatt, S. J., Chevron, E. S., Quinlan, D. M., & Wein, S. (1981). *The assessment of qualitative and structural dimensions of object representation.* Unpublished manuscript, Yale University, New Haven, CT.

Case, R. (1985). *Intellectual development: Birth to adulthood.* New York: Academic Press.

Case, R. (1992). *The mind's staircase: Exploring the conceptual underpinnings of children's thought and knowledge.* Hillsdale, NJ: Lawrence Erlbaum Associates.

Chandler, M. J., & Helm, D. (1984). Developmental changes in the contribution of shared experiences to social role-taking competence. *International Journal of Behavioral Development, 7,* 145–156.

Cohen, N. J. (1992–1996). *Psychiatrically disturbed children with unsuspected language impairments: Language, social cognition, and reading characteristics.* (NHRDP Grant No. 6606–4835). Health Canada.

Cohen, N. J., Kershner, J., & Wehrspann, W. (1985). Characteristics of social cognition in children with different symptom patterns. *Journal of Applied Developmental Psychology, 6,* 277–290.

Crick, N. R., & Dodge, K. A. (1994). A review and reformulation of social information-processing mechanisms in children's social adjustment. *Psychological Bulletin, 115,* 74–101.

Dodge, K. A. (1980). Social cognition and children's aggressive behavior. *Child Development, 51,* 162–170.

Dodge, K. A. (1986). A social information processing model of social competence in children. In M. Perlmutter (Ed.), *The Minnesota symposium on psychology* (Vol 18, pp. 77–125). Hillsdale, NJ: Lawrence Erlbaum Associates.

Felner, R. D., Farber, S. S., & Primavera, J. (1983). Transitions and stressful life events: A model for primary prevention. In R. D. Felner, L. A. Jason, J. N. Moritsugu, & S. S. Farber (Eds.), *Preventive psychology: Theory, research and practice* (pp. 199–215). New York: Plenum.

Flavell, J. H., Botken, P., Fry, C., Wright, J., & Jarvis, P. (1968). *The development of role-taking and communication skills in children.* New York: Wiley.

Gleser, G. C., & Ihilevich, D. (1969). An objective instrument for measuring defense mechanisms. *Journal of Consulting and Clinical Psychology, 33,* 51–60.

Gurucharri, C., & Selman, R. L. (1982). The development of interpersonal understanding during childhood, preadolescence, and adolescence: A longitudinal follow-up study. *Child Development, 53,* 924–927.

Hatcher, R., Hatcher, S., Berlin, M., Okla, K., & Richards, J. (1990). Psychological mindedness and abstract reasoning in late childhood and adolescence: An exploration using new instruments. *Journal of Youth and Adolescence, 19,* 307–326.

Higgins, E. T., & Bargh, J. A. (1986). Social cognition and social perception. *Annual Review of Psychology, 38,* 364–426.

Inhelder, B., & Piaget, J. (1958). *The growth of logical thinking from childhood to adolescence*. New York: Basic Books.
Keating, D. P. (1990). Adolescent thinking. In S. Feldman & G. Elliot (Eds.), *At the threshold: The developing adolescent* (pp. 54–89). Cambridge, MA: Harvard University Press.
Keating, D. P., Menna, R., & Matthews, S. J. (1992, February). *Adolescent cognitive development in everyday life*. Paper presented at the meeting for the Society for Research on Adolescence, Washington, DC.
Kernberg, O. (1975). *Borderline conditions and pathological narcissism*. New York: Aronson.
Lochman, J. E., & Dodge, K. A. (1994). Social–cognitive processes of severely violent, moderately aggressive, and non-aggressive boys. *Journal of Consulting and Clinical Psychology, 62*, 366–374.
Mead, G. H. (1934). *Mind, self, and society*. Chicago: University of Chicago Press.
Menna, R. (1994). *Cognitive and emotional factors in stress reactivity of adolescents and young adults: A developmental perspective*. Unpublished doctoral dissertation, University of Toronto, Toronto, Ontario, Canada.
Menna, R., & Cohen, N. J. (1995, March). *Dealing with stress: An examination of depressed and aggressive children's coping strategies*. Paper presented at the meeting of the Society for Research on Child Development, Indianapolis, IN.
Menna, R., & Keating, D. P. (1993, August). *Coping with worries in adolescence and early adulthood: Developmental changes*. Paper presented at the meeting of the American Psychological Association, Toronto, Ontario, Canada.
Miller, P. H. (1989). *Theories of developmental psychology*. San Francisco: Freeman.
Miller, P. H., Kessel, F. S., & Flavell, J. H. (1970). Thinking about people thinking about people thinking about : A study of social cognitive development. *Child Development, 41*, 613–623.
Oatley, K. (1992). *Best laid schemes: The psychology of emotions*. Cambridge, MA: Cambridge University Press.
Piaget, J. (1965). *The moral judgement of the child*. London: Routledge & Kegan Paul.
Piaget, J. (1970). *Genetic epistemology*. New York: Norton.
Piaget, J. (1972). Intellectual evolution from adolescence to adulthood. *Human Development, 15*, 1–12.
Quiggle, N. L., Garber, J., Panak, W. F., & Dodge, K. A. (1992). Social information processing in aggressive and depressed children. *Child Development, 63*, 1305–1320.
Rubin, K. A., & Krasnor, L. R. (1986). Social–cognitive and social behavioral perspectives on problem solving. In M. Perlmutter (Ed.), *The Minnesota Symposium on Child Psychology* (Vol. 18, pp. 1–68). Hillsdale,NJ: Lawrence Erlbaum Associates.
Schultz, L. H., & Selman, R. L. (1989). Bridging the gap between interpersonal thought and action in early adolescence: The role of psychodynamic processes. *Developmental Psychopathology, 1*, 133–152.
Schultz, L. H., Yeates, K. O., & Selman, R. L. (1989). *The Interpersonal Negotiation Strategies (INS) Interview: A scoring manual*. Unpublished manuscript, Harvard Graduate School of Education, Cambridge, MA.
Selman, R. L. (1976). Toward a structural analysis of developing interpersonal relations concepts: Research with normal and disturbed preadolescent boys. In A. D. Pick (Ed.), *The annual Minnesota symposium on child psychology* (Vol. 10, pp. 156–200). Minneapolis: University of Minnesota Press.
Selman, R. L. (1980). *The growth of interpersonal understanding*. New York: Academic Press.
Selman, R. L. (1981). The development of interpersonal competence: The role of understanding in conduct. *Developmental Review, 1*, 401–422.
Selman, R. L., Beardslee, W., Schultz, L. H., Krupa, M., & Podorefsky, D. (1986). Assessing adolescent interpersonal negotiation strategies: Toward the integration of functional and structural models. *Developmental Psychology, 22*, 450–459.
Selman, R. L., & Byrne, D. F. (1974). A structural-developmental analysis of levels of role taking in middle childhood. *Child Development, 45*, 803–806.
Selman, R. L., & Demorest, A. (1984). Observing troubled children's interpersonal negotiation strategies: Implications of and for a developmental model. *Child Development, 55*, 288–304.
Selman, R. L., Jacquette, D., & Lavin, D. R. (1977). Interpersonal awareness in children: Toward an integration of developmental and clinical child psychology. *American Journal of Orthopsychiatry, 47*, 264–274.

Selman, R. L., & Schultz, L. H. (1988). Interpersonal thought and action in the case of a troubled early adolescent: Toward a developmental model of the gap. In S. R. Shirk (Ed.), *Cognitive development and child psychotherapy. Perspectives in developmental psychology* (pp. 207–246). New York: Plenum.

Shantz, C. (1983). Social cognition. In P. H. Mussen (Ed.), *Handbook of child psychology: Cognitive development* (Vol. 3, pp. 495–555). New York: Wiley.

Simon, H. A. (1967). Motivational and emotional controls of cognition. *Psychological Review, 74*, 29–39.

Spivack, G., Platt, J. J., & Shure, N. B. (1976). *The problem-solving approach to adjustment*. San Francisco: Jossey-Bass.

Spivack G., & Shure, M. B. (1982). The cognition of social adjustment: Interpersonal cognitive problem-solving thinking. In B. B. Lahey & A. E. Kazdin (Eds.), *Advances in clinical child psychology* (Vol. 5, pp. 323–372). New York: Plenum.

Spivack, G., & Shure, M. B. (1985). ICPS and beyond: Centripetal and centrifugal forces. *American Journal of Community Psychology, 13*, 226–243.

Staub, E., & Eisenberg, N. (1981). Social cognition, affect, and behavior: An essay and review of Robert Selman's "The growth of interpersonal understanding: Developmental and clinical analyses." *Developmental Review, 1*, 385–400.

Stuart, J., Westen, D., Lohr, N., Benjamin, J., Becker, S., Vorus, N., & Silk, K. (1990). Object relations in borderlines, depressives, and normals: An examination of human responses on the Rorschach. *Journal of Personality Assessment, 55*, 296–318.

Westen, D. (1992). Social cognition and object relations. *Psychological Bulletin, 109*, 429–455.

Westen, D., Lohr, N., Silk, K., Gold, L., & Kerber, K. (1990). Object relations and social cognition in borderlines, major depressives, and normals: A TAT analysis. *Psychological Assessment: A Journal of Consulting and Clinical Psychology, 2*, 355–364.

Yeates, K. O., Schultz, L. H., & Selman, R. L. (1990). Bridging the gaps in child-clinical assessment: Toward the application of social-cognitive developmental theory. *Clinical Psychology Review, 10*, 567–588.

Yeates, K. O., Schultz, L. H., & Selman, R. L. (1991). The development of interpersonal negotiation strategies in thought and action: A social-cognitive link to behavioral adjustment and social status. *Merrill Palmer Quarterly, 37*, 369–406.

Yeates, K. O., & Selman, R. L. (1989). Social competence in the schools: Toward an integrative developmental model for intervention. *Developmental Review, 9*, 64–100.

Chapter 9

Psychological Mindedness in Psychotherapists

Barry A. Farber
Valerie Golden
Teachers College, Columbia University

We must plunge into experience and then reflect on the meaning of it. All reflection and no plunging drives us mad; all plunging and no reflection, and we are brutes.

—Goethe (cited in Becker, 1973, p. 199)

Too much awareness, without accompanying experience, is a skeleton without the flesh of life.

—Nin (1967, p. 173)

Researchers and clinicians have suggested that psychological mindedness (PM) affects individuals in both beneficial and dysfunctional ways. For example, individuals with high levels of PM are thought to be more insightful (Applebaum, 1973) and emotionally aware (Farber, 1989; Fenigstein, Scheier, & Buss, 1975) but also more interpersonally distant (Henry, Sims, & Spray, 1973) and self-critical (Farber, 1989; Levinson, Sharaf, & Gilbert, 1966) than those who are less psychologically minded. We might well hypothesize that these and other effects of PM would be manifest most acutely in psychotherapists. As a group, these individuals have often chosen their profession on the basis of feeling highly introspective and psychologically minded from adolescence onward; have exercised, examined, and refined this trait in discussions with like-minded others and in their own personal psychotherapy; have chosen to read fiction and nonfiction that reflects their enduring interest in psychological matters; have used their highly honed psychological mindedness in their work with patients; and have, in general, used this way of thinking to frame their understanding of matters ranging from the personal to the political (Farber, 1985). To many therapists, psychological mindedness is a more or less enduring way of seeing the world.

Our focus in this chapter is on the benefits and costs of high levels of PM among psychotherapists. Psychological mindedness—the tendency to look for motives, patterns, and distortions in oneself and others—is a trait, consisting of both an affective and intellectual component, that most psychologists, especially those espousing a psychodynamically oriented perspective, prize and seek to promote in themselves and their patients (Farber, 1985). Although some (e.g., Wolitzky & Reuben, 1974) have attempted to distinguish between PM and similar concepts such as introspection and self-awareness, we feel these terms are inextricably related. PM, when focused inward, is a particular form of introspection or self-awareness informed by a knowledge (not necessarily sophisticated or technical) of psychological processes. Regardless of its precise definition, however (and, as this volume reveals, there have been many), the implication of having this trait to a great degree, as many therapists do, is the subject of much philosophical, literary, and psychological speculation. This chapter deals with some of the enduring questions that have been raised, including: What are the advantages of being highly psychologically minded? What are the disadvantages? What is the price therapists and others pay for psychologically informed knowledge and understanding? When does knowledge of ourselves—the way we think, feel, and behave—get in the way of living? The battle of paradigms addressed here is between the Socratic notion that "the unexamined life is not worth living" and folklore suggesting that "ignorance is bliss."

This chapter begins with a semifictional account of the role of psychological mindedness in a clinical psychology student in the second year of training, and ends with a portrait of a psychologically minded therapist in midcareer. We delve into theology and mythology (Adam and Eve and the beginnings of self-knowledge; Prometheus), discuss the influence of psychodynamic theory on the definition of PM, examine the theoretical and research literature on the effects of psychological mindedness on therapists, and report on a recent survey conducted by the senior author of this chapter of therapists' perceptions of the ways in which psychological mindedness has affected, both negatively and positively, multiple facets of their lives.

PSYCHOLOGICAL MINDEDNESS IN A BEGINNING PSYCHOTHERAPIST

Gradually my classmates and I are being initiated into a unique culture in which psychological mindedness reigns. Many of us feel, possibly for the first time, that we are finally where we belong. We are among like-minded people who share our fascination with human nature and with other people's inner worlds. Yet, if I had to summarize my overriding impression of this stage of my training, it would be "ambiguous complexity." In developing psychological sophistication, in honing our understanding of the multiple determinants of behavior, in appreciating the numerous meanings of a single symptom, we confront the uncertain, the intangible, and the unanswerable in our patients and in ourselves.

There is the challenge of staying in touch with the patient, while simultaneously staying in touch with myself and my own reactions. There is the challenge of remaining alert to the patient's resistance while scrutinizing as objectively as possible my own hesitation to face the identical issue. There is the strain of knowing how and when to withhold my emotional reactions, no matter how intense, while recognizing that my anger, aggression, sexuality—even helplessness—are essential to my ability to work effectively with patients. I must stifle socially dictated responses in favor of a therapeutic stance whose rules seem unfamiliar.

As a graduate student in a doctoral program in clinical psychology, I spend considerable time either listening to patients or replaying what they have said to me. So much coalesces in my head at once, pressing for reconciliation: my theoretical knowledge, my experiences as a beginning therapist, my clinical training and supervision, my exchanges with classmates and professors, my personal therapy, and my personal life experiences. I have started to develop what Reik (1948) called a "third ear." I now listen both to patients and to myself, trying to hear what is said and what is not said, as if I were a third party. I track what goes into my feeling sad, angry, frustrated, or off-balance. As I fill in my emotional blanks, I come to better understand myself and the patient. The work is personally rewarding and relevant in a way that few other endeavors can match. The process is exhilarating, to a point. As is the case with any personality trait or human quality, there are two sides. At first I thought I could remain, at least in my personal life, unscathed by my professional training. I wanted to preserve my "normal" personality. I thought I could keep safely compartmentalized my budding psychological mindedness so as not to become the stereotyped therapist who sees hidden meanings in every ordinary gesture. But for all my resolve to keep the tools of my trade at arm's length, I find the work pervasively infiltrating who I am and how I live. Through clinical work, supervision, and personal therapy, I have learned to feel and hear a layer of significance in what was once insignificant, even unnoticed. It is both elusive and potent, but once acknowledged, hard to deny.

For example, when a patient wants to end therapy, it is no longer just a simple "goodbye"; I look for the underlying motives, timing, and facets of our relationship to explain its meaning. Is the patient punishing me? Do I represent some significant figure from the past? Is the move a preemptive strike so I do not hurt the patient first? Provocative behavior is no longer just aggression; I ask what purpose it serves, why it is occurring at that moment, and what my own response may be, even if I am circumspect in sharing that response. The inquiry demands not only introspection and objectivity on my part, but also the ability to step into my patient's shoes and to tolerate uncertainty.

My understanding of human nature, and of myself, has grown immeasurably. I am learning to approach people in light of a family history and an unconscious. I feel more tolerant of people for the complexities I see in their thoughts, feelings, and behaviors. What I once saw as a puzzling string of damaging relationships, I am now inclined to view as a powerful, unconscious reenactment of an unhappy childhood. In the process, however, I have lost my ability to allow people and things to be simple. I am not quite so far gone as the apocryphal therapist who thinks "I wonder what was meant by that?" when someone says "hello". Still, what used to be a simple compliment, insult, or expression of affection is now potentially other than its content suggests. Rarely does it seem that a cigar is just a cigar. I now see strong connections and unstated meanings in actions and words that meant nothing before. But assuming a therapeutic stance in my personal interactions, much as I do with patients, can leave me feeling like an outsider to my own life.

Outside the clinic and the classroom, I wonder when a friend sabotages her career: Is it her way of never outshining her competitive mother? Is it a plea for love or a hope of being rescued? When a friend forgets something we had planned: Is she angry?

Often I feel self-conscious about the meanings I feel and hear in nonverbal messages, as though I have intruded on a privileged communication between someone's conscious and unconscious. In social situations, I usually keep my internal dialogue to myself out of respect for people's emotional defenses, and because my interpretations—whether right or wrong—might cost me a friendship. At a recent party with friends, someone joked about needing a drink to combat the stress of daily life. Everyone laughed in implied agreement, then went on with social pleasantries. My inclination was to pursue the comment but social dictates held me back.

Among my classmates, the struggle to "unlearn" standard social convention and to substitute PM in its place is at once a bond and also a wedge. Our insights, although more acceptable among colleagues, are no less intrusive when levelled against each other. Conversely, of course, there is a tolerance and tacit understanding not so readily found outside our circle.

Although at times I want a break from the emotional intensity that this culture and its language create, the opposite is more typical. I feel ill at ease skating over the surface, disappointed when interactions are restricted to mere formalities. Having learned that no one's life is simple or without struggle, I feel cheated when given convenient or superficial responses. In fact, at times I unrealistically expect interactions outside the office to have the same emotional impact as those with patients. There is an alienation in honing one's psychological mindedness: Not everyone else is interested.

As with any trait, there are benefits and costs to this mindset. On balance, growing more psychologically minded has already enriched my personal and professional lives, my understanding of myself and my connections to others. The origins of my psychological-mindedness and the forces continuing to facilitate it are complex and difficult to sort out. Clearly, however, the most valuable tool of my trade is knowing myself: my conflicts, my feelings, my past, my unconscious, and most especially, those issues I least want to face in myself.

IN THE BEGINNING

In the beginning, according to the *Bible*, were Adam and Eve. They ate from the Tree of Knowledge (of good and evil) and were banished, in a state of shame, from the paradise of the Garden of Eden. Was God's banishment a divine message regarding the boundaries of mortal understanding? Is it a metaphor for the inherent price we pay in guilt and anxiety for striving to understand our needs, tensions, and mortality?

There are several theological interpretations of this account, two of which are briefly noted. The first emphasizes that the boundary transgressed by Adam and Eve was that of omniscience. That is, in eating from the Tree of Knowledge, they learned not only of good and evil but of everything in between. In learning everything, then, they approximated God too closely and were punished for their arrogance. The second interpretation focuses on sexuality. Originally naked and blissful, Adam and Eve became clothed and guilty and, even more tragically, mortal. Thus, in gaining sexuality, they lost immortality.

The common theme to both these interpretations is that knowledge has a price. Indeed, if we think of the pre-expulsion nakedness of Adam and Eve as innocence—not just of sexual matters—but of the vast corpus of human liabilities and frailties, the banishment might represent an enduring mythological theme regarding the dangers of self-knowledge. Innocence and blissfulness stand in stark opposition to knowledge, guilt, and shame. Similarly, in Greek mythology, Prometheus (whose name means "forethought") steals fire from the gods to give to mankind and, furthermore, bestows upon mankind the gift of intellect. In retaliation, Zeus plagues humans with Pandora and her box of troubles, and chains Prometheus to a mountain where an eagle preys daily on his liver. Here again, the theme of danger emerges when mankind's quest for knowledge becomes too God-like.

From another theological viewpoint, in the Buddhist tradition people are believed to have not five but six senses—hearing, sight, smell, taste, touch, and consciousness.The last of these is thought to be valuable only in such mundane matters as deciding what clothes to wear on a rainy day. Rational or reflective thought is said to impede enlightenment.

A MATTER OF DEFINITION

Before focusing on the costs and benefits of high levels of PM, it may be useful to return to the issue of definition—specifically, to the relationship of PM to psychodynamic formulation. That is, does PM, at least among psychotherapists, imply the use of certain forms of psychological thinking (i.e., psychodynamic) or can it refer to a range of psychological or philosophical constructions, from radical behaviorism to transpersonal?

In answering this question, we are reminded of a controversial paper of Arnold Lazarus' (1971), "Where do behaviorists take their troubles?" The answer to Lazarus' question (albeit 25 years ago) was to psychodynamic therapists. Seemingly, it is these individuals and their way of thinking who provide the deepest perspective on life's problems. And it does seem as though this perspective—rather than an understanding of environmental contingencies or cognitive distortions—is what lies at the heart of PM. Highly psychologically-minded individuals, we believe, are more likely to reflect and consider questions in the hope of finding meaning (or narrative coherence) rather than "scientific" answers or solutions. Indeed, we believe highly psychologically-minded individuals are attuned to a "tragic" vision of life (Schafer, 1976) in which human problems are not easily, if ever, resolved and in which ambivalence and ambiguity (rather than certainty and understanding) are inevitable in trying to come to terms with the complexity of human existence. In this regard, too—and we are aware of the irony—even such an extraordinary and influential psychologist as Skinner would not be considered highly psychologically minded. Similarly, as gifted a clinician as Rogers was, he was never truly given his due by his contemporaries, most of them psychodynamically-oriented therapists (Farber, Brink, & Raskin, 1996). To them, Rogers was not "deep" enough and not sufficiently interested in the underlying dynamics or etiology of a client's problems. Although he was viewed as empathic and exquisitely sensitive to his clients' needs, he was never considered particularly psychologically minded.

It could be argued that in light of the growing trend among clinicians toward eclectism and cognitive–behavioral therapies, and the concurrent push within the American Psychological Association for only "empirically validated therapies" to be taught in accredited psychology training programs, that the special type of PM afforded by psychodynamic language and understanding might be less valued today than in previous years. We feel this has partially occurred but only under certain circumstances. That is, we believe that the influence of psychodynamic theory has waned considerably in terms of treatment options but has nevertheless remained a powerful tool frequently used by therapists to understand themselves and their patients. (It is notable, too, that at professional conferences or meetings nonpsychodynamic clinicians seem to be as comfortable using psychodynamic concepts such as "resistance" as are most dynamically oriented therapists). Thus, we suspect there are a great many clinicians who treat problems using a cognitive–behavioral perpective but who continue to think of their own issues and those of their patients in more or less dynamic terms. Many, especially those who consider themselves eclectic, seemingly have no problem reconciling a psychodynamic understanding of issues with a more cognitive or behavioral approach to the amelioration of these issues.

It is, of course, no longer difficult to see the similarities underlying seemingly different theoretical approaches. Although once the schism between behavior and analytic therapies seemed immense and unbreachable (Messer & Winokur, 1980), recent theorists (e.g., Goldfried & Norcross, 1995) have noted commonalities in techniques and concepts that belie very different-sounding technical terms. Who, for example, could operationalize a distinction between the cognitive–behavioral notion of *schemata* and the psychodynamic idea of *internalized representations of self and others*? And who would be parochial enough to contend that only client-centered therapists are supportive in their clinical work? We suspect that it would be difficult, on the basis of transcripts alone, to consistently identify which treatments are deemed by practitioners as cognitive–behavioral and which as psychodynamic. Therapists of every theoretical persuasion often share clinical lore (e.g., "teach the hysterical patient to think and the obsessive to feel") and even techniques (e.g., helping patients identify disorted patterns of thinking). In this regard, our assumption is that many clinicians who now subscribe to a variety of theoretical approaches have embraced, from adolescence onward, a psychodynamic brand of PM that influenced greatly their career choice. These therapists' psychological mindedness, we argue, is still strongly filtered through a psychodynamic perspective.

Thus, although it might be considered progressive to embrace diversity and consider that one could be psychologically minded in numerous theoretical orientations, it seems to us this is not generally the case. The way this term (PM) is ordinarily used restricts the high end of the continuum to individuals who are introspective, reflective, and searching for meaning in ways commonly thought of as psychodynamic. The usual definitions of PM, emphasizing as they do issues of meaning and motivation (Farber, 1985, p. 170), of causes and relationships among thoughts, feelings, and actions (Applebaum, 1973, p. 36), and of reflectivity about psychological processes, relationships, and meanings (Hall, 1992, p. 137), all strongly suggest a psychodynamic bias. This is not to say that individuals who are highly psychologically minded must necessarily be fluent with metapsychological terms or complex theoretical notions. It does, however, suggest that these individuals think in ways that are consistent with psychoanalytic notions such as psychic determinism, early developmental influences on subsequent behavior, the influence of unconscious states, and the role of defenses in everyday life. That these concepts may be considered without the accompanying terminology is evident and has been demonstrated most convincingly by great writers (e.g., Dostoevsky, Lawrence, Proust, Woolf). Furthermore, all clinicians have likely encountered high levels of PM even in individuals with little formal education or artistic talent.

Thus, although we believe PM and a psychodynamic orientation enhance each other, neither guarantees the other. In other words, one can be fluent in psychodynamic jargon but unable to facilitate PM, either in oneself or in patients. Likewise, one can be highly psychologically minded without necessarily adhering to a psychodynamic model of treatment. Furthermore, as we noted, we believe that most mental health professionals, even those who later adopt a nondynamic perspective on clinical issues, have entered the field as a function of their own high levels of PM, that is, as a result of much time spent introspecting and reflecting on the meaning of intrapsychic and interpersonal phenomena. Given these assumptions, it should be clear that our discussion of PM in therapists is influenced by this psychodynamic bias, that is, by the assumption that to be truly psychologically minded, one needs to be attuned to the dynamics of inner life.

THE BENEFITS

As noted previously by Farber (1983b, 1985, 1989), to most professionals within the mental health community, PM is a highly desirable trait. It is seen as facilitating insight into oneself and others, as improving the quality and furthering the satisfaction of psychotherapeutic work, as greatly enhancing interpersonal relations, and as the mechanism by which the subtlety and nuances of life are understood and appreciated. It is used pleasurably and playfully to understand and appreciate cultural, historical, artistic, and personal events. Here is one therapist's account of how being psychologically minded has affected various aspects of his life:

> My friendships have deepened considerably in the past few years as my ability to understand and appreciate others' lives has grown. I have been told by friends that I have become more sensitive, more compassionate, and more genuinely forgiving. I also sense that I have become more critical. That is, I am able more easily to see the flaws in myself and others and the posturing in which we all engage—but I am no longer as harsh in my response to these observations.
>
> Being with a group of highly psychologically minded people is enormously powerful—a heady mixture of playfulness, competitiveness, and eroticism. It is a feeling of vitality, of being aware of primitive fantasies and possibilities, of speaking, thinking, and feeling on a level that is both thrilling and frightening. When it is working—when I sense that several people in the room, including me, are talking this language—it is a feeling of communion like no other. I feel proud that I am in a rare and special place and glad that I have learned the language.

Our sense, then, is that virtually all therapists thoroughly enjoy, appreciate, and even delight in their ability to use their PM in a creative and helpful manner. Their intelligence is often accented by their psychological understanding in ways that further their own self-esteem. Thinking psychologically is what therapists do best—and that many others respect, envy, or attempt to emulate this ability serves to reinforce its specialness. Moreover, therapists who are highly psychologically minded, able to articulate complex, dynamic formulations of a patient's pathology or patient–therapist relationship, are often highly respected by their peers and in great demand as supervisors and teachers.

In addition, increased PM is what psychotherapists often seek to promote in patients as a means of increasing their self-awareness and self-acceptance. Insight or dynamically oriented therapists of all persuasions (from classical analysts to contemporary practitioners of relationally oriented dynamic therapy) prefer their patients to be at least moderately psychologically minded prior to treatment, assume this trait will facilitate treatment (Conte et al., 1990; McCallum & Piper, 1990) and expect, too, that treatment will facilitate the capacity to be psychologically minded. In fact, some theorists (e.g., Blatt & Behrends, 1987; Loewald, 1960) believe that therapeutic benefit is directly linked to patients' ability to internalize the therapist's analytic functions and abilities. Preliminary empirical validation of this assumption has been offered by Geller and Farber (1993) who found that both during therapy and following termination, most patients—especially those who view their therapy as successful—evoke mental representations of therapy and their therapist that enable them to continue working on their problems in the ways they did with their therapist during their sessions.

Perhaps most importantly, PM is seen as the mechanism by which life's problems are best grasped and ultimately mastered. To understand the etiology, meaning, defensive purpose and adaptive function of behavior and feelings is to free oneself from the destructive potential of unworked-through events. This was Freud's message: "Where id was there shall ego be" (1933/1961, p. 80). Although the metapsychology he developed has been criticized and modified over the years, his basic assumption—that insight leads to cure—remains the fundamental principle of dynamic therapies as well as the foundation and implicit rationale for the cultivation of PM in therapists and their patients.

Thus, for the most part, excepting perhaps those who adhere to a strict behavioral orientation, therapists strive to make their patients more psychologically minded. In both implicit and explicit ways, therapists attempt to replace patients' previously held perspectives and thinking (their *assumptive worlds* in Frank's [1973] terminology) with a new, more psychologically-minded way of seeing the world. On the most basic level, this shift often occurs as patients reformulate their assumptions regarding the origins of their problems from those emphasizing fate and luck to those emphasizing inner dynamics and persistent patterns of behavior. Patients learn to take responsibility for their lives and a new way of understanding why they (and others) think, feel, and behave as they do. They learn, in Shakespeare's words (*Julius Caesar,* act 1, sc. 2), that the "fault...is not in the stars" but in themselves. They learn to adopt a psychologically minded way of framing the world and its events.

Clearly, therapists are models for this perspective. Most have been in therapy for extended periods of their lives: Pope and Tabachnick (1994) reported a median duration of 4 years in therapy among the 398 therapists responding to their survey. Many live their lives in ways that reflect their belief in the power and clarity of their psychological mindedness. And, of course, in their clinical interactions with patients (e.g., through interpretations or clarifications) they actively encourage their patients to adopt this perspective.

With these considerations in mind, PM might well be regarded as an exclusively positive trait, a way of thinking that therapists should attempt to hone (in themselves and their patients) to a maximum degree. As noted elsewhere (Farber, 1989), this perspective implies that PM cannot occur excessively and does not have dysfunctional consequences even in individuals who possess this trait in great measure. This perspective also suggests that only the most neurotic, highly defended individuals would choose "not to know," that is, would prefer ignorance to self-knowledge or impulsivity to reflectivity. As the prolific diarist and sometimes psychoanalyst, Anais Nin (1967) observed, "the discovery of significance is what deepens and embellishes experience" (p. 8). Moreover, this emphasis on the benefits of PM is consistent with the fact that most therapists value greatly their ability to be sensitive to their inner workings and those of others, and with their belief that, if this sensitivity, this high level of PM, affords a more ironic, deconstructive, and even tragic view of life that these are small prices to pay for the value received. In fact, a great many highly psychologically-minded therapists might well contend that these are not costs at all—that seeing the world in more tragic terms, for example, adds a further layer of meaning to life.

THE COSTS

Arguably, a high level of PM exacts a rather steep price, one that most individuals so afflicted cannot or will not see. More specifically, it has been posited that intensive and constant examination of one's (or another's) inner life dampens emotional experiences, impedes spontaneity, and leads to intellectualization, painful self-consciousness, egotism, and interpersonal distance (Farber, 1983b, 1989).

This view is supported by a disparate group of social scientists and writers. Sharaf (1960), for example, one of the early researchers in the area of PM (which he studied under the rubric of "intraception"), felt that intense and frequent examination of feelings could "hamper emotional experiences" (p. 23). Similarly, Burton (1972), in chronicling the lives of several prominent therapists, suggested that "the ultimately self-conscious person is apt to become paralyzed by his inner vision" (p. 24). The novelist Joyce Carol Oates (1970, p. 51) wrote that the worship of self-consciousness, that is, of constant analysis, is a "contemporary tragedy" and John Updike (1983, p. 3), in his commentary on Kafka's torturous life, suggested that Kafka had "a sensitivity acute beyond usefulness." Robert Waller (1992), in the contemporary bestseller, *The Bridges of Madison County,* has his protagonist remark: "Analysis destroys wholes. Some things, magic things are meant to stay whole. If you look at their pieces, they go away" (p. 39). And the theme of Peter Shaffer's (1974) play, *Equus,* is that in our insatiable desire to understand we may sometimes lose an essential quality of ourselves—passion perhaps, an ineffable spiritedness. In this drama, a British psychiatrist agonizes over whether to cure an adolescent boy who has tortured and blinded six horses. Wherefore the agony? Because he feels the cure would diminish greatly the boy's capacity for passion—a capacity the psychiatrist himself has long since lost and now desperately envies.

Some therapists become so "stuck" in their psychological mindedness that their "whole lives become a source of material for interpretation" (Rieff, 1959, p. 102). The potential for therapists to become pervasively psychologically-minded, to live in a "unidimensional world defined in terms of psychodynamic language" (Henry et al., 1973, p. 217), to interpret rather than react to events, and to view not only patients from a therapeutic perspective but everyone and everything else as well, has been commented upon by a number of authors (e.g., Farber, 1983b, 1985, 1989; Guy, 1987; Henry et al., 1973; Paul, 1973; Rose, 1974). Farber (1985) described some manifestations of this process:

> Relationships with relatives become understood in terms of transferential difficulties, problems with classmates are analyzed in terms of group process, unfriendly neighbors are seen as manifesting borderline tendencies, and difficulties in accepting supervisory input are attributed to unresolved oedipal issues. It is not just the language that changes; a new way of thinking has taken shape. (p. 173)

For some individuals, then, the tendency to adopt a psychotherapeutic perspective becomes a reflexive reaction to virtually all professional and personal events—a familiar, predictable, and organized system of ordering the world. The question that may be raised, though, is "What's the problem?" If PM is a gratifying and effective strategy for dealing with the world, why not use it as often as possible? The answer, in short, is that for some individuals who become "interminable analysts," a high degree of PM tends to covary with detachment and emotional neutrality; too often their analytic thinking, their psychological mindedness, becomes a way of avoiding emotionally meaningful interactions (Becker, 1973; Rose, 1974). "Stop using psychology and start relating to me with real feelings" is a complaint often heard in the treatment of couples where one partner is a therapist. As Guy (1987) noted: "Few spouses willingly endure unrestrained psychological-mindedness, constant interpretations and unceasing analysis on the part of their therapist mate" (p. 118). Similarly, children of therapists may react negatively if their behavior is incessantly analyzed and processed (Guy, 1987; Maeder, 1989).

According to Burton (1972), the separateness created by high levels of PM is often used in the service of creativity and professional productiveness. Therapists' PM, or in Burton's words, their ability to create inner dialogues with parts of themselves, may lead to loneliness, but is an essential aspect of their feeling special. Nevertheless, it is clear that this stance, even if viewed by therapists as necessary to their work and integral to their sense of self, may be distressing to friends or family members, a means by which therapists maintain too great a distance between themselves and intimate others.

Ideally, PM is used as a means to truly understand, to go beyond the obvious and manifest to the subtle and underlying dimensions of human behavior. Skilled mental health professionals are often able to enhance their own and their patients' lives through the exercise of this facility. It is ironic, then, that some mental health professionals seem particularly adept at using PM in a defensive fashion to ward off the anxiety of experiencing or expressing strong affect.

For example, an advanced doctoral student in psychology begins to explain to her therapist why she has been unable to complete her dissertation. Her mother, it seems, has been ill, which has engendered considerable transferential material within therapy, and furthermore, outdoing her mother professionally raises all sorts of oedipal issues. The therapist points out to the patient the extent to which she uses psychological concepts to push away feelings; only after much prodding does the patient acknowledge the considerable amount of shame and guilt she is experiencing.

The use of PM by a therapist to defensively ward off anxiety about a patient is illustrated by the following anecdote: The presenter at a case conference had just finished an elegant and detailed account of his treatment of a difficult and resistant patient, replete with seemingly brilliant and highly effective interpretations. Asked about his countertransferential feelings in working with this often manipulative borderline patient, the therapist paused and then said that his analytic understanding of the case—awareness that the patient's manipulations were simply a reflection of his disorder and that the patient's anger and acting-out could not be taken personally—allowed him to remain unaffected by these behaviors. The questioner persisted: "You mean when this patient tried to commit suicide it didn't bother you or make you anxious?" At this point, the therapist acknowledged that he did have some difficult moments with this patient, but that he used his awareness of these feelings, in conjunction with an awareness of his own issues, to further the treatment. "If I ever get as detached as this SOB," whispered the questioner to her colleague, "please insist that I go back into treatment."

Not only has a high level of PM in therapists been linked with emotional detachment but it has also been associated with virtually the opposite effect—the tendency to feel too much. Several psychologists (e.g., Levinson et al., 1966; May, 1958; Sharaf, 1960) have suggested that the highly psychologically-minded person, more attuned than others to inner contradictions and dilemmas, is more likely to feel guilty, insecure, or intensely self-conscious. Others, including Guy (1987), Kottler (1986), and Storr (1990), have observed that clinicians' acute awareness of others' painful issues may raise similar issues for these clinicians themselves. Basescu (1977) noted some of these aspects in his poignant and courageous paper on the "anxieties of the analyst":

> [T]he whole issue of disclosing myself in my work as a therapist is one that is shot through with nagging anxieties for me because I wonder what my real intentions are when I answer personal questions or deliberately describe something about myself—an experience, event or feeling—and I wonder about the kind of impact it has on the other person... Am I looking for attention or creating an impression? Am I playing a role? Am I giving in to pressure? Am I cooperating with avoiding something? Am I serving my needs or the other person's?... Am I conveying understanding by describing a similar experience of my own? Am I being reassured by saying, "It's all right for you to just be yourself?" (pp. 159–160)

This perspective emphasizes the frequent inability of highly psychologically-minded individuals to "leave things alone," to stop introspecting, or to accept the possibility that randomness and luck do sometimes play a role in life events. Thoroughly immersed in a model emphasizing the significance of dynamic influences and personal choice, therapists are prone to asking "What role did I play in this event–tragedy–unsuccessful psychotherapy?" even when their role may be quite insignificant. At times, high levels of PM may lead these individuals to the "correct" conclusion that their part in a certain interaction may, in fact, have been trivial; at other times, though, high levels of PM seem to catalyze an almost obsessional need to identify one's own dynamics and influence in situations where one is decidedly a minor player. Similarly, individuals who are highly psychologically minded may be vulnerable to psychological distress—to the burden of feeling flooded by endless possibilities, infinite regresses of feelings and thoughts, and countless variations on psychodynamic themes.

In addition, high levels of PM seem to be related to perceiving life in somber and tragic terms. Appelbaum (1976) noted this tendency in individuals undergoing psychotherapy:

> What does a person characteristically see when his awareness is expanded beyond those restrictions developed to narrow awareness? He sees parts of himself of which he does not approve, which may frighten, humiliate, and disgust him. He sees a life composed of choices, many he thought were never

> his to make, which he had ascribed to other people, society, heredity, or sun spots. He becomes aware that what had seemed to be unchangeable givens were self-imposed restrictions, that he had escaped from freedom while complaining that he had no freedom. He realizes that some of the choices, thus made, cannot be unmade (p. 203).

This perspective on life, this hard-edged vision, may affect all who have undergone long-term therapy, but it may be a particular vulnerability for therapists who, as a group, entered therapy with strong tendencies in this direction.

Another problem with viewing the world in exclusively psychological terms is that at times it is simply wrong—not just less useful, but a truly mistaken perspective. The history of psychology is replete with examples of mental health professionals assuming functional (psychological) causality to disorders we now understand as biologically, neurologically, or genetically derived, including autism, Tourette's syndrome, epilepsy, and stuttering. Schizophrenia and bipolar disorder may soon be definitive additions to the list. This is not to say that these disorders do not have serious psychological sequelae. It is to say, however, that explanations of these disorders that implicate faulty parenting or impaired object relationships may have been unfairly hurtful and injurious to the affected parties. That parents of autistic children were once—and in some quarters are still—blamed for their children's disorder is but the most egregious example of the misapplication by psychotherapists of psychological mindedness.

PSYCHOTHERAPISTS, PERSOAL THERAPY, AND THE FURTHER DEVELOPMENT OF PM

A central aspect of psychotherapists' training is their own psychotherapy, a process that inevitably increases their already high levels of PM. To a great extent, this is a positive development, enabling therapists to become more skilled at understanding themselves and others which, in turn, enables them to derive more pleasure and satisfaction in their personal and professional lives. On the other hand, critics have argued since Freud's time that psychoanalysis encourages too great a degree of introspection or psychological mindedness in both practitioners and patients. Illustrative of this view is Jung's (1933) contention that, as a result of therapy, patients learn much about their internal world (the "hinterlands" of their minds), but do not learn to adapt to the demands of the external world.

Even, however, if we regard such views as exaggerated, we may still legitimately consider the effects of 5 or 10 years of analysis or intensive psychotherapy (often undertaken concomitantly with taking courses and seeing patients) on already highly psychologically-minded individuals. Undoubtedly, for some, this immersion is unilaterally beneficial,affordinggreater wisdom and a greater clarity of vision, an increased ability to make sense of and control one's life, and a greater feeling of relatedness to others. For others, however, their own therapy further exacerbates tendencies to master their feelings at the expense of emotional expression, interpersonal connection, or spontaneity; it may also further narcissism and grandiosity. In addition, Garfield and Bergin (1971) suggested that, although therapy for the therapist was likely to be helpful, it could also interfere with optimal therapist performance if undertaken concurrently with learning to practice therapy. They hypothesized that this situation could occur as a result of therapists' becoming preoccupied with their own personal problems.

Furthermore, despite psychologists' tendency to glorify PM and insight, and to equate the process of becoming psychologically minded with positive therapeutic outcome, the fact is that insight and change are separate phenomena. There are many patients who have become quite psychologically minded after months or years of therapy, yet are still unable to make substantial changes in their behavior. In this regard, the report of the Psychotherapy Research Project of the Menninger Foundation (Wallerstein, 1989) noted that "the most common change in conflicts was increased awareness of them but without resolution of them" (p. 204). Among the 34 patients studied, "resolution of conflict occurred infrequently" (p. 204). For therapists, most of whom enter therapy with high levels of PM, this outcome seems all too common. We have all known therapists, who, as a result of therapy, become increasingly able to define, discuss, and understand their conflicts and those of their patients but who are seemingly as stuck as ever in their own chronic neurotic patterns. In short, although therapy offers substantial benefit to many patients, including those who are therapists themselves, for others it leads to a frustrating examination of issues without any certainty of benefit beyond that of intellectual understanding. Higher levels of PM become both the preferred defense and consolation prize of therapy.

This is not to say that all therapists become this way, nor is it to deny that long-term psychodynamic therapy has primarily beneficial effects. Moreover, the vast majority of therapists—in therapy or not—use their PM selectively: at times employing a psychologically informed understanding of their lives, at other times understanding phenomena or interacting with others in a nonpsychological manner. In fact, many therapists acknowledge that they are at times remarkably unpsychological outside of therapy, missing the meaning of what should have been obvious. Still, as a result of their own long-term therapy and its impact upon their already high levels of PM, at least some therapists, at least some of the time, may evidence ways of thinking and behaving that are seemingly dysfunctional both personally and professionally.

PSYCHOLOGICAL MINDEDNESS AND THE PRACTICE OF PSYCHOTHERAPY

In Eugene O'Neill's (1946/1967) *The Iceman Cometh*, Hickey, a traveling salesman, advises a group of alcoholics to give up their pipe dreams and illusions: You're all just kidding yourselves, he charges. Each of the characters attempts to change, tries to become productive, but each fails and ultimately returns to the previous ways of coping, including drinking and daydreaming. As Applebaum (1976) noted in his trenchant analysis of this drama, Hickey deprives his friends of their illusions by providing them with insight into their self-deceptions. He encourages them to face the anxiety and challenges inherent in change. But they take on tasks beyond their capacities; they suffer and return to the starting point. For them, a little knowledge is a dangerous thing. Only when an equilibrium based on their realistic limitations is reinstated, and they are once more shrouded in self-deception, does life become tolerable again. Still, one character, unable to re-engage his old fantasy, commits suicide.

This is clearly an extreme situation, but it still makes a point. There are those patients who are facing life situations so realistically bleak that a psychological understanding of the condition is beside the point and may only serve to exacerbate the despair. As well, there are those patients who do not want understanding—psychological or otherwise. They simply want relief from pain whether this comes from a prescription bottle, a wine bottle, or a needle. At times, solutions to problems can and must proceed without understanding causation; indeed, denial and illusions often operate in the service of the ego, preserving positive self-evaluations and useful perceptions of control and mastery (Taylor & Brown, 1988). As a particularly bright and perceptive student once asked her supervisor: "Please remind me, why is it that we want to improve everyone's reality testing?"

Many nonpsychodynamic therapies proceed without any attempt at increasing patients' psychological mindedness or insight. Gestalt therapy devalues interpretations and insight, emphasizing instead the nature of feelings in the here-and-now; behavior therapy gives short shrift to feeling states much less their childhood origins; and rational–emotive and cognitive therapies primarily bolster ego defenses, caring little about traditional notions of analytic insight. These therapies offer what many patients want and need. Jung (1933) pointed out that the therapist "may see in the mud-puddle [of the unconscious] a world full of wonders, but to the ordinary man it is something to which he prefers to turn his back" (p. 45). In short, PM is what many therapists admire and perhaps need; however, it may not be what patients want and need. In certain cases, at least, its facilitation in therapy may be inappropriate and even detrimental.

Thus, although the most salient professional effect of PM is its capacity to enhance therapeutic expertise, there is another, less favorable (albeit less common) effect: potential disenchantment with the therapeutic role as a result of too-exclusive reliance on the mutative powers of PM and insight. These elements may well be useful in promoting change but they are unlikely to be sufficient; the active practice of new behaviors or ways of thinking may be necessary (Wachtel, 1987). In addition, a patient's courage—his or her willingness to alter familiar patterns in his or her life despite inner fears and the subtle but often persistent resistance of others—may be important in effecting change. As Wheelis (1958) wrote, "the disillusionment of the analyst... begins with his [sic] awareness of the limited efficacy of insight" (p. 229). For those practicing dynamically oriented psychotherapy, the failure of psychologically oriented insights—either the patient's or therapist's—to result in positive therapeutic changes may engender frustration or even burnout.

RESEARCH

As noted, psychologists and novelists have suggested that highly psychologically-minded individuals are more sensitive and emotionally attuned, but are also more emotionally constricted, interpersonally distant, and vulnerable to psychological distress than are their less psychologically-minded counterparts. Perhaps the most direct effort to empirically investigate some of these links was a study conducted by the senior author of this chapter (Farber, 1989) in which 215 graduate students, mostly in the field of education, served as subjects. The hypothesis tested was that individuals with high levels of PM lack emotional responsiveness and suffer from low self-esteem.

Results suggested that highly psychologically-minded individuals (as measured by the Private Self-Consciousness scale; Fenigstein et al., 1975) are no less emotionally sensitive or expressive than others—at least by self-report. Indeed, on a measure that assesses the extent to which a range of emotions are experienced (the Emotion Scale; Balswick, 1975), the scores suggest that individuals in the highest range of PM more frequently experience a wide range of emotions, including love, happiness, sadness, and hate than do individuals at either a medium or low level of PM, F (2, 197) = 12.65, $p < .0001$; TukeyB at .05 level of significance. On a measure that assesses emotional expression (the Expression of Emotion Scale; Balswick, 1975), the scores of highly psychologically-minded individuals were not significantly different than the scores of less psychologically-minded individuals, F (2, 197) = 1.68, NS.

These findings seem to belie claims that a high level of PM results in emotional impoverishment. On the other hand:

> [T]hat highly psychologically-minded individuals do not appear to be as verbally expressive as they are affectively aware helps explain the depiction of these individuals (for example, psychotherapists) as emotionally distant

> or cold, or as narcissistic and self-involved...Inwardly focused attention seems to facilitate the experience of emotions; however, this heightened awareness does not seem to translate into a proportionate increase in interpersonal, verbal communication of affect...The point is that while highly psychologically-minded individuals are not actually less emotionally responsive than others, in light of their heightened awareness of feelings, they may well appear to be withholding of their feelings to others. (Farber, 1989, p. 215)

A dysfunctional consequence of psychological mindedness did emerge in this study in the area of self-esteem. High PM individuals were significantly more likely than others to have lower scores on the Coopersmith (1967) Self-Esteem Inventory, F (2, 169) = 4.50, $p < .05$; TukeyB at .05 level of significance. The tendency of a psychologically-minded individual to understand behavior in terms of narcissistic needs, instincts, compromises, defenses and the like makes seeing one's flaws easier and makes accepting positive attributes in oneself more difficult. Self-scrutiny invariably involves self-criticism (Levinson et al., 1966; Turner, Scheier, Carver, & Ickes, 1978). As Farber (1989) concluded, "highly psychologically minded individuals are wiser but also sadder" (p. 216).

This 1989 study, though perhaps of heuristic value, did not use therapists as subjects. Two studies have looked at the effects of PM on therapists. The first (Farber, 1983b) was part of a larger investigation of the effects of conducting therapy on therapists. Among other results of his interviews with 60 therapists, Farber found that many considered PM to be a double-edged sword. PM was considered beneficial inasmuch as it provides insight into others (endorsed by 45.3% of the sample) and increases self-awareness (32.1%); however, many also felt that too high a degree of PM could interfere with natural, affectively laden social interactions (42.2%).

The second study, undertaken by the senior author for purposes of this chapter, was focused more directly and comprehensively on the impact of PM on therapists. Members of the New York State Psychological Association were recruited for this study and 199 subjects (111 female, 88 male) participated. Within this sample, 76 subjects identified their theoretical orientation as psychodynamic, 66 as eclectic, 39 as cognitive–behavioral, and 6 as experiential. These therapists were primarily married (N = 151); their mean years of professional experience was 18.5.

These therapists were mailed a four-part self-report questionnaire. The first three questions addressed (a) the extent to which they experienced an increase in their psychological mindedness since beginning therapeutic practice, (b) the extent to which they perceived an optimal level of PM beyond which negative effects might occur, and (c) the extent to which they found themselves trying to confine their PM to professional interactions.

Based on a 7-point Likert-type scale, from 1 (*not at all*) to 7 (*to a great extent*), they did, in fact, report that their PM had increased significantly since they began their practice (M = 5.3); they also believed to a moderate

TABLE 9.1
Therapists' Perceptions of the Effects of their Psychological-Mindedness]

Item	Means and Standard Deviations (N = 199) *M*	*SD*
Friendships		
facilitates friendships	4.6	1.8
interferes with friendships	2.5	1.5
Intimate Relationships (e.g. marriage)		
facilitates intimate relationships	5.1	1.7
interferes with intimate relationships	2.4	1.5
Parenting		
facilitates parenting	5.7	1.4
interferes with parenting	2.0	1.2
Personal Adjustment		
facilitates personal adjustment	6.0	1.3
interferes with personal adjustment	1.7	1.0
Emotional Expressivity		
facilitates emotional expressivity	5.4	1.6
interferes with emotional expressivity	1.9	1.1
Self-esteem		
facilitates self-esteem	5.5	1.5
interferes with self-esteem	1.7	1.1
Playfulness		
facilitates playfulness	4.1	2.1
interferes with playfulness	2.7	1.7
Appreciation of art and culture		
facilitates an appreciation	4.8	2.0
interferes with an appreciation	1.4	0.9
Spontaneity		
facilitates spontaneity	3.9	2.0
interferes with spontaneity	3.0	1.8

Note: Subjects were asked to respond to these items using a 7-point scale where 1 = not at all, 4 = to a moderate extent, 7 = to a great extent.

extent that there is an optimal level of PM ($M = 3.9$) and that they do try to confine PM to professional interactions ($M = 4.2$).

The fourth question solicited therapists' opinions regarding the extent to which they perceived their PM as influencing, both positively and negatively, various aspects of their lives, including friendships, intimate relationships, parenting, personal adjustment, emotional expressivity, self-esteem, playfulness, appreciation of art and culture, and spontaneity. These were the variables that seemed to be noted most consistently in the literature on the effects of PM. As Table 9.1 indicates, as a group, therapists were consistent in their sense that their psychological mindedness is more of a facilitator of these characteristics than it is a hindrance; moreover, they viewed their PM as facilitating at least "to a moderate extent" each of these positive dimensions. PM is seen by these therapists as especially facilitating personal adjustment, self-esteem, parenting skills, and emotional expressivity. Thus, from these therapists' point of view, their psychological mindedness works in a positive direction to enhance important aspects of life, including interpersonal relationships.

Drawing conclusions from the limited research in this area is difficult. Results of studies focusing on the effects of PM in the general population are equivocal, although at least two suppositions have general support: first, that self-scrutiny, a nearly ubiquitous component of PM, leads to self-criticism; and second, that emotional responsiveness does not seem diminished in highly psychologically-minded individuals. Results of studies of PM focusing directly on therapists are also somewhat equivocal: in the first study (Farber, 1983b), in which therapists were interviewed, they seemed inclined to acknowledge both negative and positive aspects of PM; in the current survey study, therapists were far more impressed with the benefits of PM than they were with any possible drawbacks.

Not only are these lines of research limited in terms of both quantity and scope but they are also limited greatly by their reliance on self-report data. It is hardly surprising, for example, that in the current study therapists viewed PM in nearly exclusively positive terms. Cognitive dissonance theory (Festinger, 1957) and common sense suggest that when one relies consistently on a certain way of thinking to order one's personal and professional life, it is, difficult to see the flaws in that perspective or the negative consequences that may accrue as a result. This tendency becomes even greater in the absence of personal contact or indepth questioning. In this regard, too, it is interesting to note that research on the effects of PM that did not use a therapist subject pool (Farber, 1989) indicated that highly psychologically-minded individuals scored lower than others on a self-esteem inventory. By contrast, therapists in the current study perceived no such effect: They believed that their PM facilitated their self-esteem. Of course, therapists might constitute a unique subgroup of highly psychologically-minded individuals, a group that as a consequence of their own training and therapy makes more adaptive use of high levels of PM than those without this background. Nevertheless, in order to provide a more comprehensive understanding of this issue, future research is needed to investigate the perceptions of others (e.g., spouses, children, and friends) regarding the effects of PM on psychotherapists.

PSYCHOLOGICAL MINDEDNESS IN A MIDCAREER THERAPIST

As a practicing psychotherapist for 20 years, I have cultivated my sensitivity to inner states and feelings as part of my professional development. But although this is generally true, it is also too simplistic, for it reflects far too great a split between the professional and personal aspects of my life. Over time, my natural inclination to be psychologically minded transcended the professional side of my life. PM became more than just a skill to be left at the office or a tool to be picked up and put down at will. It became an automatic, integral part of me. Unlike many career pursuits in which a professional skill is applied only to a specific task, it is my person that is the central tool of my work. What began as a deliberate attempt to hone my PM in order to be a more effective therapist is now an inextricable part of who I am and how I live. I identify with Guy's (1987) notion that in psychotherapists the merging of professional and personal lives is a union between a sense of calling and lifestyle.

There have been other changes over the years. Over time, my conscious adherence to the "rules" of psychotherapeutic behavior has undergone a transformation, becoming less volitional, more integrated, more background than foreground. And it is clear to me that I have more firmly adopted a set of values (e.g., belief in the value of insight and understanding, of talking things out with others, of going beyond small talk in personal relationships) that is different from many others and may seem odd or inappropriate to all but like-minded individuals. What felt like obsessive self-analysis and rumination early in my career is less driven and self-conscious now. I am less compelled to attend to the underlying dynamics of every situation. Although still introspective and contemplative, I am more at home with my PM, more genuinely myself. The result is a less calculated, more natural self, one considerably less devoted to technically appropriate technique and less needful in both personal and professional situations of always appearing exceptionally knowledgeable or perceptive. I know—or at least trust—when my insights are appropriate to share and when it is best to stay quiet. I also feel that I am more accepting of others, including patients, friends, and family members. I feel my PM has greatly enhanced my ability to be an empathic and understanding parent. In my practice, I am more tolerant of ambiguity, both my own and my patients'. I have also grown more comfortable with my own spontaneity, trusting in myself to be appropriately empathic, confrontive, interpretive, or silent as the situation dictates. I have even noticed an ability to use my psychological mindedness in a more playful manner.

What are the costs and benefits of my psychological mindeness? On one hand, my understanding of and interest in my own and others' psyches is what allows me to make meaningful and gratifying connections with friends, family, and patients. My perceptions, sensitivity, understanding, and ability to communicate about feelings is invaluable in bridging distance with others. In this way, PM adds layers of meaning to behaviors and brings texture to interactions. And it is through the exercise of my PM that I can access primitive aspects of myself that I might have otherwise denied. Although painful, I find this self-understanding profoundly fulfilling.

On the other hand, the same perspective clearly does become its own culture, complete with its own language, thereby excluding those who do not share its fascination. Thus, having said I am more tolerant, I must also acknowledge that when others don't "get" what I see as obvious, I am still sometimes inpatient or worse still, arrogant. Sometimes, too, my psychological mindedness results in a curious passivity. That is, in my desire to understand others and empathize with their issues, I can fail to take a decisive stand or commit to a plan of action when doing so would be appropriate. Family members sometimes experience my inclination to analyze or interpret behavior as distant, intrusive, or patronizing. When I am angry I sometimes use my psychological understanding of people and situations to diminish, overpower, or exclude others.

Does the constant exercise of PM cause problems? Yes, but so does the architect's constant exercise of his or her aesthetic abilities and the lawyer's constant exercise of his or her analytic abilities. We all see the world in ways consonant with our disposition and training, in ways that necessarily magnify some aspects of life and minimize others. Thus, despite the potential pitfalls, I appreciate the depth and meaning PM has brought to my personal and professional relationships. It has shown me the duality of any human trait, its good and bad sides. It has afforded me intimate personal glimpses of other people's lives, their joys as well as their struggles. And it has allowed me to live a contemplative and emotionally rich life that feels profound and meaningful. Moreover, for me, and I suspect for most others who are highly psychologically minded, the "price" of PM is moot: We have internalized a way of being that insists on a psychological understanding of virtually all events. If the price is occasional excessive anxiety, or disengagement from others, or obsessive rumination, then this is the way it must be. I would have it no other way. I could not imagine, nor wish for, a life without psychological understanding.

CONCLUSION

What may be concluded from these studies, anecdotes, and clinical observations? We suggest the following: (a) that the positive effects of PM (e.g., sensitivity) are much more salient in the lives of therapists than are the negative effects; (b) that the negative effects (e.g., emotional distancing from others) occur to some extent in virtually all therapists, even those with only moderate degrees of PM; (c) that these negative effects of PM should be understood in context, namely, that all adaptations to life, all ways of constructing the world, inevitably enhance some aspects of life at the expense of other aspects; (d) that the emotionally barren and highly intellectualized therapist, imprisoned in a world defined by psychological principles and thinking—although not an entirely extinct species—is considerably rarer than critics of therapy, and of psychoanalysis especially, would suggest; (e) that this caricatured, negative image of the therapist reflects one pole of the longstanding love–hate relationship within this culture with the person of the therapist: a person who is needed and respected but one who is also envied and disparaged for the special expertise he or she is presumed to have; and (f) lastly, that therapists' psychological mindedness has primarily positive consequences even in those individuals with relatively high levels of this traits but, like virtually all characteristics, it can be exercised to a degree that is both self-destructive and disturbing to others.

We close this chapter by posing the following question: If therapists are highly psychologically minded, even outside their offices, and do learn to appreciate the insights that this perspective affords, are they—and their patients—losing the ability to see the world from less tragic, less ironic perspectives? Yeats (1938/1987, p. 3), in his autobiography, wrote that "we begin to live when we have conceived life as tragedy." It is a powerful thought and yet the parallel thought is how quality of life may be compromised when life is conceived only as tragedy. Thinking about origins, drives, instincts, defenses, attachment, and object relations often feels profound, even exhilarating. But if that is all a therapist does, he or she would be wise to listen to the voices of this generation's children: "Get a life." As D. H. Lawrence noted (1921/1960), "the final aim is not to know but to be" (p. 105). In the last analysis, then, self-awareness and psychological mindedness must be a pathway to, rather than the goal of, effective living.

REFERENCES

Applebaum, S. A. (1973). Psychological-mindedness: Word, concept, and essence. *International Journal of Psychoanalysis, 54*, 35–46.

Applebaum, S. A. (1976). The dangerous edge of insight. *Psychotherapy: Theory, Research and Practice, 13*, 202–206.

Balswick, J. O. (1975, August). *The development of an emotion scale and an expression of emotion scale.* Paper presented at the annual meeting of the American Sociological Association, San Francisco, CA.

Basescu, S. (1977). Anxieties in the analyst: An autobiographical account. In K. Frank (Ed.), *The human dimension in psychoanalytic practice* (pp. 153–163). New York: Grune & Stratton.

Becker, E. (1973). *The denial of death.* New York: The Free Press.

Blatt, S. J., & Behrends, R. S. (1987). Internalization, separation-individuation, and the nature of therapeutic action. *International Journal of Psycho-analysis, 68*, 279–297.

Burton, A. (1972). *Twelve therapists.* San Francisco: Jossey-Bass.

Conte, H. R., Plutchik, R., Jung, B. B., Picard, S., Karasu, T. B., & Lotterman, A. (1990). Psychological mindedness as a predictor of psychotherapy outcome: A preliminary report. *Comprehensive Psychiatry, 31*, 426–431.

Coopersmith, S. (1967). *The antecedents of self-esteem.* San Francisco: Freeman.

Dostoevsky, F. (1960). *Notes from the underground.* New York: Anchor. (Original work published 1864).

Farber, B. A. (1983a). Dysfunctional aspects of the psychotherapeutic role. In B. A. Farber (Ed.), *Stress and burnout in the human service professions* (pp. 97–118). New York: Pergamon.

Farber, B. A. (1983b). The effects of psychotherapeutic practice upon psychotherapists. *Psychotherapy: Theory, Research and Practice, 20*, 174–182.

Farber, B. A. (1985). The genesis, development, and implications of psychological-mindedness in psychotherapists. *Psychotherapy, 22*, 170–177.

Farber, B. A. (1989). Psychological-mindedness: Can there be too much of a good thing? *Psychotherapy, 26*, 210–217.

Farber, B. A., Brink, D. C, & Raskin, P. M. (1996). *The psychotherapy of Carl Rogers: Cases and commentary.* New York: Guilford.

Fenigstein, A., Scheier, M., & Buss, A. (1975). Public and private self-consciousness: Assessment and theory. *Journal of Consulting and Clinical Psychology, 43*, 522–527.

Festinger, L. (1957). *A theory of cognitive dissonance.* New York: Row, Peterson.

Frank, J. (1973). *Persuasion and healing* (Rev. ed.). New York: Schocken.

Freud, S. (1961). New introductory lectures on psycho-analysis. In J. Strachey (Ed. & Trans.). *The standard edition of the complete psychological works of Sigmund Freud* (Vol. 21 p. 80). London: Hogarth Press. (Original work published 1933)
Garfield, S. L., & Bergin, A. E. (1971). Personal therapy, outcome and some therapist variables. *Psychotherapy: Theory, Research and Practice, 8*, 251–253.
Geller, J. D., & Farber, B. A. (1993). Factors influencing the process of internalization in psychotherapy. *Psychotherapy Research, 3*, 166–180.
Goldfried, M. R., & Norcross, J. C. (1995). Integrative and eclectic therapies in historical perspective. In B. Bongar & L. E. Beutler (Eds.), *Comprehensive textbook of psychotherapy* (pp. 254–273). New York: Oxford University Press.
Guy, J. D. (1987). *The personal life of the psychotherapist*. New York: Wiley.
Hall, J. A. (1992). Psychological-mindedness: A conceptual model. *American Journal of Psychotherapy, 46*, 131–140.
Henry, W., Sims, J., & Spray, S. L. (1973). *Public and private lives of psychotherapists*. San Francisco: Jossey-Bass.
Jung, C. (1933). *Modern man in search of a soul*. New York: Harvest.
Kottler, J. A. (1986). *On being a therapist*. San Francisco: Jossey-Bass.
Lawrence, D. H. (1960). *Psychoanalysis and the unconscious*. New York: Viking. (Original work published 1921)
Lazarus, A. (1971). Where do behavior therapists take their troubles? *Psychological Reports, 28*, 349–350.
Levinson, D. J., Sharaf, M. R., & Gilbert, D. C. (1966). Intraception: Evolution of a concept. In G. J. DiRenzo (Ed.), *Concepts, theory and explanation in the behavioral sciences* (pp. 116–135). New York: Random House.
Loewald, H. (1960). On the therapeutic action of psychoanalysis. *International Journal of Psychoanalysis, 41*, 1–18.
Maeder, T. (1989). *Children of psychiatrists and other psychotherapists*. New York: Harper & Row.
May, R. (1958). The origins and significance of the existential movement in psychology. In R. May, E. Angel, & H. F. Ellenberger (Eds.), *Existence* (pp. 3–36). New York: Basic Books.
McCallum, M., & Piper, W. E. (1990). The psychological mindedness assessment procedure. *Psychological Assessment: A Journal of Consulting and Clinical Psychology, 2*, 412–418.
Messer, S. B., & Winokur, M. (1980). Some limits to the integration of psychoanalytic and behavior therapy. *American Psychologist, 35*, 818–827.
Nin, A. (1967). *The diary of Anais Nin: Volume Two (1934–1939)*. New York: Harvest.
Oates, J. C. (1970). [Review of the book, *The Perfectionist*]. *New York Times Book Review* (Section 7), pp. 5, 51.
O'Neill, E. (1967). *The iceman cometh: A play*. New York: Vintage. (Original work published 1946)
Paul, I. H. (1973). *Letters to Simon*. New York: International Universities Press.
Pope, K. S., & Tabachnick, B. G. (1994). Therapists as patients: A national survey of psychologists' experiences, problems, and beliefs. *Professional Psychology: Research and Practice, 25*, 247–258.
Reik, T. (1948). *Listening with the third ear*. New York: Farrar, Straus & Giroux.
Rieff, P. (1959). *Freud: The mind of the moralist*. New York: Viking.
Rose, G. (1974). Some issues of analysis as a way of life. Analysis interminable and interminable analysts. *International Review of Psychoanalysis, 1*, 509–515.
Schafer, R. (1976). *A new language for psychoanalysis*. New Haven, CT: Yale University Press.
Shaffer, P. (1974). *Equus*. New York: Avon.
Sharaf, M. R. (1960). *An approach to the theory and measure of intraception*. Unpublished doctoral dissertation, Harvard University, Cambridge, MA.
Storr, A. (1990). *The art of psychotherapy* (2nd ed.). New York: Routledge.
Taylor, S., & Brown, J. (1988). Illusion and well-being: A social psychological perspective on mental health. *Psychological Bulletin, 103*, 193–210.
Turner, R. G., Scheier, M. F., Carver, C. S., & Ickes, W. (1978). Correlates of self-consciousness. *Journal of Personality Assessment, 42*, 285–289.
Updike, J. (1983). Foreword. In N. N. Glazer (Ed.), *Franz Kafka: The complete stories*. New York: Shocken Books.
Wachtel, P. (1987). *Action and insight*. New York: Guilford.

Waller, R. (1992). *The bridges of Madison County*. New York: Warner.
Wallerstein, R. S. (1989). The psychotherapy research project of the Menninger Foundation: An overview. *Journal of Consulting and Clinical Psychology, 57*, 195–205.
Wheelis, A. (1958). *The quest for identity*. New York: Norton.
Wolitzky, D. L., & Reuben, R. (1974). Psychological-Mindedness. *Journal of Clinical Psychology, 30*, 25–30.
Yeats, W. B. (1987). *Autobiography of William Butler Yeats: Consisting of reveries over childhood and youth*. New York: MacMillan. (Original work published 1938)

Chapter 10

Integration of Psychological Mindedness and Related Concepts

Mary McCallum
William E. Piper
University of Alberta

In this chapter we attempt to integrate the various approaches to the study of psychological mindedness and related concepts that are presented in this volume. We organize this effort around seven common themes: development, dimensions, basic characteristics, focus, advantages and disadvantages, current state of knowledge, and future research directions associated with psychological mindedness and related concepts. Table 10.1 presents a descriptive overview of the various authors' work with respect to primary and secondary concepts, person focus, form of the measure, and samples studied. Differences in these formulations are considered under the seven headings.

THE DEVELOPMENT OF PSYCHOLOGICAL MINDEDNESS

Several chapters in this volume contribute to a discussion of the development of psychological mindedness. Hatcher and Hatcher apply a developmental model to psychological mindedness, conceptualizing it as a cognitive ability. As elaborated in chapter 3 they assess psychological mindedness by having children and adolescents respond to questions about two fairy tales and cards like those of the Thematic Apperception Test. The responses are scored on awareness of internal motivation, awareness of simultaneous conflicting motivations, and awareness and use of self-deception.

Hatcher and Hatcher conceptualize the development of psychological mindedness as being genetically predetermined. However, they also acknowledge that psychological mindedness can be fostered or inhibited by

Table 10.1
Major Concepts Presented in This Volume

Author(s)	*Primary Concepts & Definitions*	*Secondary Concepts & Definitions*	*Person Focus*	*Form of Measure*	*Samples Studied*
Conte & Ratto	*Psychological Mindedness:* An ability to be introspective about one's own feelings, thoughts, and behavior as well as an interest in understanding why others feel, think, and behave as they do. An attribute of an individual that presupposes a degree of access to one's feelings that leads, through discussion of one's problems with others, to an ability to acquire insight into the meaning and motivation of one's own and others' thoughts, feelings, and behaviors, and to a capacity for change.	None	Self & others	45-item self-report questionnaire	Mainly psychiatric outpatients; some nonpatient adults
Hatcher & Hatcher	*Psychological Mindedness:* The capacity to achieve psychological understanding of oneself and others, a complex capacity, built on both cognitive and emotional skills.	None	Self & others	4-category rating scale for answers to questions about two fairy tales; 6-category rating scale for answers to questions about stories written to TAT-type cards	Mainly students (children & adolescents)
McCallum & Piper	*Psychological Mindedness:* The ability to identify dynamic (intrapsychic) components and to relate them to a person's difficulties. The ability to reflect several basic assumptions held by psychodynamic therapists concerning human pathology.	None	Others	9-level rating scale for response to a videotape stimulus	Mainly psychiatric outpatients; some nonpatient adults
Taylor & Taylor	*Alexithymia:* Difficulty in identifying and describing feelings; difficulty in distinguishing between feelings and the bodily sensations that accompany emotional arousal; constricted imaginal processes, as evidenced by a paucity of fantasies; and an externally-oriented cognitive style.	None	Self	20-item self-report questionnaire	A diverse set of psychiatric and somatic patients; some university students
Fenigstein	*Self-Consciousness:* A tendency to direct attention and thought toward oneself	*Private Self-Consciousness:* A tendency to be aware of the covert, internal	Self	23-item self-report questionnaire	Mainly college students

		aspects of self, and to be particularly attentive to one's inner thoughts and feelings. *Public Self-Consciousness:* An awareness of an interest in the outwardly displayed manifestations of self, such as appearance, social behavior, and the impression made on others.			
Park & Park	*Personal Intelligence:* Information-processing capacities about psychological characteristics of self and others.	*Intrapersonal Intelligence:* A capacity for access to one's own feeling life—one's range of affects or emotions: the capacity to instantly effect discriminations among these feelings, and, eventually enmesh them in symbolic codes, to draw on them as a means of understanding and guiding one's behavior. *Interpersonal Intelligence:* The ability to notice and make distinctions among other individuals and, in particular, among their moods, temperaments, motivations, and intentions.	Self & others	4-item rating scale	Mainly psychiatric outpatients
Dollinger	*Psychological Mindedness:* The ability to read between the lines of what a person does or says. The ability to search beneath the surface of human behavior as well as the interest in doing so.	None	Others	10-item multiple choice questionnaire	Mainly students (high school and university)
Menna & Cohen	*Social Perspective Taking:* The ability to take others' perspectives. A developing understanding of how human points of view are related and coordinated with one another and not simply what social or psychological information may appear to be like from an alternative individual's perspective as in the construct of role-taking.	None	Self, Other & Social System	4-level rating scale or responses to interpersonal dilemmas presented in an interview	Mainly nonparent children
Farber & Golden	*Psychological Mindedness:* The tendency to look for motives, patterns, and distortions in oneself and others, a trait, consisting of both an affective and an intellectual component.	None	Self & Others	Feningsteins self-report questionnaire for private self-consciousness	Mainly graduate students and therapists

social experience. In addition, they emphasize the role of emotional development in the development of psychological mindedness. They cite Kennedy (1979) , who postulated that psychological mindedness is a two-part process involving the cognitive capacity for understanding oneself and others and the ability to tolerate painful feelings. These two lines of development are interrelated: The child's increased capacity to tolerate feelings both contributes to and is aided by an increased understanding of the meaning and nature of those feelings.

In their work with concepts involving social cognition, Menna and Cohen similarly offer a developmental model of social perspective taking. As described in chapter 8, social perspective taking refers to the cognitive mechanisms that individuals apply to social situations in order to understand them. Social perspective taking is assessed by having children and adolescents respond to dilemmas concerning conflicts with peers and authority figures. The responses are scored according to three dimensions: a structural level, functional steps, and an interpersonal orientation. The structural level dimension refers to a developmental continuum toward increasing differentiation and integration. Functional steps refer to the child's problem-solving approach, and the interpersonal orientation refers to who accommodates to whom in the child's solution.

Support for their developmental model is provided by data indicating that in cases of developmental delays, the children's responses continue to reflect a progression through the same stages and in the same sequence. Further evidence is provided by data indicating that children's performance improves as they grow older: that is, older children can focus on more than one perspective at the same time. The authors attribute improved performance among older children to maturational factors, experiential knowledge, and improved attentional capacities.

Menna and Cohen's findings are consistent with the work of Dollinger. As elaborated in chapter 7, Dollinger finds that psychological mindedness, operationalized as the ability to identify defense mechanisms reflected in stories, is positively related to age and to scores on a measure of perspective taking. Furthermore, given that Dollinger later operationalized "sagacity" as a sustained attention task, his results are consistent with Menna and Cohen's belief that improved attentional capacities contribute to improved social perspective taking scores among older children.

In addition to disruptions in social perspective-taking attributable to developmental delays, Menna and Cohen believe that perspective taking skills depend, in part, on the kind of social experiences the person has had. They also emphasize the influence of the interaction of genetic and environmental factors on the development of social perspective taking. Specifically, they discuss the association between object relations, or the relationships with people in their lives, and social perspective taking. They note that despite heightened capabilities in the area of complex social cognition, patients with borderline personality disorder (BPD) experience remarkably dysfunctional relationships. The authors cite Westen, Lohr, Silk, Gold, and Kerber (1990), who discussed the discrepancy between BPD patients' potential for healthy relationships, as reflected in high scores on tasks of cognitive complexity, and their actual relationship history, which tended to be pathological. Westen et al. (1990) interpreted this discrepancy as reflecting an interference from motivational and defensive processes. Specifically, they believed that for patients with BPD, those processes are characterized by a tendency to perceive their object world as hostile. That perception interfered with the application of their cognitive skills to actual relationships. Generalizing that discrepancy to social perspective taking, Menna and Cohen offer a compelling explanation for cases where children's scores, especially high scores, are not reflected in their actual social behavior and adjustment. If such cases exist, the discrepancy may reflect the influence of personality factors, such as object relations, in the mediation of social reasoning and actual behavior.

Their discussion is consistent with the ideas of Park and Park, who believe that BPD is a function of being innately gifted with respect to personal intelligence and being psychologically abused, probably because of that same gift. As elaborated in chapter 6, personal intelligence refers to information-processing capacities regarding the psychological characteristics of the self and others. Park and Park argue that the tenacity of personal intelligence in patients with BPD, despite its negative consequences for them, supports the idea that it is genetically based.

Park and Park recommend that personal intelligence be viewed as an exceptional inborn talent. Although they acknowledge that personal intelligence may be vulnerable to or influenced by cultural and caregiver factors, they emphasize the evolutionary advantage of personal intelligence and consider it to be a subset of social intelligence like language and symbol formation. Its evolutionary advantage is based on its relationship to empathy whereby human beings developed an altruistic response to others eliciting reciprocity and ensuring survival. Hence, defective personal intelligence is viewed as reflecting a defect in the genetically determined structures responsible for personal intelligence.

Nevertheless, the idea that the development of personal intelligence is contingent on the interaction of genetic and environmental factors is reflected in their notion of a critical period for personal intelligence. Personal intelligence must be susceptible to interpersonal and cultural influences, for its development is much like the development of language by Chomsky (1975), Park and Park argue. After listening to many examples, the child begins to induce the rules of grammar, which he or she can then apply to as yet nonverbalized ideas of his or her own while expanding his or her understanding of the language. So too, by observing others and oneself, the child begins to develop a theory of the mind, fits new information into that developing theory, and continually revises the theory. If this process of developing a theory of the mind is disrupted or compromised, the effect may be irreversible.

Taylor and Taylor also suggest there may be a critical period for developing psychological mindedness. If the opportunity is missed, it is forever lost. They base that suggestion on the finding that alexithymia tends to be rather intractable among adults. As described in chapter 4, alexithymia is presented as the obverse of psychological mindedness and reflects an impairment in the processing of emotional stimuli. Their hypothesized critical period is consistent with findings that alexithymic families do not teach or allow each other to discuss their feelings. In addition, the finding that alexithymia is related to somatization, substance use, eating disorders, and posttraumatic stress disorder, suggests that because these patients did not learn how to identify and verbalize their feelings, emotional conflict is rechannelled elsewhere. Taylor and Taylor propose a deficit model whereby alexithymia is believed to reflect an independent route of development characterized by impaired emotional functioning. Their proposal is in contrast to a psychodynamic conflict model whereby alexithymia is believed to reflect arrested development or regression to a less mature way of functioning.

Rather than assuming there is a primacy of nature or nurture in the development of psychological mindedness and related concepts, we believe that it is advantageous to remain open to the likelihood of an interaction between the two. A developmental delay can interfere with positive social experiences, which can further interrupt developmental progress. Hence, those with fewer skills engage in fewer positive experiences, which compounds the problem in that the skills do not have the opportunity to develop. A genetic weakness may be reinforced and exacerbated by negative social experiences. In the case of patients with BPD, we suggest that whether or not there is an inborn deficit or inborn gift, consistent exposure to a pattern of significantly negative social experiences inevitably disrupts their social, emotional, and psychological development. The development of personal intelligence or social cognition among patients with BPD may reflect their attempt to identify and anticipate the moods of those in their environment in order to avoid even more frequent incidents of abuse. We believe that negative social experiences may disrupt, pervert, delay, or accelerate the social, emotional, and psychological development of children with or without a genetic abnormality.

UNIDIMENSIONALITY OR MULTIDIMENSIONALITY OF PSYCHOLOGICAL MINDEDNESS

The authors in this volume differ on whether psychological mindedness is conceptualized as a single concept or as a set of related concepts. In our own attempts to predict patients' response to psychodynamic psychotherapies, we conceptualized psychological mindedness as only one of many important predictor and process variables that interact to determine whether a patient will remain, work, and benefit from therapy. Consequently, we chose to operationalize psychological mindedness as a narrowly defined construct. Our scale, the Psychological Mindedness Assessment Procedure (PMAP), consists of a hierarchy whose scoring criteria reflect basic assumptions of psychodynamic theory. These basic assumptions include psychic determinism, internal conflict or ambivalence, and defense mechanisms. The scale's higher levels incorporate criteria from the lower levels such that each level becomes more comprehensive and complex in its focus. However, it could be argued that each level of our scale reflects a distinct construct. For example, the identification of a defensive process, the criterion for scoring at the higher levels of the scale may not necessarily presuppose the identification of conflict, the criterion for scoring at the middle level of the scale.

The scale developed by Hatcher and Hatcher reflects three of the same basic assumptions of analytic theory incorporated in the PMAP, that is, psychic determinism, conflict, and defense. In contrast to our work, however, these authors present these concepts as distinct lines of development rather than as a hierarchy. There are no empirical data to help clarify whether these concepts build on each other, as we believe, or whether they represent distinct lines of development as Hatcher and Hatcher believe.

Dollinger's early research focused on one of the same three concepts mentioned here, that is, defense. As described in chapter 7, Dollinger and McGuire operationalized "defense understanding" as the ability (of children) to explain the motivations of characters in stories as reflected in responses that tie together affect, behavior, and the situation. Dollinger's subsequent research also investigated subjects' ability to see through defenses. In that line of research, he focused on the Word Association Implications Test (WAIT).

The WAIT assesses the ability of adults to "read between the lines" of what another says as reflected in the correct identification of a(n actor–) thief using the thief's responses to a word association test. Judgments concerning the subject's ability to read between the lines are based on his or her correct or incorrect identification of the thief. Dollinger attempted to identify components of that ability. The components included sagacity, acumen, empathy, and game strategy. These components are presented as internal aspects of the ability to see through the thief's word associations in determining his or her culpability. In addition, the components appear to be theoretically related to psychological mindedness. However, we suggest that the components may represent separate variables. The problem with defining a psychological concept in terms of other psychological concepts is that the approach to assessment often becomes indirect and diffused.

Park and Park experienced a similar difficulty in operationalizing personal intelligence. As elaborated in chapter 6, and summarized in Table 10.1,

Park and Park developed a scale that faithfully reflects the definition of personal intelligence offered by Gardner (1983). Items on their scale encompass the two types of personal intelligence (intrapersonal and interpersonal) as well as the concepts believed to be associated with them. The scale's four items are:

1. Intense preoccupation with or talented access to one's feelings;
2. intense preoccupation with or sense of the feelings of others;
3. three perceptive intuitions or insights about others;
4a. capability of empathic concern for important others; and
4b. grandiosity, devaluation, and envy are not pervasive.

Accordingly, the first three items attempt to detect perceptual competence. In addition, the authors include an assessment of a preoccupation with using this competence. This inclusion reflects their belief that personal intelligence is genetically determined. They also include an item to detect empathy—(4a). Finally, they include an assessment of low level grandiosity—(4b). It is not clear whether these additional concepts are considered to be a reflection of personal intelligence or independent concepts that may be associated with it. In either case, the concept of interest becomes rather diffused and complex.

Sometimes what is conceived as a unitary concept changes as a function of research findings. As elaborated in chapter 5, the findings of Fenigstein consistently indicated that the supposed global concept of self-consciousness is actually composed of two distinct components, one private and one public. What began as a unidimensional concept evolved into a multidimensional concept as dictated by the data. Given that the two concepts were found to be independent, it followed that there could be a discrepancy between someone's public and private selves. Identifying such a discrepancy is related to the previous discussion on the role of identifying defensive processes when operationalizing psychological mindedness. Being able to distinguish between apparent versus real motives suggests being able to identify a defensive process. Rather than referring to concepts such as defense or self-deception, however, Fenigstein refers to concepts such as impression management. In other words, Fenigstein is interested in the distinction between another's real versus apparent motives.

The concept of social perspective taking is presented as the most multidimensional of all the concepts in this volume. Menna and Cohen conceptualize social perspective taking as encompassing three dimensions: structural level, functional steps, and interpersonal orientation. There are four structural levels: egocentric and undifferentiated, subjective and unilateral, self-reflective and reciprocal, and third person and mutual. There are four sequential problem-solving steps: (a) defining the problem, (b) generating alternative strategies, (c) selecting and implementing a specific strategy, and (d) evaluating outcomes. There are three interpersonalorientations:self-transforming,other-transforming,andcollaborative. It is not clear whether these are subcomponents of social perspective taking or whether they represent distinct skills.

Ambiguity concerning whether psychological mindedness is a unidimensional versus multidimensional construct is reflected in the work presented throughout this volume. In addition, we believe it is contradictory to conceptualize a scale as being both multidimensional and internally consistent. For example, in the case of the Psychological Mindedness Scale (PM Scale), Conte and Ratto report an alpha coefficient of .87. An alpha this size may create the impression that the items are homogeneous, that is, highly intracorrelated, and that the items represent one concept or factor. However, a factor analysis conducted on the scale's items yielded some 14 factors. Because no factor after Factor 5 had more than two items with a factor loading equal to or greater than .40, a five factor solution was accepted. Those five factors consist of: (I) avoidance of insight and reluctance to discuss one's problems; (II) openness to new ideas and capacity for change; (III) access to one's feelings; (IV) insight through discussing one's problems with others; and (V) interest in the meaning and motivation of one's own behavior and that of others. The number of factors revealed by the principal components analysis suggests that the items are not highly intracorrelated. As Briggs and Cheek (1986) explained, a high alpha coefficient does not necessarily indicate that items are highly intracorrelated, because it is sensitive to other characteristics such as the number of items. Factors derived from factor analyses are often correlated with one another when applied to a particular data set.

Similarly, despite reporting an alpha coefficient of .81 for their (revised) Toronto Alexithymia Scale (TAS–20), Taylor and Taylor conceptualize the concept of alexithymia as being multifaceted and comprised of three independent factors: (I) difficulty identifying feelings and distinguishing them from bodily sensations that accompany emotional arousal; (II) difficulty describing feelings to others; and (III) externally oriented thinking. However, as with their original scale, they report that the first two factors are highly correlated. In reality, for both scales, there is probably a considerable range of item intracorrelations with an average intracorrelation of moderate size. Thus, instruments such as the PM Scale or the TAS–20 are in all likelihood neither unidimensional nor multidimensional in the extreme sense. This fairly common state of affairs creates difficulty in understanding and conceptualizing concepts such as psychological mindedness. Moreover, by including other variables, such as motivation or positive response to interpretation in the definition, we believe that the construct, becomes diluted and perhaps confounded.

BASIC CHARACTERISTICS OF PSYCHOLOGICAL MINDEDNESS AND RELATED CONCEPTS

Stability

Implicit in many of the ideas discussed concerning the development of psychological mindedness and related concepts is the assumption that psychological mindedness is a skill or ability tending to be relatively stable after a person reaches adulthood. That belief is reflected in the work of Conte and Ratto (chap. 1). Their scale's high test–retest reliability reflects the stability of psychological mindedness as operationalized by them. Results of our investigations with the PMAP (chap. 2) also suggest that psychological mindedness tends to be a stable characteristic. Although manifestations of the ability can be influenced by motivational factors, psychological mindedness has not been modifiable even by participation in intensive psychodynamic psychotherapies! Taylor and Taylor believe that alexithymia is a stable personality trait. Dollinger implies the stability of his concept of sagacity when he concludes that it cannot be modified by training.

Conversely, Menna and Cohen believe that although social perspective taking is acquired in early childhood, it continues to be differentiated and integrated throughout life. They also find that children improve on their measure of social perspective taking following clinical and school interventions. Unfortunately, they do not report whether an improved score translates into improved behavior and adjustment. We suspect that the child's motivation may mediate the application of those skills. The influence of motivation is an important idea to consider. We see the acquisition of the ability to be psychologically minded as separate from the motivation to explore or display that ability.

In contrast to our viewpoint, Conte and Ratto incorporate items assessing motivation into their psychological mindedness scale. Although most authors suggest that motivation can mediate the display of psychological mindedness, Fenigstein (chapter 5) argues that self attention is an interest that stems from wanting to distinguish between real and apparent motives. He continues by stating that psychological mindedness refers to a preference, rather than an ability.... We suggest that in many instances interest and ability tend to covary; we become interested in activities at which we are skilled and bored with activities at which we are unskilled. However, we believe that no amount of interest or motivation can compensate for a lack of skill.

The stability of the concept of psychological mindedness has implications for training psychodynamic therapists. In chapter 9, Farber and Golden depict the experience of a graduate student being exposed to a psychodynamic world. It is unclear whether such exposure actually increases the student's level of psychological mindedness or whether it merely provides him or her with new insights about psychodynamic processes and theories. The distinction we are making is between the process of using psychological mindedness versus the outcome of that process in terms of acquiring insight. A related question is whether the process associated with psychological mindedness is a means to an end or an end to itself. That question is addressed in the following subsection.

A Means or an End. In their discussion of the advantages and disadvantages of being psychologically minded, Farber and Golden (chap. 9) phrase the question of whether psychological mindedness is a path or a goal. The process by which the patient attempts to understand his or her problems is what we refer to as evidence of psychological mindedness. The process is conceptualized, therefore, as a manifestation or a reflection of an underlying cognitive structure. When the structure is applied to information, the application is reflected in a process whereby the patient considers and categorizes information. That process eventually results in an outcome of some kind, usually insight. Let us review the various definitions of psychological mindedness and related concepts as presented in this volume and as summarized in Table 10.1. We emphasize the parts of the definitions that support our contention that psychological mindedness tends to be identified with a *process* reflecting a *structure* leading to an outcome.

Conte and Ratto's (chap. 1) definition of psychological mindedness includes the idea that it is "an *attribute* of an individual...*that leads,* through discussion of one's problems with others, to an ability to acquire *insight*...." (p. 21). Hatcher and Hatcher (chap. 3) define psychological mindedness as "the *capacity to achieve* psychological *understanding*...." (p. 66). We define psychological mindedness as the *ability to identify* dynamic (intrapsychic) components and to relate them to a person's difficulties (p. 28).

It is important to note that our definition of psychological mindedness is distinct from our definition of psychodynamic work. We conceptualize psychological mindedness as an ability to identify intrapsychic phenomena and relate them to a person's difficulties. We conceptualize psychodynamic work as the application of that ability to patients' problems in a group therapy situation. Specifically, it is defined as an attempt to understand the problems of one or more members of the group, or the group as a whole, in terms of conflict among dynamic components. Accordingly, we operationalize psychological mindedness as a process whereby subjects' responses to a videotape of simulated patient disclosures are rated according to their identification of intrapsychic components such as wishes, fears, defensive processes. We operationalize psychodynamic work as a process whereby patients' responses to group therapy patients' disclosures are rated according to their identification of intrapsychic components.

Dollinger (chap. 7) defines psychological mindedness as "the *ability to read* between the lines of what a person does or says; the *ability to search* beneath the surface of human behavior...." (p. 169). Finally, Farber and Golden define psychological mindedness as "the tendency to look for motives, patterns, and distortions in oneself and others..." (p. 212).

Regarding the concepts related to psychological mindedness, the emphasis on process is also present. Taylor and Taylor (chap. 4) define alexithymia as "a difficulty in *identifying and describing* feelings; a difficulty in *distinguishing* between feelings and bodily sensations...." (p. 79). Fenigstein (chap. 5) defines self-consciousness as "a tendency to *direct* attention and thought toward oneself" (p. 105).

Park and Park define personal intelligence as "information-processing capacities about psychological characteristics of self and others" (p. 133). Finally, Menna and Cohen (chap. 8) define social perspective taking as "the ability to take others' perspective" (p. 190).

Clearly, psychological mindedness and concepts relating to it are repeatedly conceptualized as a means to an end versus an end to itself. Because we consider adjustment, rather than psychological mindedness, as a goal or an end, psychological mindedness is not regarded as an index of adjustment. Our repeated finding that psychological mindedness, as assessed by the PMAP, is not significantly associated with (pretherapy) measures of psychiatric symptomatology or psychological distress supports the independence of psychological mindedness and mental health. Even the most psychologically minded person can be profoundly disturbed. Rather than representing a treatment goal (outcome criterion), we contend that psychological mindedness should be viewed as a useful tool by which one can engage in a psychodynamically oriented therapeutic process to arrive at a beneficial outcome.

Let us consider some analogous examples that involve other approaches to therapy. Although recording incremental fear responses to phobic stimuli is a method by which one engages in behavior therapy, recordkeeping is not an indicator of mental health in and of itself. Although free association is a method by which one engages in psychoanalysis, free association is not an indicator of mental health. Although psychological mindedness facilitates a method by which one engages in psychodynamic psychotherapy, it is not an indicator of mental health. Conte and Ratto (chap. 1) concur with this point and suggest that, similar to ego strength, psychological mindedness may represent an intervening variable between certain predictor variables and therapy outcome.

If psychological mindedness provides the means or the path, then insight is the end or the goal. In the same vein, Fenigstein (chap. 5) argues that attention to the self does not necessarily equal an understanding of the self. He argues that self-focused attention, directed toward past or present psychological events, does not necessarily facilitate accurate insight. He interprets his data as suggesting that thinking about the self can result in a biasing of mental judgments, and a decrease in the validity or accuracy of self-predictions. He cautions that when a psychologically minded patient believes and accepts a therapist's psychodynamic interpretation of his or her problems, that acceptance may only reflect patient conformity rather than a meeting of minds. Fenigstein's argument tends to question the validity of any insight, including those based on psychodynamic theory. His position concerns the issue of whether one can distinguish between absolute or objective reality and one's subjective perception of reality. This issue is addressed in the next subsection.

Objective Versus Subjective Reality. We believe Fenigstein raises a fundamental question relating to epistemology: How do we know what we know is valid? It is an intriguing question. For example, if I believe I am sad, how accurate is that belief? If I believe I am sad because my father died, how accurate is that insight? The situation becomes even more difficult if we include the concept of self-deception. For example, how does a recently divorced woman determine whether her new suitor is boring or that she holds that opinion because she is afraid of being hurt again, or whether both appraisals are accurate? One problem associated with determining the validity of psychological phenomena is that they can seem valid one moment but invalid the next. The fact that the perception of psychological phenomena shifts need not make the perception inaccurate or invalid. That the perception of psychological phenomena can be distorted by defensive processes is one of the reasons that people utilize psychological mindedness in an attempt to know themselves better. It is one of the reasons why highly psychologically minded people seek therapy, given that they are unable to bypass their own defenses to gain insight on their own.

Let us consider the following example. A patient reports that his mother never loved him. When he confronts his mother regarding her neglect, she insists that she does indeed love him. Which belief is valid? In working with the material, the therapist accepts that the patient never felt loved. The epistemological question is whether the patient is accurately labelling the sensation he is feeling as one of being unloved. The therapist looks for inconsistencies and finding none, accepts the patient's perception of never feeling loved as "valid" in that it is how he really feels. The therapist invites the patient to explore this feeling and its role in leading to all kinds of negative consequences for him, such as depression, avoidance of intimacy, and so forth. The therapist's task is to understand the patient's point of view, to challenge it, to offer alternative points of view, and most importantly to impress upon the patient that his point of view is subjective and not an absolute truth as such. The patient may never know how his mother truly feels about him. However, one goal of his therapy might be to realize that whether his mother loved him or not, he felt that she did not convey love in a way that was recognizable to him. Furthermore, the patient might benefit from realizing that this feeling of being unloved has led to many problems for him. The challenge for the patient, therefore, is to diminish the negative impact that his perception of his mother has had on him.

The distinction we are making is between objective and subjective truth and is consistent with the work of Rosen. Rosen (1977) distinguished between two types of truth statements, causal propositions and entailment propositions. The former characterize physics and can be subjected to the usual experimental–statistical methods of validation for scientific hypotheses. Conversely, entailment propositions characterize symbolic or historical events. They are statements about meaning whose truth can only be tested by logical analysis. Although causal propositions are interested in effects, entailment propositions are interested in meanings. To illustrate the distinction between cause and effect versus meaning, Rosen (1977) reviewed the revision of Freud's seduction theory. The original theory postulated that adult hysteria was caused by childhood sexual abuse. Further patient disclosure convinced Freud that much of the childhood abuse had taken place in fantasy. The theory was modified to reflect the idea that the meaning of events and of the fantasies associated with them are more important in understanding symptom formation than are the events themselves. In other words, it is the intrinsic meaning of events to the patient that determines their impact rather than the events themselves.

The Person Focus of the Measures

That the acquisition of self-knowledge can be impeded by one's own defensive processes poses a problem for these measures of psychological mindedness focusing on the self as opposed to others. As summarized in Table 10.1, there are differences among the measures concerning their person focus. The measures of Taylor and Taylor and of Fenigstein focus solely on the self. Our measure and the measures of Dollinger focus solely on others. The measures used by Conte and Ratto, Hatcher and Hatcher, Park and Park, Menna and Cohen, and Farber and Golden focus on both the self and others. However, Farber and Golden do not differentiate between psychological mindedness with respect to the self and others. Rather, they believe that when psychological mindedness is focused inward, it is a particular form of introspection or self-awareness informed by a knowledge of psychological processes.

A valid assessment of psychological mindedness is contingent on eliciting representative samplings of psychological mindedness unconfounded by other factors. Hatcher and Hatcher (chap. 3) identify a problem associated with assessing psychological mindedness directed toward the self. That problem involves a possible confound due to differences among patients regarding the relevance of stimuli. By relevance, they mean the similarity between the conflict depicted in the stimuli and the person's own intrapsychic conflicts. Some patients may experience difficulty responding to TAT-like cards that they find irrelevant, whereas other patients may experience difficulty responding to cards that are all too relevant or "too close to home." To control for such confounding factors, Hatcher and Hatcher suggest the assessment should include the use of several different stimuli, which in their case are TAT-like cards. Park and Park concur by stating that assessments of intrapersonal intelligence tend to be influenced by defense mechanisms and the unconscious.

Hatcher and Hatcher also suggest that the assessment of psychological mindedness directed toward others is more straightforward because it does not involve self-reflection. They caution, however, that the stimuli may still differentially activate patients' own conflicts, thereby confounding the assessment, although to a lesser extent than when the focus is the self.

Menna and Cohen report that subjects scored higher on their measure of social perspective taking when hypothetical versus real life dilemmas were used. They interpret this result as reflecting the interference of the emotionally charged situations associated with the real life dilemmas. Apparently, the real life dilemmas involve the subject, whereas the hypothetical dilemmas only involve other people. Their results also support the contention that it is more difficult to focus these skills on oneself than others.

Although it appears easier to achieve a valid assessment of psychological mindedness when the focus is on others, it is important to know whether the ability to understand others generalizes to an ability to understand the self. Conceivably, the psychologically minded patient will achieve self-knowledge when he or she focuses that skill on him or herself. Dollinger states that the relationship between psychological mindedness with respect to the self versus others remains an empirical question.

For us, the question of whether psychological mindedness toward others generalizes to psychological mindedness toward the self has implications for the predictive validity of our measure of psychological mindedness, the PMAP. In our clinical trials, we attempt to predict how patients will respond to psychodynamic psychotherapy based on how they view another person, the patient on the PMAP videotape. To benefit from therapy, we believe that the highly psychologically minded patients must take their ability for understanding other people's problems and apply it to their own problems. In constructing the PMAP, we expected that psychological mindedness toward others would differ from psychological mindedness toward oneself because the latter is influenced by the subject's defensiveness or emotional response. This is one reason why we use a standardized stimulus for assessing psychological mindedness; we want to assess the person's ability to understand problems in a way that is consistent with psychodynamic theory without the assessment being significantly confounded by the person's own defensive processes. We questioned whether this skill would generalize to the therapy situation. As presented in chapter 2, for the purposes of selecting patients for group therapy, the PMAP's focus on another may be quite appropriate. In group therapy, each patient is expected to contribute to the therapeutic process of all group members. Nevertheless, the question of whether the ability assessed by the PMAP generalizes to the person's understanding of his or her own problems remains.

Advantages and Disadvantages of Psychological Mindedness and Related Concepts

In this section, we consider advantages and disadvantages associated with being psychologically minded. Most clinicians, especially those who follow a psychodynamic theoretical approach, value psychological mindedness in their patients and their colleagues. With one exception, all of the authors who have contributed chapters to this volume seem to believe that psychological mindedness is more associated with positive events than negative events. However, as with any strength or ability, there are also disadvantages associated with high levels.

The exception is Fenigstein who is skeptical regarding the merits of psychological mindedness. He reports that self-focused attention can exacerbate anxiety, depression, and paranoia. He believes that the process of self-focused attention or psychological mindedness can be detrimental to the person. In addition, as previously mentioned, he doubts the utility of that process in terms of gaining insight because his data suggest those insights to be inaccurate. He does grant, however, that people may benefit from the perception of knowing themselves because that perception would heighten their sense of having meaningful control over their behavior.

The position of Fenigstein is consistent with material from the chapter by Park and Park. In their work with personal intelligence, they posit that infants who are highly reactive and easily distressed may be high in personal intelligence. Such infants are also hypothesized to be more depressed, anxious, and to have lower self-esteem. Complicating these infants' lives even further is the authors' contention that children with high personal intelligence can be perceived as threatening by their parents, especially narcissistic mothers. The authors believe that this interaction is fertile ground for the development of BPD. If personal intelligence and psychological mindedness refer to similar phenomena, then the child who is born with a tendency toward developing psychological mindedness is at risk for heightened levels of anxiety, depression, and parental abuse.

Using Fenigstein's instrument as a measure of psychological mindedness, Farber and Golden (chap. 9) found results that were consistent with those of Fenigstein. They report that subjects scoring high on the measure tend to question their own role in events even when they are insignificant. Finding that high public self-consciousness was negatively correlated with self-esteem, Farber and Golden agree with Fenigstein that self-scrutiny involves self-criticism. However, they are not so pessimistic as Fenigstein regarding the merits of psychological mindedness. They conclude that a high level of psychological mindedness is associated with an ironic, tragic vision of life where ambivalence and ambiguity is an integral part. As such, they believe in the merits of self-knowledge but warn that there is also a danger to self-knowledge. In their words, the highly psychologically minded person is wiser but sadder.

Farber and Golden present psychological mindedness as a personality trait that has both advantages and disadvantages. They creatively present the costs and benefits associated with high levels of psychological mindedness by depicting two psychotherapists, one in training and one in mid-career. The disadvantages associated with high levels of psychological mindedness include the loss of the ability to allow people and things to be simple. In addition, highly psychologically minded people risk feeling alienated from others who are not highly psychologically minded. The authors warn that this feeling of alienation may render them feeling lonely. This loneliness seems to relate to feeling disappointed with the superficiality of interactions with people low in psychological mindedness. Highly psychologically minded people may become reserved from fear of being unwittingly intrusive, or from feeling awkward as if they are eavesdropping on someone's unconscious. The highly psychologically minded person may tend to feel like an outsider to his or her own life.

The authors also point out that in addition to feeling like an outsider, the high psychologically minded person may feel special. Other advantages associated with high levels of psychological mindedness include an increased tolerance for the complexities of people, which can lead to becoming a more sensitive, compassionate, and genuinely forgiving person. Psychological mindedness can also be used pleasurably and playfully to understand and appreciate cultural, historical, artistic, and personal events. This can be an exhilarating experience. Ultimately the goal of psychological mindedness is for the person to know himself or herself. Toward this end, psychological mindedness can help the person become free from unconscious controlling impulses.

Farber and Golden conclude that there is a need for balance between the seductiveness of inner world exploration and outer world exposure and adaptation. They further state that this balance can be facilitated by seeing psychological mindedness as a mechanism by which life's problems are best grasped and ultimately mastered, that is, as a path rather than a goal.

Using the PM Scale developed by Conte and colleagues, Conte and Ratto interpret their results as suggesting that psychological mindedness facilitated behavioral adjustment, but intensified subjective distress. These results are consistent with the wiser but sadder idea Farber and Golden propose. In addition, we suggest that these results support our contention that there is a distinction between the process and outcome of psychological mindedness. With regard to process, psychological mindedness may be a way whereby the person attempts to understand and thereby adjust to the world. This process helps the person make sense out of a seemingly random environment. However, the insights the person gains from his or her attempt to understand the world may be distressing. Consider the following example.

> A psychologically minded man comes to understand that his wife's occasional withdrawal from him is not random. Rather he begins to appreciate the fact that she withdraws following times of particular closeness. The husband adjusts to his wife's ambivalence regarding closeness by respecting her privacy. He no longer feels responsible for her withdrawal or even particularly rejected by her. He trusts that she will soon return to him. After some time alone, his wife appreciates the fact that he has respected her privacy. She no longer feels trapped or suffocated. She relaxes and joins him in front of the television. They experience closeness and the marriage feels rewarding. However, the husband begins to feel sad during such times of closeness with his wife because he knows it will be followed by her withdrawal. He begins to feel ambivalent toward times of closeness with his wife and this realization further saddens him.

As this example depicts, the psychologically minded person appreciates the complexity and ambiguity characterizeing intimate relationships. As one loves, appreciates, and moves closer to the other, so too does one anticipate and dread the loss of the other, and moves away from the other. The challenge for the psychologically minded person is to tolerate the ambivalence that this view of relationships elicits. This challenge includes the relationship with oneself. As one gains an appreciation for the gift life represents, one simultaneously gains an appreciation for its fragility. As one becomes aware of one's strengths, one becomes simultaneously aware of one's weaknesses. By integrating all aspects of the psyche, the petty and flawed aspects as well as the generous and courageous aspects, we believe an individual can find a realistic balance in his or her life whereby the glass is both half-empty and half-full, where every beginning is also an ending, where every tragedy is also an opportunity. In brief, we are more optimistic regarding the benefits of self-knowledge; we believe there is a self acceptance that comes from self knowledge.

CURRENT STATE OF KNOWLEDGE AND FUTURE DIRECTIONS FOR THE MEASURES

In this section, we summarize the usefulness of the concept of psychological mindedness by briefly reviewing what the various measures successfully predicted. We also offer some suggestions regarding possible future directions for the authors who contributed chapters to this volume.

Conte and Ratto report that pretreatment scores on the PM Scale were found to be significantly and directly related to the number of psychotherapy sessions attended. With regard to outcome, the results were inconsistent. In one study, psychological mindedness was found to be significantly and directly related to an increase in global functioning and a decrease in psychosocial symptoms and problems. However, these latter findings were not replicated in a subsequent study.

Our own work has also yielded varying findings. In all three clinical trials, pretherapy scores on the PMAP were found to be significantly and directly related to effective work in psychodynamically oriented therapy. In terms of attrition, psychological mindedness was related to remaining in short-term analytically oriented group therapy for loss, but not in the two intensive day and evening treatment programs.

With regard to outcome, in the day treatment program, psychological mindedness was (significantly and directly) related to positive outcome. In the loss group study and the evening treatment study, it was not. The inconsistent results concerning outcome in our studies may be partly attributable to statistical artifacts. The high attrition by low psychologically minded patients in the loss group study, and the restricted range of outcome variance in the evening treatment study, may have precluded a valid test of the hypotheses. The inconsistent results may also be due to the influence of other important variables (patient personality, therapeutic alliance, therapist technique) intervening between the onset and completion of therapy. The outcome of therapy is multiply determined.

As previously mentioned, it would be helpful if our future investigations could provide empirical support for the PMAP's hierarchy. In this way, we might determine whether each level builds on itself or reflects a different aspect of the psychological mindedness construct. In addition, it would be important for us to acquire further information about how nonpatient populations perform on the PMAP.

Research involving the TAS–20 focused on associated features of alexithymia. For example, alexithymia was found to be significantly and directly associated with the tendency to somatization, and is prevalent among patients with substance abuse problems, eating disorders, and posttraumatic stress disorders. These associations do not provide information, however, about the response of clinical populations to treatment. Future research that focused on the scale's predictive validity may provide data alerting the clinician that patients belonging to specific diagnostic groups may be less suitable for psychodynamic approaches to therapy.

In terms of future directions for the TAS–20, it would also be informative to know whether alexithymia is indeed the "obverse" of psychological mindedness. To date, Taylor and Taylor found a significant and negative correlation between scores on the TAS–20 and the PM Scale of Conte and her colleagues. If that (negative) association was replicated with other measures of psychological mindedness, it would be helpful to understand the implications. For example, we would be particularly interested to know whether alexithymic patients can be taught to describe their feelings. Perhaps such an endeavour would demand a more comprehensive approach than described in chapter 4. It certainly would be an exciting area of research to explore. We encourage Taylor and Taylor (chap 4) to continue their goal of developing a precise definition and measure of alexithymia.

Menna and Cohen (chap. 8) focused on developing a valid assessment of social perspective taking. Their review of the literature revealed that social perspective taking was found to be associated with forming and maintaining friendships (Selman, 1981). Because the presence of a social support network was found to positively influence a person's ability to cope with stress, particularly loss, Menna and Cohen's measure of social perspective taking might prove useful for identifying high-risk populations. Unfortunately, their research has yet to reveal whether scores on their measure of social perspective taking translate into behavioral adjustment. There is a paucity of clinical research in this area. We encourage those researchers to apply their measure with clinical populations.

The work by Park and Park (chap. 6) reflects their rich clinical experience. Although it is true their research is based on clinical practice and must be considered exploratory, nevertheless we believe their chapter emphasizes some of the most intriguing questions of today's clinical practice. We eagerly await the continued application of research methodology to their clinical hypotheses, especially with respect to hypothesized genetic determinants of psychological mindedness.

As we encourage Park and Park to continue to apply research methodology to their intriguing clinical hypotheses, we encourage Dollinger (chap. 7) to expand his research to include clinical populations. His work represents a careful and methodical approach to the study of psychological mindedness. He reports that children's defense understanding consistently correlated with age, verbal intelligence, and perspective taking. In addition, Dollinger and McGuire found that children in their study perceived various defense mechanisms (as depicted in the stimulus stories) differently. Less valued defense mechanisms created a negative halo effect for the story characters displaying them. In addition, specific defense mechanisms were attributed more to one gender than the other. Unfortunately, his findings are inconsistent concerning the relationship between defense understanding and defense use. In addition, an adult version of the defense understanding task was not found to be significantly related to the psychological mindedness scale of the California Personality Inventory (CPI). Dollinger devoted substantial attention to the other measure developed for use with adults, the WAIT. He reports the consistent finding that intellectual competence plays an important role in scoring well on the measure. Unfortunately, to date, his measure has evidenced a limited ability to predict behavior. We encourage Dollinger to investigate what his measure predicts in this regard. In particular, we are curious to know how his findings generalize to a clinical population.

We offer a similar recommendation to Fenigstein. Fenigstein used his measure primarily with college students. Farber and Golden have used Fenigstein's measure primarily with psychotherapists, including those in training. Given the finding that his scale is related to depression, anxiety, and paranoia, it would indeed be informative to use it with a clinical population.

We also offer this recommendation to Hatcher and Hatcher and to Menna and Cohen in reference to their work with children and adolescents. In particular, regarding the work of Menna and Cohen, we encourage those authors to explore their measure's predictive validity in terms of children's behavior.

CONCLUSION

We believe that psychological mindedness and related concepts represent a promising area of investigation to theoreticians, clinicians, and researchers alike. There is much diversity among the authors' approaches to terminology, conceptualization, and measurement. By assembling their work, we hope we brought the reader an appreciation of this enduring concept. Although the psychotherapy literature evidenced an ebb and flow in attention to other concepts relevant to psychodynamic theory, research, and practice, psychological mindedness remains central. Furthermore, as this volume documents, the scope of its investigation evolved throughout the years and has broadened to include other areas of psychology. We hope we provided readers with sufficient information to choose approaches that best serve their own applications. The belief that understanding what makes human beings "tick" is of particular interest to us as a species, and the idea that humankind is always in search of meaning underlies this volume.

REFERENCES

Briggs, S. R., & Cheek, J. M. *(1986). The role of factor analysis in the development and evaluation of personality scales. Journal of Personality, 54,* 106–148.

Chomsky, N. (1975). *Reflections on language.* New York: Pantheon.

Gardner, H. (1983). *Frames of mind: The theory of multiple intelligences.* New York: Basic Books.

Kennedy, H. (1979). The role of insight in child analysis: A developmental viewpoint. *Journal of the American Psychoanalytic Association, 27* (Suppl.), 9–28.

Rosen, V. H. (1977). The nature of verbal interventions in psychoanalysis. In S. Arkin & M. E. Jucovy (Eds.), *Style, character, and language* (pp. 220–239). New York: Aronson.

Selman, R. L. (1981). The development of interpersonal competence: The role of understanding in conduct. *Developmental Review, 1,* 401–422.

Westen, D., Lohr, N., Silk, K., Gold, L., & Kerber, K. (1990). Object relations and social cognition in borderlines, major depressives, and normals: A TAT analysis. *Psychological Assessment: A Journal of Consulting and Clinical Psychology, 2,* 355–364.

REFERENCES

de Carufel, F. L., & Piper, W. E. (1988). Group psychotherapy or individual psychotherapy. Patient characteristics as predictive factors. *International Journal of Group Psychotherapy, 38,* 169–188.

McCallum, M. (1989). *A controlled study of effectiveness and patient suitability for short-term group psychotherapy.* Unpublished doctoral dissertation, McGill University, Montreal, Quebec, Canada.

McCallum, M. & Piper, W. E. (1987). *The psychological mindedness assessment procedure.* Unpublished manual and videotape.

Piper, W. E., de Carufel, F. L., & Szkrumelak, N. (1985). Patient predictors of process and outcome in short-term individual psychotherapy. *Journal of Nervous and Mental Disease, 173,* 726–733.

Piper, W. E., Debbane, E. G., Bienvenu, J. P., & de Carufel, F. L. (1987). A system for differentiating therapist interpretations and other interventions. *Bulletin of the Menninger Clinic, 51,* 532–550.

Piper, W. E., Debbane, E. G., Bienvenu, J. P., & Garant, J. (1984). A comparative study of four forms of psychotherapy. *Journal of Consulting and Clinical Psychology, 52,* 268–279.

AUTHOR INDEX

C

D

E

J

K

L

Y

Z

SUBJECT INDEX

W

CONTRIBUTORS

Nancy Cohen, Ph.D.
Clinical Psychologist, Associate Professor and Director of Research at C.M. Hincks Institute, Department of Psychiatry, University of Toronto

Hope Conte, Ph.D.
Professor of Psychiatry, Department of Psychiatry,
Albert Einstein College of Medicine at Yeshiva University, Bronx, New York

Stephen J. Dollinger, Ph.D.
Department of Psychology, Southern Illinois University, Carbondale, Illinois

Barry A. Farber, Ph.D.
Department of Psychology, Teachers College, Columbia University, New York, New York

Allan Fenigstein, Ph.D.
Department of Psychology, Kenyon College, Gambier, Ohio

Valerie Golden, Ph.D.
Doctoral Student, Clinical Psychology Program, Department of Counseling and Clinical Psychology, Teachers College, Columbia University, New York, New York

Robert L. Hatcher, Ph.D.
Director, Psychological Clinic, University of Michigan, Ann Arbor, Michigan

Sherry L. Hatcher, Ph.D.
Adjunct Associate Professor of Psychology and Clinical Area Associate Chair, Department of Psychology, University of Michigan, Ann Arbor

Mary McCallum, Ph.D.
Assistant Clinical Professor, Department of Psychiatry, University of Alberta; Research Associate, Department of Psychiatry, University of Alberta Hospital Site; and Private Practice, Edmonton, Alberta, Canada

Rosanne Menna, Ph.D.
Clinical Psychologist, Assistant Professor, Department of Human Development in Applied Psychology, University of Toronto/Ontario Institute for Studies in Education, Toronto, Ontario, Canada

Lee C. Park, M.D.
Associate Professor of Psychiatry, Department of Psychiatry and Behavioral Sciences, Johns Hopkins University School of Medicine, Lutherville, Maryland

Thomas J. Park, Ph.D.
Assistant Professor of Biological Sciences, Department of Biological Sciences, University of Illinois at Chicago

William E. Piper, Ph.D.
Professor, Department of Psychiatry, University of Alberta; and Coordinator, Research and Evaluation Unit, University of Alberta Hospital Site, Edmonton, Alberta, Canada

Rosemarie Ratto, Ph.D.
Member of the Adjunct Research Faculty, California School of Professional Psychology, Berkeley/Alameda campus.

Graeme J. Taylor, M.D.
Staff Psychiatrist and Professor of Psychiatry at Mount Sinai Hospital, University of Toronto, Toronto, Ontario, Canada

Helen L. Taylor, B.Sc.
Research Assistant, Department of Psychiatry, University of Toronto, Toronto, Ontario, Canada

For Product Safety Concerns and Information please contact our EU representative GPSR@taylorandfrancis.com Taylor & Francis Verlag GmbH, Kaufingerstraße 24, 80331 München, Germany